On an Irish Island

On an Irish Island

ROBERT KANIGEL

ALFRED A. KNOPF   NEW YORK   2012

THIS IS A BORZOI BOOK
PUBLISHED BY ALFRED A. KNOPF

www.aaknopf.com

All permissions to reprint previously published material may be
found immediately following the index.

Library of Congress Cataloging-in-Publication Data
Kanigel, Robert.
On an Irish island / by Robert Kanigel.—1st ed.
p. cm.
"This is a Borzoi book"—T.p. verso.
ISBN 978-0-307-26959-1
1. Great Blasket Island (Ireland)—History. 2. Great Blasket Island (Ireland)—Biography.
3. Great Blasket Island (Ireland)—Description and travel.
4. Adventure and adventurers—Ireland—Great Blasket Island—Biography.
5. Travelers—Ireland—Great Blasket Island—Biography. I. Title.
DA990.B65K36 2012
941.9'6—dc23   2011028159

Jacket photograph: Children by the Waves. *Unknown
photographer. Courtesy of Ionad an Bhlascaoid/The Blasket Centre
Jacket design by Joe Montgomery*

Manufactured in the United States of America

First Edition

For Dottie, Peg, and Elaine
City Slicker Farm, 1959–1960

Contents

On an Irish Island

Prologue

Nineteen twenty-three was barely yesterday, a lot like today. People lived in suburbs and commuted to work. They traveled by tram and subway. They drove automobiles. They went to the movies, subscribed to magazines, looked up in the sky to see airplanes. Vaccines, flush toilets, best-seller lists, billboards, cameras, and power lines were part of their lives. Their memories were fresh with visions of a war that killed with industrial efficiency. Picasso, Stravinsky, and Virginia Woolf had taught them to see through fractured lenses. Telegrams, telephones, newsreels, and radios had shrunk the world. If you were part of the great and growing middle class and lived in a place like Chicago or Berlin, London or New York, life could be pretty fast. You had your ambitions, you wanted more, you lived a busy life.

In the spring of 1923, George Thomson, a nineteen-year-old English boy, finished his first year at King's College, Cambridge. He'd grown up in a suburb of London. His father was a chartered accountant who hoped his son would follow in his footsteps. He was smart, had won a coveted scholarship to King's, was destined for distinction. At the university, he was a student of the classics, and later, when he took its daunting Tripos exams, he'd earn first-class honors.

But had he been able to, George Thomson later said, he would have taken a different path. All through his last years of secondary school, while studying Euripides and Plato, Ovid and Cicero, and then on into his first year at King's, he had been distracted by the events of the world. During his first two years at Dulwich College (a preparatory school), European armies still grappled along the blood-drenched Western Front. Yet it was not the Great War that compelled George's adolescent attention, but events in Ireland. Little rural Ireland, off the main stage of the world, had, beginning in 1916, endured seven years of rebellion and war—first against England, then in a cruel civil war that shed more Irish blood than had the British. It was Ireland, and all things Irish, that captivated young George Thomson.

Now, in August 1923, with the violence stilled at last, it could seem that the whole tortured recent history of Ireland had conspired to propel him across England, across the Irish Sea, across the breadth of Ireland, to a tiny quay at the foot of a precipitous cliff on the Dingle Peninsula. He was at the westernmost tip of Europe. He was in one of the wildest corners of Ireland, so forlorn, neglected, and poor that its people had been leaving it for America for almost a hundred years. George was bound for a tiny village perched on the eastern face of a great rock rising from the water three miles off the coast. Rowed by rough-hewn, wool-sweatered men across this unpredictable stretch of cold Atlantic to that tiny backward slip of an island, he would step from the modern world into what novelist E. M. Forster would call, with only modest exaggeration, a "neolithic civilization." When he left the island six weeks later, he would be close to tears. The island would grip his imagination, grant him friendship and love that would overfill his life, forever alter his ideas about what life could be at its sweetest, and about how the world ought to be at its best.

The Great Blasket island, or An Blascaod Mór, as it was rendered in Irish Gaelic, is the largest among a group of seven small islands just off the west coast of County Kerry. For at least two centuries before Thomson's coming, about 150 people lived there, in stone houses dug into the slope of the hill facing the mainland. Virtually all were fishermen who, with their families, wrested precarious livelihoods from the sea that washed the island's shores. They hunted rabbits, harvested oats and potatoes from mediocre soil. They had limited relations with towns on the mainland, which they rowed across open water in small boats to reach; evil weather sometimes kept them on the island for weeks at a time. They had no electricity, no plumbing, no church, no priests, no police, no taverns, no shops. They spoke Irish, though few could read or write it. English was for most of them unintelligible.

One summer's day in 1923, the way he told the story later, an islander, Maurice O'Sullivan, was "looking after a sheep on the hill-side, the sun yellowing in the west and a lark singing above." On the path ahead he saw a man approach, someone in "knee-breeches and a shoulder-cloak, his head bare and a shock of dark brown hair gathered straight back on it. I was growing afraid. There was not his like in the Island."

"God save you," said the stranger, in English.

"God and Mary save you, noble person," said O'Sullivan in the Gaelic ritual reply.

The young men sat down for a smoke. The visitor "tried to say something in Irish," O'Sullivan recalled. He couldn't, and tried again in English.

The Englishman was George Thomson, and after six weeks with O'Sullivan, talking together as they tramped over the hills and across the beach, his Irish grew readier and more fluid. Year after year Thomson returned to the island, his friendship with O'Sullivan deepening. Bound for international distinction as a classical scholar, he would encourage O'Sullivan's exuberant memoir of growing up on the Blaskets, *Fiche Blian ag Fás,* and help translate it into English as *Twenty Years A-Growing.*

"There is no doubt but youth is a fine thing, though my own is not over yet and wisdom comes with age," O'Sullivan begins the story of his life. It's a high-stepping affair, brimming with energy, filled with youthful adventure, the inspiration for a film script Dylan Thomas left unfinished at his death. E. M. Forster wrote the introduction. It would be reviewed adoringly in Europe and America, appear in numerous translations, earn a permanent place in the Irish literary tradition. For Thomson, the companionship he enjoyed with O'Sullivan and the other islanders with whom he played, worked, danced, and traded tales reached deep into him. He'd remember always the bleak beauty of the Blasket, its conviviality, the warmth of his relations with the villagers. His friendship with Maurice was the most important of his life.

Even in stripped-down form this makes for a nice story. Yet, astonishingly, it was not the first time, or the last, that it or something like it had been enacted on the Blaskets. Eighteen years before, in 1905, the playwright John Millington Synge, a key figure in the Irish literary revival and friend of the poet Yeats, visited the Great Blasket; the island touched him, too. Anyone who'd lived with Irish peasants, he wrote in the preface to his most famous play, *The Playboy of the Western World,* "will know that the wildest sayings and ideas in this play are tame indeed" compared with those heard in the Aran Islands, which he'd also visited, or on the Blaskets.

That's how it was all through the first decades of the twentieth century: Thomson and Synge were just two in a line of scholars and writers who first came to the Blaskets to learn spoken Irish, influenced islanders to see themselves through new eyes, and helped spawn a remarkable literary flowering—a succession of books, originally in Irish, but later widely translated. First Tomás O'Crohan's *The Islandman,* in all its dignity and grace. Then O'Sullivan's joyful *Twenty Years A-Growing,* and Peig Sayers's bleak and wrenching *Peig.* Though stylistically distinct, each told of a vulnerable, wave-lapped few square miles, breathing its own unlikely island air, aware of its historical fragility. "I have done my best" wrote O'Crohan, "to set down the character of the people about me so that some record of us might live after us, for the like of us will never be again."

With the success of these first books came other memoirs, collections of letters, works of history, linguistics, and folklore. All billowing up from a tiny, sea-bound community largely cut off from the twentieth century. "If we put them all together, side by side," George Thomson said years later, "we have a little library of fifteen or sixteen volumes, the Blasket Library. And this is something unique. There's no such collection in any other language, a collective portrait of a pre-capitalist village community, made by the villagers themselves, at the very moment of transition from speech to writing." Several of the books achieved international renown. Many remain in print. One was required reading in the Irish national school system for three decades. Together, they represent a poor Irish-speaking peasantry, their hard lives close and cooperative, rich with story, song, and dance, cut off from the clamor of modern life—and, inevitably, reflecting back at us our own soft, technology-thick lives.

On an Irish Island tells the story of George Thomson and the other scholarly visitors to the island in the years after 1905, their impact on the island and its literary legacy, and on the islanders to whom they grew so attached. It tells of a dying language and what hope of its revival meant to Ireland in the early twentieth century; of the Irish oral tradition as it was lived on the Great Blasket and embodied in Ireland's most famous storytellers, and in the lilting cadences of Irish and its stage-Irish imitators; of life on this stone outcropping in the Atlantic before it was abandoned, its residents dispersed to the mainland and to America, its life cut short by the irresistible forces of modernity.

I learned the rudiments of the Blasket story only in 2005, on my hon-

eymoon in western Ireland, where my wife and I had gone on the recommendation of friends. On our second day there, in the tiny sea-facing
town of Dún Chaoin, we visited the Blasket Centre, established by the
Irish government in the 1990s—on the mainland, just up from the sea,
within sight of the island—to tell the Blasket story. And there, as it happens, Sarah and I had our new marriage's first, um, *tiff.*

We had been at the Centre for several hours, viewing a documentary,
taking in images and artifacts from a vanished world, wholly absorbed.
But enough is enough, and by now it was late afternoon. I was in the
bookshop, irretrievably lost among the Blasket writers. But Sarah was
finally ready to go—and by now a little put off by her new husband's
seeming obliviousness to all but these books. Were we to spend our *entire*
honeymoon in the Blasket Centre?

We left. We returned to America. But the Blaskets had gotten under
my skin. And it wasn't alone the islanders who fascinated me, but the
visitors—writers and scholars from Oslo and London, Dublin and Paris,
city people all, who'd left behind their libraries and dusty archives, traveled across the breadth of England and Ireland, and found friendship, and
sometimes love, in this harsh, remote, astonishingly beautiful place.

I didn't just then think about writing about the Blaskets myself; that
came some months later. I'd been reading a book on quite a different subject, one with no trace of Irish content. It was called *Wrapped in Rainbows,*
Valerie Boyd's fine biography of the legendary African-American novelist
Zora Neale Hurston, author of *Their Eyes Were Watching God.* During the
1920s, when Hurston was a graduate student in anthropology at Colum-
bia University, her adviser sent her to America's black rural South to collect folklore—songs and stories and old ways of knowing—from her own
people. There, a world opened up to her, unseen, unknown, disappearing,
that her city friends could scarcely have imagined.

Reading Boyd's book, I was struck by how similar it seemed to the
vanished world and culture of the Great Blasket. And on both sides of
the Atlantic, in Hurston's black South and at the edge of West Kerry, and
at almost the same time, people realized that it was only so long before
the lore of the people, their old rural community life removed from the
clamor of the city, was gone entirely; that in its disappearance something
precious was being lost; that vanishing with these slower societies were
just those sweet, simple satisfactions and deep human relationships that
modern life seemed to elbow out of the way. The Blasket story, I came to
realize, wasn't only about one little corner of Ireland. In telling it, I could

get at a bigger, more urgent story, as central to this century as to the last, about how we live now, what we've left behind, and at what cost.

Gifted as they were, the Blasket writers would not have reached the rest of the world with their life-tales and sagas were it not for the superbly educated men and women, so different from themselves, who visited their island. George Thomson and the others came from the great intellectual capitals of Europe, looking for something. But what they found, it turned out, meant more to them than what they had come to find. And it is this surprising, almost freakish collision between two worlds that lies at the center of my story. It is a story of friendship, fellowship, and love across a great cultural divide—between a bare speck of village and the great world of literature and learning; between peasant fishermen and scholars mostly still in their impressionable twenties who, before coming to the island, led bookish lives cloistered in seminar room and library, caught up in a twentieth century that sometimes seemed too shallow and too fast.

The word "friendship" is not entirely unproblematic, or without irony. Money sometimes changed hands between visitor and villager. Favors were traded. But whatever they exactly were, these relationships forged in work, song, and talk around the fire blossomed again and again on this enchanted isle, and often proved lasting, deep, and loving. That's about how it was for a tall, imperious Norwegian who'd go on to become one of the world's leading linguists, Carl Marstrander, twenty-three when he visited the island in 1907; for a Yorkshireman more at home in the Middle Ages than in his home in London, Robin Flower, twenty-eight on his first visit in 1910; for a lonely Irishman with a wild heart from Killarney, Brian Kelly, twenty-eight; for a charming and brilliant Frenchwoman, product of Paris's elite academies, Marie-Louise Sjoestedt, twenty-three; for Synge, thirty-four; and, particularly, for George Thomson, twenty.

It would be hard to imagine a coterie of people more brilliant, more adventurous, more deeply interesting than these. Brian Kelly's short life is shrouded in mystery. Marie-Louise Sjoestedt's, too, ends prematurely, in tragedy, in German-occupied Paris. Each is unforgettable in his or her own way. But it would be useless to deny that Thomson holds a special place among them for me; his story touches every facet of the Blasket saga and ranges across this book from end to end.

His innocuous, overfamiliar name might suggest a white-bread sort of Englishman; he was anything but. He had enormous spirit and integrity. He was moved by the injustice he saw around him; he would become a Marxist, visit the Soviet Union, later serve on the Central Committee of the British Communist Party. Arriving in Ireland deficient in modern Irish, he would come to speak a Blasket Irish the equal of any of the islanders'. He was a passionate, caring, loving man, would write to his wife that Irish had thirty-nine ways to express "darling" and bestow on her a bountiful sampling of them.

Thomson's fascination with all things Irish was stirred and enriched in the Blaskets, but began earlier. His father was an Ulsterman. Both parents showed Irish republican leanings. While a student in prep school, he followed with revulsion accounts of the Black and Tan massacres, when British mercenaries, apparently picked for their brutality, laid waste to Irish homes. Come Monday afternoons, he'd tear off his school uniform and take the train into London for classes in Irish at the Gaelic League. And long before being rowed across to the Great Blasket that day in 1923, before even going up to King's, he gathered books of Irish verse and grammar and, at age seventeen, inscribed them with his name in Irish: Seoirse Mac Tomáis.

Chapter 1

The West

[1905]

Before George Thomson, of course, others had crossed the three miles of Blasket Sound that separated the Great Blasket from the mainland, or had explored the smaller rocky islands, mostly uninhabited, that were its neighbors, the so-called Lesser Blaskets. They recorded bird sightings. They took geological samples. Most never said much about their visits—or, left unaccountably unmoved by the awful splendor of the islands, perhaps had nothing much to say in the first place. Revenue agents of the English king occasionally appeared; at least once, the story goes, islanders pelted them from the overhanging cliffs with rocks, chasing them back to their boats. Protestant missionaries visited, too, determined to turn islanders away from dark Papist ignorance.

In 1843, Mrs. D. P. Thomson, wife of a Protestant cleric on the mainland (and unrelated to George Thomson), visited the Great Blasket. It was difficult even to get onto the island, she wrote in a book published a few years later, since one must "take advantage of the swell of the wave and leap on the rocks" from the shifting, unsteady platform of the boat. Once on land, she "was more affected than I have the power to describe, by witnessing human nature reduced to the savage state it is among these islanders, within almost ear-shot of religious light and civilization." Mrs. Thomson told of local women and children crowded into the schoolroom, "chewing seaweed incessantly," who pressed lengths of it "into their mouths with their thumbs in a most savage manner, and spat about unceremoniously at will; they touched my dress, turned me round and round to look at every separate article, laughed with admiration at my shoes and gloves, kissed and stroked my old silk gown." After submitting to this inspection, she proceeded to speak to them of Jesus Christ.

In 1892, Jeremiah Curtin arrived on the island. An American from Milwaukee, Harvard-trained, Curtin was a linguist visiting West Kerry in search of folklore. New Year's Day found him in Tralee. He took the train to Dingle, came around through Ventry and the neighboring villages, visited Ballyferriter, and finally was rowed out to the Great Blasket. There he found "perhaps 20 straw-thatched cabins, the thatch held in place by a network of straw ropes fastened down with stones." Piles of manure stood in front of each, cattle being kept in them at night. Curtin was in search of Gaelic myths he'd been assured he'd be able to gather like flowers from a field. But the pickings were slim: "I care more about getting the price of a bottle of whiskey than about old stories," one man told him. Curtin soon left, gleaning for his trouble only a photo or two of the thatched-roof village he had too briefly visited.

The first to see the island with new eyes and tell the world about it was John Millington Synge. This preternaturally gifted playwright, this quiet brooding literary force, discovered on the island in 1905 something of the luminous spirit later visitors would find as well. He was thirty-four at the time and had less than four years to live. But in his short life, he'd already gained stature as a notable figure of the literary revival then washing over Ireland. Three of his plays had been produced by the Abbey Theatre in Dublin or its predecessor companies. In the time he had left he would write another, *The Playboy of the Western World,* swollen with such luscious language that, by one estimation, it added up to "the most fertile and vigorous poetic dialogue written for the stage since Shakespeare." Its incidents, characters, and speech were rooted in the spoken Irish Synge heard on his visits to Ireland's west, including the Blasket. Gone, from his rendering of the island, was the ugly primitivism marking earlier accounts. He found instead among the peasants there an abiding grace and dignity.

Those earlier visitors had come to the island lugging heavy loads of cultural baggage . . . and so did Synge. For, by the time of his visit in 1905, the Blaskets weren't just islands in the farthest western reaches of Ireland. They were The West, which had come to stand for the deepest, purest wells of Irish nationhood.

In those days Ireland, or Eire, didn't exist as an independent state; Ireland was British. To any self-respecting Irishman of republican sympathies, of course, Ireland was *never* British, merely occupied by them. Still, for seven hundred years Ireland had been variously invaded, conquered, and colonized by England, and for centuries England's reigning monarch reigned over Ireland as well. Since the capitulation following the Battles of the Boyne and Aughrim in 1690 and 1691, feeling against the English ran deep. The Catholic-Protestant divide that had split Europe since the Reformation played out in Ireland, too. Catholics were barred from voting, serving in the Irish parliament, or sometimes even practicing their religion. Protestant landlords owned most of the land, evicting impoverished Catholic tenants at their whim. The murderous Famine of the 1840s, though set off by crop failure, had been exacerbated by English indifference. Periodically, resistance to British rule took violent form, but more often it was purely political, as in the nineteenth-century struggle for "home rule," Charles Stewart Parnell's Irish Parliamentary Party, and various republican brotherhoods and kindred nationalist groups.

In the closing years of the nineteenth century, fresh interest in the Irish language further confounded Ireland's tortured relationship with England. Late in the same year as Jeremiah Curtin's visit to the Blaskets, on November 25, 1892, Douglas Hyde went before the newly formed Irish National Literary Society in Dublin and delivered a lecture that one critic, Declan Kiberd, would call "Ireland's declaration of cultural independence." It bore the title "The Necessity for De-Anglicising Ireland."

A thirty-two-year-old linguist, son of a Church of Ireland rector, Hyde had grown up hearing old people in his native County Roscommon speaking Irish, and through them glimpsed a rich Gaelic culture he'd never encountered among his own family and their friends. *That* Ireland, he declared now, was dying. Ireland's problems lay in its rejection of all things Gaelic, and its embrace—sometimes willing, sometimes forced—of everything English. In Anglicizing themselves, he declared, the Irish "have thrown away with a light heart the best claim which we have upon the world's recognition of us as a separate nationality." It was, he asserted, "our Gaelic past which, though the Irish race does not recognize it just at present, is really at the bottom of the Irish heart."

The Ireland of the seventh century, he reminded his listeners, was "then the school of Europe and the torch of learning"; the Dark Ages had been brightened by the wit and intellect of Irish monks, bards, and scholars. But over the past century, Ireland had become cut off from its roots. Irish had fallen into disuse. O'Mulligans had taken English names like Baldwin, O'Hennesys were now Harringtons, Eibhlins were Ellens. Pipers and fiddlers were disappearing. The harp, long a symbol of Ireland, was becoming extinct. Irish jerseys had given way to shoddy cast-off clothes from Manchester and London.

Needed was, for example, to "set our faces against this aping of English dress, and encourage our women to spin and our men to wear comfortable frieze suits of their own wool, free from shoddy and humbug." Irish autonomy demanded sweeping de-Anglicization. "We must strive to cultivate," declared Hyde, "everything that is most racial, most smacking of the soil, most Gaelic, most Irish, because . . . this island *is* and will *ever* remain Celtic at the core."

The following year, Hyde helped establish the Gaelic League, which for the next two decades would champion a revival of Irish culture and language. Forget politics, Hyde as much as said; the core of Irish identity lay in the Irish language. "My own ambition," he would write later, was "language as a neutral ground upon which all Irishmen might meet." Through the last years of the nineteenth century and first decade of the twentieth, the League's influence spread. "Whatever it was ten years ago," a Dublin professor wrote in 1907 of Gaelic, "it is very much alive now. . . . You see Gaelic inscriptions over the shops, Gaelic on the street labels, Gaelic in advertisements, a Gaelic column in newspapers. . . . The Gaelic League is everywhere." Irish youth might not much care for French or German, but during these years they did for Gaelic, for Irish: "They want to learn Irish, as they want no other language on earth." And when leaders of the language movement looked around Ireland for exemplars of all that was Irish at its purest and best, they looked fixedly *west*.

Think of Ireland as two hundred miles across and three hundred miles north-to-south and you won't be far wrong. Across this breadth, however, its population is, and was, distributed unequally. Its two largest cities, Belfast and Dublin, both lay off inlets to the Irish Sea and faced east, to Scotland and England. The weight of its bigger, stronger English neighbor was felt unevenly across the country, too. The English first invaded in the twelfth century, expanding and colonizing from east to west, bringing with them English place-names, English families, English castles. After the Reformation, Protestantism made its strongest inroads in the east, encroaching but feebly in the west. The English language, meanwhile, squeezed out Irish until, by the 1850s, little of the native language could be heard outside parts of Counties Donegal, Mayo, Galway, and Kerry, all in the west.

So by the time our story begins in the early years of the twentieth century, "Ireland" meant, roughly speaking, two Irelands—split not along the familiar divide of Northern Ireland and the south of recent political history, but along an east-west axis. The east was overwhelmingly English-speaking, included substantial Protestant minorities, and boasted big cities that looked like those of England and Scotland, with all their coal dust, clamor, and corruption. The poor, rural, mostly Roman Catholic west, with its Irish-speaking enclaves, was typically seen as a throwback to a simpler, purer past that elsewhere in Ireland had been overrun by the noisy and the new.

Here, though, could be found the precious seed that one day might be planted in an Irish political soil more hospitable to its growth. To Irish nationalists, historian Kevin Whelan would observe, the rural west was "the authentic Ireland, a materialization of an unsullied primordial past," the Irish-speaking Aran or Blasket islander its exemplar. To another scholar, Kevin Martin, the western islands were "part of the creation myth" of a new Ireland aborning.

And this was The West that, with its distinctive dialects, drew John Millington Synge.

Born in 1871, Synge had come out of the Dublin Ascendancy; that is, his family was long and deeply Irish, but Protestant—landed gentry from Wicklow on his father's side. The son of a barrister, he'd studied languages at Trinity College, Dublin, at the time virtually reserved for Protestants. Settling on becoming a musician, he lived in Germany, Italy, and France. In Paris, at the Sorbonne, he came under the influence of one of Europe's foremost Celtic scholars, H. d'Arbois de Jubainville, who nurtured in him a love of Irish. Also in Paris, he met William Butler Yeats, already a major literary figure, who recognized his talents and, in the familiar story, bestowed on him among the most famous hard nubs of literary advice ever

Playwright John Millington Synge, around the time he visited the Great Blasket in 1905

offered and accepted. "Go to the Aran Islands," he told Synge. "Live there as if you were one of the people themselves; express a life that has never found expression."

Before Synge went to the Blaskets, then, he went to Aran, three remote islands in Galway Bay, across from the mainland wilderness of Connemara. He made his first trip there in 1898, being rowed out the first time in a curragh. "It gave me a moment of exquisite satisfaction," he wrote later, "to find myself moving away from civilisation in this rude canvas canoe of a model that has served primitive races since men first went to sea." Between then and 1902, he returned to Aran four times, for four and a half months all told, his mastery of Irish improving with each visit.

Synge was a swarthy, thick-necked man with a great shock of dark hair and a bushy mustache, and had all the hallmarks of healthy, virile manhood to him. But in fact he was sick much of his life—with asthma in his youth and then Hodgkin's disease, which began to afflict him in his late twenties and would kill him before he turned forty. He was, though, an energetic walker, tramping across the hills and down the dusty roads. He'd go up and talk to anybody he happened to meet. Yet he was essentially shy, his seeming gregariousness more spur to the stories and speech of others than sign of any great need to speak himself. As every portrait of him somehow suggests, his was a silent absorbing presence. To the Aran Islanders, one critic noted, Synge was "so strange and silent that no one actually knew him." His gift was to listen through those deep moody eyes, and transmute the language of fisherman and peasant, weaver and tramp, into art. First, in 1903, came *In the Shadow of the Glen,* a grim one-act comedy in which an old peasant feigns death to test his wife's fidelity. Then *Riders to the Sea,* a one-act tragedy exhibiting, by one estimation, "an almost Aeschylean starkness and grandeur."

Synge's accounts of his Aran visits had not yet been published when, early in the new century, he was drawn to another Irish-speaking enclave in the west. Separated from one another by broad ranges of English-speaking Ireland, the last remaining Irish-speaking areas, each more and more unto itself, had split into distinctive dialects. There was Donegal Irish to the north. And Connemara Irish, which is what the Aran Islanders spoke, down the coast. And Munster Irish in the southwest, which included County Kerry. The differences were notable. Most spoken Irish, for example, stressed first syllables; Munster sometimes shifted emphasis to the last. Words known in Ulster were unknown elsewhere. The country's zealous language enthusiasts exhorted Irish-learners to explore them all.

Synge felt the tug. His brother Robert had recommended a Kerry family with whom he could stay, with whom he might unearth a new bounty of Irish stories and Irish expression. During parts of four summers Synge would visit Kerry; these yielded dialogue, plot material, and idiosyncrasies of language that would inform his later work. And on one of these trips, in July 1905, he wrote to Willie Long of Ballyferriter, County Kerry, at the western tip of the Dingle Peninsula, seeking a place more pristinely Irish yet.

If there was anything like a local aristocracy in this far-off, underpopulated little town, Long—well off, loquacious, a bit of bluster to him—was it. He was a forty-six-year-old father of four sons and two daughters, a well-connected merchant, innkeeper, and schoolteacher. Local ordinance apparently barred teachers from keeping inns. So, to get around it, the low-ceilinged, two-story little place on the main street of Ballyferriter over which he presided bore the name of his brother instead.

Three shillings sixpence per night, or twenty-four shillings a week—that's what Synge's stay would cost, Long wrote him on stationery bearing his name and address in a riot of different typefaces. "Of course my place is not an out-and-out Hotel but I guarantee you quiet, clean & good accommodation. . . . The worth of your money you'll have." As to Synge's abiding concern, Long reassured him: "Myself & household all speak Paddy's language still, so there is no need of any cottage for getting it." In other words, Synge could get his fill of Irish right there in Willie Long's parlor.

The gateway to the Dingle Peninsula was Tralee, a town of about ten thousand lying most of the way southwest across the country from Dublin. Forty miles of formidable mountains stood between it and Ballyferriter, but by 1891, a little narrow-gauge steam railroad had been slipped in among the mountains. It boasted the steepest track of any line in Ireland or England. The train never scuttled along faster than about twelve miles an hour, and often broke down. But for the first time it linked Dingle and its nearby villages, including Ballyferriter, Dún Chaoin, and the Blaskets themselves, to the rest of Ireland.

In Tralee, Synge found a boy to carry his bag across town to the depot, scene of "a confused mass of peasants struggling on the platform with all sorts of baggage." Synge's narrow car was soon "filled with sacks of flour, cases of porter, chairs rolled in straw and other household goods." Under way, he overheard a woman in a shawl tell of a son who had left for England, leaving his elderly father bereft in loneliness. " 'Ah, poor fellow!' she said. 'I suppose he will get used to it like another; and wouldn't he be worse off if he was beyond the seas in Saint Louis, or the towns of America.' "

Long had written Synge that he'd arrange to pick him up where the chugging little train dropped him off in Dingle. Sure enough, when Synge arrived he found a cart, pulled by a tall mare, to take him the ten miles or so to Ballyferriter. The driver needed a little while to hoist his bags aboard and fasten them, but finally they were on their way, over and through the hills rising behind Dingle. "As the night fell the sea became like a piece of white silver on our right; and the mountains got black on our left, and heavy night smells began to come up out of the bogs."

From Long's on August 4, 1905, Synge wrote Lady Augusta Gregory, his aristocratic patron in Dublin. Like Douglas Hyde and Synge himself an upper-class Protestant, Lady Gregory had grown up in a great house outside Dublin, where her playmates among the Irish Catholic help piqued her fascination with their world. Later, she would collect folklore and write plays, most of them serviceable if not inspired. But it was in funding and nurturing the Abbey Theatre, dedicated to making a national theater shot through with Irish sensibility, that she became best known. And Synge was one of her eternal triumphs. It was largely through her energies that his first two plays were produced, garnering much acclaim. Now, in Ballyferriter, her protégé wrote to her. He was "in the centre of the most Gaelic part of Munster," making progress with a dialect that, after Aran, seemed almost foreign. "I have realized that I must resuscitate my Irish this year or lose it altogether, so I am hard at work." Near Bally-ferriter, lined up along the northeastern flank of a wide-necked peninsula, rose the companionable little prominences known as the Three Sisters. Jutting into the Atlantic just to the west stood spectacular Sibyl Head. One day, Synge climbed it, arriving "suddenly on the brow of a cliff, with a straight fall at one's feet of many hundred feet into the sea. It is a place of indescribable grandeur." Why did anyone remain in Dublin, London, or Paris, he mused, when it would be better "to live in a tent or hut with this magnificent sea and sky, and to breathe this wonderful air."

But it wasn't for the sake of the scenery that Synge had written Willie Long in the first place; he needed someplace cut off from English, thick with Kerry Irish. And, it turned out, he wasn't getting his fill of "Paddy's language" after all; even this far west, English was too strong. So he was setting out for a more purely Irish-speaking milieu yet. As he wrote Lady Gregory, he expected it to be "even more primitive than Aran and I am wild with joy at the prospect."

On August 14, he recorded in his notebook, "I came off yesterday to the Great Blasket Island."

That first day, a local holiday, he had gone out to the island with Long and a couple of other locals, three oarsmen powering them over the tricky swells in a *naomhóg*, pronounced "nay-vog," a craft of wood lathing covered in canvas painted with black tar. The day was clear, the sea and sky blue.

As we came nearer the island, which seemed to rise like a moun-tain straight out of the sea, we could make out a crowd of people

The lower village of the Great Blasket, the fields beyond it, the White Strand below and to the right

in their holiday clothes standing or sitting along the brow of the cliff watching our approach, and just beyond them a patch of cottages with roofs of tarred felt. A little later we doubled into a cove among the rocks, where I landed at a boat slip, and then scrambled up a steep zig-zag pathway to the head of the cliff, where the people crowded round us.

It was a reception virtually identical to those other visitors would receive over the next forty years.

He stayed in the house of *an rí*, the king, who was no hereditary ruler at all but simply acknowledged for his strength and personal stature, much as tribal chieftains were in times past. His name was Pádraig Ó Catháin—Anglicized, it would be Patrick Keane—and he spoke a little English, being among the few on the island who did. Synge was given a small room just off the stone house's main room, known simply as the kitchen. The house stood midway up the hill to which the village clung. Synge could look out his window and see the mountain before him, green with grass but barren of trees, its steep slope silhouetted against the sky.

"I have been here for a week today," he wrote Lady Gregory on August

20, "and in some ways I find it the most interesting place I have ever been in. I sleep in a corner of the King's room and in the morning—on state occasions—the princess" (he meant the king's younger daughter, Cáit; he never grew tired of such winking references to island "royalty") "comes in when we awake and gives us each a dram of whiskey and lights our pipes and then leaves us to talk." They talked mostly in Irish—his being better than the king's English. In the evenings the house filled up with some-times twenty or thirty people, talking, drinking, and dancing.

All during his island stay, he kept up his correspondence. He wrote to Max Meyerfeld, his German translator, helping him with Irish-tinged obscurities in his stage dialogue; "reeks" were mountains, "creels" were wicker baskets for fish or turf. He wrote to Lady Gregory: eating, reading, and writing in the ever-busy kitchen, he explained, he'd not yet been able to read her latest play, but on a jaunt out on the cliffs he'd dipped into it and liked it. He wrote to Yeats, commenting on Lady Gregory's play and other matters of the big world. And each day he spent among the island-ers, hiking around the island, playing music, happy in the company of his host and hostesses.

He kept a notebook—"Notes in Ballyferriter and the Great Blasket Island, August 1905"—but also took pictures. And both tell of a place far better off than others, like Jeremiah Curtin or Mrs. Thomson, had intimated a generation before. The villagers were poor, certainly. But the period right after the turn of the century was a relatively prosperous one, and you can see it in Synge's photos. In one, taken in front of the king's house, the sun streams in from high overhead. The men, in sweaters and caps, don't look ragged. They don't look forlorn. The king himself, head amiably cocked, a little welcome smile on his face, a picture of confidence and composure, wears a jaunty flared hat. His daughter Cáit could pass fashion muster even today. She wears a long skirt, perhaps from America, with a cinched waist, decorated with fabric strips at the hem; a belt with a metal buckle that looks like the Celtic pewter you find today in Irish handicrafts stores; a string of beads down the front of her long-sleeved blouse, with little flounces at the wrists.

Not present in the photo is Cáit's elder sister, the king's other daugh-ter. Synge would refer to her in his notebook as "the little queen," and in the published account of his visit as "the little hostess." Her proper name was Máire Ní Chatháin, or Mary Keane. On the island she was Máire Pheats Mhicí—Mary, daughter of Pádraig, granddaughter of Mike. Born in 1882, she'd lost her mother when she was about eight, soon after the birth of her youngest brother, Seán. When Synge arrived on the island that August, she had been married since the previous February to an island man, Mícheál, but was still tending her father's house, where Synge was staying. "She is a small, beautifully-formed woman," Synge wrote, "with brown hair and eyes—instead of the black hair and blue eyes that are usually found with this type in Ireland—and delicate feet and ankles that are not common in these parts."

It is this beautiful woman of twenty-three who, it's been said, was Synge's inspiration for one of the immortal figures of stage history, a character named Pegeen Mike.

On his first visit to the Aran Islands, in 1899, Synge wrote, he'd "heard a story of a Connaught man who killed his father with the blow of a spade when he was in passion, and then fled to this island and threw himself on the mercy of some of the natives with whom he was said to be related." The story lingered with him because, in September 1904, about a year before his visit to the Blaskets, he began work on a new play built on such a premise, *The Playboy of the Western World*. The words of the title carry different currency to modern readers; Synge's "playboy" was a kind of trickster or rogue.

Into a "country public house or shebeen, very rough and untidy," according to Synge's stage directions, stumbles Christy Mahon, ragged, dirty, and frightened. Pub denizens crowd around him. What has he done? An ordinary thief, is he? No, nothing so small, he says; he's killed his father. With each new horrific detail, admiration for Christy unaccountably grows, which spurs him to ever more articulate, even poetic descriptions of his crime. Soon, there he is, fairly standing taller on the page, rogue and hero, recruited for organized sport on the beach, and winning, sought by all the women and girls.

A play that makes its protagonist the killer of his father, and shows the local peasantry as sympathetic to him and the women among them fawning over him, might be expected to encounter a hostile notice here and there. And, indeed, when, in early 1907, it was produced at the Abbey, *The Playboy of the Western World* raised a fury. Many in the audience hooted it down. Police had to be called in to contain the crowd. Night after night the protests went on. Editorials lambasted the play for unpatriotic heresies and as an affront to Irish womanhood. The Playboy Riots, they've been called since.

But *The Playboy* is no trifling asterisk of theatrical history. It is unforgettable, wondrous, and strange, clothed in exotically heightened language far removed from any English we recognize, its dialogue stocked with peculiar constructions, unfamiliar turns of phrase. Sometimes its words are not English at all but borrowed from Irish—like *streeleen* for "idle conversation"—that Synge took down from Blasket Islanders and recorded in his notebook.

When his boasts of a wicked crime are first doubted, Christy replies, "That's an unkindly thing to be saying to a poor orphaned traveller, has a prison behind him, and hanging before, and hell's gap gaping below." But while some of the best lines go to Christy, many others go to the daughter of the pub owner, Margaret Flaherty, or Pegeen Mike—roughly, "Little Peg, daughter of Michael." She's "a wild-looking girl," as Synge describes her, about twenty. As the play opens, she's supposed to be marrying an oafish, inconsiderable local boy, Shawn Keogh, toward whom her attitude veers between teasing and contempt.

Enter Christy. When Pegeen Mike first hears his father-killing story, she believes not a word of it. "You're only saying it," she says. "You did nothing at all. A soft lad the like of you wouldn't slit the wind pipe of a screeching sow." But soon she's won over by an eloquence that, stirred by his strangely welcoming reception from the others, fairly leaps up from him. Pretty soon she's addressing Christy with what Synge describes as "a honeyed voice." She falls for him, hard. "And to think it's me is talking sweetly, Christy Mahon, and I the fright of seven townlands for my biting tongue. Well, the heart's a wonder."

An early critic, Percival Presland Howe, called Pegeen "one of the most beautiful and living figures in all drama." Who in Synge's life might have inspired her? Maybe, from a literary imagination as fertile as Synge's, we have no business asking for any such too-easy correspondence between life and art. And yet the question beckons. Distinguished Synge scholar Ann Saddlemyer, an editor of Synge's plays and correspondence, favors actress Molly Allgood, Synge's love during the final years of his life; Allgood would herself play Pegeen when *The Playboy* premiered in Dublin. Synge's biographers David H. Greene and Edward M. Stephens, on the other hand, assert without qualification that the "prototype" for Pegeen Mike was his "little hostess" on the Blasket.

But if Máire Ní Chatháin somehow inspired the immortal Pegeen, one wonders just how. Did she make a physical impression on Synge? Something in her personality? In how she spoke? Certainly Synge's seemingly domestic Blasket "hostess" does not at first blush suggest fiery Pegeen.

Just as certainly, though, she is the most memorable figure in Synge's Blasket account—just as Pegeen is in *The Playboy*. Synge devotes to her a closely observed poem, "On an Island," warmly appreciative of their time together:

> You've stuffed my pillow, stretched my sheet,
> And filled the pan to wash your feet,
> You've cooped the pullets, wound the clock,
> And rinsed the young men's drinking crock;
> And now we'll dance to jigs and reels,
> Nailed boots chasing girls' naked heels. . . .

The real Máire and the fictional Pegeen are about the same age. Both tend to their father's affairs, presiding over the place where most of the action takes place. Both do so ably; all their actions suggest competence and lively intelligence; Máire, like Pegeen, is a "big" figure, no mere drudge supplying a servant's labor in exchange for the ten pence a week Synge paid for room and board. And just as Pegeen showers Christy with attention once she falls under his spell, so Máire does Synge.

On several occasions, they are alone together. On his first night on the island she actually puts him to bed, just as Pegeen Mike does Christy at a gentle moment in the play—chastely, to be sure, yet with a warming intimacy. She lights a candle, carries it into his room beyond the kitchen, removes her apron, fastens it to the window in lieu of a blind, only then leaves him to himself.

Once, when returning in the evening from a walk along the island ridge, Synge is joined by two young women, with whom he walks back to the village. An old woman laughs at the sight of them. " 'Well, aren't you in good fortune this night, stranger,' " she says, in Synge's telling, " 'to be walking up and down in the company of women?' " " 'I am, surely,' I answered. 'Isn't that the best thing to be doing in the whole world?' "

Indeed, Synge was always more at ease with women than with men. "He was shy and inclined to silence with men," his biographers write of him, "but all too willing to lay bare his troubles and his dreams to a sympathetic and sensitive woman." Women drew him out, much as Pegeen and the other island women do Christy. He'd observed of Aran that "the direct sexual instincts are not weak on the island," the women apparently less troubled by Victorian fastidiousness than in Dublin or London; as he put it, they were "before conventionality." Something similarly free applied to the Blaskets; both in his notebooks and his published account, Synge pictures an unexpectedly easy and porous border country between the sexes.

So it is, certainly, between him and Máire, the little hostess. She seems so *interested* in him, so frankly curious about all he does and says. After a hike around the island, he returns to the house to write letters. She finishes up the breakfast chores, comes over, sits by him on the floor, pulls out her hairpins, and begins combing her hair, idly questioning him about his correspondents: Who is this that you're writing to? Where do they live? Are they married or single? How many children have they? Later, Synge takes out some photos from his travels, which Máire, and some other women, examine closely. She is especially taken with those showing babies or children. "As she put her hands on my shoulders, and leaned over to look at them, with the confidence that is so usual in these places, I could see that she had her full share of the passion for children which is powerful in all women who are permanently and profoundly attractive."

Máire may or may not have directly inspired Pegeen. But something in Synge's island flirtation with her—for that, surely, is what it was—recalls Christy and Pegeen; the situation, I think, as much as the person, left the lasting imprint. Like Christy Mahon in the glow of Pegeen's attentions, we can almost see Synge puff up with masculine pride in the warmth of Máire's closeness and the fullness of her attentions.

When an editor asked him for a series of articles devoted to the Blaskets like those he had done about the Arans, Synge wrote back to say he hadn't enough material. But his trip to the Great Blasket had touched him deeply, in some ways more even than his Aran visits; in his introduction to a collection of Synge's travel essays, Nicholas Grene calls it "the most intimate experience Synge had of the lives of the people." And of course he *did* write about it. Much of what the world first learned of the Blaskets owes to Synge's account of his West Kerry travels, first published in 1907 in the journal *The Shanachie* and later appearing in book form along with some of his other travel writings.

His West Kerry account, spanning some seventy pages, was studded with song lyrics and conversations with men and women he met along the way. He told of a man lamenting the death of the Irish language, of the circus in Dingle, of hikes among the sea-facing cliffs, of Kerry's "wonderful air, which is like wine in one's teeth." He wrote of the Great Blasket's cottages, its rabbit-riddled mounds, its children, its dancing, his tramps across the island. One time, he

> walked through a boreen towards the north-west, between a few plots of potatoes and little fields of weeds that seem to have gone out of cultivation not long ago. Beyond these I turned up a sharp, green hill, and came out suddenly on the broken edge of a cliff. The effect was wonderful. The Atlantic was right underneath; then I could see the sharp rocks of several uninhabited islands, a mile or two off . . . the lesser Blaskets. The whole sight of wild islands and sea was as clear and cold and brilliant as what one sees in a dream, and alive with the singularly severe glory that is in the character of this place.

Despite its seeming warmth and sympathy, its interest in the islanders and delight in their surroundings, Synge's published account did not exempt him from criticism. Some islanders saw some of his descriptions as slights: Did the apron-on-the-window story suggest Máire's care and hospitality . . . or a lack of proper curtains? At least one scholar, Irene Lucchitti, would write him off as a "cultural tourist." To her, Synge's "emphasis on wildness suggests a primitive simplicity that denies the social complexities of living in such a tightly structured society." His social reticence, his tendency to *take in* rather than volubly express himself, "shows him to be a silent observer who took what he needed yet gave little of himself."

This, I think, is harsh. Synge's account was probably the first to imbue with sympathy and dramatic force a place that in the past, when it had come to the attention of the world at all, had typically been treated badly. It is a commonplace, of course, to say that anything a writer writes says as much about him as it does about his subject. Synge *was* selective; he saw what he saw and not what he didn't see, extracting from his time on the island those elements he wished, or needed, to express, and not others. He wrote much about what he had seen on the island, but, inevitably, left out much as well—including a number of insights and observations, excluded from the published account, that he recorded in his journal.

It is late August. After sixteen days, Synge is leaving the island. His host heads down to the slip to prepare the boat. Máire offers to slice some bread and wrap it in a clean handkerchief to take with him. But he might never be able to return it to her, he says. Don't worry, he has her telling him, surely her handkerchief is "a nicer thing to have round my bread than a piece of paper." Finally, the king rows him across the sound and arranges with a local farmer to take him and his bags to Ballyferriter. The king kisses his hand in farewell, he's loaded on a cart with an old woman and a little girl, and he's off, the island consigned to memory.

At Willie Long's in Ballyferriter, Synge sits down to dinner in the parlor, caught up in a bout of longing. "I am sitting within the four white-washed walls of this little hotel," he writes, "with a book and a lamp and paper and ink and a pen. That is my world, instead of the living world I have come from, where there is the princess, and the little queen, and the old king, and all their company." He imagines them on his departure wandering back from the head of the cliff in twos and threes and gathering again in the kitchen of the king. "The two worlds, their world and mine, are very different."

But then he crosses out this last sentence. "They have an island," he writes instead, "and I have an ink-pot."

A few months later, in January 1906, Synge got a brief note from the island king in awkward English, thanking him for a letter and pictures Synge had sent. The king forwarded the best wishes of Máire and her younger sister, wrote of the lovely weather, of boats coming back each day stuffed with fish. Reaching Synge at almost the same time was a letter from Berlin, advising him of harsh business realities, of German theater managers disdainful of English plays. "Do let me have the Ms. [manuscript] soon," he was implored.

Synge was a man of Dublin, Paris, and Berlin, and of the Aran Islands and the Blaskets, too. He was thirty-four when he came to the island. In his short life, he'd been raised a Protestant by a pious mother, but rejected religion. He had once seriously weighed becoming a musician. He'd led the bohemian life in Paris, with early loves there and in Germany. He'd studied languages in the Sorbonne; written plays performed in Dublin and elsewhere in Europe; formed attachments with Yeats and Lady Gregory—but also with an Araner he gave the name Michael, and with Máire on the Blasket. He was an inveterate student of human personality, an artist of consummate genius who created a whole new language of mixed Irish and English that was entirely his own. He was a complex man, who led a complex life in brain, body, and heart, a friend of fishermen, a creator of immortal art.

René Agostini, a scholar who wrote of Synge's relationship to the peasants he met in the Arans and Blaskets, described him as "aspiring to simplicity but incapable of it"—which could just as well describe most of those who would follow Synge to the Blaskets.

Chapter 2

The Fine Flower of Their Speech

[1907]

The islanders whom Synge met in 1905 could trace their roots on the Great Blasket not to the immemorial past, or even to the Middle Ages, but only to the eighteenth and early nineteenth centuries and the arrival from the mainland of fewer than a dozen families. To give them, for the time being, their more familiar English names, they were Kearneys, Guiheens, Dunlevys, Crohans, Sheas, and Keanes, and a little later O'Connors, O'Sullivans, Dalys, and a few others. Island lore and archeological evidence tell of people who lived earlier on the Great Blasket and its smaller neighbors. One was poet and warrior Pierce Ferriter, who gave the town of Ballyferriter its name, and who reputedly stood fast against the English from a protected cove along the northern flank of the island where he could slay them with impunity; he was executed by them in 1653. The vestiges of a small fort halfway back along the ridge of the island attest to still earlier inhabitants, as do the remains of some stone huts perhaps associated with an early Christian monastic settlement. But it was only with the Kearneys, Guiheens, and the others that the first permanent community emerged on the tip of the island that faced the mainland.

Shards of island history tell of rents paid to distant landlords, of a ship from the Spanish Armada flung on the rocks of Blasket Sound, of other shipwrecks and their cargoes helping islanders get through the Famine. But Synge and subsequent visitors saw little by way of historical remnant. What struck them as they trudged up the zigzag path from the break in the rocks that served as pier was bustling life—children, women, and men setting out in the boats, hunting rabbits, cooking, cutting peat, tending to animals, talking a stream of Irish among themselves. After three miles of open water in a little boat, the visitor was abruptly *there,* in a stone village dug into the side of the hill that shot up from the sea's edge, the mainland now seeming inconsiderable and remote.

The island itself was about three miles long and half a mile wide, shaped like an ineptly cut arrowhead aimed southwest. On its northeast flank (farthest from the point, where it might be affixed to the arrow shaft) stood the village itself, with its twenty-eight houses. That, anyway, is the figure normally given. The roofless ruins today, plaited with outbuildings and low stone walls, don't make for easy counting.

But the houses were mere backdrop for the animal strivings of 150 humans, as well as the donkeys, chickens, and sheep that were as much a part of village life. Typically of one or two rooms, the houses were tied together by interlaced paths gradually worn into, or cut into, the sloping ground. From their chimneys issued smoke from fires built from peat gathered on the back side of the island, dried in little stone structures there, then borne across the island on the backs of donkeys laden with wicker panniers. There were no trees, none. There was plenty of living green, but it was all pasturage, over wide stretches of the island, and bog, and a few low bushes.

It was a place of sheer rock faces, eroding gullies, sharp projections into the sea, seabirds in flight hundreds of feet below, a place of stark contrasts and extraordinary beauty. Vistas could change within a few steps; there was no disguise, no shelter, no privacy granted by copse or wood, only by the spatial irregularities of the island, where the curve of a hill or the descent into a crevasse might abruptly lose you to another's sight. Several peaks shot up from the landmass. The one to which the village clung rose to more than seven hundred feet. Along the back of the island, you'd encounter two more, reaching higher yet, to almost a thousand feet. A few paths, more or less level, emerged from the village and wrapped around the hill. Depart from these thin ribbons of horizontality and you could imagine rolling or sliding down the sheer slope.

Yet, however steep, it was a plump pillow of green compared with the cliffs by which the island finally dropped away to the sea. Abruptly, the earth was gone, and there were only the rocks and crashing surf a hundred or two hundred feet below—everywhere along the island's circumference, mouthfuls of land chomped out by some great sea monster, each its own gnarled universe of rock, softened just a bit with growths of sea pink or other vegetation. Each was alive in the minds of the islanders with its own name: Cuas Fhaill Beag, little cliff cove, on the long north face of the island; or Cladach an Chapair, copper beach, a little to the west, where a wrecked ship had once deposited a load of copper bolts; or Rinn na Croise, point of the cross, on the south. There were scores of them, no hundred yards of shoreline failing to get its own name and coloration in the island's collective mind.

In this rhythm of cove and point, there was one exception. Not the village itself, which dropped to the sea much as the rest of the island did, to the wave-lapped inlet where the *naomhógs* were brought ashore. Rather, it was north of the village and visible from its heights: a cove where the cliffs fell not into the sea but into a soft swathe of fine white sand three hundred yards across. An Traigh Bhan, the islanders called it, the White Strand. It was close to the village, but not quite of it, just below the gentler slope of land where most of the island's few crops were grown. A stretch of shore that was sweeter, more forgiving, where you didn't need to watch your footing, as you did everywhere else on the island. Here driftwood washed ashore, seals beached, children ran barefoot in the wet sand.

In 1907, two years after Synge came and went, the island received a new visitor, a tall Norwegian, Carl Marstrander. "All the bridges to the outside world were . . . broken," he would recall of his time on the island. "On this St. Helena I lived for five months in voluntary jail, in a world so different from the one I up to then had been living in." Young Marstrander had been identified by his professors in Oslo as an unusually gifted student of linguistics. But, visiting the Great Blasket at the age of twenty-three, he'd been thrust into an alien world that, when he came to write about it two years later, still left him befuddled, unsure of what to make of its maddening contradictions.

"Children of nature," he termed his island friends, or neighbors, or hosts, or objects of study, or teachers, or whatever they really were. "They are rather unstable in their mind, like a lot of Celts, and one doesn't have to do much to make them happy." Sadness never lingered with them,

The young Carl Marstrander was an athlete. On the Blasket he'd use a naomhóg *mast to demonstrate pole vaulting to the islanders.*

but passed "like the short summer showers in Kerry that come and go. They do not seem to think of a day after today. They do not know," he wrote, "the slow patient work which will bear fruit in years to come. But whatever will give them profits at the moment gives them enormous energy."

Marstrander pictured the islanders as forever joking, prone to exaggeration, inexorably drawn to "the strange and horrible." They were "superstitious and blinded by many prejudices," prey to demanding priests, yet quick to disregard their pastoral injunctions. One priest, angry at being ignored, cursed them, according to Marstrander, going so far as to offer prayers "that the Almighty might lead your boats into destruction on the sea." For a few days, at least, the islanders, white with fear, forsook whiskey, gave up dancing and song. Impossible for one priest's intemperate reproof to exact such a price? No, wrote Marstrander, "the West of Ireland still lives in the dark middle ages."

The islanders, he was convinced, were all but incapable of introspection. They were preternaturally social creatures, unable to be at once happy and alone. Evenings brought them together for singing, dancing, and storytelling. "It's from these evening gatherings," he wrote, "that I have my most wonderful memories and my most lasting impressions from the Blaskets." Everyone would climb the path to the house of the king, boys in blue sweaters and heavy boots, girls barefoot and wrapped in shawls. "I have never seen such beautiful and stylish dance as in the Great Blasket. The men are champions. Every beat, every little change in the music, even the smallest, is mirrored in their dance, whether it is by a movement of their foot or a bend of their wrist or knee."

He marveled at how, when weatherbound for weeks at a time and unable to fish, they rarely put the time to productive good use, as with handicrafts. They didn't often cross the sound for Mass, yet their morale was "healthy and high. Particularly is this true of the sex life, which is told boys and girls from childhood." While their elders looked on benignly, everyone joked about sex, "the boys caressing the girls even in the presence of older people." Yet they managed to stay pretty much out of trouble.

There among the islanders on that barren outpost of Europe, Marstrander found a strange, unaccustomed mix of customs and social practices that even in retrospect he could not resolve. "I have never met people who have demanded so little of life," he wrote. "I am often thinking back on them and get a feeling of great attachment, or pity. I do not know." Their outward lives were miserable, yet perhaps—he simply couldn't say for sure—they were happy. "The wet cliffs out there are their whole world. They have no longing for a richer life led under brighter conditions, because they have never known anything better." He felt bound to them, he wrote after his return to Norway in late 1907, "with the strongest ties of friendship."

Blue-eyed, fair, lean, and tall, his erect carriage contriving to make him seem taller still, Marstrander was the son of the principal of a local college whose overfull library was stocked with works on, among other subjects, European linguistics. Young Marstrander took an interest in the field, including Celtic languages, even before enrolling at the University of Oslo, then called Christiania, in 1901. Over the next six years, the faculty came to see him as blessed with a remarkable ear for languages and a deep, developing understanding of them. His special talents, they determined, needed nurturing. One day in early 1907, he was summoned to the study of one of his professors, Sophus Bugge.

Bugge, seventy-four years old, a comparative linguist, was among those Norwegian scholars and artists tantalized by their country's ancient ties to Ireland. Just two years before, in June 1905, Norway had pulled free from Swedish rule for the first time since the Napoleonic Wars. Nationalistic fervor swept the country. Interest blossomed in the country's roots, culture, and very identity—especially in its heroic Viking past, when the original Norwegians, the Norsemen, marauded the coasts of Western

Europe, plundering, forming settlements, and mixing with local peoples, including the Celts, forebears of today's Irish. All this needed study, and Marstrander was to be enlisted in the new work. He was to go to Ireland, Bugge told him, and learn modern Irish; the Old and Middle Irish he'd studied in school were too remote from the way it was spoken now. A special scholarship had been secured for him. Was he ready to go?

How long did Marstrander weigh his answer? One wonders because of how he later described the scene. He had been named to the Norwegian Olympic team, in pole vault, for the 1908 games in Athens; he was torn about what to do, and said as much to Bugge. (Of course, the 1908 Olympics were held in London, not Athens, so the story loses some veracity.) Bugge would have none of it. *Hic Rhodus, hic salta,* he replied, referring in Latin to an Aesop's fable Marstrander would have known: An athlete back from games on the isle of Rhodes boasts of his formidable long jump there and swears he can produce witnesses to his feat. Don't bother, he's enjoined, simply repeat it: *Here's your Rhodes; let's see you jump.* Bugge needed an answer then and there.

Soon, Marstrander was on his way to Dublin, where he was a guest of Richard Irvine Best, secretary of the new School of Irish Learning there. Then he headed west across the barren, mostly flat plain to Galway, and from there reached West Kerry—Kerry, perhaps, because the Donegal and Connemara dialects had been explored, whereas that of West Kerry represented still fertile scholarly ground. In Tralee, he stayed at a place he remembered as the Teetotal Hotel, which "served whiskey from morning till night." The locals spoke as little Irish as he did.

After taking the same train across the peninsula as Synge had, he arrived in Dingle. There, by one account, a former islander advised him that if it was "the living Irish" he wanted he should head for the Blaskets. No need for that, someone else told him—there was plenty of Irish to be heard right there in Ballyferriter. Besides, " 'there's not much sense in going into the island and drowning yourself.' "

In Ballyferriter he stayed at Willie Long's, where, like Synge, he was soon disappointed. "I did not get in contact with the ordinary man," he wrote, which was necessary if he hoped to learn "the difficult Irish language." Long, he concluded, was too big a local figure; people were afraid to open up in front of him. Marstrander was treated "like a bust on a pedestal." Local farmers to whom he was introduced clammed up. Conversations stopped when he entered the room. One scholar has noted how Gaelic League organizers during these years found many people "ashamed to admit they knew Irish," which was associated with illiteracy and poverty; even in Ballyferriter, Irish was deemed inferior, unsuitable for church, school, or commerce. Once, in a local pub, Marstrander was again assured that Ballyferriter ought to suffice for Irish. No, he said, nodding to a conversation going on beside them in English, "my enemy is just behind my ear."

It was time to get out. One day in early August, he packed his bags, hired a donkey to get him to Dún Chaoin, made his way down the steep path to the little quay at the base of the cliff, and was rowed over to the Great Blasket.

What happened next is today firmly enshrined in Blasket lore, not least because Marstrander so delighted in telling it. On his arrival, he was met by a delegation of villagers. The king welcomed him with an old Irish greeting. Marstrander expressed thanks in his best Irish, *Ta buiochas agam ort a Ri,* making "an honest attempt to get my tongue right for this unusual sound." He failed, utterly. Um, yes, the king replied with consummate grace, the Norwegian language was quite a nice one.

Since at least the late 1800s, scholarly interest had grown in the origins of language, in early Irish texts, in Old and Middle Irish and their origins in a conjectured root language common to most European tongues. Scholars plumbed the sacred texts of the early church. They studied fragments of Irish bardic poetry that had come down through the centuries. Later, the world would marvel at the extraordinary contribution of this small country to English-language literature, theater, and poetry, at Synge, Yeats, Beckett, Shaw, Heaney, Joyce, and the rest of the great Irish pantheon.

But theirs was *written* language. Just now, at the time of Marstrander's visit, English's grip on the country having tightened for three hundred years, the Irish language was hardly written at all. Virtually no Irish-language literature was being produced. There were a handful of Irish-language newspapers, a few Irish-language scholarly journals. The Gaelic League inspired a degree of fervor, but its achievements, set against the sweep of recent Irish history, were still tenuous and slight. And the few tens of thousands of people, mostly in the west, who spoke Irish daily mostly couldn't read or write it; this was true on the Great Blasket just as it was in Kerry generally and the other Gaeltacht areas of the country. What was left of Irish was the spoken language—not, it should be said, as a sad second-best to the written, but as something full and rich in itself. It was this Irish that Synge had traveled to the Aran Islands and the Blaskets to learn. Now so did Marstrander.

To learn the spoken tongue meant learning its vocabulary, of course, but also, with greater difficulty, learning its sounds. Much in Irish would prove daunting to any newcomer, but the words themselves were probably the least of it. Irish is part of a family of Gaelic languages, with strong links to Scots Gaelic, Welsh, Manx, and Breton, spoken across the English Channel in Brittany. More broadly, it is part of the larger Indo-European family of proto-languages; some of its grammatical features and even vocabulary are shared with linguistic distant cousins, including English, Italian, and Russian. "Two" in English is *dva* in Russian, *due* in Italian—and *dó* in Irish. "Mother" in English is *mater* in Latin—and *máthair* in Irish. Scholars have found all sorts of linguistic connections, many of them transformed or misshapen, to Irish's roots in what some have called Common Celtic. At least when pointed out, then, some Irish words can seem to an English-speaker surprisingly comfortable and familiar. The word *patir* in early Celtic, "father," became *pater* in Latin, but along the way lost its initial "p," turned into *atir,* and finally into the Irish *athair.* Irish, then, was not Korean or Swahili; its kinship with other European languages meant its vocabulary, at least, was not always so fearfully alien.

Its pronunciation, though, was another story.

All languages have their distinctive sounds, even before you can make sense of them; every journeyman actor invoking a cruel German *Kapitän* or snooty French waiter capitalizes on that fact. A set of the mouth, a play of the tongue, French nasality and rolled "r"s, guttural German, musical Italian. Clichés, certainly, but they emerge from characteristic sounds. English has forty-four distinct sounds, or phonemes; Irish, depending on the dialect, has sixty—which, absent firm command of the phonetic alphabet, can be difficult to describe and classify. There could be a whispery twang to Irish. There were sounds reminiscent of the Scottish *loch,* and variations-on-a-nasal-theme that might remind you of gargling, vowels getting lost in the back of the throat never to return. Even ears new to the language would never confuse it with German, say, or English. You could listen to Irish in full flight and come away certain that none of its consonants—and none of its vowels, either—were quite like anything you'd heard before. In later years, a brilliant French linguist visiting Dún Chaoin and the Blaskets would write that, although her Irish was improving, "when I compare it with the splendid soft language of this place, I get disgusted and pessimistic."

Before coming to the Blaskets, Carl Marstrander had been pronounced a gifted linguist by his professors. He would go on to a lifetime's career in the field. He already had some English, and good German, as well as his native Norwegian. He had studied Old Irish. He could probably point out Scandinavian influences on the language; "shoe" is *bróg* in Irish, *brok* in Old Norse. On the mainland, he'd already had several weeks' exposure to spoken Irish. But none of it seemed to do him much good. "After a fortnight in Ballyferriter," he would write, "I could hardly understand more than the usual hello and goodbye." Indeed, right there in front of the villagers on his first day on the island he had been unable to express the simplest greeting, could not *get my tongue right for this unusual sound.*

"The speech is like a big river flowing from the lips of these islanders," he would write. "The ends of words and small words almost disappear in the ordinary day-to-day language." His knowledge of the written language helped him little. For nine hundred years, written Irish had remained largely fixed, representing the language as it had once been spoken; but in that time, spoken Irish had veered off. Who, Marstrander wondered, on "hearing the word *drar,* [would] think of the written *dearthair,*" or hearing *dreafu* think of *driosūr?*

Irish consonants took two quite different forms, resulting in two nearly complete sets of sounds for each. "Broad" and "slender" were the terms customarily used to describe the difference, both intimately linked to the vowel sounds to which they were applied. In English the "c" in "call," and most other words in which it is followed by the vowels "a," "o," or "u," sounds different from the "c" in "cell," and in other words with the vowels "e" and "i." In Irish, *most* consonants went through such a shift. With some of them, like "b," "m," or "p," broad or slender determined whether the lips were relaxed or tensed. With others, like "d," "n," or "t," the difference resided in whether the tongue was pressed against the upper teeth or against the hard palate. Fiendishly complex sound-changes that Irish grammarians labeled eclipsis and lenition figured in as well. Pronunciation was more than usually entwined with grammar and meaning; words sounded different depending on their role in a sentence, the differences significant enough that, reduced to print, they had to be spelled differently, too. "Horse" is *capall.* "Horses" is *capaill.* "The horse's hooves" is *crúba an chaipaill.* "The horses' hooves" is *crúba na gcapall.* And all these horse words *sounded* different.

Was everyone to gather "at the top of the big cliff"? Well, top was *barr,* cliff was *faill,* and big was *mór.* But you'd hear nobody say "err baur un fayll moore," which is about how *ar barr an faill mór* would sound if anyone were saying it. Nobody would say it, of course, because it was wrong. Thanks to the peculiar rules governing the genitive case, all the familiar words shape-shifted into new forms, the phrase becoming *ar bharr na haille móire*—which, resplendent now in a whole new necklace of sound, would come out "Err vaur na halla mora."

In the end, most consonants, depending on whether they were flanked by a "broad" vowel, meaning "a," "o," or "u," or a "slender" vowel, "e" or "i," or whether they were "lenited" by virtue of the word's role in the sentence, could be sounded in up to four different ways, the tongue moving up, down, and around the palate, the sound aspirated, or trilled, or sometimes disappearing altogether. A "d" could sound close to an English "th" or more like a regular "d," or else a "y," or something like a growled "gr."

These mysteries Marstrander was determined to penetrate.

Marstrander arrived on the island on a Sunday, briefly lolled about the village, inquired where he might stay for the night, and was directed to the king's house. Why, he was asked the next day, had he left Ballyferriter? Not enough Irish there, too much English, he replied; as an islander put it later, "His business was to get the fine flower of the speech," and the best Irish was presumably right there on the Great Blasket.

Who, he asked the king, could teach him?

He knew just the man, the king said. His name was Tomás Ó Criomhthain, pronounced something like "o-*krih*-in," and in English rendered as O'Crohan. Like everyone else on the island, he made his living from the sea, but, unlike most everyone else, he could read and write Irish. And of course he spoke it—beautifully, correctly, precisely.

Marstrander approached him. Did he know English?

Not much, replied Ó Criomhthain.

Fine with him, said the Norwegian.

And so it began. For two or three hours a day they'd meet, from seven or so to ten in the evening, in Marstrander's room in the king's house, talking, reading, and writing Irish. Toward the end of his stay, Marstrander advised Ó Criomhthain that he'd not be able to spend so long on the island as he'd hoped: Could they meet more often, perhaps twice a day? By now it was fall, the days growing shorter, Ó Criomhthain's time out on the boat at night longer. But he agreed, apparently squeezing in a session around midday. "We'll manage," said Ó Criomhthain. "I won't refuse you."

After two months, Marstrander composed a letter in Irish in which he declared that spending time like this with the islanders was the surest way to learn the language. He was "improving moderately. I could now express what I wish in Irish, which pleases me, for I had hardly any word when I left Dublin."

He kept lengthy vocabulary lists. He drew (or had drawn for him) rude sketches, their features identified in Irish: A *fear,* or man, rows a *bád,* or boat, across quiet waters. A *sliabh,* or mountain, rises behind him. He learned not just from Tomás but from everyone. Socially, a great gap existed between the university-educated Norwegian and these peasant fishermen. "Marstrander bridged this gap," it was said of him when he died in the 1960s, "simply by acting as if it didn't exist." Later, he'd impress his colleagues as an immaculate dresser, a lavish entertainer, and a natural aristocrat. But on the island, he fell in with the villagers, fishing with them, cutting turf on the hills, riding the donkey home at night. He "had little spare flesh on him but he was as healthy as a salmon," Ó Criomhthain's son Seán would say of him. He liked to show off his pole-vaulting skills. "He would catch hold of a naomhóg mast," Seán recalled, "make a dash, take a running jump, stick the end of the mast into the ground and rise as high as the tops of the houses"; by one surely exaggerated account, he vaulted himself *over* the houses.

Around the village he was An Lochlannach, the Viking, a particular hit among the old women, as well as among the boys, whom he taught athletic skills; sometimes he'd gather half a dozen of them together, clamber aboard their joined hands, and then, on the count of three, have them heave him into the air. Exploring the island, he learned of its superstitions and folktales, like that of a female spirit, or *púca,* that lived under a seaward cliff and "charms the young ones with her tempting voice." After five months, he wrote, he was "accepted like one of their own, as an Islander."

"A fine man," Ó Criomhthain would call him, "with the same manner to low and high." Whatever Marstrander's private, more nuanced views of his island friends were, he treated them as if their language and culture *mattered.* After all, they could do something, speak Irish, that Norwegians couldn't do, that Englishmen couldn't do, that even most other Irish couldn't do. Blasket Irish, they came away half convinced, wasn't just Irish, but the best Irish, the purest. Marstrander lent them stature. They were fishermen? Yes, but something in how they lived was precious and rare.

More than Synge's brief visit, Marstrander's laid the ground for the unlikely literary phenomenon that was to blossom on the Blaskets. "It was Marstrander who started the whole thing," declared Bo Almqvist, Swedish folklorist and Blasket scholar, a century later, at a celebration of Marstrander and Ireland's Viking links in Dún Chaoin. Marstrander was a student of myth, yes, but also a creator of myth. He "convinced the people of the island that they were a special people." Without Marstrander, Almqvist added, "there would hardly be a Blasket culture, and no Blasket writings."

Around Christmas, Marstrander returned to Norway. He and Ó Criomhthain corresponded for a while. He asked his teacher to compile a list of island flora and fauna—birds and eggs, bog grass and meadow foxtail, each with its name in Irish—and sent him the paper he'd need to do it. With the help of an Irish-language teacher then visiting the island, Ó Criomhthain obliged. Marstrander sent him money—Ó Criomhthain would call it "yellow gold"—and later, probably at Christmas 1910, a pipe. After this flurry of activity, however, their correspondence lapsed. "I haven't heard anything from him," Ó Criomhthain would write in the late 1920s, "for many a long day."

Marstrander, we might say today, was launched on his career trajectory, destined to become among the most distinguished linguists of his day. In Oslo, he won a scholarship in comparative linguistics and continued his Celtic studies. By 1909, he was back in Ireland, the holder, at an astonishingly young age, of a coveted position with the new School of Irish Learning in Dublin.

The school was the brainchild of Kuno Meyer, an energetic little German with a great mustache and a passion for all things Irish. An "evangelist for the Irish language," someone would call him. He had spearheaded the emerging field of Celtic studies first while on the Continent, then through his appointment at University College, Liverpool.

For the ten years after Douglas Hyde's 1892 speech calling for the de-Anglicization of Ireland, the Gaelic League had done much to foster a resurgence of the language. Among its innovations were local festivals in celebration of Gaelic culture; a *feis* included dancing and singing competitions, sporting events, and prizes to schoolchildren for proficiency in spoken Irish. The culmination of the year came with the annual *oireachtas,* a much-anticipated Ireland-wide *feis.* And it was at one of them, in 1903, held in the Concert Hall of the Rotunda in Dublin's Parnell Square, that Meyer made a long, impassioned plea, in English, for the formation of a new school of Irish learning and literature.

Meyer, forty-four, described the League-inspired revival of interest in Irish language and culture as "one of the most remarkable and unexpected national movements of our time. . . . It is one of those almost elemental phenomena, the suddenness and force of which seems to carry everything before it." This, of course, was bald overstatement, a pep talk for an audience already won over to the cause. "Wherever one goes now," he continued, "one finds men and women, young and old, able to speak and read and write Gaelic; it is taught in the schools; ancient customs are revived; papers are springing up; Irish literature is being printed; the interest in the history and traditions of the country and the race is widening and deepening."

But this pretty picture, he allowed, was blemished. Many remained indifferent to Celtic studies. Those wishing to acquire "the spoken language in all its idiomatic force, and with all its dialectical varieties," had few places to turn. Needed was the encouragement of serious Irish scholarship. The language movement should give students of the language access "to the higher regions of study and research" and so "bring about a second golden age of Irish learning," rivaling, presumably, the Middle Ages, when little Ireland served as scholarly incubator for all of Europe.

Six weeks later, a new School of Irish Learning was already taking shape in Dublin. Meyer was its first director.

Right from the start it succeeded, drawing students and scholars from around Europe. For a time located in a three-story house at 33 Dawson Street, down the street from Trinity College and virtually across from the Lord Mayor's residence, the school offered training in linguistics, philology, and textual studies. Five years after its founding, one of its key figures, Osborn Bergin, left. Marstrander was named to replace him.

Marstrander taught his first class in April 1910, and that summer three more—in Old Irish, Middle Irish, and the *Tain Bo Cualinge,* a legendary tale with pre-Christian roots. At one point in the summer, he and his students gathered for a garden party at the home of a Mrs. Eason. When they rounded up everyone for a photograph, Marstrander sat near the center.

Carl Marstrander and Robin Flower met at the School of Irish Learning in Dublin in 1910. In this photo taken at a garden party for teachers and students that summer, Marstrander sits near the center, fourth from the left, Flower almost directly behind him.

Arrayed around him were men in jackets, high-collared shirts, and ties, and women in great broad-brimmed hats and light summer frocks. Just behind Marstrander stood a boyish-looking man actually two years older than he, his straight dark hair parted crisply to the side, Robin Flower.

It was probably within days of the party at Mrs. Eason's that Flower wrote a colleague at the British Museum that he was making good progress with Irish. By now, "infixed pronouns, the vagaries of the copula, vocalic changes and the like have no terrors for me." But it was Marstrander himself who was leaving the deepest imprint on him.

> I am working under the finest scholar and one of the most admirable men I ever met in my life, Carl Marstrander, a Norwegian of extraordinary abilities, who knows all the languages of the earth (Sanskrit, Armenian, Phrysian and the like), is the finest comparative philologist and my very good friend. I could exhaust myself in eulogy and leave the rudiments of his praise unshaken. I praise God for him daily.

Four years earlier, Robin Flower had been named assistant keeper in the Manuscripts Department of the British Museum; "keeper" was English parlance for what Americans would call "curator." Soon after settling into this august preserve of imperial culture, he had taken on an ambitious new project. The Museum held a great store of Irish manuscripts, ancient tracts, and poems in Old and Middle Irish, which no one had ever worked all the way through. An earlier scholar, Standish Hayes O'Grady, had begun to catalogue them in the 1880s. A seven-hundred-page fragment of his work had been printed and bound for use around the Museum. But it had never been published, the project as a whole languished, and Flower had proposed to finish it.

The Old Irish he'd need to tackle the venerable texts, someone later observed, was "by common consent the most difficult of the Indo-European tongues." On his own, Flower began taking Irish lessons, but progressed little and asked for help. In June 1910, he was awarded three weeks' leave and fifteen pounds for expenses, to go to Dublin and attend lectures at the School of Irish Learning.

The school left him fairly giddy. "What human beings Celtic students are! They have a grace from God, the gift of eternal youth." As for Marstrander, "I dine with him every night after the classes," his letter continued. "It's a good life. I am taking lessons in modern Irish and am making progress." And, oh, one more thing, he wrote: after Dublin, if several practical difficulties could be resolved, he proposed to visit the Blasket Islands.

He had heard about them, of course, from Marstrander—the purity of the Irish spoken there, the islanders and their hard lives, all doubtless enriched and embellished; Marstrander, Bo Almqvist has suggested, was "a bit of a trickster" and, like any good teacher, he could spin a story. Whether in class, or over beer and wine at dinner, Marstrander told Flower of his arrival on the island and the laughably miscued Irish between him and the king. Folklorists today report surprisingly similar stories, at other cultural and linguistic divides, going back centuries, but Flower was hearing it for the first time. To him, Marstrander was larger than life, like a soldier back from the front replete with war stories, improbable tales from the edge of the known world. Flower lapped them up. Two months later, like Synge and Marstrander before him, he was in the home of the island king.

Robin Ernest William Flower was born in Leeds, England, in 1881, son of a portrait painter who'd for a time served in the American Civil War as a Confederate soldier; he eventually deserted and made his way to

Canada, then returned to England. Marmaduke Flower was his name, and he had ancestral ties to Northern Ireland. Robin's mother, Jane, though born in Yorkshire, came from a Galway, Ireland, family. Robin Flower himself graduated from Pembroke College, Oxford, but after graduation he foundered, apparently suffering some sort of breakdown; his health was never robust. He spent time in Cologne, Germany, and in the Orkneys, applying for this or that position. Finally, in 1906, the call came from the British Museum. He never left it.

Flower was the consummate bibliophile, a compulsive consumer of the written word. Island photographs of him sometimes show him with a cigarette dangling from his mouth, hand thrust into pants pocket, looking very much the man of the world. But one of him from around 1910 shows him as he more often was, reading, sitting back in what looks like a tufted leather high-back chair. His head was forever in a book. While still in school, his son Patrick recounted later, he'd head off for the woods on his bicycle, his cat Appleby perched in a string bag suspended from the handlebars, reading as he rode. When he was twelve, a school friend recalled, "his pockets always bulged with cheap magazines"; late to class, he'd be seen "trying to read and run at the same time," working his way up from boys' fiction to Swinburne, Shelley, and Keats. When sometimes

*Robin Flower, about the time of his first
visit to the Blasket in 1910*

a teacher would search his pockets, his classmates were left rapt in wonder at how much reading matter he'd managed to stuff into them.

What might better suit Robin Flower than the British Museum? Located in London's Bloomsbury, off Great Russell Street, founded in 1753, it had grown into one of the world's great cultural institutions, repository of all Britain could draw into its outsized imperial hands; it had the Benin Bronzes, the Elgin Marbles, the Rosetta Stone. Its Manuscripts Department, during the four decades Flower worked there, held ancient and medieval books and manuscripts taken from all over the world. It occupied a group of rooms, or saloons, to the southeast of the great Reading Room on the ground floor, all dark wood and coffered ceilings, tiers and tiers of ancient books, along with low glass-topped wooden cabinets for their public display.

For most of his life, his son wrote later, the Museum was "home from home for the great reader. Thousands of lovely books and manuscripts to absorb." Early on there, his biographer, Idris Bell, wrote of him, Flower would indulge "his practice of wandering about the Department and taking down from the shelves any manuscript which caught his attention"— Elizabethan literature, or Oliver Goldsmith, or even, as a colleague chided him, "Mexican hieroglyphics." His intellectual interests, it would be said of him, were "inexhaustible." Once, Flower translated an eighth-century poem written in Old Irish, "Pangur Ban," which tells of a monk, cat by his side, and the surprising similarities of their work.

> Oftentimes a mouse will stray
> In the hero Pangur's way;
> Oftentimes my keen thought set
> Takes a meaning in its net.
> . . .
> So in peace our tasks we ply,
> Pangur Ban, my cat, and I;
> In our arts we find our bliss,
> I have mine and he has his.

Flower had been at the Museum for four years when, in August 1910, age twenty-eight, he arrived in the Blaskets. He wrote, with characteristic lightness, from the house of the king: "I am safe here in the royal palace, which consists of a fair-sized cabin with an earthen floor and two small rooms built on it to accommodate visitors." He briefly described the village, the houses "thrown down anywhere where they can find a bit of reasonably level ground," the *naomhóg*s and their curiously stunted oar-blades. He was finally learning to row them, he wrote, after earlier being unable to synchronize with the man behind him. He was happily boating, bathing, reading. "I lead the life," he wrote, "of Tír na nÓg here."

The reference, one any self-respecting Celticist would know, was to perhaps the most famous legend in the whole Irish canon, part of the mental landscape of any Irishman even lightly attuned to his culture. It told of a mythical place, beyond any map, located on an island far to the west that could be reached only through an arduous voyage or by invitation of one of its fairy residents. It was a place without sickness or death, full of music, food, drink, and pleasures of every sort, of tireless strength, unending bliss, life lived to the full. It was the Land of the Young. Listen to its music, Flower exhorted his readers in a poem, "Tír na nÓg," that appeared in a slim volume published the year he visited the island:

> And you shall hear it chanting in one triumphant chime
> Of the life that lives for ever and the fugitives of time
> Beyond the green land's border and the washing wastes of sea
> In the world beyond the world's end, where nothing is but glee.
>
> The magic waters gird it, and skies of laughing blue
> Keep always faith with summer, and summer still is true;
> There is no end of dancing and sweet unceasing song,
> And eyes to eyes make answer and love with love grows strong.

Especially pleasant, he wrote near the end of his stay, was "talking with Cáit Ní Catháin, the Princess, who's teaching me Irish at a great rate." Cáit, then about twenty-four, was the younger daughter of the king and sister of Máire, Synge's little hostess. In one of Flower's sessions with her, a boat approached the island, and while it was yet distant, Cáit identified who was aboard. "I tried to say," Flower wrote, " 'You've got good eyes,' but what I said was, 'You've got pretty eyes' (which by the way is quite true). Cáit's answer was 'So have you.' " Abruptly, he realized his error, and they both burst out laughing, agreeing it was "a pardonable mistake."

Flattered by the islanders that his still-fumbling Irish at least boasted "the proper island *blas,*" or accent, he was plainly making progress. He would be leaving on Saturday, he concluded his letter, and back at work the Monday after that. "Remember me to everybody and tell them I am working hard, learning Irish from the prettiest girl on the island."

When he returned the following summer, Flower brought with him his new wife, Ida Mary Streeter, the youngest sister of a friend from Oxford. They had met and fallen in love while he was still a student there and she attended an art school in Hertfordshire of which Flower's father was director. They went on to meet at London's Royal Academy, or the National Gallery, where art students needn't have chaperones. While enjoying his island lessons with Cáit, Flower may already have been engaged to her. He'd been back in London just a few months, living near Leicester Square with his friend Vivian Locke Ellis, a poet, when, in January 1911, the Museum granted him a special two-week leave to be married. The ceremony took place on February 4. The couple went to live in a Chelsea flat, and that summer he brought her to the island.

Later, Flower wrote Richard Best in Dublin of their "glorious time there. The weather was too hot, and I was too tired for any serious work, but I got to be able to speak and understand pretty well. . . . My wife enjoyed herself thoroughly," he added, "and did some rather nice sketches of the island."

They were better than nice; our feeling for the village in that summer of 1911 owes as much to her as to him. While he worked on his Irish, Ida, who was pregnant at the time, roamed the island with pencil, sketchbook, and drawing board, making finely detailed renderings of the village and its cozy interiors. Together, they bathe the village in a balmier, more settled light than that by which it's more often seen. Maps and surviving photographs don't suggest a place that could have leapt intact from a Hollywood soundstage. Ida Flower's drawings do.

A pen-and-ink she made of the interior of the king's house suggests all the comforts of home, rudimentary though they were. In the middle, the *croch,* or fireplace crane—the sturdy, trusslike structure from which pots were suspended over the hearth. The settle, a bare wood bench, off to the side. A beam reaching across the breadth of the room, supporting a loft, a kind of rude attic, bearing household gear. All modeled by soft window light. Three years earlier, Marstrander judged the house to represent "as good lodgings as I found in Ballyferriter," meaning Willie Long's place, a commercial inn. It still was.

Island houses were truly *homes,* some imperfectly maintained, others neat, warm, and snug. Floors were of beaten clay, the area around the fireplace stone-flagged; sand brought up from the White Strand would be scattered on the floor and, with any animal waste, swept out daily. The largest houses were about twelve by twenty-five feet on the inside; most were smaller. With a few exceptions, they were oriented the same way, their front doors facing south, one of the short sides dug into the hillside, offering the smallest target for prevailing westerly winds and rain. *Cluthair,* meaning cozy or snug, was the ideal. On the sheltered side of the house it was as if you were "in another country," poet Máire Mhac an tSaoi, who spent the summers of her youth across the sound, in Dún Chaoin, has noted of similar houses on the mainland. "The old houses had their own charm and they were very comfortable. Mind you, when you got out of one of those westerly gales . . . into the warm kitchen it really was the height of luxury."

During Flower's earliest visits to the island, big changes were in the works, altering the village more than anything in the last century. Like much of West Kerry, the island had in 1907 been declared a "congested district." In fact, such districts were in no way congested the way Dublin and Belfast were, with crowds of urban dwellers, but distinctly rural. They were "congested" only in the particular sense of being so poor, so barren of industry, jobs, or opportunity for life at anything but bare subsistence, that they were thought to hold more humanity than they could support.

The Congested District Board bought up Blasket croplands owned for ages by the Earl of Cork and reorganized the system of land tenure. It repaired and improved village paths, put islanders to paying work. It condemned some houses as unfit, and built five new ones, in the upper village, in three structures. To this day, even from across the sound in Dún Chaoin, they stand out from the rest of the village. They sit higher on the hill, farther west, a little apart from the other houses. They have two stories, not one, with interior staircases leading up to an additional room. Built of concrete, not stone, they have staircases and floors made of timber brought across the sound to the treeless isle.

Another project was to improve the slip where the *naomhógs* docked. Among those who worked on it—on his first visit to the island, in the summer of 1910—was Flower. A photo shows the work crew posed beside the slipway with their spades and pails, rubble and stone. They are a serious-looking bunch, wearing hats, vests, sweaters, and heavy boots. But Flower stands hatless, shoeless, and sockless, his head swung up toward the camera in a broad smile. At the British Museum, of course, he was hardly used to physical labor, so the work took its toll in blistered hands. "My high-spirited friend," an islander with whom he'd worked, began a letter to him later, in Irish, thanking him for gifts he'd sent from Dingle. And then: "Are the pickaxe marks still there?"

As we've seen, Flower returned to the island in 1911; then he came again every year through 1914. In 1913, he wrote Kuno Meyer that he'd had a productive time, transcribing island stories for three hours a day, hunting rabbits with the king's son, Seán. In 1914, he was on the island when word reached them that the Austrian archduke had been assassinated, setting off the Great War. It was 1925 before Flower returned, this time with his children, as he would many times more over the rest of his life.

At least from 1912 if not before, he was called "Bláithín" on the island, Irish for "Little Flower." Of all the distinctions and honors awarded him over the years, it was noted in a radio talk a few days after his death, this "honour from the little island kingdom was that which Robin Flower appreciated most of all."

On his first visit to the island, Flower became aware of changes the Congested District Board was making in how fields were allotted for cultiva-

Hatless, shoeless, and, it seems, callous-less: Robin Flower on a crew helping to build the village's new pier—work from which the London scholar's hands came away well blistered. Tomás Ó Criomhthain stands to Flower's left.

tion. In the old "rundale" system, which went back to the Middle Ages, each family owned strips of land scattered widely over the island. In the new system, each family got land concentrated in a few areas. "You may imagine," he would write, "the process of ingenious and complicated judging by which this metamorphosis was effected." Most of these intricate debates, however, went right by him. "It is one of the great regrets of my life that this happened at a time when my knowledge of Irish was so rudimentary that I could not follow the arguments that went on round me." He remembered "foaming crests of rhetoric." But just then, in August 1910, he could understand little of it.

Given how adept he became in Irish, it may be hard to imagine a time when he wasn't. But at first, Flower struggled with it like everyone else. Indeed, although the pickax letter cited previously was written in Irish, its author appended a few sentences in schoolbook English. "Dear young gentleman. I don't like to finish this letter in Irish for fear that you couldn't understand the whole of it." It was signed Tomás Ó Criomhthain.

Ó Criomhthain, of course, was Marstrander's teacher. He had become Robin Flower's. And it is perhaps time we addressed him as Flower would all his life, and as he was generally known by the visitors who revered him: *Tomás*—just the one name, confused with no one else on the island. Flower would write of returning to the island, being greeted by the villagers, doling out sweets to the children, watching them run out the door and onto the hill with their prizes. And then:

> A sudden feeling comes upon you of a new presence in the room. You look up and see, leaning against the wall almost with the air of a being magically materialized out of nothing, a slight but confident figure. The face takes your attention at once and holds it. This face is dark and thin, and there look out of it two quick and living eyes, the vivid witnesses of a fine and self-sufficing intelligence. He comes towards you and, with a grave and courteous intonation, and a picked and running phrase, bids you welcome.

This is Tomás. It should be plain by now that he was no simple fisherman.

Chapter 3

Brian's Chair

[1917]

On an island where hardly anyone knew how to read and write Irish, Tomás learned to do both. The wonder is, how?

By one strand of evidence from 1936, a Gaelic League teacher came to the island in 1905, when Tomás was about forty-nine. From him, Tomás learned to read his native language, then taught himself to write by imitating what he found in books.

That's one possibility. Another is that Tomás may have learned to read a little Irish in the Protestant school that, back in the 1860s, when he was of school age, still had a place on the island. Around the time of the Famine, Irish Protestants set up schools throughout the country that dispensed soup and other needed nourishment, along with liberal doses of theology, and instruction through the Irish language. "Soupers," Catholics called these proselytizing Protestants. On the Great Blasket, the Scoil an tSúip was located down the hill, near the approach to the village. Tomás may for a time have attended.

If so, when he got the chance to tell his story later, by which time the Protestant presence on the island was gone, he'd hardly have wanted to bruit it about. His own account, certainly, makes no mention of it, but credits his introduction to written Irish to the very end of the nineteenth century. It seems that, when bad weather left him stuck on the mainland with his boat, he'd often stay in the Dún Chaoin house of a cousin, whose children were by now being introduced to Irish in school. They read to him, the way Tomás tells it, "until I got a taste for the business and made them give me the book." He caught on quickly, his stock of spoken Irish alchemically transmuting the ink squiggles of the books into order and sense. "My head was full of it, and, if I came across a limping sentence, all I had to do was to hunt for it in my own brain." In time, he gathered a few books himself and took to reading them to other islanders. It gave him pleasure. He never wearied of it, "for I was red-hot to go ahead." By the time Carl Marstrander showed up on the island, Tomás was a decade into working with the language, and the villager best equipped by far to help the visitor with it.

Tomás was a proud man, especially of his abilities in written Irish. Among a group of letters he wrote in the early 1920s, some, treated purely as objects of calligraphic art, must be reckoned minor gems. Written in the old style, where pronunciation changes of consonants are marked by little dots rather than the auxiliary "h"s they get now, they rarely show so much as a smudge or cross-out. The "fadas," accent marks, are spare, graceful slashes, like the fine lines of an etching. When signing his name, Tomás does so sometimes with a flourish that hints at the outsized sense of self behind it.

He was born in 1855 or 1856, grew up in "a cramped little house, roofed with rushes from the hill." Hens nested in the thatch and laid eggs in it. He lived there with his parents and older siblings, together with their cow, ass, and chickens. His father's family had come from Dún Chaoin and married into the island. "My father was a marvellous fisherman and a great man for work"—a stonemason, a boat's captain, and altogether "handy at every trade." So was Tomás. He was probably in his teens when he began his life as a fisherman.

As part of a boat crew, young Tomás would sometimes visit Inishvick-illaun, one of the Lesser Blaskets, a few miles away. A single family lived there, the Dalys, with their five sons and five daughters. To young Tomás, it has been written, Inishvickillaun "was Tír na nOg, with sport and fun and company, and fine, lively, beautiful girls with big hearts." He fell in love with one of them, Cáit. On one visit, Tomás would write, Cáit "went out the door and, as she went out, waved me out too that I might follow her." Follow her out he did, "not pretending anything." It was a fine November day in 1877. It seemed possible they would marry.

But larger family interests intervened. Cáit's family lived a hard *naomhóg* row away, not right at hand when help was needed. A better match, Tomás's older sister insisted, would be a young Blasket woman, Máire Mhici, sister of the future island king. Weeks later, in February 1878, the two were married. Some controversy lingers as to whether a sad, lonely song Tomás sang at the wedding in Ballyferriter was just a pretty song or amounted to a public lament for his lost love. "I well knew how to deliver it," Tomás recalled. "You would think that there was no other voice in the house, loud or soft, until I had finished it."

The loss of Cáit was hardly his last. All told, he had ten children with Máire Mhici; she died in childbirth with the last of them, in about 1902. One child, aged seven, fell to his death from a cliff. Two died of measles. One immigrated to America. Tomás would one day record this sad litany under the heading of "The Troubles of Life," describing them in language so spare and unadorned as to seem coldhearted. "I was told he was very hard and tough in his youth," his grandson, Pádraig Ua Maoileoin, would assert. That's just how the Ó Criomhthains were, "like iron in body and soul. It was difficult to make them cry, or shed a tear. It was difficult to imagine them mourning someone's death."

But at least once, Tomás did. In the early summer of 1909, Eveleen Nichols, a student at the School of Irish Learning in Dublin, and already, at twenty-four, a rising figure in the language movement, visited the island; the Gaelic League was by then encouraging people to visit West Kerry to better learn the language. She took to the island right away, making friends with Tomás's daughter Cáit. "One day they would be on the hill," Tomás would remember, "another about the strand and the sea; and when the weather was soft and warm they used to go swimming." One August afternoon, the sea was breaking hard on the beach and they got caught in the tide. They tired. They called for help. Tomás's eighteen-year-old son, Domhnall, was digging potatoes in a field above the beach—accounts differ on this and other details of the tragedy—when he heard the commotion and realized they were in trouble. He threw down his spade, bolted to the beach, and, still in clothes and shoes, ran into the surf. When he found his sister safe, he swam out to save Nichols. Both of them drowned. Tomás and brother Pats were returning from the day's fishing and spied boats bringing to shore two lifeless bodies. When he reached the confused scene, he saw first the boy's shoes—or, rather, their soles, with a nail pattern he recognized at once; he'd repaired them himself. "He let out a scream," someone said later, "that could be heard on the two sides of the village."

Tomás would tell of brothers and sisters dying; of islanders hurt or killed in accidents and drownings; of casting a crab-baited line for rockfish and getting the hook stuck in his finger. But he told of wakes and Christmases and weddings, too, of dripping lobster pots, of hiking up the hill to cut turf. He played hurling on the beach in his bare feet. He made windows from driftwood washed up onto the shore. He made panniers for the donkeys. He built himself a house. He hunted seals and rabbits. He fished.

But he was never an ordinary fisherman. At the island school, Tomás had learned to read and write—read and write English, that is—better than most other islanders. At least once, when the teacher was laid up, he and another older boy were delegated to fill in for him. Tomás was a natural pick: "Dónall's Scholar," they sometimes called this son of Dónall Ó Criomhthain. By 1907, certainly, he had a reputation as a man of studious temperament, interested in books, reading, and learning; small wonder that Marstrander and other Irish-language devotees were sent his way. And for all the push for English in those days, the Irishness rose up in him. In the 1901 census, he gave his name as Thomas Crohan; in 1911, he was Tomás Ó Criomhthain, the only island name recorded that year in Irish. He'd early grown interested in the work of the Gaelic League, which even in tiny neighboring Dún Chaoin had a presence, and at some point began sending brief stories to Irish-language publications.

Later, when books bearing his name appeared in print, reviews were apt to picture them as the work of an Authentic Blasket Islander, unmediated by art, a peasant incarnate, profoundly *of* his island home; indeed, that was made to seem the rare wonder of them, that they'd come from so unpromising a source, from so ordinary a peasant fisherman. But Tomás Ó Criomhthain, it stands repeating, was no ordinary anything, much less fisherman. By any standard, whether of his time or our own, he was "gifted." And all the visitors knew it. Marstrander did. So did Robin Flower.

Thinking back to his early days with him, Flower described Tomás as "a small, lively man, with a sharp, intelligent face, weathered and wrinkled by the sun and rain and the flying salt of the sea, out of which two bright, observant eyes looked critically upon the world." Together they'd sit in Tomás's house, or in the king's kitchen, or under the lee of a turf rick, Tomás disgorging "tales and poetry and proverbs," together with "precise explanations of difficult words" and lively observations of the island world around him.

The two of them, said Flower's daughter Síle, who saw them together a lot on the island in the 1920s, became "tremendously close friends. I think he must have been one of his best friends in life. . . . They loved each other," and had a great deal in common. After Flower's first visit, in 1910, the two of them kept in frequent touch. Tomás wrote him about the island roads and houses they'd worked on together, congratulated him on his marriage. Flower sent him tobacco, and money, too. One time, Tomás wrote back about the hit he'd made with some money Flower had sent, distributing it among the islanders in the form of beer. Typically, he'd write to Flower in Irish, often appending a letter in English to Mrs. Flower as well, thanking her for the calendar she'd send him each Christmas. Once the war was over, he told her in a 1915 letter, he would "cross the Irish Sea out to him. Then the children might have Irish out there. He might laugh when he will hear this. . . ." Tomás concluded with a few words in Irish

His face "is dark and thin, and there look out of it two quick and living eyes, the vivid witness of a fine and self-sufficing intelligence": Tomás Ó Criomhthain, as Robin Flower described him, shown here about 1925.

to her husband, then added: "May the Almighty God protect and save ye from all danger's that's going about."

But by 1916, the world war had been on for two years, and it had been that long since the two men had seen each other. Flower was in London, but just then relieved of his regular job at the Museum and assigned to translating foreign newspapers, sometimes more than a hundred a week. "At present I am in despair under the weight of the Dutch and Belgian press," he wrote late that year. "It is horrid work."

By this time, Tomás stood off to the side of his island brethren—or in some ways, it's difficult to deny, above them. He couldn't have been immune to the attention and respect he'd gained. It had to have been exhilarating to be singled out, introduced to the Norwegian linguist, to work with him, teach him, be sought after for knowledge. And likewise to engage in far-ranging conversations with the scholar from the great museum in London. Tomás might reasonably have concluded, and with some satisfaction, that he had transcended by far what might otherwise have been his lot. Or else, in a darker, elegiac mood—he was now about sixty, wizened, past his physical prime—he might have concluded that he had done all of noble note he would ever do.

But then, in the middle of the war, as Europe shed the blood of its young, Brian Kelly arrived on the island.

Brian Albert Kelly was twenty-eight at the time, from Killarney, a mid-sized town fifty miles or so east of the Blaskets, yet worlds apart. His family was well off, had a drapery shop and a hotel in town, the Crystal Palace, their children mostly destined for careers in law, medicine, and the church. Brian attended Dublin-area schools and went on to Trinity College, from which he graduated with a bachelor's degree in 1911, having studied the classics, modern history, English literature, and Old Irish. For at least five years, even after his graduation, he remained active in the Dublin University Gaelic Society.

Then Kelly got caught up in a nasty bit of international intrigue. In April 1914, after a year in Paris, he'd gone to Germany to study history, and completed a term at the University of Marburg. But with the onset of the war, he'd been gathered up in a sweep of foreign students and landed in prison. He wrote to Kuno Meyer, of the School of Irish Learning, whom he had known in Dublin, and who might have some pull with the authorities. But Meyer was out of the country, so it fell to his sister Antonie to pull strings on Kelly's behalf, get him out of prison, and connect him with Roger Casement.

Casement: rebel, revolutionary, martyr. A memorable figure who in the years since his death has inspired a whole raft of biographies. An Irish-born diplomat, he had only a few years before, in 1911, been knighted by King George V for his work illuminating human-rights abuses in Congo and the Putumayo River region of Peru. But with the start of the war, his anti-imperialistic streak and deep sympathy for the Irish national-ist cause led him to Germany. He had a plan—to form an Irish brigade from Irish prisoners-of-war that, German-armed, would fight England from Irish soil. The plan went nowhere. Meanwhile, word got out of his apparently promiscuous homosexuality. In August 1916, despite pleas for a reprieve from George Bernard Shaw, Sir Arthur Conan Doyle, and other luminaries, he was hanged for treason.

But not before he had responded to Kelly's plea from prison and brought him to Berlin, where the two of them met. Casement tried to enlist him in his plan to recruit Irish POWs, briefly embedded him in a prison camp in Limburg where twenty-five hundred of them were held, and finally had him released, as promised. As Kelly put it in a secret report to the British authorities early the following year, Casement seemed to him an "impulsive and excitable man," who saw England as the destroyer of European peace, Germany the nation of the future, and Ireland its natural friend. "Unhinged" was his ultimate assessment of him.

By the time Casement went to the gallows, Kelly was back in Killarney, probably living at home, recovering from his brush with dangerous men and tumultuous times. And it is at this point that his fifty-six-year-old mother, Bridget Kelly, steps into our story. Was Brian, after his war-time ordeal, unable to take any firm next step for himself? Or was Mrs. Kelly simply better connected around Killarney and thus better suited to make inquiries on his behalf? In any case, it was she who, in the fall of 1916, a few months after the Easter Rising, approached Mr. Pádraig Ó Siochfhradha—in English this was usually spelled, and pronounced, "Sugrue"—a Gaelic League teacher prominent in those parts. Might he, she asked, come to their home and, once a week, give her son lessons in spoken Irish? Brian had studied Old Irish in school, but modern Irish was the new badge of Irish republican sensibility. And he, like many with their heads in books, could not speak it.

To hear Ó Siochfhradha's account, he and Brian got on well. "We understood each other," he wrote later. "He enjoyed my friendliness and my understanding; he was gentle, shy, and, I'd imagine, inclined to be a loner. But when he'd sense the good will and friendliness in a person, he'd open up." Over the course of half a dozen sessions, Kelly improved considerably. Yet, if he was to make further progress, they agreed, he needed to go where Irish was spoken, the *Gaeltacht.* He had no job, family, or money worries to stand in the way, so he was soon off to the Blaskets, letter of introduction in hand for Tomás Ó Criomhthain.

In April 1917, he landed on the island, remaining there for the rest of the year.

It is a calm day on the Great Blasket. Tomás is gathering mussels at the water's edge when he looks up to see two young women. "Are there limpets here, Tomás?" There are, he replies. But how, he asks, do they propose to scrape off the tenacious little mollusks? All they have between them is a broken pair of scissors and an iron bolt. Maybe they should send their mothers instead: "Wouldn't they have more skill and craft for the work?"

But if their mothers did it, one of them says, how would they learn to do it themselves? Besides, "isn't it grand to be here by the sea's edge at low tide? The lovely smell that's there when everything that was under the sea before is under the sun now and its mouth gaping."

We say Tomás Ó Criomhthain "told" this story because it appears in a book listing him as author. In Irish it was called *Allagar na hInise,* published in 1928 by Government Publications, Dublin, later translated into English as *Island Cross-Talk,* published in 1986 by Oxford University Press, and still in print. An extraordinary transformation had taken place. Blasket stories, for generations told around peat fires or at the village well, had been catapulted into the world beyond the island, given fixed and permanent form on paper, bound between the covers of books. A man who had grown up on a treeless island and made his living from fishing and farming, who had never seen Dublin, or even Tralee, or ventured beyond the next peninsula across Dingle Bay, who was largely illiterate for at least the first forty years of his life, was now an author. It was like the First Books all over again: however they'd first come into the world, books had somehow been reborn on this little island where almost no one knew how to read. *How was this possible? How could this be?*

In fact, even before Brian's coming in 1917, the printed word was not quite so alien to the Great Blasket as it once had been, or as it might have seemed, say, from Dublin. The Gaelic League issued two Irish-language publications—*An Claidheamh Soluis,* sword of light, and *Fáinne an Lae,* dawn of day—and Tomás, who'd by now been reading and writing Irish for fifteen or twenty years, had contributed to both of them. He had served as Marstrander's research assistant—*research assistant?* what else would you call him?—compiling lists of local flora and fauna and sending them to Oslo. In 1915, he had written a founding member of the Gaelic League, Seosamh Laoide, about a book he had recently read, *Tonn Tóime* (the great wave, said to have borne the legendary Oisin to the Land of the Young). In both English and Irish, he observed, small words, the pebbles of language, mattered more than did the big, imposing ones.

Tomás, then, was already linked to a larger world of language and ideas. After Robin Flower's second Blasket visit, Tomás felt qualified to congratulate him on his improved Irish. A few years later, after the birth of Flower's daughter Síle, he appended a note to Mrs. Flower, saying, "I am going to help Mr. Flower to be an Irish Professor, the same as Mr. Marstrander." Tomás Ó Criomhthain, then, had become the island's resident intellectual. He was mentor to his young scholarly friends. He was master of Irish, and knew he was. If he had something to say as a writer, he would probably be able to say it.

But when Brian Kelly—or Brian Ó Ceallaigh, as he was known in Irish—came to the island, he found Tomás jotting down folktales and song lyrics. How long, one wonders, and under what circumstances of trust and friendship, did it take him to get Tomás to write about his life on the island, about *himself*?

Oh, but "everyone knows what life is like here," Kelly reported Tomás as replying when he finally did ask. And it was true: most everyone Tomás knew lived on the island, knew its life intimately; they'd all probably by now heard many of his stories, nuggets of personal wisdom, choice bits of folklore. But Kelly was thinking bigger, of a different, larger audience, *off* the island. He said so later—that he'd tried to make Tomás realize how interesting the life of the island could be "for people who were accustomed to a more comfortable and uncomplicated existence." He wanted more from Tomás. He had *ambitions* for him! Set against Tomás's limited experience, that might be seen as unreasonable or unrealistic. But Kelly persisted. He pushed. He prodded Tomás to write. He practically dragged it out of him.

One evening, while walking along an island path, Brian suggested to him that he write something about emigration—or started to suggest it, anyway, because just then they came upon some island women, walking in pairs, singing. *No,* said Brian, all but amending his advice in mid-stride, "Write about what you see at this moment." Tomás did. It was called "An Guth ar Neoin," or "The Voice in the Afternoon," and it managed to link the women they'd met with Brian's original suggestion. The women were singing "in lively, eloquent Irish," Tomás wrote. That made for a lovely and memorable sight, sure to leave a bystander feeling right with the world. But the *words* of their song, carried by that "voice in the afternoon," were bleak: if only they had the passage money, the girls sang, they'd be on a boat for America. Later that year, Tomás's story was published in *An Lóchrann,* the lantern, an Irish-language monthly.

Tomás often gathered turf along the hillside, or fished from a rock as the sun set, reveling in the sheer beauty of God's creation. Write about it, Brian urged. "You can't live on scenery," Tomás shot back. Yet, spurred by his Killarney friend, he wrote just such a piece, which was published the following year. It was about a field at the edge of the White Strand where the two of them would sit and talk. Brian would plunk himself down on a particular rock that Tomás called "Brian's Chair." And from that anointed spot, late one afternoon, Tomás described the vista, the sun spreading above him to the north, the cliffs on the mainland, no two the same color. "I don't think, and I wouldn't think, that there could be any other colours in the world than these." To the editor who published the essay, Brian reported, "it proved that a feeling for nature, akin to that of Wordsworth, existed among the Gaelic-speaking people."

That was just the beginning; once Brian Kelly got to him, Tomás's output never flagged, his days with Brian forever bathed in a golden light of memory. Many gentlemen came to the island, he wrote to Flower after the war, but "no one of them ever looked after Tomás but one"; he *didn't* mean Flower. In a letter he wrote to Brian himself, in 1921, he composed this lonely poem:

> The nights are getting longer and the days are shortening
> On the fields of the Great Blasket.
> If only I could see Brian this year
> On the fields of the Great Blasket.
> It is very true that life is troubled
> Every year since we parted from one another
> But we will be reunited one day
> On the fields of the Great Blasket.

What breed of magic did Brian work on Tomás? What imagination, what urgent caring and love, did he lavish on Tomás that led to a succession of sustained creative acts culminating in two accomplished works of literature? How did he pull it out of him? How did he overcome whatever grip of assumption and expectation might otherwise have bound Tomás to the past and limited his aspirations? What did he bring to his friendship with Tomás that, for example, Robin Flower did not?

Oddly, Brian's own stunted career may have left him more receptive to Tomás's potential as a writer, more approachable; compared with Flower—who, his biographer could write, was "exacting in his standards and not without his prejudices"—he was probably easier to please. When he came to the island in early 1917, he was twenty-seven. He had time on his hands. He had no job; he had apparently never held a proper job, was still rooting around for what to do with his life. Some accounts suggest he was unsettled, and lonely. He had, though, a degree of literary discernment. That was the verdict, anyway, of Irish nationalist leader and scholar Eoin MacNeill, cofounder of the Gaelic League, after Kelly's death: "He had an instinct for the values of language," MacNeill wrote of him, and "true literary taste." Moreover, Kelly had only just awakened from his dark, values-challenging night of war, imprisonment, and treason, and may have come away with looser, less received notions of how the world was supposed to work. It took imagination, and a certain distaste for hierarchy and prejudice, to see Tomás as someone who, despite his want of education, could create written language that was beautiful, heartfelt, worthy.

Before he left the island and returned to the mainland at the very end of 1917, Brian supplied Tomás with a stock of ink and paper, the oversized kind known as foolscap, and asked him to write bits and pieces of his experience and post them to him. Not once in a while, but regularly, so many pages at a clip. And, to seal the bargain, he bestowed on Tomás a gift, his own Waterman fountain pen.

Tomás cherished that pen, according to his son Seán, a teenager when Kelly left the island. After dinner, around eight in the evening, Tomás would pull up to the table beside the fireplace. A lamp high on the wall, with two thick wicks and a mirror behind it, shed plenty of light. Tomás would draw up to the fire, light his pipe, "smoke a fine blast" of it, lay out his paper, and set to work in the quiet of the house, till maybe ten o'clock, or half past. And when he was finished, Seán recalled, "he'd dry it with a piece of cloth and a bit of paper and put it away. If a butterfly or a cricket

Part of a letter, in Irish, from Tomás Ó Criomhthain to Brian Kelly, who more than anyone else encouraged him as a writer.

in the corner as much as touched it he'd nearly kill them. Not a hand was to be laid on the pen in case it might be damaged."

At first, Tomás wondered if maybe Brian wanted his scribblings merely to assure himself a steady stream of Irish, to keep up his language skills—or so he said later, out of who knows what false modesty. But he came to understand that Brian wanted the best for him. "He said it would be a pity if I were idle."

Tomás had told Brian about one day in his youth, on a turf-gathering expedition to the other side of the island, when he'd been waylaid by Seán Ó Duinnshlé, or Seán Dunlevy, an island poet who died in 1889. "Well, isn't it a pity for you to be cutting turf on such a hot day," said the poet. "Sit down a bit, the day is long, and it'll be cool in the afternoon." As the two of them lay out in the sun, Dunlevy recited a long, angry poem about a sheep killed by neighbors:

> Aréir is mé go haoiblhinn
> Is mé sínte ar mo thaoibh deas
> 'Sea tháinig aisling taoibh liom
> Do sprioguigh mé thar meón . . .

At the end, according to Tomás, Dunlevy asked if he had something to write it down with: "The poem will be lost if somebody doesn't pick it up." Tomás fished out paper and pencil and, in some crude English-based phonetic script, recorded it. Now, these many years later, Brian was making a similar plea. "I thought it a pity that [the life of the island] would die, unrecorded, and I felt that Tomás could make it live on paper for future generations." He needed to write about the ordinary and everyday in island life.

And so Tomás did, for five years the flow never abating. Sharply observed little stories, rarely more than a few paragraphs, a few hundred words at a pop; short gathered dialogues; moral lessons; bits of light comedy. The first to make it into *Allagar na hInise* (which represented only about a third of Tomás's output), was dated April 1919. "Seamus and His Cravings," it was called in the book's English translation, *Island Cross-Talk,* and it describes men working in the fields who stop for a smoking break. Another tells of an island character, Tadhg the Joker, who hears a cuckoo but fears no one else has. A third pictures as many women gathered at the village well "as there are in Killarney. . . . They drowned the noise of the King and the noise of the ocean too." We learn the price of sugar, flour, and tobacco, island blessings, ornate curses. Some stories carry a bitter tang, reflect the harshness of island life. Others are warm and wise. Still others express moments of idyllic beauty. And inevitably, right in the middle of things, stands Tomás.

"The mountains were aglow with every hue," he writes in the spring of 1920.

A fire was burning here and there, tokens that people were cutting turf in various parts of the bog. The sea was calm with currachs coming and going. Seán Léan was rowing a currach, all by himself, as proud as the Prince of Wales in his stately yacht. The fish were lifting their heads out of the water, the birds singing their music and on land the people were stripped to their shirts, re-earthing the potatoes. Groups were coming down both sides of the hill with bundles of furze, and children raced east along the slope after morning school. Smoke was rising from every house at this time—dinner on the way surely.

A vignette recorded a few months earlier suggests how the island's "simple life" could be anything but. A neighbor walks by Tomás's house and the two stop to chat. "I have the seven cares of the mountain on my shoulders," Seán Shéamais tells him. "I need turf. I have sheep to dip. I need flour. I have a wall to repair. I have a shed to rebuild. I have a trawl-line to see to and a net to prepare." He can't decide what to do first and in frustration has "left the house now to have a day away from it all." Tomás is not sympathetic.

For all the iconic status granted Ó Criomhthain's later work, *The Islandman*, some hold *Island Cross-Talk* to be more interesting. "I had forgotten that it contained such fine things," observed George Thomson after reading it again in Irish many years after its first publication. "Yes, indeed, it does recall Irish nature poetry, and Shakespeare's sonnets as well." Pádraig Ua Maoileoin, Tomás's grandson, called it "the great pearl of Tomás's writing," praising it for "nice little scenes beautifully assembled and polished," like stones on the shore worked and polished by the waves.

"A long-distance conversation with his friend Brian"—that's how Blasket scholar Muiris Mac Conghail described it. But, although encouraged by Brian, Tomás probably never felt wholly free to express all that he saw and felt. His family, friends, and neighbors were crowded one on top of another in a tiny village at one end of an island. Everyone was a cousin of everyone else, the families entwined by marriage. He had gumption to write about them as honestly as he did, but there were limits. Tomás changed names. He held back. He didn't always "manage to describe what was in his heart," said Pádraig Ua Maoileoin. "There was no way that poor man could do that and live within that community. They lived [there] in each other's shadow."

But what he did he did. "He was a mason as well as a fisherman," Brian said of him, "accustomed to put up a house stone by stone. 'Do the same with words as you would with stones,' I used to say to him." The pages of foolscap in Brian's care piled up, 189 of them before Tomás was finished. An entry for April 1922 tells of a Clare man seeking an islander to improve his Irish, leading Tomás to mention Brian Kelly by name: "I don't know whether anyone else in the country has as much written Irish in front of him as he has to hand." And then he adds: "Wouldn't it delight my heart to be able to read a book of my own before I died."

We enjoy here the hindsight of history, sure that Tomás's efforts will bear fruit, that his work ultimately will get bound between covers and set before the world. But Tomás wished for this in 1922, and it would be many a long year of uncertainty and doubt, demanding more than anything Brian Kelly could give it, before he'd be able to pose for a photograph, leaning against the low stone wall in front of his house, with his own book in his own hands.

Tomás's stories were almost all rooted in the life of the island itself—acts of kindness, foolishness, or bravery, clever repartee, chatter at the village well, accidents and injuries, and always the changing weather. But news of the big world did sometimes make its way across Blasket Sound. Twice a week in good weather, the king brought mail by *naomhóg*. And the islanders were always much attuned to prices in the mainland markets, on whose whim their livelihoods depended. In June 1919, mackerel went for four shillings a hundredweight in Dingle, lobsters for a shilling a piece. In September, in the wake of a carters' strike in Dún Chaoin that kept their catch from market, villagers groused that an ounce of tobacco cost almost a shilling, a new net four pounds. The island stood apart from the rest of Ireland—but not entirely so.

In November 1919, the islanders learned that Éamon de Valera, a leader of the 1916 Rising, was in California, raising money for the nationalist cause. What would freedom mean? asked Séamaisín, in one of Tomás's vignettes. "One crowned King of England and another crowned King of Ireland—that," said Tomás, "is something you'll never see, Diarmaid, so long as the sun is in the sky. If there is a crown on a King in Ireland it will be England's crown he will have to wear."

"I hope you're proved wrong!" said Diarmaid Bán.

In the spring of 1920, Tomás noted the death of the Mayor of Cork, shot by British soldiers.

Then, a little later: "A currach has come in with the news that every train in Ireland was halted." Food was scarce. Men were dying in a hunger strike. Serious fighting was expected.

July 1921 brought talk of home rule, following a truce in the Anglo-Irish War. Negotiations were to follow in London.

In fact, the years of Brian's visits and Tomás's *Island Cross-Talk* stories corresponded to the most tumultuous time in Ireland's recent history. The 1916 Rising, today an iconic moment in Ireland's struggle to become itself, began when a few Irish republicans took over Dublin's General Post Office and declared a provisional government. "Irishmen and Irishwomen: In the name of God and of the dead generations from which she receives her old tradition of nationhood, Ireland, through us, summons her children to her flag and strikes for her freedom."

It was lofty talk, and most Irish didn't at first pay it heed. But then the leaders of the rebellion were summarily executed by the British; martyrs all, they became. Public opinion shifted. A general election two years later brought loud calls for independence from the Crown. Elected Members of Parliament representing Ireland convened an Irish Parliament, or Dáil, and proclaimed an Irish Republic. The British refused to accept its legitimacy, touching off the War of Independence that ground on from January 1919 to July 1921. Among the British ranks were seven thousand soldiers, recruited by advertisements in Britain as willing to take on a "rough and dangerous task." They were furnished with dark-green and khaki uniforms that led them to be called the Black and Tans. They proved notorious for their brutality.

The truce in July 1921 was followed by a treaty in December. It called for the British to leave Ireland; Northern Ireland to remain part of the United Kingdom; members of a new Irish parliament to swear allegiance to the British Crown. Irish opinion split. Brother divided against brother. The resulting civil war between pro- and anti-treaty forces was as terrible as the War of Independence, took more lives, and in the scale of its atrocities was just as cruel.

On the first day of January 1923, Tomás concluded *Island Cross-Talk*.

"I am writing this at the start of the New Year in God's name, and if we spent the Old Year well, may we spend the New Year seven times better. . . . Since our people throughout Ireland cannot understand each other, may God grant the grace of understanding to them before the year is long gone."

In May, a cease-fire ended the civil war.

In August, the first elections of the Irish Free State were held.

Late that month, George Thomson, straight from King's College, Cambridge, and bound for the Blaskets, arrived in Dingle while elections were in progress, arousing the suspicions of Irish police.

Chapter 4

Nice Boy with a Camera

[1923]

A few months before he left for Ireland, George Thomson had finished up his first year at King's College, among the oldest and most storied of Cambridge University's two dozen or so colleges, founded in 1441. A scholarship student in classics, he occupied rooms looking out onto Chetwynd Court, adjacent to a classroom whose leaded-glass windows whispered church as much as college. Above him lived another classicist, below a budding mathematician admitted to King's the same year he was. Both had gone to distinguished English public schools dating back to the fifteenth and sixteenth centuries—one to Saint Dunstan's, the other to Christ's Hospital School, which counted Samuel Taylor Coleridge and Charles Lamb among its "Old Blues." Thomson himself was a product of the similarly venerable Dulwich College.

George's father, William, was a chartered public accountant, not especially wealthy, but hardworking. Family lore and correspondence establish him as the illegitimate son of a British judge long stationed in India, Sir William Markby, and a French peasant girl he'd met in his mid-thirties on a trip back to England before his marriage. William was taken in by a Scottish carpenter and his family in the north of England; Markby contributed to his care and, later, his education.

Early in the new century, on June 6, 1900, thirty-seven-year-old William Thomson married Minnie Clements, twenty-three, daughter of a civil servant. On hearing of the impending wedding, Markby wrote William, signaling his approval—he knew the bride's father—and sending him a check as a wedding present. George Derwent Thomson had two older sisters, but was the oldest of their three boys, born August 19, 1903; his middle name owed to the picturesque Derwentwater area of the Lake District, which his parents liked to visit. When the family sat for a photograph in the summer of 1920—all of them clustered around the dark-complexioned paterfamilias with his big drooping mustache, the women in their long summer dresses and high collars or chokers—the five children made for a fresh-faced, singularly handsome brood.

In 1916, when he was about twelve, George set up a lending library out of his home, stocked with Macaulay and Ruskin, Dickens and Scott, Austen and Thackeray. The holdings of what he variously called his "Select Library," or " 'Den' Library of Famous Literature," were listed in a hand-inked catalogue, broken down into biography, fiction, and poetry, peppered with charming little graphic devices, and setting out a formidably starched list of rules worthy of libraries anywhere. Books needed to be returned within fourteen days, though exceptions, George allowed, were permitted. His library, he advised readers, comprised "nearly one hundred & fifty volumes of all that is best in English and Foreign Literature and is always increasing in numbers." Whether slavishly following the grown-ups or poking fun at them, young George was surely adept at verbal mimicry.

West Dulwich, where George lived at the time he went up to King's, was one of a cluster of towns bearing the name "Dulwich" spread across the far southern limits of London. He and his family lived in a two-story semi-detached house on Lovelace Road, one among a gentle sweep of similar houses with bay windows and stained-glass detailing built soon after the war; it was new, comfortable, and amply scaled, though hardly palatial. From the front windows, or anywhere in the house, really, you could look across the street to All Saints Church, a towering Victorian Gothic extravaganza in red brick with stone accents that, when going up in the 1890s, had for a while been envisioned as the Anglican cathedral for all south London. Though ultimately scaled back, it was hard to miss, for its arches, its flying buttresses, the sheer mass of it.

Before moving to Lovelace Road, the family had lived nearer to Dulwich College, the old public school around which the Dulwich communities had grown up. It had been founded in 1619 by a well-known actor of his day, Edward Alleyn, a regular in Christopher Marlowe's plays, and possibly Shakespeare's, who made a big success of it as part-owner and manager of the Fortune Theatre, rival of the more famous Globe; Dulwich College graduates were called Alleynians. By George's time, the school was housed in a cluster of buildings that had gone up during the Victorian era, all cloisters and spires. If it was not first among English public schools, like Eton or Harrow, Dulwich had a distinguished enough pedigree of its own. Along with the usual admirals, archbishops, and cricketers, author Raymond Chandler had gone there. So had Sir Ernest Shackleton, the Antarctic explorer. So had that quintessential observer of English manners, P. G. Wodehouse, author of the Jeeves novels, whom college records show in cricket flannels in 1900. Instead of the adolescent angst more characteristically suffered by writers in school, George Orwell once said of Wodehouse, Dulwich was for him "six years of unbroken bliss."

George Thomson's time wasn't so idyllic, though he seems not to have been acutely miserable, either. He had little use, it is true, for school sports; one time, his wife would remember him confiding, he'd forged a letter saying he was to be excused from some intolerable game or match. He bristled at school discipline, too, sometimes slipping out of home-work. But on the whole, he was not being stuffed into academic garb that didn't suit him. The first of his family to attend university, he truly liked to learn.

George was enrolled in what at Dulwich was called the Classical side—as distinguished from the Modern side, for boys intent on business and civil-service positions; the Science side; or the Engineering side. The Classical side aimed expressly for admission to Oxford and Cambridge, and was loaded up with Latin and Greek, mathematics and modern languages. In his first year, George was introduced to Greek grammar, and in time was reading Thucydides, Euripides, and Homer, along with Caesar, Cicero, and Virgil. Each year in June, on Founder's Day, students put on a classical Greek play in translation. One year they did Aristophanes' *Clouds*. Playing one of Plato's disciples was George, photographed for the occasion with the other boys, sprawled on the grass in chiton and sandals.

Sometime in 1921, just eighteen and still at Dulwich, George saw a pro-duction of the *Oresteia*, Aeschylus' classic trilogy of murder and revenge. It was directed by J. T. Sheppard, an Alleynian from the previous generation. Sheppard had gone to King's, where he'd become a fellow, and then to renown as a classical scholar. "A missionary for the Classics," someone once called him, known for a "dynamic personality and his histrionic gifts as a lecturer." For thirty-five years, he would direct productions of his own translations of Greek plays, and it was one of these George saw in 1921. "At the risk of appearing sentimental or gushing," he wrote to Sheppard a few years later, "I feel I must write and tell you how much I owe to you in the study of Classics." That production of the *Oresteia* had fixed him on learning Greek, he said. During his three years as a King's undergraduate, George saw much of Jack Sheppard, whom he would esteem as mentor and credit with influencing his whole approach to the field. "Ever since I have been at college the chief enjoyment I have had from reading has been due to you."

Still, his daughter Margaret Alexiou insisted later, "Classics was second best" for George Thomson. At King's, where he held a scholarship (thus ensuring his name would be permanently enshrined on the Honours Board in Dulwich's Great Hall), he might have preferred to study Gaelic. But there *was* no Gaelic Studies at King's in those days. George would go on to earn a permanent and distinguished name in the classics; in doing so, he endured no serious deprivation. Still, this other, seemingly discordant thread, Gaelic and all things Irish, would wend through his mental universe always.

It must have happened early, while he was still at Dulwich. During his first years there, until he was past fifteen, the Great War raged. Notices of Alleynians killed in action, five hundred of them by war's end, darkened the life of the school. One Alleynian was killed leading an infantry charge, in October 1916, about the time George first enrolled. Another's plane crashed on return from a raid, killing him, in George's third year. Yet, as close to home as it must have seemed, the European war apparently did not afflict him as much as other events partly coincident with it but cresting later. By these I mean the seven years of trauma in Ireland, from the Easter Rising in 1916 through the end of the Irish Civil War in 1923.

"During the last years of my high school studies," Thomson wrote later, "the Irish rebellion against the English colonial occupation began and the hard struggle of the Irish people for their liberation moved me deeply." He asserted, and it was repeated later in the family, that his mother's ardent Irish nationalism—she was of Northern Irish descent on her father's side—accounted for Ireland's hold on him. That doubtless figured in. But just as important was that these struggling Irish represented an oppressed peasantry, chafing under the boot of a great monolith of an industrial power. In George's adolescent imagination, it was not abstract Ireland with a claim on him, but its suffering people.

The home library George catalogued when he was twelve or thirteen included no works of Thomas Hardy, in particular not his novel *Tess of the D'Urbervilles,* which George read later, when he was sixteen. It was the formative literary experience of his life. *Tess* tells the story of a peasant girl, daughter of a farm laborer, in Wessex, the fictional rural landscape Hardy created for his novels. She is seduced by a local squire, then "rescued"— this was George's word when he wrote about it later—by a parson's son, Angel Clare, who has decided to educate himself about the realities of rural life. Living there among the peasants, he falls in love with Tess. For a time it seems they will marry. But the story darkens. He forsakes her. She kills her original seducer, a D'Urberville, and goes to the gallows. The book's last paragraph tolls an ironic bell: " 'Justice' was done. . . ." George would recall "the burning anger with which I read that last paragraph," his hatred for a society whose cruelties led to Tess's tragedy "and contempt for those who tried to justify it." When he read *Tess* again, in the 1950s, while visiting China, he needed to ingest it only a little at a time, he wrote, because it "evokes so many forgotten memories." It was just too intense. "Again and again I find myself recalling my feelings at the very first reading." It, and indeed Hardy's whole oeuvre, with its grand narrative of a peasantry laid waste by the modern world, would resonate through George's life.

Hardy's fictional Wessex was a thinly veiled version of his ancestral home, Dorset, a largely rural and agricultural county on England's south coast. "As a schoolboy," George would write, "I spent my holidays in Dorset, cycling around and staying with the poorest cottagers I could find"— descendants, very likely, of those who had inspired Hardy a half-century before. Later, he adds, "I came to know the Irish peasantry as well as anyone could who was not one of them." There is perhaps a boastful tincture to this claim to hard-won knowledge of plain folks. But more significant is the close mental link it suggests between the Hardy-like figures from Dorset he met as a boy and the Blasket Islanders he'd befriend later.

The Irish tragedy playing out in the newspapers while he was in high school and in his first year at King's consumed him. Later, he'd cite particularly "the Black-and-Tan terror in Ireland," which he connected in his mind to the injustices visited on Tess. He became "an ardent Sinn Feiner," referring to the militant nationalist movement that, beginning late in 1917, came under the dominion of a new chief, Éamon de Valera. When George was about seventeen, he joined the Gaelic League and began attending Irish-language classes at its London branch. "As soon as he'd get home he'd throw off his cadet uniform" and head off, his wife recounted later. The West Dulwich train station was a short walk away. Fifteen minutes later, he'd be in central London's Victoria Station.

Meanwhile, he amassed texts and literature in Irish. Like *The Pursuit of Diarmuid and Gráinne,* which joined his library around Christmas 1921. George's edition of this ancient Irish tale of three-cornered love was published by the Society for the Preservation of the Irish Language, in Irish and English, with a notes section and glossary to help new students. Invariably, George would write his name in these volumes, often with rather a flourish. Much as teenagers often try out different signatures, George tried out different names. Sometimes it was just "G. Derwent Thomson." But often it was one or another version of his name in Irish.

Into the front cover of his *Concise Irish Grammar,* George recorded this poem:

> Idly I scan the unillumined page
> And slowly con the grave grammarian's vale
> Of "fear" and "ban" and "rann," and "cwail le cwail" . . .
>
> I read the strange script of a vanished age
> And follow threads which this with that word bind
> In close-wrought vocal tapestries entwined.
>
> Then the print fades, the book slips from my hands.
> My eyes are clouded and my spirit sees
> Long dances in the fairy forest-lands
> And black-haired Deirdre laughing in the breeze.

He wrote the poem in March 1922, while still in Dulwich.

One day probably early the following year, his first at King's, George was in Jack Sheppard's rooms in Wilkins Hall when he met another Kingsman, Arthur Waley. George said he was thinking of heading off to the Gaeltacht, the Irish-speaking part of Ireland, to learn the language. Waley, thirty-three, was no Celticist, having trained in the classics at King's and then gone on to teach himself Chinese and Japanese. But just then he was at the British Museum, as its assistant keeper of Oriental prints and manuscripts. If George wanted to sample the Gaeltacht, Waley suggested, he'd probably want to meet a colleague of his at the Museum, a Mr. Robin Flower.

When the two men met, Flower urged George to go to the Great Blasket. The term at King's was over in May, so George doubtless went home to Dulwich first. But late that summer, on a wet day in late August, a little after his twentieth birthday, he arrived in Dingle. It was the day of the general election marking the first real peace after seven years of war. George asked directions, in English. Who *was* this Englishman who spoke a little Irish, worried the police, and what was he doing there? He was stopped, questioned, perhaps arrested, though if so not for long. The issue was soon settled; apparently he was no spy or provocateur.

The next day—Sunday, August 26, 1923—George reached Dún Chaoin. At some point, he made his way down the steep snaking path carved into the side of the cliff that led to the slip. From there he was rowed across Blasket Sound to the island.

Máire Maidhc Léan, aged fourteen and "just a slip of a school girl," as she remembered herself, saw a boat approaching the island that day and went down the hill to greet it. "Out of the currach," she recalled, "stepped a courteous, slightly built young man with dark hair and a pleasant smile." George wore a raincoat, something she'd never seen. She "gave him a thousand welcomes and was delighted that he understood me, that he had some Irish."

That evening, at her family's whitewashed stone house midway up the hill, across a path from the king's house, George was shown to the room where he was to stay. They sat him down at the table, served him tea, invited him to sit by the fire. Soon, Máire recalled, he was "pointing to the pot rack and asking what it was called in Irish. I told him. He continued asking me the name for this and that." Her father sat on the long wooden bench nearby, the settle, and soon was likewise being pelted with questions.

The children had a school assignment, to memorize Tennyson's "The Brook": "For men may come and men may go, / But I go on forever." At the end of that long day, George was exhausted, but couldn't sleep, was too tired to sleep, didn't *want* to sleep, charmed as he was "by listening to them reciting it by heart."

. . .

So, George was staying with the Maidhc Léans. Or that, at least, is what the family was called on the island. In fact, no census recorded any such name. In English, their family name was Guiheen. In Irish, by one spelling, it was Ó Guithín. (The prefix "Ó" or "Mac," literally "son" or "grandson," means "descendant of"; "Ní," "daughter," does the same for women.) Máire was formally Máire Ní Ghuithín, the interpolated "h" altering her surname's pronunciation from the familiar hard "g" to something like a French rolled "r" and, grammatically, representing the genitive case, making Máire *of* that family. On the island, though, she would more often have been called Máire Maidhc Léan.

For an Englishman from London like George, a thicket of confusion obscured the names of his new acquaintances. This was no trifle on a par with whether Edward goes by "Ed," "Teddy," or "Ted." Nor was spelling really the problem; the island's was an oral culture, most islanders being illiterate in Irish, so spelling needn't have much troubled him. Rather, the confusion stemmed in part from the fact that most of the island population, about 150 at the time, derived from only a handful of families. There were lots of Guiheens on the island, just as there were lots of Keanes, Kearneys, and O'Sullivans, to momentarily cede them the Anglicized forms of their names. Refer to "that Guiheen girl" and you might leave the listener hopelessly unenlightened: *which* Guiheen girl? Nor was "Máire Guiheen" much better; there were only so many families, but also only so many given names, like Máire, Eibhlín, and Nóra, or Seán, Pádraig, and Tomás among the men and boys. During one period, the village was home to six Seán Ó Cearnaighs.

How to distinguish the many Guiheens one from another? This particular Mary Guiheen—Máire Maidhc Léan Ní Ghuithín—was the daughter of Maidhc and the granddaughter of Léan. Her mother, Maidhc's wife, was Máire Ní Chatháin, Synge's little hostess, now about forty; island women often retained their maiden names. But because there might well be other Máire Ní Chatháins—as indeed there were—the little hostess was also known as Máire Pheats Mhici—or Máire, daughter of Pádraig, granddaughter of Mícheal.

But we are not done yet. The islanders often bore distinguishing nicknames unrelated to genealogy. Pádraig Ó Catháin was, as we've seen, *an rí,* the king. One particular Tomás Ó Cearnaigh, who had immigrated to the States only to return, was known as An Poncan, the Yank. Eibhlín Ní Shé was known as Nelly Jerry. In one of his books, Tomás Ó Criomhthain dubbed a villager Tadhg the Joker. Mícheál Ó Gaoithín, when a bit older, was usually just An File, the poet. His mother, island storyteller Peig Sayers, was almost never known as Máiread Sayers Uí Ghaoithaín, her proper name; she was simply Peig, or sometimes Peig Mhór, Big Peig.

This way of names had emerged naturally enough in use. But to anyone new to the island, and certainly for an Englishman encountering it for the first time, it posed problems—as it does for us here, in print, lost among Irish names thick with seemingly familiar English consonants and vowels that nonetheless don't add up to familiar English sounds. In Irish, "Siobhán" is pronounced "Shivanne." "Ó Laoghaire" is "Ó Leary." To vex us the more, Irish spelling changed during the years our story spans; for instance, the name for Ireland's Irish-speaking area went from "Gaedhealtacht" to "Gaeltacht." Names changed, too. Nóra Ní Shéaghdha, an island schoolteacher who later wrote a book under that name, might have been known a few years later, or had she immigrated to America, as Nora O'Shea.

But Nóra Ní Shéaghdha *didn't* immigrate to America and would not have been known by an Anglicized version of her name—except, perhaps, to English-speaking merchants in Dingle or tourists who didn't know any better. In this book, islanders most often retain their Irish names. So do Irish scholars and writers, such as Muiris Mac Conghail or Pádraig Ó Fiannachta.

Leslie Matson, an Irish schoolteacher who in the late 1950s took an interest in Dún Chaoin and the Blaskets, later prepared a compendium of brief island biographies, "Blasket Lives," for which, as helpful resource, he prepared lengthy lists and cross-lists of each islander's Irish name, Anglicized name, maiden name, nickname, or pet name; that was one good answer to a problem with no perfect solution. George Thomson himself, in a note to one of his translations from the Irish, would write, "With regard to the spelling of proper names I have sought rather to help the English reader than to be consistent. Some Irish names have an English form, others have not; and we have used one or the other, whichever seemed the more convenient." In these pages, I steer close to Thomson and adhere to no one fixed method or system. Rather, I have tried to let the story itself, as it develops, suggest which name to use when, and so, just possibly, keep things straight.

George Thomson, we've said, would become an eminent classical scholar. But just then, it needs saying, he was a kid—a university student just turned twenty. He was handsome, amiable, and deeply interested in every-thing around him, so it wasn't long before he fell in among villagers his own age. One was Mícheál Ó Gaoithín, or O'Guiheen in English (who, about George's age, looked something like the young John Lennon). "We became close friends," George recalled. "He was different from the other boys—studious and introspective." And compulsively superstitious: once, when a boy he didn't see threw pebbles at him, he was sure the fairies were attacking him. He was imaginative, smart, and one of only a few islanders who could read and write in Irish; when just fifteen, he had a poem published in a national Irish-language publication. "There never were children with cleverer heads for books," his mother once told Robin Flower. On September 7, 1923, Mícheál noted in his journal that he and Seoirse—George's name on the island—went down to the slip. "He's a nice boy. He has a camera." And he was snapping pictures with it like the tourist he still was.

Mícheál's journal was one of at least three being kept on the island that year. Another, as we've seen, was that of Tomás Ó Criomhthain. The third, also likely at Brian Kelly's behest, was that of Eibhlín Ní Shúillea-bháin, a round-faced woman just a bit older than George. "I have not seen the young Englishman since he came to the village," she wrote on August 30. But just three days later, she and her friends were hanging out with him and another visitor, a Tipperary boy whom she described as "great fun and a joker." Not so George. He was "very friendly altogether, but I don't think he likes the joking at all." At this point, he had little Irish, but she did her best to engage with him. Did he have a girlfriend? Eibhlín understood him to say that he did, one of recent vintage, that the girl was on the island, right there among them. Repeatedly, according to her diary entry, he said "he had a pain in his heart because of her."

How much of this flirtatious muddle owed to the language barrier, how much to nerves or youthful cluelessness? In any event, a severe tooth-ache kept Eibhlín home for three weeks, and not until the day before his departure did George reappear in her journal. She wanted him to take a picture of her, but all morning it was foggy. That afternoon, though, the sky cleared, and George lined her up with five other young people. He snapped them all together, the low, grassy little island of Beginish just behind them, the mainland off in the distance.

But George wanted one of just her, too. She grabbed her brother's cap and planted it atop her head, brim backward. Don't laugh, said George. She wore a dark sweater, gently scalloped at the neck, with tapered sleeves that stopped a few inches short of her wrist. A wisp of hair peeking out from under her cap blew in the breeze. A perfect little triangle of light settled on her cheek.

She hoped George would send her the photo, she wrote in her journal that evening, "because I've never seen my own picture."

Eibhlín's younger brother was named Muiris—or, in English, Maurice—and was just George's age. His mother had died when he was just a babe. Whereas Eibhlín stayed on the island, he'd been shipped off to an orphanage on the mainland. When he was seven, in July 1911, his father brought him back. By that time, he spoke only English. But back on the island he absorbed Irish quickly and, by the time he met George, had taken his place among the other young Blasket fishermen. The two of them would become lifelong friends.

Maurice loved teasing, pranks, and every kind of deviltry, and his joie de vivre, when it didn't curdle over into depression, was the delight of his friends. He'd make up stories for the old women, a cousin remembers, tell them "that this girl was going to get married, that this fella had made a match. And they'd believe him." One time, he dressed up in his dead grandmother's old clothes, a ghost in her coat and shawl, leaving his sister and her friend to scream in terror. Another time, he loaded up George with such a weight of heather on his back that he keeled right over. "He was great fun," said this cousin, Máire Mhic Ní Shúilleabháin, in 1993, and "great company for George."

A few years later, when Maurice described meeting George Thomson for the first time, he recalled encountering him on the path one bright sunny day, stopping for a smoke, and trying to talk across the language gap. *Beware the laugh of an Englishman,* Maurice had been brought up to think, but George was the happy exception. "George and I spent the next six weeks walking together on strand, hill, and mountain," he wrote, "and after spending the time in my company he had fluent Irish." If he did, of course, it was because he worked at it; that first summer, he'd endlessly repeat Maurice's "words under my teeth before I could understand them." On his part, Maurice saw in George a rare devotion to Irish. "If everyone in Ireland were as eager as he for the language, the people of old Ireland would be Gaels again without much delay." It was the beginning of a beautiful friendship, Maurice offering a lightness of being that was welcome balm to George's overheated intellectuality. Later, Maurice would have much to learn from George. Now George had everything to learn from him.

Islanders seated on the wall are, left to right, Seán Ó Criomhthain, Eibhlín Ní Shúil-leabháin, Micheál Ó Gaothín, and, melodeon on his lap, Maurice O'Sullivan.

One hot day that first summer, the two young men and Maurice's father hiked, "happy as children," to the back side of the island to retrieve two sheep. At a gloriously situated spot along the hillside about two miles west of the village, looking south to the Skelligs, they sat down to rest. Were the Blaskets much different from London? Maurice's father asked. They were, said George.

"It is a pity I am not in the city of London now," said Maurice, "for it is a fine view I would have."

George, his unlined young face scrunched up into a frown at the idea, looked at Maurice sharply. "Indeed, you would not," said he, as Maurice told it later, "but the heat killing you and your health failing for want of air. And as for the view, you would be looking at the same thing always—people walking the streets with nothing in them but only the breath, and believe me if one of them could see this view out before me now, he would give his riches for it."

That first summer, George came under the spell of Maurice's grandfather, Eoghan Ó Súilleabháin—Eugene O'Sullivan, or "Daideo," as George came to know him. He was a heavily built man of about seventy-five with a good singing voice, a bent for argument, and a head full of traditional lore. Maurice delighted in his company, as did George. Years later, while visiting China, George met a frail old professor who chanted a Chinese poem for him, head thrown back, eyes shut, the same deep feeling in his voice, and that was all it took to transport him back to the Blaskets. "If I had been listening with eyes closed, having forgotten where and when it was," he'd write, "I should have imagined that I was listening to Maurice's grandfather." Just before he returned to England, it was Daideo who said to him, "*Casta na daoine ar a cheile ach ni chasta na croic ar na sleibhte*": "Men meet but not the hills or mountains," a nod to the tenacity of human connection. "I never took much notice of it," George would write in a letter to a friend many years later, "beyond thinking it was rather an odd idea, not more odd however than other Irish proverbs." But then he encountered Daideo's parting remark in other languages, countries, and contexts, its layers of ambiguity never for him quite resolved.

"George left us today," Eibhlín wrote in her journal on September 30, "and we are rather lonesome after him. . . . Few people have ever left this place without feeling lonesome and George was near to tears."

Late one afternoon two weeks later, she went down the hill for the mail, which hadn't reached the island in a week, hoping for a book she was expecting. It hadn't come, but what had come was a letter for her in Irish, in an unfamiliar hand. When she tore it open, a picture slipped out. She looked at it and laughed. It was the one George had taken of her, cap turned backward, sent to her from England.

Back in Cambridge, George had spacious new rooms at King's. He was in Bodley's Court now, a range of four-story stone buildings at the far end of the college from the great chapel frequented by the tourists—up a winding stone staircase, leaded windows at each landing, to the top floor. From a bank of windows in the big front room he could look down over the Backs, the great green expanse between the university colleges and the river Cam, spanned by little King's Bridge. It was the iconic Cambridge scene. He was back in this cradle of scholarship, of privileged people with time to read, write, and think. It was the world for which he had been groomed and where he excelled. He might have been pardoned for thinking those six weeks on the island had never happened.

But they had happened. They had changed him. He was different now. "I went to the Blasket Island in order to learn the language," he would write, "but when I got there I found something even more significant and attractive—the people that spoke it."

After that first visit, he would go back again and again, once a year, for ten or eleven years running. At summer's end, he would return to his life as student and scholar. At Christmas, he'd send the islanders gifts, such as chess sets—he'd taught several of his friends to play. Or a toy railroad for the Maidhc Léan children that was soon monopolized by their father. And then, each summer (and one Christmas, too, perhaps in 1925), he was back. Year by year, his ties to the island strengthened. His friendships with the islanders deepened. His Irish ripened. In the end, Tomás Ó Criomhthain's son Seán had to notice: "George had better Irish than Muiris himself," meaning Maurice O' Sullivan, "indeed than all the rest of us."

Over the years, his head brimmed over with memories.

Rowing in to the island and out in a canvas canoe, the waves lapping at its sides, the rhythmic slap of the narrow-bladed oars.

Pulling the table up to the fire at Maurice's house, a book between them.

Children lined up on the beach for a photograph, the girls in their dark pinafores, demurely kneeling in the sand, the older ones hamming it up for the camera.

The boy who cut himself while digging and tried to staunch the blood with a fistful of dirt.

The old woman at the village well who'd filled her buckets and now stood looking out to sea, lamenting the loss of seven sons to America.

Sitting by the fire in Peig Sayers's house, Peig lapsing into a poetic lament that for all the world could have been a Shakespearean sonnet.

Always, stories rising up, unbidden, at the scantiest excuse, from everyone on the island, Fenian tales drawn from Irish tradition, prose that verged on poetry, poetry prose.

And then, of course, there were the moonlit nights, and the music, and the dancing, high on the cliffs above the pounding surf. . . .

Especially after it was abandoned and reduced to ruins, it would be easy to imagine that the Blasket community had been around since antiquity, or at least since the Middle Ages, or at any rate was steeped in ageless tradition. But the settlement of the Blaskets was recent enough, the generations going back to the early settlers few enough that creation myths of a sort around this or that aspect of village life sometimes took hold. One of these concerned its music.

The way Seán Ó Criomhthain liked to tell the story later, an islander, Mike, one day crossed the sound, hoodwinked a Dingle man into letting him take a fiddle he didn't pay for, brought it back to the island, and learned to play it. "That was the first fiddle of their own which the island-ers had." They called it a sliver, for its shape. Ultimately, Mike left for America, but not before two other islanders learned to play his fiddle and saved up to buy their own. Soon, "all the lads on the Island were becom-ing interested in the fiddle and some of them set about making one." For strings, they used fishing-net cord; if the instrument showed special prom-ise, they'd contrive to get proper strings for it. "Within a few years there was a sliver in every house in the village . . . [and not] a boy or girl on the Island who couldn't knock some smattering of music out of it."

Following the fiddle onto the island was the melodeon, or "box," a small accordion introduced early in the twentieth century and catching on quickly. At the height of the melodeon craze, nightly dances sometimes kept the young people up almost till morning. "They had little else to do during the day," Seán seemed to grumble, "except to bring a couple of loads of turf from the hill and dress themselves up for the night." Some fine evenings, they'd bring a visiting box-player over to the Spur at Seal Cove, near the northern tip of the island. Out of sight of the village itself, it was large enough and level enough to accommodate two dance sets at once and, said Seán, "many other activities if you so wished!"

In the village itself, it was often Peig Sayers's house where the furni-ture would be cleared for the evening's dance. "The room would be lit by a turf fire, and an oil lamp, and a tiny red lamp before the holy picture," remembered Robin Flower's daughter Síle, a teenager at the time, who visited the island during some of the same years George did. The room was full to bursting, the boys "crouching on their haunches," ready to jump up and ask a girl to dance before the music started. "And then it was very, very lively dancing, reels and sets." At evening's end, in the blackness of the night, they'd wend their way home. "The boys were dying to get a kiss from us. We thought this was terrific at the age of fourteen or fifteen," she remembered. "Finally we arrived home, and this howling mob of boys would be outside the window, waving through the window and blowing kisses at us."

It was impossible not to be moved by weeks or months spent in a set-ting so alive, in the shelter of the darkness, to the lilt of song, the whine of the fiddle, the drone of the melodeon, the play of dancing feet, the aban-doned pulse of young bodies. No visitor was immune to it. "The sharp sounds of their heel irons are still ringing in my ears," wrote Marstrander of the dancers. Synge wrote of four Blasket couples dancing a polka:

The women, as usual, were in their naked feet, and whenever there was a figure for women only there was a curious hush and patter of bare feet, till the heavy pounding and shuffling of the men's boots broke in again. The whirl of music and dancing in this little kitchen stirred me with an extraordinary effect. The kindliness and merry-making of these islanders, who, one knows, are full of riot and severity and daring, has a quality and attractiveness that is absent altogether from the life of towns.

Robin Flower captured the dancing in verse:

"Rise up now, Shane," said a voice, and another:
"Kate, stand out on the floor"; the girls to the men
Cried challenge on challenge; a lilt in the corner rose
And climbed and wavered and fell, and springing again
Called to the heavy feet of the men; the girls wild-eyed,
Their bare feet beating the measure, their loose hair flying. . . .

Now, the island, one needs reminding about now, was not some easy-living tropical paradise. It was a hard and unforgiving place, difficult to wrest a living from. Clinging to its precipitous cliffs, rowing and sailing over its roiling waters, you couldn't long forget the essential seriousness of life. Marriage mattered; so did birth, so did death, and not much else. The islanders, many said, possessed dignity and poise, heroic grace. Many of them tapped a deep religiosity. Given the pleas to Jesus and Mary marking everyday Blasket speech, it would be possible to imagine the island as pious or prudish. And many islanders did hold firmly to the tenets of their faith and conform to every standard of decorum between the sexes.

All this was true.

But also true was that the Great Blasket was an island. And islands are famously places of freedom and abandon, of rules relaxed, of stricture and release held in balance. Synge's *Playboy* idea—a man kills his father and is hailed for his manly daring—was hatched on an island, in Aran. The Blaskets inspired in him another idea, for a play set on an "island with a population of wreckers, smugglers, poteen makers . . . startled by the arrival of a stranger." No priest inhabited the island; one was rowed in for the Stations, to take confessions and say Mass at the school, but that was just once a year. Otherwise, the church, its institutions and representatives, could seem far distant indeed. "While life was reasonably good there was little talk of priests or ministers," recalled Seán Ó Criomhthain. "The ordinary person doesn't spend his life talking about religion." The great litanies of the ought-and-should could seem remote, mainland verities not so much rejected as forgotten or ignored.

Sometime before George came to the island, an English translation of Boccaccio's *Decameron*, his collection of lubricious tales of love and sensuality set in medieval Florence, found its way to the island; George once saw a tattered copy of an English edition of it in Maurice's house. Using Irish names and place names, Mícheál O'Guiheen would translate several of Boccaccio's stories into Irish, leaving scholars to debate just how much, or how little, he'd cleaned them up. Delving into the story, folklorist Bo Almqvist concluded that O'Guiheen, very simply, was no prude, that the appeal of the Boccaccio stories for him and other islanders lay in their similarity to Irish folktales that could be "every bit as earthy and bawdy as any Boccaccian tale."

"On our way back to the village," wrote Synge of what he observed following an evening's dancing,

> the young girls ran wild in the twilight, flying and shrieking over the grass, or rushing up behind the young men and throwing them over, if they were able, by a sudden jerk or trip. The men in return caught them by one hand, and spun them round and round four or five times, and then let them go, when they whirled down the grassy slope for many yards.

Marstrander, likewise, recounted the flirtatious horseplay that sometimes accompanied these evening dances.

> The girls are shouting at the men. *Earg, earg,* stand up, and dance, but they are standing seriously and careless, as if they didn't hear anything. Then the girls shower them with jokes and sarcasms, threats and rude stories. They shall be teased to dance, just as the heroes of old are geared for battle with abuse from his friend. No method is forbidden. No secret is taboo. "Get up Seán, or will I tell them who put her white arms around your neck yesterday, get up Seán." Seán got up very fast, blushing. . . .

It was a small island, but it wasn't as if you couldn't slip away—you could. The village itself might seem claustrophobic, a few minutes' walk from one end to the other. But its few houses were really just a speck of urban adornment to an otherwise wild countryside of pasturage, mountain, bog, and cliff; it could be two hours over the back of the island to Ceann Dubh, or Black Head, at the island's far southwestern tip. To any red-blooded island boy or girl, there were plenty of less traveled areas to get away to. Close by was the White Strand, with rock-sheltered corners lying behind the cliffs, invisible to the prying eyes of the village. Or else a couple "might hop in over a fence or up the hill a bit," remembered Seán Ó Criomhthain of his youth. "They'd go some place where people didn't usually go." The island was too small, making it hard to find such a spot? "Not at all. It was easy to find a place there if you wanted to." Young men he termed "the real experts . . . brought the girls up the hill."

It is many years later, and George Thomson is being interviewed for a television documentary. He's on the mainland, sitting on the grass as he speaks, the island rising across the sound behind him. He is an old man now, and he remembers: "There were lots of young people on the island" in the 1920s. Dances were frequent. On nights when the weather was bad, they'd gather at Peig Sayers's house. "There was a good floor there, as it was one of the new houses"—concrete, not dirt. Or "sometimes we'd have a great night in the schoolhouse. We'd dance all night."

Among reminiscences delivered in George's memory at the time of his death was one from Pádraig Ó Fiannachta, a Roman Catholic priest reared in West Kerry who'd befriended him. "I am certain that dear George is dancing steps in Paradise with the people of the Island now," he wrote, "and that he has the sets better than he had them long ago." He was probably not a naturally gifted dancer, though "he couldn't have been as unmusical as he seemed," suggested daughter Margaret years later, perhaps influenced by standards set by her mother, a musician. But on the island, raw energy trumped any natural want of ability. Sometimes George, Maurice, and one or two other men could be seen dancing on the beach, pipes hanging from their mouths all the while. One old islander, Seán Ó Guithín, remembered George with his jacket off, stripped to his shirt. Oh, he said, "he could step it out with the best."

Sometimes, on moonlit nights, the young people would drift from the village en masse, cut across the northeast face of the island, beside the fields above the White Strand, to Speir Chuas na Rón, Seal Cove, the brink of which fell precipitously to the surf crashing up against the rocky cove below. As he remembers those nights of dancing there now, George sits propped on one elbow, his other hand idly fingering a workman's cap by his side, an errant wisp of hair slipping down across his forehead. . . . And then, from that wizened old face, a secret smile breaks free.

"I suppose he had a few girls on the island?" one of his old friends is asked.

"Oh, he did indeed!" says he. "There was one girl in particular. . . ."

It couldn't have been long after his arrival on the island that he met Mary Kearney, which is how he referred to her when he mentioned her in a letter written years later. Máire Pheats Tom Ó Cearnaigh was her proper island name: Mary, daughter of Tom Kearney's son Pat. She lived in a new house at the top of the village with her parents, brothers, and sisters.

She'd entered the world in 1908 through the ministrations of the island midwife, Méiní Dunlevy, in a house toward the middle of the village that shared a stone wall with the island school. When she was about five, her growing family—by now she had two more sisters and a younger brother along with older siblings—moved to the upper village; she may have remained there briefly in her grandparents' coddling care before moving up the hill. Her family's new Congested District house had a concrete floor, wooden stairs to a second level, a slate roof, and a back door

Island children. Mary Kearney, George Thomson's girl, is fourth from the left in the middle row.

(atypical for the village) facing the hill behind it. A little road—a wide path, really—passed in front, leading in a lazy arc to the north side of the island. Below, the surf billowing onto the White Strand seemed somehow close by; only a few fields stood between them and the sea. On a fair day, Beginish, the nearest of the Lesser Blaskets, small, flat, and green, punctuated by scattered rocks, could seem practically out the front door.

Mary's fisherman father, known as Peats Tom, a trim, handsome man with thick eyebrows and a big fluffy mustache, was apparently the soft touch of the family. One time at dinner, the children were horsing around, making a god-awful racket, when their mother, the sterner of the two, decreed silence. So there they sat at the table, silent, obedient, stifling their giggles . . . until Peats Tom stage-whispered a barely audible "tee-hee" that reduced them to hilarity all over again.

Mary's younger brother, Seán, remembered her as a sweet, lively young thing who delighted in the animals of the island. A day off from school and she'd be roaming the hillside to play with the sheep and lambs. As a child, she and her friends played with homemade dolls that used hair made from frayed rope. She may always have had something of a religious bent; her brother more than once found her on her knees, praying to the Virgin Mary. One day, a framed image of the Virgin fell off the wall onto her as she slept. The glass broke, but Mary came away unscathed. This, anyway, is the story Seán told much later.

When Swedish folklorist Carl von Sydow visited the island in 1920, he photographed Mary. She was twelve then, and wore the white pinafore with lacy decoration most of the girls her age wore. When von Sydow returned in 1924, he again took a picture of her, this time in a dark dress, signifying a young woman, no longer a girl. Mary had brown eyes, thick black brows set below a high forehead, and black hair. But her smile! She smiled as if she couldn't hold it back, and wouldn't want to, and why would you ever? In an audio recording made when she was much older, her laugh is fresh, strong, and youthful.

She was fifteen when George arrived on the island, and his bewitchment may have come early. A photo of the two of them together survives from that first summer. They sit in the sun, their backs against a "ditch," or embankment, lined up for the camera beside two other islanders. Mary squints, her head cocked a little to the side, her thick hair pulled back into a bow, hands set demurely on her lap. George, beside her, looks less like the young man he really isn't yet, more the boy he still is. He wears a suit of what appears to be heavy wool, a jacket button cinching him at the waist. He looks as no Blasket boy ever looked, as if he were just off the boat from college, which is about what he was. It is the summer of 1923, and he seems perfectly delighted to be where he is.

From the moment he stepped onto the island, George had been a hit, falling in easily with his age-mates. If at age twenty he showed even a dash of the sincerity and intelligence his friends unfailingly remarked on, he could hardly have failed to excite interest. He was handsome and, in his way, exotic, certainly in those years before the island saw so many visitors from beyond Ireland. It's not surprising that Mary Kearney would be drawn to him.

What happened between her and George in whispered conversation on the White Strand, or on paths along the back of the island, or while dancing at Peig's or above the Gravel Strand, or in chance looks or tender moments amid the crowded company of the others, is lost to us. "I remember the times on the Blasket Islands very well" was all Mary would say years later, on a tape she knew he'd hear. "We had a great time, George."

Certainly they spent plenty of time together. He met her family, her sisters and brothers, sometimes played chess with them. He must have learned early on that Mary's father, in his early forties at the time, was

Mary Kearney and George Thomson are at the right.

something of a celebrity. Back in 1909, he'd jumped into the water and helped save Tomás Ó Criomhthain's daughter Cáit at the time of the Eveleen Nichols drowning. He had a bronze medal to show for it, from the Royal Home Society, patronized by the King of England himself, "for having saved life from drowning." He wasn't shy about wearing it. Mary's father must have seemed to George no idle, clever talker, like some of the effete boys and men he knew at King's, but an authentic Irish hero.

For George, a new world was opening up, and an extraordinarily happy time. He was not by nature carefree. His sister-in-law would later recall him as a formidable presence, with scant time for idle chatter and "no patience with the frivolous or mediocre." His idea of a good time at age twelve, remember, was setting up a lending library. And in later years, as we'll see, he took nothing so seriously as, by his lights, setting the world aright. "Deeply serious, dedicated and preferring silence to small-talk and frivolity"—that's how one respectful obituary judged him. In family photographs, he always looks about the same—placid, earnest, his even features rarely corrupted into a smile, his great thatch of straight hair flopping down over his forehead. In one photo from about three years before he went to the Blaskets, younger brother Hugh has a winsome look to him, whereas George is all sharp, straight lines; as well as you can tell from an old studio portrait, he seems *closed*. He is certainly good-looking, but in a way more befitting an older man than the seventeen-year-old schoolboy he was at the time.

It is unlikely, then, that, before reaching the Great Blasket, George was ever much the life of the party; or that the mischievousness, the sheer antic frivolity, of young Maurice O'Sullivan could have seemed to him anything but welcome counterpoint to the stresses of school; or that the convulsive, spirited laugh of Mary Kearney—his "black-haired Deirdre laughing in the breeze"?—could have seemed to him anything but captivating,

"I'd say he was in love with her," said one of the old islanders. "He was very fond of her. He'd've married her if she would have had him."

Would he? Would he *really*?

George from London, fresh from Cambridge University, his academic career primed to take off, was giving serious thought to marrying this barely schooled young girl from the island? She was Roman Catholic and he was not. How could they marry? Through some mysterious alchemy of love, a summer flirtation had bubbled up into a full-blown crisis—for George, certainly, and perhaps for Mary as well.

At one point, Mary's brother Seán reported, George approached their father, who did nothing to scuttle the match. "Well," Seán has his father saying, "it's not me that will marry you. . . . If you like her, and if she likes you, you can't be kept apart, and I suppose it's a mortal sin to keep two people who are in love apart."

But even if George was smitten, and her father willing, Mary herself may never have given herself over to the idea. The island was the only world she'd ever known. He was from a faraway world she could scarcely imagine—perhaps not someone, ironically, to take seriously. Her faith, meanwhile, she took very seriously, and George's religion, or lack of it, erected a formidable bar. At some point, or perhaps several—the chronology is muddled—George told her just how he felt. Either she rebuffed him altogether, or simply explained to him she could never marry a non-Catholic. Probably on one of his visits to the island—1926 is as good a guess as any—George, lost and lovestruck, looked into converting.

"I remember him coming to our house in An Cill. He wanted advice from my uncle Pádraig as to whether he should convert to Catholicism. The girl wouldn't marry him unless he became a Catholic."

The speaker was Máire Mhac an tSaoi—Mary McEntee—one of Ireland's most distinguished poets and writers. An Cill was the house her uncle had had built in Dún Chaoin—on the mainland, within sight of the Blaskets—in 1925. Her uncle was one of the leading intellectual lights of Ireland, Monsignor Pádraig de Brún, otherwise known as Paddy Browne.

A Roman Catholic priest and holder of a doctorate from the Sorbonne, de Brún had in 1913 taken a position teaching mathematics at Saint Patrick's College in Maynooth, Ireland's premier seminary. He was brilliant, the proverbially smartest person in the room, a true polymath, his mind ranging freely over an intellectual landscape encompassing mathematics, the classics, poetry, and the Irish language. He would long serve as president of one of Ireland's national universities, and near the end of his life was named chairman of the council of Dublin's Institute for Advanced Studies.

He had built An Cill, his niece explained, as refuge, balm for the grief he'd experienced in Dublin with the 1916 Rising and the execution of a friend, Seán MacDermott, one of its leaders. The house was of modest size but glorious prospect. Made of creosoted wood, virtually unknown in those parts, its front door green, its pyramidal roof bright-red felt, it stood on a hill near the ruins of an old church, overlooking the Atlantic. Its rear windows faced the Blaskets. From the front door you could look out at the hills rising above Dún Chaoin, and, from anywhere else, hear the seas

In the doorway of his house in Dún Chaoin, mathematician-scholar-priest Father Paddy Browne about the time George Thomson approached him for advice about his relationship with Mary Kearney

crashing below. And here it was, Máire Mhac an tSaoi remembered, that George Thomson came to talk to her uncle.

In Dún Chaoin, with its few score houses scattered across the landscape, everyone knew everyone; George would certainly have known of Father de Brún. With his dark hair, deep hooded eyes, and rich baritone voice, the irrepressible de Brún would come to be seen as a "maverick . . . altogether uninhibited and irreverent, caring not a fig for theological caution . . . impish and mischievous in his humour," fond even of off-color limericks. But that was later. More recently, he had been reproved for his open support of the republican cause by his superiors at the seminary.

He was no average country priest, yet he *was* a priest in the Roman Catholic Church. Just what did young George expect of him? How did he frame his request? With what hesitancy or conviction did he, at twenty-two or twenty-three, assert his love for the island girl and seek an opinion, a ruling, a morsel of advice, that might leave her his?

Máire Mhac an tSaoi was only a girl at the time—her memory of George Thomson, she reports, extends only "from the knees down"—and her recollection may have been enriched by later accounts of the story from her uncle, who died when she was in her late thirties, and with whom she was close. In any case, here is how she told it in her old age:

> My uncle Pádraig advised him not to convert simply in order to marry her. He was an atheist. If he couldn't say with honesty that he was no longer an atheist it would only be a cause of sorrow for both of them. The marriage would be based on a lie and nothing good would come of it.

George did not convert.

At some point, Mary left the island, to take a position as servant to a doctor outside Dublin.

Later, George went to see her there.

At first, George's times on the island with Mary, Maurice, and the others must have been just so much raw, undigested experience; *he,* barely in his twenties, was still raw, awash in the alien sounds of a new language, trying to make sense of so much else that seemed exciting, novel, and strange. In the end, though, his Blasket summers changed his mental makeup. They influenced his scholarship. They tinted his writing; they gave him a stock of raw material that would find its way into his stories, poems, and translations. They would shape his values and help make him the man he was to become.

One day many years later, while visiting China, rereading *Tess of the D'Urbervilles* a few pages at a time each evening, he felt an acute and sudden tug of awareness. He'd been reading chapter 25, in which Angel Clare reflects on his time at Talbothays Dairy in Wessex, where he'd met and fallen in love with Tess. Angel came to the dairy, Hardy wrote, sure his brief stay would be "the merest episode in his life, soon passed through and early forgotten," an interlude during which to reflect on the great world and its work. But, quite the contrary, it was the great world on which he soured, "dissolved into an uninteresting outer dumb-show; while here, in this apparently dim and unimpassioned place, novelty had volcanically started up, as it had never, for him, started up elsewhere. . . . It was amazing, indeed, to find how great a matter the life of the obscure dairy had become to him."

There in China, George was just two pages into the chapter when "it struck me suddenly," as he wrote in a letter home, "that Angel Clare, who came to Talbothay to study farming and found something unexpected, was not unlike me, who went to the Blasket Island to study the Irish language and found there something unexpected.

"But there, I am slipping into daydreams again, and it's bedtime."

Chapter 5

Inishvickillaun

[1926]

It was a fine summer morning in the year 1926, three years after George's first visit to the island.

> White streaks of foam were passing up through the Sound to the north and they nicely gathered together on the surface of the sea. They would turn in on each other till not a trace of them was to be seen. There was a wonderful stillness. The mountains were clear before me, nodding their heads above in the sky. Isn't it they that are proud to have power to be higher than the rest, thought I.

So Maurice O'Sullivan would recall the day. He, his father, and his uncle were making for Inishvickillaun, one of the Lesser Blaskets, a six-mile row distant. Maybe George wanted to go with them? Maurice crossed the village to the Guiheen house, where George was staying. Of course, said George, he'd love to go. Mrs. Guiheen volunteered to pack them lunch, and soon they all were off, Maurice and George rowing along the big island's long, craggy southern flank, the sea a dead calm. When they looked toward Slea Head, on the mainland, "there was nothing but a path of sparkling light from the sun which shone without spot in the sky."

Seven islands counted as the Lesser Blaskets, clustered round the great island like escort vessels round a battleship. Each had its distinct shapes, proportions, and colors, its flora and fauna, its legends and peculiarities. One of them, Inishtooskert, looked from the mainland like a reclining man. Tiaracht, a rocky ziggurat aimed almost seven hundred feet straight up, had since 1870 been home to a lighthouse; waves buffeted it so relentlessly that Richard M. Barrington, a naturalist visiting in 1880, concluded that no plants could survive in its first 150 feet above the sea. Inishnabro seemed to Barrington "a cathedral," all towers and spires etched in rock. Most all the islands, as you drew near them from a *naomhóg* perched a few inches above the water, loomed as ominous hulking masses of granite and green, birds skimming above them. None, by Maurice's time, were any longer inhabited.

Inishvickillaun, the island to which Maurice, George, and the others rowed now, had perhaps the most distinctive character of them all. It stood in relation to the Great Blasket much as the Great Blasket did to the rest of Ireland—just off to the southwest. About a mile long and a half-mile wide, it had one high grassy plateau, punctuated by two distinct peaks, which over the years had sometimes been farmed for potato, cabbage, onion, and oats; it was good land. Tomás Ó Criomhthain would write of a land agent taking men there to shear sheep kept on the island, of a three-day visit to hunt rabbits that storms stretched to a week. The island had been inhabited by one family until as recently as 1904, and Synge noted the following year that old Maurice Daly, a Blasketer, planned to spend the coming winter there alone. The island held ruins of cottages, and of an ancient chapel. It had a small graveyard. Puffins and storm petrels called it home now.

All this, however, was only the visible Inish—as Inishvickillaun (which is spelled in dozens of different ways) was known among the Blasket Islanders. There was another Inish, one invested with magic. "The whole island," observed Robin Flower, "is inhabited with the sense of loneliness; it is as though it were at the last end of things, dwelling in a silence which the ceaseless murmur of the sea round its base and the whining gulls about its summit rather accentuate than disturb." Something in this peculiar place—"the most pleasant and mysterious of the Blaskets," George would one day call it—made it seem haunted by spirits, fairies, and the dead.

It was Inishvickillaun that spawned a tune much loved by the islanders, the "Song of the Fairies." The strains of what one scholar has termed this "musically eccentric" air seem to come from far away, as a distant fiddle sound, persistent, rising, unearthly. No hearing of it suggests anything but some other world, remote, cut off from our own. Robin Flower wrote how, according to local lore, a man once sat there on the Inish alone, playing his fiddle, tossing off the usual "jigs and reels and hornpipes, the hurrying tunes" that so inspired the dancers. But then, as he sported with the familiar music of his day, a wholly different tune rose up, unbidden. He could not tamp it down, this rebellious, mournful sound. It "passed away to the cliffs and returned again, and so backwards and forwards again and again, a wandering air wailing in repeated phrases." This fairy music, as Flower interpreted it, was "a lament for a whole world of imaginations banished irrevocably now, but still faintly visible in the afterglow of a sunken sun."

When, in 1930, a visiting Jesuit priest came to hear it, only one young island girl could actually play or sing it; yet all knew where it had originated—on Inishvickillaun. And the Inish, drowned in magic even in the clear light of summer, was where George, Maurice, and the others were bound today, rowing resolutely along the southern precipices of the big island. They passed seals in pairs on the reefs, crying, keening, sturgeons leaping, splashing back into the sea.

"Before long," Maurice wrote of their trip later,

> we reached the strand of the Inish and the two of us turned our faces up into the island. The sky was cloudless, the sea calm, sea-birds and land-birds singing sweetly. The sight of my eyes set me thinking. I looked west to the edge of the sky and I seemed to see clearly the Land of the Young—many-coloured flowers in the gardens; bright houses sparkling in the sunshine; stately, comely-faced, fair-haired maidens walking through the meadows gathering flowers.

Here again was Tir na nOg, which Flower had written of to a fellow Celticist on first coming to the Blaskets in 1910. That same year, he'd published a book of poems, one of which bore the same name:

> The magic waters gird it, and skies of laughing blue
> Keep always faith with summer, and summer still is true;
> There is no end of dancing and sweet unceasing song,
> And eyes to eyes make answer and love with love grows strong.

Like most visions of paradise, of course, Tir na nOg's was darker and more ambivalent. The Land of the Young was one of perfect happiness, yes, but always beyond one's reach, impossible to attain lastingly. In one version of the story drawn from Irish myth, the poet Oisin, from Fionn Mac Cumhail's band of legendary heroes, is chosen by a beautiful maiden, Niamh of the Golden Hair, to join her there. For three hundred enchanted years they enjoy bliss, never growing older. But Oisin cannot forget the world he's left behind. Niamh understands, gives him a magical horse to bear him back for a visit, but warns he must never actually set foot on the mortal earth. Of course he does, is forever denied Tir na nOg, and instantly becomes old and blind.

Now, though, at least in Maurice's fertile imagination, it could seem they were almost there, fairly imbibing its fragrance. "What do you see in the west?" asks George, who has thrown off his jacket and sits on a rock looking down at him. "Upon my word, George, it is at the Land of the Young I was looking."

In a moment, though, his vision shape-shifts into something else entirely. "I looked west at the edge of the sky where America should be lying," he wrote,

George Thomson, on a northern slope of the island

and I slipped back on the paths of thought. It seemed to me now that the New Island [America] was before me with its fine streets and great high houses, some of them so tall that they scratched the sky; gold and silver out on the ditches and nothing to do but to gather it. I see the boys and girls who were once my companions walking the street, laughing brightly and well contented.

America, land of the young, of opportunity, of gold and riches, was beckoning to Maurice, as it did every islander.

George, who was returning to England the next day, "looked at me between the two eyes," Maurice recounted. " 'There is no one but the two of us on this lonely island,' " he said by way of preamble, " 'and so I hope you will put courage in my heart. . . .' "

"I knew well what was the question he had to put to me," Maurice wrote, for his friend had asked it many times before.

" 'The question is,' said George, 'have you cast America out of your head?' " He wanted to know, in other words, was Maurice staying in Ireland or immigrating to the New World?

Numbers matter. It's not enough to coolly report that many Irish immigrated to Australia, Canada, and America. It may be truer to say that, from before the Famine to the time of George and Maurice's visit to the Inish, *most* Irish emigrated. In the early nineteenth century, Ireland's population was eight million; by 1926, fewer than four million; its rural west, especially, was decimated. A letter to the editor of *The Irish Statesman* in 1927 asked readers inexplicably left unmoved by emigration whether they had "ever travelled through the empty lands, empty now of even the bullocks? To any sane person a perusal of the last census is terrifying; the evidence afforded to the eye of a deserted countryside and a swelling group of dingy, decaying towns filled with beggars is overwhelming."

When, later, he'd come to compare Ireland to the ancient world of the Greeks, George Thomson would liken the Blaskets to Ithaca, which Odysseus endorsed as "a rough place, but a fine nurse of men." A Kerryman from near Dingle would, in the 1950s, use a similar image in a sadder way: Ireland, he said, had become "a nursery for raising human beings for export." First, aboard wooden sailing vessels, the famine ships, that bore emigrants to America; then, in Maurice's day, in the great six-hundred-foot steamers. Many Irish immigrants made good lives for themselves in America, and their children still better ones. They built America's railroads. They tended the sculleries and nurseries of brownstones in Boston's Back Bay. They filled the ranks of the police and fire departments of American cities and later commanded them. Today forty million or more Americans trace their roots to Ireland. Yet, if the loss of so many of its youngest and most spirited counts as Ireland's tragedy, maybe the greater tragedy lies in the conditions that drove them to emigrate in the first place.

The Congested District Boards, like the one that, around 1910, built the new houses on the Great Blasket? Such districts were "congested," recall, because their populations were too great to support at any level above bare subsistence; "excess" Irish men and women clambered aboard ships, especially for America. The Famine was horrific, but conditions in Ireland all through the rest of the nineteenth century and into the twentieth were never much better; poverty took deep and persistent hold. Steel factories? Great textile manufacturers? Save for Belfast, in the North, there was nothing like that in Ireland. Rural Ireland was cut off from a rapidly industrializing world that had left it economically almost irrelevant. Synge found Aran and the Great Blasket irresistible; but he realized as clearly as anybody that "nearly all the characteristics which give colour and attractiveness to Irish life are bound up with a social condition that is near to penury."

Emigration was so ingrained in the national culture that it came to be seen as routine and expected, as a first job, or marriage, or bearing children was elsewhere. Custom and tradition built up around it; there was Irish music, Irish Catholicism . . . and Irish emigration. In the 1950s, an American scholar, Arnold Schrier, drew up a questionnaire on emigration that, under the aegis of the Irish Folklore Commission, went out to thirty specially selected folklore collectors. In it, he pointedly asked about such icons of emigration as the "emigrant letter" and the "American cheque."

The emigrant letter was the invariably sunny missive reciting the emigrant's accomplishments and good fortune in America, passed around from person to person or read out loud by the parish priest at social gatherings, and often containing money. So predictably upbeat were they, Schrier's folklore collectors were reminded, that ultimately they became "an object of sarcastic cant." For example, an innocuous "How are you doing?" might get the sardonic reply, "Oh, fine, like an American letter," any darker truths papered over. The gifts, money, and relentless good cheer from America, observes Kerby Miller, a University of Missouri–based authority on Irish emigration, "inspired dissatisfaction with customary life-styles, while the steady drain of young people weakened" traditional life back home. Emigration fed on itself. The number of Irish-speakers fell. The cultural glue of traditional music and folklore weakened.

The American cheque was looked forward to eagerly come Christmas or Saint Patrick's Day; it cleared debts with the village shopkeeper, paid funeral expenses, or supplied passage money for the next family member bound for America. The sum was often exaggerated, an empty letter never admitted; its value, after all, was the ultimate measure of how your Seán or Máire was doing across the sea. "Nobody was supposed to be poor or out of work in America."

Schrier asked his respondents about the American wake, too, the traditional leave-taking ritual for the emigrant and his family. One Kerry informant described it as "a combination of joviality and sorrow. The young people sang and danced. The older people were usually sad and silent, especially the parents of the intending emigrants." There were rounds of tea, refreshments, and drink, on into the morning. And sad songs of emigration, which became so common that they, too, came to be seen as traditional. A young man "to his love did say":

> Oh Molly, lovely Molly
> No longer can I stay,
> For the ship is waiting at Queenstown
> And her anchor now is weighed
> But where I be I'll think of thee
> My lovely Irish maid.

To which she replies:

> When you go o'er to the Yankee shore
> Some Yankee girls you'll see
> They will all look very handsome
> And you'll think no more of me.
> You'll forget the vows and promises
> That you to me have made,
> You'll forget them all you left behind
> And your lovely Irish maid.

The American wake was a sad, recurrent part of Blasket life. "I have a great mind to go to America," Maurice records his sister Maura (Máire) abruptly announcing one day while she's washing the dishes and the rest of the family sits by the fire. Next day she writes to her aunt in America for passage money, and some weeks later it arrives. In the ensuing month, the household is consumed with the specter of her departure and that of her friend Kate. The old people lament no one will be left to bury them.

The day approaches. "A mournful look was coming over the very walls of the house. The hill above the village which sheltered the houses seemed to be changing colour like a big, stately man who would bend his head in sorrow."

Finally, on the last night, everyone gathers at the house for the American wake, all "dancing and mirth" mixed with "a mournful look on all within. No wonder, for they were like children of the one mother, people of the Island, no more than twenty yards between any two houses, the boys and girls every moonlit night dancing on the Sandhills or sitting together and listening to the sound of the waves from Shingle Strand." Maura collapses into Maurice's arms. "Oh, Mirrisheen," she says, using an affectionate diminutive, "what will I do without you?"

"Be easy," Maurice tells her: he'd probably be joining her before long. "Strike up a tune," he says to a neighbor with the melodeon. "He began to play," Maurice writes. "Four of us arose and I called my sister for the dance."

In America, the Irish didn't settle willy-nilly across the great land but, like most immigrants, were drawn to specific, mostly urban enclaves. Many Irish countrymen, writes Kerby Miller, learned so much about America that they came to see it as scarcely foreign at all. "Western peasants often knew far more about Boston or New York than about Dublin, Cork, or even parts of their own counties." Blasket Islanders, as it happens, made a cluster of towns along the Connecticut River centered on Springfield, Massachusetts, their new home.

They, and immigrants from Dún Chaoin, Ventry, Dingle, and other West Kerry towns, settled into small houses on the north side of Springfield, took jobs at local factories, later worked their way into bigger houses on Hungry Hill, or in neighboring towns, some of them over the state border in northern Connecticut. Springfield itself, with a population of about 140,000, was the fourth-largest city in the state and a great Irish ghetto, with a bar, Irish-catering grocery, or funeral home on every corner. Sheehans, Guiheens, and Sullivans were all close by, comfortably nestled into parishes anchored by big Roman Catholic churches. In Maurice's account of his sister's coming emigration, she and her friend talked "of nothing but America. They would run across to the wall where pictures from Springfield were hanging. 'Oh,' Kate would say, 'we will go into that big building the first day.' "

Despair mounted among those who feared being left behind. "This place," Maurice's sister Eibhlín wrote in her journal the day George left the island in 1923, "is like a drowned vessel now. Everyone wants to leave when they get the chance." Indeed, by the time of George and Maurice's trip to the Inish in 1926, she had left for America. Sister Maura, of course, had recently left, too. And now, as George and he sat on Inishvickillaun looking out to sea, maybe it was Maurice's turn.

George had never been to America, through all his long life never would go, and, according to his daughter Margaret, developed no little antipathy for it. Even by 1926, America had become a symbol to him of all that was too rich, frenetic, and cruel in modern life. Nor was he alone in seeing its vaunted opportunity, its Hollywood glitter, its cars and skyscrapers, as just a cover for a place that ate up immigrants and consumed their souls, its stopwatch-clicking efficiency experts and gang bosses squeezing the life out of them. "There's a curse on America if this place," the Blasket, "is any better," says Séamas, one of Tomás's stock characters in *Island Cross-Talk*. "You're better off working anywhere but where you'd be under somebody's eye day in and day out." Yes, says Séamaísin, Séamas's foil, "it's a corner of hell," the condemned forced to go "without sleep or rest in their struggle to make a living." In America, the good, gentle virtues of rural Ireland stood no chance.

For many Irish priests, according to Kerby Miller, America was "a vicious, materialistic, 'godless' society, which corrupted the emigrants' morals and destroyed their religious faith." For some, America was the consummately un-Irish place, where neighborliness had been banished, where people loved only money, where, it was said, "rosy-faced, fair young girls, so pure, so innocent, so pious," were dragged down into corruption. One Kerryman, his carefully penned reminiscence today preserved in a green leather-bound volume at the Delargy Centre for Irish Folklore in Dublin, told how Irishmen viewed compatriots returning from America, gold watches suspended on chains from their waistcoats, as hard-hearted and callous. "Having had the experience of life in America where it was a case of 'every man for himself,' they had lost the kindly good-natured ways of home."

That was America to some Irishmen. And that, or something like it, was America to George Thomson. Just twenty-three years old—and just twenty-three years old in the intensity of his opinions—he had plainly imbibed such values and understandings. "Listen here," he told Maurice now:

> If you want the history of America look at the Yank who comes home; think of his appearance. Not a drop of blood in his body but he has left it beyond. Look at the girl who goes over with her fine comely face! When she comes home she is pale and the skin is furrowed on her brow. If you noticed that, Maurice, you would never go to that place.

There was no future for Maurice on the island, George realized, but that didn't mean he had to leave Ireland. Why not, he'd importuned him before, stay in Ireland and join the Civil Guard—the Garda Síochána, the Irish national police formed after the establishment of the Free State. With them, he'd find good opportunities. "There was the reluctance of the world on me to do as he said," Maurice would write. But he had to decide one way or the other. "Both of us knew that if I did not agree with him that day I would be gathered away [to America] before the summer was come again."

Finally, he yielded. He would forsake America. He would enlist in the Guard.

That evening, just before George's departure the following day, Maurice took down his fiddle and headed over to George's place, where he found him seated on a stool by the fire. They talked a while, his friend at one point replying with a local idiom.

"'Tis the fine, rich Irish, you have now," he told George.

"And if it is, it is you should be thanked, for isn't it from yourself I learned all I have!" George replied.

Then it was up to the house at the top of the village, strains of music reaching them, everyone soon dancing, "George stripped to the shirt like themselves, for the night was soft." When they took a breather outside, George reminded his friend that, once on his way to Dublin to enlist, Maurice had but to telegraph him and he'd be there at the station to greet him.

It took him six months or more to build up to it; George, who by now had graduated from King's and was living in Dublin, encouraged him by mail all the while. But finally, on March 14, 1927, as his father sat by the fire reading a letter from America, Maurice delivered the news: he was leaving the island, joining the Guard, heading off for Dublin the next day: "I give you my blessing," his father said, "for so far as this place is concerned there is no doubt but it is gone to ruin."

Maurice's journey to Dublin proved exhilarating, sad, confusing, and even, at least to us today, comic. There was nothing routine to any of it. It was all firsts. He was starting out on a new life—going where he had never gone, seeing what he had never seen. Each obstacle encountered, person met, or mistake made propelled him to some new height or depth of feeling.

The king, on his regular mail hop, rows him over to Dún Chaoin, "my back to the Island of my birth and my face to the mainland." He hears his dog, Rose, back on the island, "howling as she saw me departing from her. I crushed down the distress that was putting a cloud on my heart."

All is unfamiliar. On the mainland he must pick up a certificate from the parish priest, in whose Ballyferriter rectory he encounters a young woman who understands nothing he says. "Well, thought I, isn't it a strange thing to meet already a girl without Irish!"

Tramping to Dingle, he follows the line of telegraph poles. At the house of a family friend, where he's to stay, he's at first not recognized. He reveals himself as if by riddle: he's no Irishman, he says, though he has Irish blood, and has arrived in Ireland this very day.

How, then, has he picked up his fine Irish?

"Arra, my dear sir, isn't it we who have the best Irish?"

But if not an Irishman, what, then, is he?

"I am a Blasket man, my boy."

That night, his sleep is blighted by visions of railway tracks running this way and that, people like ants, all confusion. "Three nights I lived in that night." After breakfast, he makes his way to the station, tortured by the sense that everyone is staring at him. The train pulls out. Green fields and unfamiliarly abundant trees sweep by him, "houses in every glen and ravine, the Blasket Island and the wild sea far out of sight. They were gone now and I a lonely wanderer, and as the old saying goes, 'Bare is the companionless shoulder.' "

The train stops. People start to get out. Is this Tralee, where he must get out? No, it's Annascaul; he's mistaken a town of a scant few hundred for one of ten thousand. Yet he's relieved now, counts himself lucky not to face a trek back to Dingle.

Another stop. He grabs his bag. No, he learns, not this, either. He's thrilled by one simple, irrefutable fact: so far, he's not lost. He draws out his pipe, puffs at it with satisfaction.

Finally, it's Tralee. In the station, with four hours to kill, he stashes his bag against a wall, careful not to let it out of sight. But when he spies other waiting passengers hand over their luggage for red tickets, he does the same. "I was well pleased with myself now, and why wouldn't I be, and every knowledge coming to me."

He steps into the telegraph office to wire George in Dublin. The girl behind the desk is reading a book, and it's all he can do to get the telegraph form from her; they exchange scarcely a word. " 'There is no fear, my girl, but you are a stiff one,' said I in Irish, knowing she would not understand me."

" 'Good day to you, sir,' " says she in English, finally. And that "sir" gladdens him! Has he now the look of a gentleman? "My heart was now rising continually the way I was getting knowledge of everything."

Small triumphs of understanding follow one another. On the platform he sees "boxes thrown out of the train without pity or tenderness, big cans, full of milk as I heard, hurled out on to hard cement." Then, back on board, he looks out the window as his own train makes a long, sweeping turn; he can see its whole length yet can't see what drives it. Confusions and uncertainties. Irish gone, all is English.

In Mallow, he gets off. "Change for Dublin! Change for Cork!" he hears. He follows a savvy-looking woman he has met to the Dublin train, settles into his seat, and falls asleep—until the conductor comes to punch his ticket. "I think you have made a mistake," he's told. "You are halfway to Cork." Doubts overtake him. It's not the Dublin train at all. He glares at the woman. "I was unable to crush down the ill will I felt towards her."

But in Cork all is resolved, and he's directed to the next train for Dublin, at no extra fare. " 'A thousand thanks to you,' said I . . . , as pleased as any other mother's son from here to Halifax, as an Islander would say." He telegraphs George with the change of plans.

At nine that night, the train for Dublin pulls out of the station. Maurice sleeps until a cold shiver wakes him.

> The night had a lonesome look. It was sharp and cold, nothing to be heard only the duga-ga-dug, duga-ga-dug of the train and now and again the fairy music of the wind as it ran against the windowpanes. It is far away my thoughts were at that moment—far

west in the Blasket. I see the curraghs back beyond Carrig Vlach
and hear the glug-glag of the ripples on their sides. I see others
off the strand of Yellow Island and yet others down to the west of
the Tail, the nets stretched back out of the sterns and phosphores-
cence around them. I see again the old crew—Shaun Liam, Tigue
O'Shea, and Tomás O'Carna down at the Tail, their nets in the
sea and they talking. Look how they strike their arms together to
keep themselves warm!

The train pushes through the night until they reach the edge of Dublin. It is three in the morning. At this unholy hour, will George really be
there?

The train was entering the station, my heart beating. It stretched
alongside the platform. There was no one alive to be seen, only a
big fat policeman, covered well up under his chin. I took my bag
and stepped out, and I tell you I hated the thought of that city.
    As I leapt out who was before me but George!

The young man who welcomed Maurice to Dublin in March 1927 already
had close ties of the heart to Ireland, the Irish people, and the Irish language. But professionally and intellectually, it bears repeating, he was a
student of the classics. For at least ten years, since he enrolled in the Classics side at Dulwich College, the world of Homer and Aeschylus had been
his intellectual home. Most of the books he'd write over the years per-
tained to ancient Greece, not modern Ireland. In the months between
his visit to the Inish with Maurice and their reunion now, he had been
finishing a thesis that would become the first of them, *Greek Lyric Metre*,
upon which his scholarly reputation rests in part even today.
    His thesis was titled "The Prometheus Trilogy of Aeschylus, with an
Appendix on Greek Lyric Metre"—two sharp divisions, his acknowledgments section sounding two chimes of thanks. First to Jack Sheppard, his
mentor at King's; his own work, George wrote with a twenty-three-year-old's
overwrought deference,

is merely a corollary of Mr. Sheppard's work on Greek tragedy. I
am digging with the tools he has put into my hands in a corner

of the field which he has not had time to explore so thoroughly as the rest, and, if I have succeeded in striking water at any point, it is because the genius of the diviner first showed me where it lay.

As to the second part of his thesis, it represented "the first results of an attempt to apply the metrical principles laid down by the late Walter Headlam in 1902." This other King's classicist had died young, at forty-two, but not before contributing what George termed "a brief but brilliant" article in the *Journal of Hellenic Studies* on meter in Greek lyric poetry. In it, Headlam had asserted that due appreciation of Greek poetry meant bringing to it an insistently musical ear: "The principles of Form in modern music are the very principles then followed in Greek lyric metre." Headlam's paper had attracted scant attention in England and Germany, but, George wrote,

> as soon as I read it, I felt that he had touched the heart of the matter. Not only did the principles he enunciated seem to my ear completely satisfactory, but the examples he gave of their application did more than carry conviction—they revealed beauties in the poems concerned which had hitherto passed unnoticed.

If Sheppard was his literary father, he wrote now, Headlam was his literary grandfather. "I am an unworthy descendant," he concluded, "but not, I hope, lacking in filial piety." He signed his name and dated it, "Dublin, Dec. 9th, 1926."

Dublin. The city had been George's home since fall, as it would be for most of the next five years, ending in 1931. Summers, he was off to the Blaskets; at least once he went to Greece; and for the year spanning 1928 he was back in Cambridge. But mostly during this period Dublin was the center of his life, a place more congenial to him than Cambridge or London would ever be, furnishing him a store of fond memories. What helped, too, of course, was the delicious freedom he enjoyed thanks to his success at King's.

Students at Cambridge University took a formidable university-wide examination known as the Tripos, in two parts, separated by a year or more. George scored "firsts," or first-class honors, in both. In 1926, the same year he earned his B.A., he had been awarded a prestigious fellowship called the Craven Studentship, for "advanced study or research away from Cambridge in the Languages, Literature, History, Archaeology or Art of ancient Greece or Rome." It was a good gig: at a time when many a whole family scraped by on a hundred pounds a year or less, the Craven assured its fortunate young recipient two hundred; the assistant librarian at King's made only 235. With Craven in hand, George was off to Dublin for the academic year 1926–27, nominally enrolled at Trinity College. Especially once he'd put the finishing touches on his dissertation, at the end of 1926, he was free to throw himself into the life of his vibrant new urban home.

Dublin was Ireland's capital and largest city, population about 400,000, storied in recent revolutionary history. The façade of the General Post Office, off O'Connell Street, still bore bullet holes from the Rising of April 1916. The imposing legal complex known as Four Courts, which Michael Collins's men shelled in the early days of the Irish Civil War, was still largely in ruins. The Abbey Theatre, on Lower Abbey Street, with its gabled wrought-iron canopy, was the site of the Playboy Riots. James Joyce had made the Dublin of a single day—June 16, 1904—the stage set for his epochal *Ulysses,* published in 1922. Dublin's streets were crowded with automobiles, motor-driven trucks, horse-drawn cars, and bicycles. Double-decker trams barreled through College Green, between Trinity College and the Bank of Ireland building across the street, bearing ads for Savoy Chocolate and O'Mara's Bacon and Hams. Dublin was in its heyday, busy, crowded, and culturally vibrant.

Just now, George was living in books-and-papers-crowded rooms on Leeson Street, near Saint Stephen's Green. But he was frequently in Raheny, a well-off enclave in the northern outskirts of the city, home to Moya Llewelyn Davies, a local grande dame, beautiful and rich, who lived in a fine old mansion there known as Furry Park. Maurice didn't know it when he stepped off the train in Dublin early that morning in March 1927, but Furry Park was their destination, he and George being guests for the week of Mrs. Davies.

From the station, at three-thirty in the morning, George and Maurice are driven off in a car, courtesy no doubt of their hostess. "I was blinded by the hundred thousand lights," Maurice wrote later, "lights on every side of me, lights before me, and lights above my head on the tops of poles." A car slices toward them along the other side of the road, "and yet another, our own making rings around the corners and blowing the horn without ceasing. I don't know if I am in a dream. If not, it is the Land of the Young without a lie."

Eventually, they stop outside what Maurice remembers as "a big castle, magnificent lamp alight above the door, the walls covered in ivy, up to twenty windows in it, big and broad." Silently, like robbers, waking no one, George lets them in. They enter a large room, elaborately furnished, with "pictures of noblemen long dead hanging on the walls," fine furniture, lush curtains.

Late next morning, "the sunbeams were pouring in through the curtains and the two of us awake, talking and conversing of the affairs of the island." A week before, Maurice was sleeping in a stone cottage. Now he enjoys the comforts of Furry Park. There's a knock on the door. In comes

George Thomson with Maurice O'Sullivan in his new Civic Guard uniform, a few years before Maurice began work on the book that became Twenty Years A-Growing

Moya, "young, handsome, brightly laughing . . . the flower of nobility."
She serves them tea.

"Isn't that a handsome girl?" says Maurice, once she's left.

At one point he steps out among the trees sheltering the grounds.
Leaves flutter. Birds sing. A scene to glory in. "Isn't it a fine life is given to
some rather than to others!" he muses. "I don't know what in the world
could trouble the man who lives there, though I have often heard it is they
who are the worst for discontent." Not for a minute does he buy *that* one;
a "great lie," he calls it. A man "would need only to sit outside his castle listening to the music of the birds for all sorrow to be lifted from his heart."

That evening, George takes him into town for a movie. Maurice sees
clean streets, happy couples with apparently nothing else to do. "Isn't it a
great pity entirely for the poor lads back in the Island," he ruminates, "with
nothing for them to see or hear but the big rollers coming up through the
Sound and the howl of the wind blowing from the north-west across the
hills, and often for four weeks without news from the mainland!"

They reach O'Connell Bridge, which spans the Liffey at the heart of
the city, with "trams and motors roaring and grating, newspaper-sellers
at every corner shouting in the height of their heads, hundreds of people
passing this way and that without stopping, and every one of them, men
and women, handsomely got up." The traffic is so heavy he and George
can't at first get across the street. It's worse "than to be back off the quay of
the Blasket waiting for a calm moment to run in."

They continue, probably straight up O'Connell Street in all its imperial width, finally turning in to Prince Street. There, facing them, a hundred yards back from O'Connell, where the street narrows, is the Capitol
Theatre. Its blinking marquee lights—CAPITOL—seem to Maurice as if on
fire. He exclaims at the sheer spectacle of it. George acts astonished, too,
but Maurice suspects he's being kind. "Well, well, said I to myself, I must
change and not show my wonder at anything else."

The Capitol, where Fianna Fail, the new republican party, had held its
inaugural meeting a few months before, lies practically in the shadow of
the bullet-riddled General Post Office. Built originally as an opera house,
it now presents movies as well as live shows. It is grandly overdone, with
cafés, lounges, and ballrooms, seats for fourteen hundred people, three
tiers of private boxes and cantilevered galleries—just the thing to impress
a boy from the country.

It does. "It took my senses from me," Maurice would write. "Stars
came before my eyes with the sight—the cleanliness and the splendour

of the place within. It was impossible to comprehend it. Wonderful is the power of man. We went up a staircase as twisty as a corkscrew and my delight was so great that I thought of heaven."

They take their seats. The great curtains part. The Blaskets are far, far away.

Chapter 6

The Last Quiet Time

[1929]

George Thomson's first time on the Blaskets came in 1923; his trip to Inish-vickillaun with Maurice in 1926; Maurice's journey to Dublin in 1927. The first of the books that would begin to draw interest to the Blaskets were published in Irish in 1928 and 1929. The 1930s would bring to the island journalists, curiosity seekers, language enthusiasts, and film crews enough, it could seem, to crowd out the islanders themselves; this flood of attention and publicity, coupled with the worldwide economic depression, the gathering toll of emigration, and other factors, would change the face of the island forever. The mid-to-late 1920s, then, was the last time when the island was still something like what it long had been, before it became something else.

Day by day, season by season, the familiar rhythms of island life played out. Smoke curled up from the hearths of the village's felt-roofed stone houses. Young girls gathered turf. Boys played football with old socks stuffed with hay or straw; or they'd steal out from school for a swim, charging down to the slip, throwing off their clothes, and hurling them-selves into the sea. Women met around the well at the top of the village, bantering, exchanging news, their jugs slowly filling. Men in threes and fours hoisted atop their heads the black beetlelike *naomhóg*s, carried them down to the slip, and headed out to sea to fish. The island king rowed to the mainland twice a week to pick up letters and parcels; the villagers gathered round him on his return. Once a year, the priest would be rowed into the island to take confessions and say Mass. There'd be dancing at An Dáil, the village's "parliament" of a house, or at Peig Sayers's. There was no doctor on the island, no proper nurse; a Massachusetts-born woman reared in her grandparents' house in Dún Chaoin and married into the island in the 1890s, Méiní Dunlevy, served as midwife. There was no plumbing; when you felt "the pressure," you went outside by a fence to relieve yourself, men and women alike. From time to time, the islanders made forays to the mainland and into Dingle to pick up provisions.

Dún Chaoin and the nearby mainland towns—Ventry, Ballyferriter, and the western peninsula's market center, Dingle, population about eighteen hundred—were tied to the island by bonds of marriage, kinship—and misunderstanding. Mainlanders sometimes saw the islanders as wild tricksters; islanders were apt to see the mainlanders as money-grubbing. Dún Chaoin, directly facing the island, was less a village than a collection of houses spread across the sloping highlands that stood back from the sea; it was more rural, really, than the island itself, whose compact village asserted an almost urban density. Years later, a filmmaker contemplating a documentary about western Ireland came away discouraged that "hardly any of the villages had a close clustering of houses that could *look* like a village" on film. Local jurisdictions were many and overlapping. Corca Dhuibhne was the broad ancestral region, the western part of County Kerry. Then there were parishes, and named towns, and the little townlands that made them up, which rarely appeared on any map. The puffs of white that were sheep ranging over the West Kerry hills were more numerous by far than people.

A big moment in the year came in November, with the Dingle Fair. Island sheep were fattened; the villagers rounded them up, brought them down to the slip, loaded them into *naomhóg*s, and rowed them across to Dún Chaoin. There, they'd tie them up two-by-two, walk them up the path to the top of the cliff, and then the dozen miles to Dingle, where they'd often spend the night. "You'd have a drink," Seán Ó Criomhthain remembered, "and when that went down you felt as happy as if you never had a poor relative."

Near the center of Blasket village stood the island school. It was one of the larger buildings, about twenty-five feet long, set, like most of them, so

In the decades before this picture was taken in about 1930, as many as fifty students attended the island school; by 1941, when it was closed down, there were just three.

its long axis followed the slope down the hill; its short northeastern wall was common to the house next door, belonging to one of the Kearneys. Beginning in the fall of 1927, Nóra Ní Shéaghdha, straight from teacher-training in Limerick, became head teacher: "I was young and light-hearted," she remembered. About a quarter of the island's population—forty-two by her memory—were students there. Attendance was no problem, "because there was nothing to keep them at home," and because no one had to come very far. "Even if a gale of wind was blowing they'd still have to come to school." In fact, her own attendance proved more the problem. Friday afternoons, she'd be rowed back across the sound, intending to return to the island on Sunday, but sometimes a storm marooned her on the mainland; the authorities in Dublin were not sympathetic. In time, she took to staying on the island.

At school, there was no place to hang coats, and the children would sometimes run in drenched. "They'd shake it off like ducks," said Ní Shéaghdha, "because they were accustomed to having the salt water blowing into their faces every day of the week and every day of the year." She and the assistant teacher seated them at long benches, in two groups, the younger children toward the fire, the older ones toward the door. Her pupils, she remembered, were all "very keen on English. Who could blame them? [Even] if they only went down to Dingle they'd need it, and at that time there was nothing in their heads but America." That and poetry. "They were extremely interested in English poetry just as they were in Irish poetry. They had poetry in their blood, I suppose, and they found it easy to learn." Seán Ó Criomhthain recalled from an earlier period that he and his classmates had studied *Macbeth,* and loved it, and were always more interested in learning English than Irish. "We were thinking of another country and of life beyond the Island. It was then the intention and plan of everyone on the Blaskets to go to America."

During the summer, the men would fish five or six days a week for lobster; during the winter, for mackerel. After a night's fishing, the crew would row over to Dún Chaoin, stow their boats, and carry hundred-pound sacks of fish up the cliff path from the slip; what they got for their trouble was at the whim of the market. The early years of the century, when Synge and Marstrander visited, were good ones. But now, big French trawlers, which could fish farther out to sea, were competing more successfully with the little island *naomhóg*s. And in 1927, the United States imposed a tariff on salted mackerel. The market softened. The hard lives of the island fishermen grew harder. "It was our business to be out in the night, and the misery of that sort of fishing is beyond telling," wrote Tomás Ó Criomhthain, who up to about 1926 was still sending his perfectly penned epistles to Brian Kelly. "I count it the worst of all trades."

The *naomhóg*s, bow and stern lifting high above the water, were instantly recognizable. On land, perched upside down on wooden posts flanking the path up to the village, black-bottomed, thick with repeated tarrings, they looked like works of nature—truly like the giant beetles visitors reliably said they resembled. Yet turn them over and slip them into the sea, and the human artifacts they were became apparent. Four bench seats were spaced along their twenty-six-foot length. The tight wooden latticework visible from inside looked like nothing so regular and measured as an engineer's graph paper.

They were in many ways better than the big seine-boats they'd replaced in the 1880s, which had been seized for failure to pay rent and, Seán Ó Criomhthain would report, allowed to rot away on a quay in Dingle; the little *naomhóg*s, on the other hand, weren't worth a rent collector's trouble. They could be fitted with a single sail, but were more often rowed by three or four men using peculiar small-bladed oars. A Norwegian fisherman "would laugh at this little toy," noted Carl Marstrander. But the life of the island depended on them; a census counted four hundred of them west of Dingle in 1921, the island itself good for several dozen.

It took a lot to sink them—heavy seas, gross overloading. They were remarkably maneuverable, easy to slip into the gap between the sea-splashed rocks, tucked away at the base of the cliff, that passed for a harbor. The men would bring the boat to an almost braked sudden stop as they approached shore, manage a graceful little 180-degree twirl, step lithely out, pass up the oars, turn the boat upside down in a single swift, graceful movement, their heads disappearing in the beetle's carapace, and march it up the hill in stately procession. Stored bottom-up, the boats obligingly presented cuts or other damage for repair.

Of course, the seeming vulnerability of the little craft was not all illusion. The crew might carry a wooden bowl to bail water, a sock to plug a leak. Visitors found passage into the island memorable, thrilling—or downright terrifying. Robin Flower's son Patrick remembered how as a boy, probably in the late 1920s, he was literally tossed from shore to a big islander in the boat, his mother "huddled in a lump in the well of the boat," the two of them ill the whole way across. "All I could hear was the roar of the wind and [the crew leader's] called instructions as we breasted each wave." It was daytime, Patrick knew, but it felt like darkest night.

A striated checkerboard of arable field above the White Strand, about sixty acres of the island's eleven hundred, constituted the island's farm. Oats and rye, along with potatoes—planted in ridges, each furrow dug, each sod turned, by hand—were the chief crops; in 1925, a hundred pounds of potatoes might be worth six shillings, but the islanders normally consumed all they harvested. Cabbage, turnips, and carrots were also grown. The sheep that grazed the green island slopes supplied wool for clothing, mutton for food, and a little ready cash when taken to market; in winter, island women cleaned, carded, dyed, and spun the wool that they later made into jerseys and shawls. Another source of income was rabbit pelts, which islanders sometimes mailed off to Cork or Dublin, maybe three dozen at a time, fetching perhaps three shillings.

Another "crop" was the peat (the first stage in the transformation of vegetation to coal) used to heat every house on the island. Some years later, Mary Kearney's younger brother, Seán, would demonstrate for the cameras just how you harvested it. Wearing boots, pants with turned-up cuffs, a thick open-necked sweater, and wielding a long-handled bladed implement, Seán cut straight down into the turf. Each piece was about a foot square. Cutting out the top layer, vegetation still attached, he turned it over with the same tool and tossed it aside. At the next layer down, he did much the same, the clumps of peat liberated this time resembling squares of dark, moist cake. These would be collected and left in small stone enclosures on the far side of the island to dry. In winter, when storms made fishing impossible, the islanders would recover them and bring them down to their houses.

Accounts of objects and materials of value washing up on the Gravel Strand, to the north of the village, or on the White Strand, or elsewhere around the island, occur often enough in local lore to suggest a surprisingly reliable source of village livelihood. Driftwood shaped by island carpenters became part of many a window frame or *naomhóg*. Shipwrecks, too, con-tributed to the wealth of the island, enough to galvanize the whole village when they were reported. U-boat sinkings during the Great War were, during the 1920s, objects of recent memory. "Thanks to the submarine campaign," an islander told one visitor, "the Great War was a prosperous era." Crates of oranges. Canadian potatoes. Onions from Spain. Barrels of wine. Linens and porcelains: "You see these cups that are so pretty? They came to us like that from the sea." Perhaps the biggest haul came with the running aground of the *Quebra* in 1916, which left long stretches of shoreline crowded with "wreckage and wood and chests and barrels and cotton," recalled Méiní Dunlevy, with "flour and meat and fat stranded on the beach for us." The islanders gathered up all they could. "It wasn't the Island of Hunger in those years, but the Island of Plenty."

The island endured. Its people endured. "The world is said to change every twenty years," Seán Ó Criomhthain said when he was in his sixties. But all through the late 1920s, the island stayed much as it had long been. The hill rising above the village remained, and the ever-shifting play of light, and the grand views, and the growing green. Year by year, the tide streamed through the narrow rock-encumbered channel that was Blasket Sound. The waves ran up on the beach, wore away at the ancient cliffs. Trees, as always, were nowhere—hard to accept for those from milder and more familiar climes, but true: no trees. No river, either, and no lake. There were no hares, no stoats, no weasels, no frogs, no foxes, no badgers, no hedgehogs, no newts. Plentiful were seabirds; an 1880s naturalist counted 174 species on the Blaskets, including puffins, razorbills, guillemots, storm petrels, and gulls. From the heights of the village—or most anywhere on the island, really—they were forever swooping above or beneath you.

Constant, too, in their inconstancy were irresolute skies that changed with astonishing frequency, the west wind blowing in something new every time you looked up. It rarely snowed on the island, and the cold never grew bitter, thanks to the Gulf Stream. It didn't even rain that much, not if you were totting up annual inches of precipitation. But it rained *often*. And when not raining it was misty, foggy, or gray, the sun at best irregular. In December, high up north as the island was, at the latitude of Labrador, islanders got an average of less than one and a half hours of sun out of the twenty-four.

Still, the familiar comforts of nature offered balm. "You'd go back the hill, yourself and another lad or two, looking at sheep," Seán Ó Guithín, who was seventeen in 1928, would remember. "A rabbit might jump out and the dog would chase him and if there was anything troubling your mind, that would help you to forget it."

Did the islanders live in poverty? Was this the precise and responsible word to describe their condition? Asked many years later, Nóra Ní Shéaghdha couldn't quite settle on how to answer the question. Well, yes, she concluded at last, some "were certainly poor and could have done with more if they had it." After all, the harsh life of the island was one reason they left. Emigration sapped the island community, yet enriched it, too; many families lived better thanks to money from America. In the end, marriage itself became problematic, for there was almost no one left to marry. Tomás's son left. Mary Kearney's older sister left in 1925. Mícheál O'Guiheen emigrated in 1928, though he returned the following year, close-mouthed about his bad time in America. "My two eyes were red from crying," he wrote later about leaving the island. "Son of my heart," said his mother, "it is a poor place where you wouldn't be better off than here. Don't you see that everyone is running away from it if he can?"

The young people left. A trickle of visitors arrived.

Almost invariably, like George Thomson, they came for the Irish, but found much else to occupy them and enjoy. "They had dancing and music and fresh fish and every sort of sea-food to munch," recalled Seán Ó Criomhthain of this period, from the early 1920s on, so "they felt they were in heaven."

One visitor, for about two weeks in 1920, was forty-eight-year-old Swedish folklorist Carl von Sydow, who wrote of the islanders, "They can't speak English, and they are renowned for the beauty of their Irish"; this was already something of a formula. Earlier, on the mainland, he'd stayed at Willie Long's place in Ballyferriter, the two of them discovering a mutual interest in botany. On the island, he stayed with the brother of the king, shared a bed with a schoolteacher from Cork, heard folktales from Peig Sayers, met her son Mícheál, became friendly with Tomás Ó Criomhthain, and took lots of pictures. In 1924, he was back, taking more pictures, including one of Tomás, bundled up in wool without his familiar porkpie hat, standing in the doorway to his house. Von Sydow was recording what would prove to be this last quiet time in the life of the island. When he left the second time, George Thomson was on hand to snap a picture of him as he was rowed away.

At least twice before 1922, Seoirse Mac Cluin, a young Catholic priest, visited the island. Compiling an Irish phrase book, he put islanders to work on his behalf, asking them to use odd or distinctive words and phrases in sentences. Soon, the island schoolchildren were busily beseeching the old people for words. The biggest help, of course, came from Tomás. They worked together, morning and afternoon, for most of a month.

In 1925, after a decade away, Robin Flower began returning to the island for vacations. The end of the war in 1918 hadn't itself been enough to bring him and his wife back to the island, probably because they were busy making babies—four of them between 1912 and 1921. "Talk Irish to Barbara," Tomás wrote to Flower in 1912, soon after her birth; Barbara was the first of the four. Nine years later, in 1921, Flower wrote Richard Best, his colleague at the British Museum, "We have a real boy baby at last, of name Patrick and of disposition angelic. He is to go to the font next Sunday, and will you be his godfather?" Patrick was the last. In between came Síle and Jean. All had Celtic-studies masters as their godfathers; Barbara's was Carl Marstrander.

Beginning in the mid-1920s and on into the '30s, the children regularly accompanied their parents on their four-week August vacations; indeed, vacations they were, as much as research trips. "The girls," Flower wrote Best from the Blaskets in 1929, "are having the time of their lives here, running about and dancing and picking up bits of Irish. The weather has been wonderful this last fortnight and now with sun all day and a full moon over the island at night it is a heaven to be here." Each year, they'd stay briefly in Dún Chaoin, Patrick would remember, then cross to the island the next day, their big clan spread between two island houses. Soon, the children would be running around barefoot as if they always had. Barbara, who picked up the language easily, sometimes went along with Síle to the island school. "We children had the most idyllic time those summers," Patrick would recall. One photo of him at six or seven shows him with his father and sisters, leaning against a sheer rock precipice. Flower's wife, Ida, befriended Cáit, daughter of the king. "It was an incredibly primitive life compared to what she must have been used to," Síle said of her mother, "but she loved it." As for Flower himself, islanders sometimes spotted him sitting alone against a bank, hands cradling his knees, staring across to the mainland, lost in reverie. His Blasket holidays, according to Celtic scholar Seán Ó Lúing, were the happiest times of his life.

His Irish was good by this time, though he always spoke it with an English accent; sometimes he had trouble getting his mouth around particularly stubborn Irish phrases. But in returning to the Blaskets after the war, he felt almost like an islander himself, the émigré restored to his roots. He grew into a familiar figure, like a lovable if not rich uncle. He'd come with sweets for the children. He'd read stories to them. He mixed with everyone. He was known as a great scholar, yes, but he was light and easy company. At Tomás's, he'd eat roasted mackerel with his fingers, lick them contentedly, then toss the bones to the dog.

Flower was a bit broader around the middle now; he was forty-four in the summer of 1925. Professionally, he was well established. In 1927, University College, Galway, had awarded him an honorary doctorate in Celtic literature. The year before, the first volume of his *Catalogue of Irish Manuscripts in the British Museum* finally came out, all 670 pages of it; it was to grapple more ably with this daunting project that, back in 1910, he'd first enrolled in the School of Irish Learning, met Marstrander, and come to the Blaskets. One reviewer caviled that the *Catalogue* was too preoccupied with medieval literature. A more recent view held that, most of a century later, it "has all the freshness reserved over time only for works of real artistic merit." In the end, the project was of a piece with his Blasket experience. "In the Blaskets he learned Irish and legends," Seán Ó Lúing has written; "in the Museum the literary manifestation of the same world unfolded from the pages of old writing."

The year Robin Flower returned—1925—a new visitor arrived on the island. Her name was Marie-Louise Sjoestedt, a French woman of Swedish extraction. Save for Flower and Thomson, none among the Blasket visitors would return so often, and over so long a span, as she. She vis-

Marie-Louise Sjoestedt, a French woman of Swedish descent, in a photo from a memorial volume dedicated to her after her premature death in 1940: a student of West Kerry Irish, she visited the Blasket all through the 1920s and into the 1930s.

ited again in 1926; then in 1927, 1928, 1929, 1933, and for the last time in 1936. Her earliest visit came before any of the Blasket books had been published; when visitors to the island were still few enough to stand out fresh and distinct in the minds of the islanders; when the island was still an exotic, faraway enclave known but to a few. She visited for the last time when all three of the first-generation Blasket books had seen print, when the Blaskets were known beyond Kerry, beyond Ireland, beyond Europe.

She was extraordinarily gifted, a sterling product of the French academic system at its best. Marie-Louise Sjoestedt was twenty-four when she first came to the Great Blasket in July 1925. Six years before, in the spring of 1919, scant months after the end of the world war, she had appeared at the Sorbonne in Paris asking to study with the eminent linguist Joseph Vendryes and embark on the next step of the academic ladder, the *licence*.

She'd come out of Laon, in northeastern France, her un-French name that of her father, Erik-Valentin Sjoestedt, a diplomat with the Swedish Embassy in Paris. Her mother, from an old Corsican family, was a novelist and essayist. The family lived in an apartment on Avenue Malakoff in a fashionable district near the Arc de Triomphe that attracted artists, writers, and diplomats. Marie-Louise lapped up all that swirled around her of ideas, language, the arts and sciences; precocious she was if anyone was. When Vendryes met her for the first time, she was barely eighteen, but he came away already impressed with what he called "her solidity of thought and sureness of judgment." She was ready to work and learn, a natural scholar, with a bent for original work, someone who ought never be allowed to sink into one of the low-level niches of intellectual work to which women were so often relegated.

Linguistics was the discipline in which she proceeded to gather *licence, agrégation, diplôme,* and the other badges of the French system. "Who does not remember," recalled a classmate who took a course with her devoted to the Greek verb, "that striking young girl, with the pretty, appealingly childlike face, in her pearl necklace, leaning wisely, almost severely, on her notebook?" She studied Latin grammar. She studied Czech; she spent the summer and early fall of 1921 in Bohemia. She studied Russian, flirted with Slavic studies, later traveled to the Soviet Union. Always it was language, in all its intricacies, that beguiled her.

She had many choices as to what to do next—in a way, too many. Her family was well off; the immediate prospect of a job needn't contaminate her choice. But one of her advisers, Antoine Meillet, one of France's most esteemed linguists, perhaps determined not to see an intellect of such promise lost to dilettantism, pointed her firmly toward Celtic studies. For the academic year 1924–25, she was awarded a lectureship that left her amid the stone quadrangles of Trinity College, Dublin. There she met Osborn Bergin, T. F. O'Rahilly, and other key figures in the field. And there, too, almost certainly, she met Seán Cavanagh.

As it appears today on a plaque on the Dún Chaoin house in which he lived for many years, a few hundred yards from the sea and across the sound from the Great Blasket, his name was Seán Ó Caomhánaigh; in English that became Seán Cavanagh. But so universally was he known by a nickname, that it, too, appears on the plaque—Seán an Chóta, Seán of

*Seán an Chóta—adventurer, novelist, lin-
guist, raconteur, and companion of Marie-
Louise Sjoestedt on her visits to Dún Chaoin
and the Blaskets*

the Kilt, for the garb he wore in his youth. That's how Marie-Louise may
have known him even in Dublin—that is, if she didn't simply call him
Seán Óg, young Seán, as she did later when inscribing a book to him.
Born in 1885, he was actually older than she by fifteen years.

Seán was an adventurer, a year and a half out of jail when Marie-Louse
met him; he'd taken the "wrong," anti-treaty side in the civil war, and
wound up in the Curragh Military prison. Before that he'd spent six years
in the States. As girls and young women in the parish remembered him,
he was a roguish charmer, a lover and admirer of all womankind. In prison
he'd tell of sexual jaunts in a turf rick with a Dún Chaoin woman when
he was fifteen, she forty-five. He was oddly handsome, with a luxuriant
head of dark hair and exotically high cheekbones—"a prize-fighter's face,"
according to one who knew him in prison, "mobile, humorous, Bohemian"—with a gold-crowned tooth and a winning smile.

Seán is something of a Zelig to our story. It was he who, back in 1907, brought a prominent Gaelic Leaguer to the island looking for, but never finding, Carl Marstrander. Two years later, he helped row Eveleen Nichols to the island on the ill-fated visit that culminated in her drowning and that of Tomás Ó Criomhthain's boy. A year after that, he stood for the same group photo as Marstrander and Robin Flower at the garden party at Mrs. Eason's for students and faculty of the School of Irish Learning.

In 1915, age thirty, Seán left for America. Whether he intended to emigrate or not is unclear. What is clear is that he didn't settle in Springfield, Massachusetts, like so many Kerrymen, or in Boston. He didn't settle for long anywhere, in fact, but traveled round the country. He worked as a riveter in a New Jersey shipyard, in a Chicago steel mill, on ranches in the Dakotas. When he returned to Ireland in about 1922, he wrote an Irish-language novel based on his experiences. It was published in 1927 as *Fánai,* the wanderer. This Zane Grey–like adventure yarn, thick with ranch life and black-hatted villains, spiced with romance, takes place in a town near the border between North Dakota and Minnesota, the last stop on the line north to Canada. When a train loaded with farm workers pulls into the depot, most of them head off to the riverbank to fill their rusty pots with water and light campfires. One of them, though, lies by himself on the grass, stiff from work, before finally trudging off alone to town. A classic American Western in the making, except that the protagonist isn't some Luke, or Jed, but Seán Ó Lonargáin, Irishman, thoughtful and bookish, who's drifted west, by one telling, "in response to the undefined promptings of his heart."

Seán Ó Lonargáin's free-spirited creator was the man Marie-Louise befriended when, after her year in Dublin, she first visited Dún Chaoin and the Blaskets. "He was from the first day I landed in the parish my kind, loyal teacher," she wrote later of him, "a guiding light for me, with eternal patience, a co-researcher who shared with me his knowledge of the people and of the area. It fails me to describe the value of his help." Both loved language; Seán, whose first language was West Kerry Irish, had taught Irish under the auspices of the Gaelic League, and even in prison he ran Irish-language classes for fellow inmates. Kerry Irish was his passion, as it now was hers. For long stretches, set against the area's rocky coves and precipitous heights, they were inseparable. Roasting mackerel on open fires. Rowing together across Smerwick Harbor, into a rising gale, the little bay's waters rough and turbulent around them. Basking in summer-soft seascapes, he her teacher, she his brilliant French companion, tall, pretty, and fresh.

Under the circumstances, it would have been easy for something to develop—a friendship, an abiding intimacy, a full-blown affair—and something did. Sometimes, by what we can glean from Seán's writings, they'd head off for a rocky precipice high above the sea within sight of the Blaskets that today's maps call Clogher Head, or Ceann Sraithe. It looked like the site of some cataclysmic eruption—great gray boulders heaped atop one another, lichen and bits of vegetation clinging to them, interspersed with soft sheltered beds of turf speckled with wildflowers. The sea breeze might roar in from the north, but here, in these nooks among the upturned rocks, they'd be protected against wind, or prying eyes. If they wanted to be alone, way out from the coast road, this was the place. Here, there were "only sea-birds around us," Seán would recollect, "and the sound of the surf; beautiful, peaceful, without a sorrow in the world."

If Seán's perhaps fevered memories are to be trusted, Marie-Louise—"Máire," to him—was at one point ready to marry him. He procrastinated. When he realized, too late, what she meant to him, and said so, she was cool to him. One story heard in Dún Chaoin has him going to Paris to see her, her spurning him, him tossing the engagement ring he had for her into the Seine.

Did Marie-Louise merely use Seán as an entrée to the world of Dún Chaoin and the Blaskets? Or, to resort to an equally pat and proverbial formula, was she simply too good for this West Kerry yokel? The classicist Stephen MacKenna once intimated of Seán an Chóta that he was more "an artist in life" than creative *artiste* himself. He possessed a gift for jest and conviviality, a wanderlust. He was an eloquent raconteur, a fine talker; he must have been great to pal around with in Dún Chaoin and on the island. But for all the encomiums Marie-Louise lavished on him in print and the good times they spent together on those rocky headlands, she may never have considered him a potential life's companion.

Later, when it was all over between them, Seán set to compiling a written record of Kerry Irish; the final treatise, never published, fills twenty-nine handwritten volumes in the National Library of Ireland. His way of getting at an odd word or phrase was to offer a dictionary definition, a few sample usages, then sometimes a brief scenario or vignette to express its meaning. "Above all the beautiful women in the world," he wrote, "Máire was my sweetheart, the one I loved with all my heart"; that's how he illustrated one West Kerry usage. In fact, when Seán's biographer, Niall Ó Brosnacháin, counted vignettes that seemed to refer to Marie-Louise, he came up with forty-two. Most tell of a broken heart, fairly writhing with loss and longing, as in "My girl abandoned me, the woman I loved and courted." But for the word *feart,* "miracle," he wrote: "I never met anyone who understood the miracle of Irish as Máire did."

Celtic Gods and Heroes, published in 1940, and the work for which Sjoestedt is best known today, explores mother goddesses, chieftain gods, the Fianna myths, the Land of the Young, and countless other features of Celtic mythology and legend, all richly flavored with the fantastic. Of course, grown-ups are rightly skeptical of accounts of two-headed monsters or children who cleave dragons. And yet, Sjoestedt argues, to dismiss the bearers of such tales, the earliest Celtic mythographers themselves, poses grave risk to understanding. The authors of the oldest texts were Christians not long removed from paganism; their manuscripts went back sometimes to the eighth century, when Ireland's conversion to Christianity, begun three centuries before, "was neither very remote nor, probably, very profound." It was imprudent, therefore, to repudiate the ideas these authors held of the Celts' mythical world. "There is a greater risk of error," she writes, "in too much skepticism than in too little."

I find charming this seemingly artless welcome of the fantastical, and I think it suggests something of what Marie-Louise brought to the Blaskets—a willingness to give herself over to aspects of language, personality, and belief that, for a Paris sophisticate, might at first have seemed outlandish. All the weight of her education had taught her to be skeptical, reasoned, careful. But the island and its people simply won her over. Three weeks into one visit that included a visit to the island, she wrote from Dún Chaoin, in English, "I cannot help but feel regretful at going away so soon. I am greatly taken with this place, lonely and wild as it is. I don't think I shall ever get tired of it." She couldn't know for certain she'd be back, but if she was, she wrote, she hoped to remain on the island for some months. "The people of the island are companionable and joyous, very fond of music and dancing and company." She'd get on well with them, she was sure, because "I am full of roguery—just like themselves."

That was in 1925. In a letter she wrote from the Blasket eight years later, the island had lost none of its hold on her. "What fertile imagination," she wrote of an old island woman she encountered, "what liveliness of language, what humor, what emotion! They are rather an extraordinary race these old fishermen of the West. It is quite exciting to work with them."

One of her visits came in winter. She had just spent four months on the mainland, Seán an Chóta her guide and tutor. Now, for six weeks, she was on the island, in the house where George Thomson had also stayed, with Máire Ní Ghuithín. A dance was being held at Peig Sayers's place, the two of them were going, and Marie-Louise was determined to give her island friend a proper Parisian coiffure. She washed her hair, heated the special tongs she'd brought from Paris. . . . And then, of course, the door opened, Máire turned, and burned her ear. But Marie-Louise finally finished the job and offered Mademoiselle Ní Ghuithín a mirror: "Look, aren't you beautiful." Máire slipped into the red blouse and black skirt Marie-Louise had brought her, and the two of them went up the hill to dance. And endure. The island boys teased Máire mercilessly: Oh, and what have we here, a lady from France? Learning any Irish is she? All evening it was like that. Better that Marie-Louise had left her hair alone.

But that was the slightest snag to a warm friendship. "Even though she was from Paris, France, you would think her an island girl," Máire Ní Ghuithín wrote later. "She was so humble and simple in her character." She wore a black shawl like those the women wore when they went to Mass on the mainland. In the evenings, she'd help Máire and the others with their schoolwork, teach them a little French. The rest of the time, she pursued the maddeningly elusive sounds of Irish. " 'Sound-info' she used to call it," remembered Máire. When, years later, Marie-Louise published her *Description d'un parler irlandais de Kerry* (description of a Kerry Irish dialect), she dedicated it to Antoine Meillet, her adviser in Paris, but also thanked her Blasket informants, including Máire.

Marie-Louise Sjoestedt's two most important technical treatises on West Kerry speech would appear in the 1930s. But even by 1928, after parts of three years' close listening in the company of Seán an Chóta, she was ready to say something about English's influence on the local dialect, the subject of a paper she wrote that year. It was here in Dún Chaoin, the Blaskets, and neighboring parishes, after all, that the two languages, English and Irish, butted up hardest against each other. Here Synge, Marstrander, and Flower, at the head of a procession of writers and scholars, had come to hear pure spoken Irish. But as Sjoestedt discovered, it was *not* so pure after all; English was leaving an imprint.

Books and journals in English were no big problem, she found, but the area's English-speaking merchants did contribute to Irish's decline. So did the schools. So did returned émigrés from America. Ironically, even students visiting the area to acquire Irish sometimes made things worse, teaching the locals more English than they absorbed of Irish. Generally, teenage girls used more Anglicisms and loan words than did the boys, tried more ardently to learn English—no doubt, Marie-Louise hazarded, because they were coolheadedly looking ahead to their future in America.

By 1928, in any case, evidence of Irish's decline in West Kerry was inescapable. In the intimate retreats of rural life, or in nature itself, the language remained largely untouched. Everywhere else, though, English knocked at the door. Clothes were mostly English now, words near to "hat," "apron," "pocket," and "gown" all making their way into Irish. The effect would grow, Marie-Louise wrote, "in proportion that these urban modes spread to the country." The black peasant shawl called *brat* was now more often called . . . a shawl; the English term, even in Dún Chaoin and the Blaskets, seemed "more elegant, more fashionable than the Irish term. The word for style, *faisiún,* is itself English." Everyday foods stayed Irish, but those the least bit exotic became English; cheese figured little at peasant tables, so the Irish *cáise* was fading away, giving way to "cheese." Irish had a word for what the French called *confiture,* "but my hosts never used it on their own; they always served the English word *jam.*" Insults, such as Irish near-equivalents to "drunkard" and "blackguard," often owed to English—"epithets that a supposedly more cultivated population willingly applied to a population deemed inferior . . . and that they, in turn, came to adopt." Through recourse to French, Irish, English, and Latin, Marie-Louise wove a rich scholarly tapestry of all she had heard and learned. The loan words she cited, she wrote, represented changes to these rural enclaves influenced by, and in imitation of, modern urban life.

Over the years she visited Dún Chaoin and the Blaskets, Marie-Louise had become protective, passionately so, of the Irish language. But she was clear-eyed about its prospects. If Irish was to take its place as the language of cultivated Ireland, she wrote two years later in *Revue celtique,* no task was more urgent than the encouragement of Irish-language books. Not textbooks stocked with vocabulary, though. Needed was "a literature in Irish that one could read for love of Irish." For too many, the "Gaelic baggage" they picked up in school would "join the piles of knowledge one acquired in college only to forget as soon as you'd left." Meanwhile, all the best intentions of the state to support Irish-language authorship risked encouraging writers "with no other talent than to write Irish more or less correctly," and no other calling than to get published and paid; and risked, besides, imposing moral and intellectual standards on serious readers more appropriate to high-schoolers.

When the day came, however, that all the literary dross was pared away, she declared, sure to be counted among true Irish-language classics was "the work of the peasant, fisherman, and storyteller Tomás Ó Criomhthain."

Chapter 7

Gorky's Peasants

[1929]

In *The Islandman*—or *An tOileánach,* as it is called in Irish—Tomás Ó Criomhthain tells of his life from childhood in the 1860s to old age in the 1920s. It's an autobiography, then, or a memoir—except that some critics value it more as anthropology, seeing its scenes, incidents, and personalities as bearing more on Tomás's faraway island community than on him. He fishes, hunts, marries, endures the death of children. QED: island life personified. To me, though, even rendered into what its translator termed a "plain, straightforward" English and thus deprived of the flavor of the original Irish, Tomás's book satisfies most reliably through its vibrancy and bite, the incisive, sometimes caustic eye with which Tomás views himself and his fellow islanders.

> I was born on St. Thomas's day in the year 1856. I can recall being
> at my mother's breast, for I was four years old before I was weaned.
> I am "the scrapings of the pot," the last of the litter. That's why I
> was left so long at the breasts. I was a spoilt child, too.

So it begins. Tomás had four elder sisters and one older brother. "They were all well grown when I was a baby, so that it was little wonder that

I was spoilt among them all. Nobody expected me at all when I came their way."

Whereas his earlier writings for Brian Kelly were self-contained snippets of stories, *The Islandman* was a single more or less continuous narrative, wrought from memory, bearing a sense of transition and flow. Always, and even in English, his personality percolates up from the page as he describes his fellow islanders. Like the woman across the yard, who was "in and out of our house all day long. . . . She was a little, undersized, untidy-haired babbler with a sallow face, not much to look at—a gossip, always hither and thither."

Or one of his early teachers, who didn't last long on the island: "A great mug he had on him, hollow eyes, and a sleek swarthy complexion. He had prominent teeth, and a bush dripping from his nose like a goat's beard. But the bush wasn't the worst part of him, for it was fair in colour and hid his ugliest feature."

Or his sister's husband, who "couldn't keep a glass of whisky or a pint of porter long between his hands without pouring them down him, and he never enjoyed the taste of anything he paid for with his own money, but liked it well when another man jogged him in the back to have one with him."

The book's chapters bear prosaic names like "My Schooldays," "Gathering Seaweed," and "The Little Canoe." But the author's voice counts for more than any structural features. On young Tomás's first visit to Dingle, his father buys him his first pair of boots. His sister Eileen doesn't recognize him when he returns to the island, Tomás writes, so distracted is she by "the shining glory about my feet."

A tiny island-of-an-island stood off the shore of the Great Blasket that could sometimes be reached at low tide in order to collect limpets and winkles. One day there, Tomás sees his mother "gathering her skirts together and bringing them forward between her legs. I didn't mind a bit that the world should see my mother's legs and calves, for there was nothing stunted or lumpy about her: she was a fine well-grown woman, fair-skinned and bright from crown to heel."

And so the story goes, earthy and wry. One critic, John McGahern, has pointed out that Tomás doesn't actually depict the island itself much, its exquisite scenery only a frame through which to view richly lived lives: "A field is only described as it is reclaimed and cultivated. A strand is there to be crossed, a sea to be fished, a town to be reached, a shore to be gained, walked upon, lived upon. These are all near and concrete realities but so stripped down to their essence . . . as to be set free of all local characteristics." "Set free," like a balloon, from the restraining tether of the little village, bigger and more than the island, bigger and more than Tomás himself.

An tOileánach "has a flavour, a quality of goodness you can almost taste," Máire Mhac an tSaoi, writing as Máire Cruise O'Brien, once put it, "like the goodness of fresh bread or of a sound apple." The book has been frankly adored by its readers, set up on an Irish-language pedestal, admirers forever finding new superlatives with which to laud it. Author and literary theorist Declan Kiberd discerns a "Hemingwayesque quality to the writing, of grace under pressure." For Seán Ó Coileáin, professor of modern Irish at the National University of Ireland, Cork, "there's an authenticity in that book that I don't find anywhere else in modern Irish"; here was "the real thing, the bare rock, the foundation." Ó Coileáin says this having edited a later edition of *An tOileánach,* published in 2002, which he deemed closer to Tomás's original intention. Yet he admits that that first, imperfectly "authentic" edition, which he reports reading every year since he was fifteen, "will always remain *The Islandman.*"

An tOileánach was first published in the summer of 1929 in a printing of three thousand. But its origins went back seven years, to 1922, when Tomás was still sending Brian Kelly the diary entries that would become *Allagar na hInise,* or *Island Cross-Talk.* Kelly, muse and mentor, ever confident of his friend's ability, wondered whether the spark might be in him for a grander, more ambitious work. At some point, probably while living in Dublin, Kelly broached the idea to his Irish teacher from early Killarney days, the man who'd encouraged him to visit the Blaskets in the first place, Pádraig Ó Siochfhradha.

Ó Siochfhradha had grown up on a little peninsula beside Dingle Bay, in an atypically tree-shaded area that included the estate of Lord Ventry, whose forebears had planted widely, and for whom his father worked as groundskeeper. He grew up speaking both Irish and English. But one day when he was an impressionable eighteen, which would have made it about 1901, he heard a fiery Gaelic Leaguer in Dingle proclaim that, were Ireland ever to throw off the English yoke, Irishmen needed to speak Irish. After that, as a relative told the story, "I don't believe he ever spoke a word of

English," at least publicly; once, years later, when he had to sign his name in English in order to be nominated to a high position with University College, Dublin, it was enough of an event to make the newspapers.

Soon he learned to read the language he'd grown up speaking. He equipped himself with dictionaries, began teaching local youngsters the rudiments of the language, became one of the Gaelic League's *muinteoirí táistil.* These itinerant teachers typically got around their districts by bicycle, "backs bent, eyes gleaming, hands asweat or frozen on the handlebars, their feet going round endlessly on a glorious treadmill," as one writer immortalized them. Working in Cahircaveen, on the peninsula just across the bay from Dingle, Ó Siochfhradha might teach a class at five in the afternoon in one town, then another at seven that evening in a town miles away. Like a hawk, all fierce, single-minded energy, he'd swoop down by bicycle on each town to bestow a little Irish learning. "An Seabhac," "The Hawk," pronounced roughly "ahn showk," became his nom de plume. And nom de guerre as well. He would go on to lead a battalion of the West Kerry brigade of the Irish Volunteers, run arms, and several times be jailed. He would work in the language movement all his life, becoming a powerful force for Irish culture and literature.

An Seabhac had been teaching in Killarney, and active there in nationalist recruiting, for several years when, in late 1916, as we've seen, he heard from Mrs. Kelly, took on Brian as his pupil, and sent him to the Blaskets. During the years since, the two of them had maintained contact, and now they conferred once more. Tomás was still churning out his short journal entries, but now Brian wanted him to tackle something more avowedly literary. Might Tomás be induced to compose, purely out of his imagination, a fresh story? Brian and An Seabhac didn't think so. What they cooked up instead, the way An Seabhac told it later, were the bare bones of a story to which Tomás would presumably add the meat, namely this: A beautiful girl arrives on the island on a sailboat with her wealthy father. She becomes interested in the island, stays to learn Irish, falls in love with an island lad. At first he can't admit that he loves her as well, but finally he does, and they marry. The end.

Um, no. On a trip to the island, Brian laid their skeleton of a story before Tomás. He wanted nothing to do with it. Nothing like that had ever happened on the Blasket, An Seabhac pictured him saying, "and it shouldn't be associated with the island. It was a lie!" Readers shouldn't be asked to believe what wasn't so.

Brian got another idea. Maybe he could get Tomás to write his autobiography—not little vignettes this time, but a serious, connected life story. Tomás wasn't interested.

Brian persisted. Tomás made as if to acquiesce by filling a scant few pages of foolscap: There you go.

Well, Brian replied, that wasn't exactly what he had in mind.

Why, asked Tomás, by now maybe a little annoyed, would anyone want to hear the story of his life? He was a fisherman. His snippets of island lore were one thing. But his *life?* Who'd care?

Brian found a way to answer him.

Just a few years out of Trinity College, he was well educated, well read, and well versed in the literary currents of his time. And one such current was the rediscovery, through literature, of peasant cultures. All across Europe, slow-paced rural life was being routed by the relentless forces of modern civilization and high-strutting technology. But as village life was swept away, some writers were making it the subject of their work.

Late in the previous century, as we've seen, in novels like *Tess of the D'Urbervilles* and *Jude the Obscure*, Thomas Hardy, a stonemason's son, brought England's vanishing rural world vividly to life. Around the same time, in France, appeared Pierre Loti's *An Iceland Fisherman,* about the harsh lives of Breton fishermen who plied the waters around Iceland. A little later, in Russia, in an autobiographical trilogy the first two volumes of which had appeared by 1916, Maxim Gorky wrote of growing up in a hardscrabble Russian village. All were writing about working people, fishermen and peasants, in natural settings largely untouched by the modern world. On at least one visit to the Great Blasket, An Seabhac reported, Kelly brought with him books by Loti and Gorky and took to reading from them to Tomás.

"Time after time the codfish let themselves be hooked in a rapid and unceasing silent series. [One man] ripped them open with his long knife, spread them flat, salted and counted them—which upon their return would constitute their fortune—and piled up the lot behind them, all still redly streaming and still sweet and fresh." That's from *An Iceland Fisherman;* Pierre Loti, the pen name of Louis-Marie-Julien Viaud, was a French naval officer who took scant interest in sophisticated Paris, much in the lives of ordinary men and women. In *My Childhood,* Maxim Gorky told of growing up in his grandfather's house, with its "endemic plague of hostility. . . . All the adults were fevered with it and even the children were

infected." His aim, he wrote in an early chapter, was to "disown" the grim
story he had to tell: "Such dull savagery on the part of one's own tribe is
too wounding to acknowledge. But truth outweighs pity."

No countesses or kings here, no great high-minded truths, only the
eternal struggle for existence on the high seas or in a muddy village, of
people not so very different from Tomás himself. To anyone inclined to
reckon the life of an island rustic as not worth telling, they must have
seemed a revelation. Loti's fictional Yann was a fisherman. Gorky's autobiography was that of a peddler, scullery boy, gardener, dock hand, and
tramp. Yet apparently *they* mattered enough to wind up within a book.
Loti's book (which had accompanied Synge on his first trip to the Aran
Islands) didn't touch Tomás that deeply. Gorky's, though, did. "I declare
to the devil," his son Seán has him saying, "he's a fellow just like myself."

That, of course, was just the idea.

Making even more of an impression on him, Seán would report, was a
novel appearing in Norwegian in 1917, and in English soon thereafter—a
great, sprawling tableau of a book, *Growth of the Soil.* Its author was Knut
Hamsun, awarded one of the first Nobel Prizes, in 1920. In it, a burly,
laconic peasant ekes out a living from the Norwegian wilds. Isak is an
Everyman, a reminder, at a time when industrialization strode unimpeded
across Europe and America, of how dearly civilization depended on faceless men and women still close to the elemental earth.

As different as these books were, they told a similar story of poor
people, in difficult circumstances, making a go of it—a theme much alive
in the Ireland of the day. Through them, writes Australian scholar Irene
Lucchitti in a 2005 doctoral thesis that became a book, *The Islandman:
The Hidden Life of Tomás O'Crohan,* "Tomás was offered one story after
another of hard and primitive ways of life in places of extreme and dangerous beauty." Together they suggested that he wouldn't be the first who
made his living from the earth and sea with a story to tell, that others like
him had told theirs, that he could do it, too.

By mid-1922, Tomás had set to work, apparently clear that he'd begun
a wholly new project. Brian sometimes turned to masonry metaphors with
him, and one that stuck with Tomás, as he told it later, was that "the cornerstone should be established before my work could begin." That's what
he did now, casting aside any mental cornerstones representing *Island
Cross-Talk,* so "there would be no connection between the work I had
completed and the work I had yet to complete." In short, a fresh start, a
new literary design.

Soon, he was sending Kelly batches of pages, and by late 1924 or early 1925, he had more or less finished the book. I say "more or less" because the book wouldn't be published until midsummer 1929, and in the intervening years it would change—change under influences literary, personal, and political, in ways both trifling and significant, that have intrigued scholars since. During these years, the manuscript would pass out of the hands of Tomás and into those of outsiders to the island, first Brian Kelly, then An Seabhac.

Back in 1918, Kelly had become a "junior inspector of National Schools," as his title dignified him, a position for which he apparently had little interest and less aptitude, and which he abandoned after a year. For a while he lived with his older brother, a Dublin priest. The next few years were ones of drift and, probably, severe personal distress. "Brian did not have an easy life," An Seabhac summed it up. He and Brian met from time to time over the years, in Dingle and, beginning in 1922, in Dublin. "Anybody who understood Brian would have to be fond of him, but it's few people who really understood him. He was gentle, quiet, a loner." When they could sit by the fire, just the two of them, "all the shyness and quietness would disappear, and he'd be bright, good company, and full of stories." But that school inspector's job, it seemed to An Seabhac, had "upset his gentle kind mind, and this left him unhappy with himself and with many other things also." If this seems mysterious, it has remained so. Finally, Kelly left the country, taking Tomás's mostly finished manuscript with him.

In London, he took it, and perhaps *Allagar na hInise* (*Island Cross-Talk*) as well, to the Irish Texts Society. They could do nothing with it, he was told; it needed too much work, even just to sort out its unorthodox spellings and idiosyncratic script.

He took it with him to Paris; nothing there for it, either.

Returning briefly to Ireland, he approached the minister of education. But this early in the new state's history, the government wasn't publishing much of anything; An Gúm, its new publishing agency, wasn't established until 1926.

What to do? How to get Tomás's work published? By the end of 1925, according to An Seabhac, Kelly was "disappointed and discouraged." All through those months together on the island, and those years in correspondence, he had prodded Tomás: Go to your pen and paper each day. Write your story. Brook all discouragement. This Tomás had done. Kelly felt a responsibility to him, yet now seemed unable to discharge it.

It was around this time that he approached An Seabhac with the manuscript. Kelly was again leaving Ireland, for the Continent, where he would spend the remainder of his life. Perhaps he knew he was lost in some down-spinning personal crisis, opaque to us now; one Irish scholar, Seán Ó Coileáin, thinks Kelly may have been homosexual, no easy burden in Catholic Ireland. Desperate, he approached An Seabhac: would he accept responsibility for doing all he could on behalf of Tomás's manuscripts? Of course, his old teacher assured him, provided "I could use them, or part of them, in whatever way I saw fit," and as long as he had Tomás's blessing.

Here things get complicated. An Seabhac did secure Tomás's blessing, and was not shy about using the editorial prerogatives granted him. Some decisions he made did not please everyone; indeed, they entirely pleased no one. Both *Allagar na hInise* and *An tOileánach* were, as we've seen, later translated into English, stirring some controversy among scholars and critics. But no less controversy surrounds how *An tOileánach* was prepared for publication in *Irish*—a translation, too, after all, from the spoken language to the written.

Scholars have compared the original Irish manuscript with what later appeared in print and, with perplexity, annoyance, or alarm, noted numerous discrepancies: the sacrifice of quirky spellings that nonetheless aptly reflected the spoken word; a chapter inserted at the editor's request; a new ending; missing scenes, seemingly arbitrary deletions, undue preoccupation with convention. In her 1930 review of *An tOileánach,* for example, Marie-Louise Sjoestedt thanked An Seabhac for letting her see the original manuscript, said she understood the reasons for his editorial alterations, but lamented that some episodes, "entirely innocent in their naiveté, have been . . . sacrificed to pedagogic requirements and to 'respectability.'"

One scene no doubt on her mind was one where young Tomás and a friend, the future island king, go swimming, both of them buck naked.

> When we turned around, what did we find but three big lumps of girls looking straight at us. The king became embarrassed a lot quicker than I did, and he turned towards the sea with his back to them, trying to hide from them. I remained standing exactly as I was when I entered this world and it occurred to me that there was no reason for me to take fright rather than them.

Two girls turned away, "but there was never three women who didn't have a bold one in their number," and he and the third girl just stood there, shamelessly provoking each other, until she at last yielded. The girl "who was giving me the cheek," Tomás concludes the story, "saw a baptism before she ever saw a wedding. And, of course, the signs were on her with her display that day."

For purely linguistic reasons, Sjoestedt was troubled, too. Though Tomás's writing and spelling were "often simply arbitrary," they nonetheless pointed up key "traits of the local dialect"—translating voice to print "with remarkable exactitude." That was gone now from the published text, the spelling cleaned up and made more regular—precious witnesses to the spoken word, embodied in Tomás's spelling, sacrificed to editorial convention.

In 1973, Tomás's grandson, Pádraig Ua Maoileoin, would issue an alternative edition of *An tOileánach*. Yes, it "preserves the odd earthy expression and episode that An Seabhac felt 'not fitting to be so set down,'" Máire Cruise O'Brien would write. But Tomás's first editor, she went on, "shows perhaps more finish in arrangement by chapter and paragraph." She found but a single instance—the restoration of a scene from Tomás's wedding—where the new edition got the better of An Seabhac's.

Actually, Ua Maoileoin's edition had cuts and additions, too. No book is ever published just as its author originally sets it down. Few fail to profit from an editor's ability to stand apart from it, smooth its rough edges, and steer it through sometimes dangerous shoals to publication. All this is normal and necessary. The manuscripts Tomás sent to Brian and that ultimately reached An Seabhac were those of a novice author, however gifted, who had somehow slipped the bonds of illiteracy; they needed editorial attention, and got it.

An Seabhac had his hands full with both of Tomás's manuscripts. The Irish Texts Society in London, recall, had told Kelly that to take them on would be just too much work. As An Seabhac saw it, he made cuts, yes, but none undermining the story's essential truth. He altered Tomás's homegrown spelling system. He massaged Tomás's West Kerry dialect to make it less foreign to other Irish-speakers. He edited out repeated storms, near-drownings, and other features of island life that seemed to him repetitive.

In so doing, it struck Irene Lucchitti, An Seabhac failed to "recognise that repetition inhered in Island life and that by removing the artistic rendering of this fact, he was falsifying or, at the very least, distorting Tomás' record of Island life." Now, nonfiction literature does not work like some meteorological instrument whose pen slavishly records every dip and rise in barometric pressure; no writer is obliged to transpose all of his subject mechanically, as if he could, onto the unwilling page. Even with An Seabhac's cuts, some found *An tOileánach* repetitive: "Anyone at all would grow tired after reading some of it," a 1931 convention of Irish schoolteachers heard Mícheál Breathnach complain, "because it is the same thing page after page, with little happening and few changes of scene." Irish scholar James Stewart, who disapproved of some of An Seabhac's edits, terming them "textual tampering," nonetheless conceded that many of them—"the pruning of unwieldy phrases, unnecessary illustrations and pious untruths, and the replacement of somewhat inelegant words—would by many be regarded as an improvement in the texture of the narrative." In the end, it seems plain, *An tOileánach* profited from many of An Seabhac's editorial interventions—and from Tomás's good sense in agreeing to them.

In a few instances, An Seabhac wanted not cuts but additions, and went back to Tomás for them. "I may as well give some brief account of the way we managed things in this Island when I was young," chapter 3 leads off, going on to describe village houses by size, design, and furnishings. The house he'd built with his own hands, Tomás notes, wasn't large, but "if King George were to spend a month's holiday in it, it isn't from the ugliness of the house that he would take his death." None of this was part of the original manuscript; An Seabhac had asked him to supply it, and he did. Seán Ó Coileáin has suggested that therefore it was not what Tomás truly *meant* to write, and thus in some degree inauthentic. But more justly, I think, An Seabhac can be seen as a sagacious editor, alive to his readers' needs, helping his author better satisfy them. By no means dismissive of Tomás, he was taking him seriously, grooming him, helping to "professionalize" a novice author.

The final chapter of the published book, not included in what Kelly had amassed from Tomás and delivered to An Seabhac, serves as valedictory. He writes of cold nights struggling against the sea, driven by the waves. "The swell would be rising to the green grass, the storm blowing out of the north-west, and the great waves breaking. . . . You may understand from this that we are not to be put in comparison with the people of the great cities or of the soft and level lands." Evenings spent with friends and a drop of drink leavened sea-borne troubles. But all that, he continues, is "gone by now, and the high heart and fun are passing from the world. Then we'd take the homeward way together, easy and friendly after all our revelry, like the children of one mother, none doing hurt or harm to his fellow." Tomás wrote this, and wrote it with heart. And he did so at the urging of An Seabhac.

The manuscript An Seabhac got from Brian probably lacked some of the structural connective tissue of the final book, which remains a little episodic. For what became *Allagar na hInise,* Tomás had penned self-contained little stories, a book page or two long; crop out the weaker ones, string along the remainder in chronological order, and you had a book. As he posted the pages of his autobiography to Brian, Tomás may have seen little reason to alter this approach, which made for good stories, but not necessarily a book bound tightly into a coherent whole. In a paper given at a conference in Sardinia in 1994, Joan Fitz Gerald went so far as to picture Tomás as "untrained in the craft of writing continuous narrative," so that "the weaving of the separate anecdotes or tales which make up each chapter into a narrative whole is left to a writer [An Seabhac] who knows how to construct texts." An Seabhac's nephew (who is also named Pádraig Ó Siochfhradha) reports seeing some seventy or eighty pieces of editorial correspondence between the two men; his uncle, he says, repeatedly asked Tomás, "What do you mean by this?"—paring away ambiguity, building coherency over the long line of the emerging book. "He had tremendous stickability," he says, smiling at his own coinage. "He saw it through."

An Seabhac was no hack. He had a long history with the Irish language and was himself an author of some repute; he'd written a volume of humorous sketches, a picaresque novel, and, in 1922, a much-loved children's story, *Jimín Mháire Thaidhg,* which led one pundit to refer to him as "the greatest humourous writer the language movement has produced." He had become involved in the nascent Folklore of Ireland Society and, in January 1927, would be elected its first president. He was a versatile and experienced professional who would become principal editor of An Gúm, the government publishing agency. Just now, in his early forties, he was in his prime. In 1957, Ireland issued a pair of postage stamps to honor Tomás Ó Criomhthain. In 1983, it issued one in honor of An Seabhac, picturing him with black beret perched atop his bald pate, arms clasped in front of him, all intellectual bravado. Every writer needs an editor, and Tomás got one worthy of him.

Indeed, An Seabhac's most lasting contribution on behalf of Tomás's books may be that they were published at all. The Irish Free State in the

In English, he was Patrick Sugrue; in Irish, Pádraig Ó Sioch-
fhradha. But more often than either, in print and by reputation this
distinguished author, editor, and champion of the Irish language
was known by his pseudonym, "An Seabhac," the hawk. He helped
shepherd Tomás Ó Criomhthain's books into print.

late 1920s was gripped by puritanical sensibilities growing out of the influence of the church. State censorship was a fact of life. Priestly complaint
was enough to get Seán an Chóta's novel of the American West, *Fanai,*
withdrawn from circulation and cleaned up before being reissued with
offensive material—tame scenes of courtship and kissing—removed.
Tomás's tale of himself, naked before the island girls, would likely have
compelled the censor's hand, too. If any one principle dominated An Seabhac's approach to *An tOileánach,* it may simply have been the avoidance
of trouble.

His nephew pictures him as religious, sensitive to anything that might
do harm or cause embarrassment; so he may have needed no outside goad
to avoid controversy. Many cuts he made, James Stewart has observed,
"were made to save face rather than space, because, mistakenly, they were

believed to show the Islanders as either too punchy, too sexy, too sly or too slanderous." But they did achieve their goal. Ó Coileáin, certainly among those to rue some of An Seabhac's editorial changes, concedes that *An tOileánach* would not have been published without them. "He said he never regretted doing what he did," Pádraig Ó Siochfhradha says of his uncle. "He said it *had* to get into print."

Irene Lucchitti insists that the similarity of the Loti, Gorky, and Hamsun stories offered to Tomás as models "made clear that he was being asked to write a particular kind of story," one exemplifying "an authentically Irish hero." Ultimately, though, Tomás's books were his own. *The Islandman,* wrote Robin Flower in the foreword to his English translation, tells his tale "with perfect frankness, serving no theory, and aiming at no literary effect" (though the highest literary effect can be the one not aimed for). Kelly and An Seabhac, each in his own way, influenced Tomás; as products of their times and of their own temperaments, they could hardly have helped it. They were not a malignant influence on Tomás's work, but on the whole a happy and productive one, culminating in two Irish-language classics. "I would not have left two books behind me, were it not for the man who got me working," Tomás once said of Brian. He could well have said something similar, if probably not so warm and heartfelt, of An Seabhac. Tomás's books, like those of most authors, emerged with a little help from his friends.

In introducing his English translation of *Allagar na hInise,* Tim Enright aptly described its reception in Irish: "It was a wonder to the Gaelic world for it had been written from within the oral tradition, capturing the moment of transition from speech to writing." It is hard to do justice to this transition today. We readers must imagine every bit of news or information originating outside our familiar world of print; every fact, urgent or trifling, every opinion, every poem, every insult or blandishment coming to us "live," on the wings of the human voice. A visitor to the island in the early 1930s said of Tomás's own voice, it "still lingers in my ear, clear and musical like a silver bell."

It cannot be surprising that a world alive only in evanescent sound, cut off from the written word, can be hard to write about—for bookish sorts, hard even to think about. "The effects of oral states of consciousness are bizarre to the literate mind," Walter Ong wrote in *Orality and Literacy.* More difficult yet may be to imagine a culture of sound and gesture not as primitive precursor to a higher and better kingdom of Print but rich in its own right. Robin Flower would write, in *The Irish Tradition,* how, while walking one day along a Blasket path, he met an old man brimming over with "the strength and happy spirit of his youth." Together they sat down in a field, and the old man, without "preamble or explanation . . . fell to reciting Ossianic lays," ancient ballads that sang of the heroic exploits of the legendary Fionn Mac Cumhail, a kind of Irish counterpart to King Arthur and his knights:

> At times the voice would alter and quicken, the eyes would brighten, as with a speed with which you would have thought beyond the compass of human breath he delivered those highly artificial passages describing a fight or putting to sea, full of strange words and alliterating rhetorical phrases which, from the traditional hurried manner of narration, are known as "runs." At the end of these he would check a moment with triumph in his eye, draw a deep breath, and embark once more on the level course of his recitation.

> I listened spellbound and, as I listened, it came to me suddenly that there on the last inhabited piece of European land, looking out to the Atlantic horizon, I was hearing the oldest living tradition in the British isles. So far as the record goes this matter in one form or another is older than the Anglo-Saxon Beowulf, and yet it lives still upon the lips of the peasantry.

On the Blasket, Flower's old man was no aberration. The standards for speech were high there. The islanders *spoke well.* Tomás's life, Declan Kiberd would observe, was "built around admiration for people who used words and used them well. It was a life structured between morning songs, morning prayers, work songs, evening recitations, formal storytelling. It was in many ways a much more artistic life than the kind that is lived now by the citizens of Dublin in their suburbs." Talk and turn-of-phrase as art: what was *Allagar na hInise* (which one scholar prefers to translate as *Island Repartee)* but a succession of scenes showing off the wit and genius of the islanders as jokers, performers, quibblists, rhetoricians. The island's rich oral culture, someone once said, ranks as "the chief surviving element of Gaelic civilization"; from it stepped Tomás, with what Flower called his "inborn genius for speech." The irony of it, of course, was that the oral culture of the Blaskets should make its most lasting impact through print.

In 1962, the curmudgeonly Irish writer Myles na Gopaleen described the original Irish-language edition of Tomás's memoir as

> among the most important life-stories of this century, mainly for its account of custom, isolation, the savagery of island life, the gallantry of the islanders but, above all, for the astonishing precision and beauty of the Irish itself, immense in its profusion of vocabulary and idiom and having a style that is quite out of another age.

And Daniel Binchy, who visited the island and met Tomás in 1928 or 1929, for his part admitted that, until the appearance of *An tOileánach*, he had been "profoundly skeptical of the value of modern Irish as a literary medium." He wasn't any longer, not when it was in the hands of a writer like Tomás. "But," he wondered, "where shall we find such another?"

Chapter 8

Interminable Procession

[1929]

It is the fall of 1929, a few months after publication of *An tOileánach*. Marie-Louise Sjoestedt is back in West Kerry. The automobile that's brought her from Dingle stops, amid a patchwork of open fields, at a familiar thatched-roof house. "A woman comes out to kiss me. 'Welcome, Marie,'" she says, her voice stressing the "a" of Marie-Louise's name, giving it a "caressing" inflection. "The older people of the house rise with a familiar dignity to greet me: 'God protect you in this house.'" She's being welcomed once more to this "secret world of an old culture . . . poor by the standards of the world, but rich with inner treasures."

Marie-Louise's visit here is part of a research trip, the basis for two long articles to appear the following year, together titled "L'Irlande d'aujourd'hui," Ireland today. They will offer a look, new to most of her French readers, of the Ireland that's emerged from seven years of strife, and now a few of peace. One article draws on interviews she has conducted in Dublin with political and cultural leaders like Maud Gonne, the English-born Irish revolutionary, muse of Yeats, and widow of John MacBride, martyr of the Easter Rising; and Éamon de Valera, the George Washington–like Irish national father figure. She talks with them of the Irish language, of Catholic-Protestant relations, of the economy, of Ireland's future. It is garden-variety journalism, stocked with facts, figures, and quotes.

The other article is more personal and impressionistic. It takes her to The West, into Gaelic Ireland, to the Irish-speaking parts of the country that exert such a hold on her. Of the Free State's twenty-six counties, she informs her readers, nineteen are wholly English-speaking, and seven have Irish-speaking pockets. "It is towards one of them, one of those rare parishes where English has not yet penetrated, that the Tralee train carries me." Tralee itself she finds lifeless and dispirited. But soon she's headed farther west yet, to Dún Chaoin and the Blaskets, by the same narrow-gauge train Synge took across the mountains in 1905.

She is not shy about linking the dramatic countryside to visions of rebellion and romance; here are "hills as supportive of guerrilla war as the Spanish Sierras, as hospitable to outlaws as the Corsican maquis." She tells of "the nobility of a naked land . . . of its supreme harmony of proportion." She is moved by the beauty of it all. Finally, when she reaches the coast, the Blaskets come into view, a "magnificent chorus" of island topography that reminds her of the Greek islands.

On the Great Blasket, she learns that the king is dead: "I see him, as I often did in winter when, alone in his canoe, rowing with powerful strokes, he took the island's mail to the mainland." There's much more like this. She is reliving all that the island means to her. She remarks on the extraordinary courtesy she finds. She reports that horses are unknown, that the old men remember when there weren't even donkeys. She tells how the women gather peat, their panniers overflowing, babes in arms all the while. "Deprived of all material comfort," she writes of the islanders, they enjoy "a social life more intense in this restricted community than in all the scattered parishes of the coast. . . ." Practically all are "singers, poets, and musicians, without thinking of it," instinctively drawn "to all that is powerful or strange."

Her account is warm and evocative, but no mere travelogue. She sees the beauty and oddity of this outpost of civilization on the far fringes of Ireland. But she sees, too, and with icy clarity, its troubles, in particular the emigration of its young.

To reach western Ireland from Paris, she tells you, you can take the usual route—twenty hours, across two national borders through London to Dublin, and thence across the country. But there is another way, the one she makes her own: from Cherbourg, on the French coast, board one of the great transatlantic steamers that will stop at Queenstown, on Ireland's southwest coast, chief point of embarkation for immigrants to the United States and Canada; of six million who left Ireland in the century after 1848, almost half left from Queenstown. Able reporter that her essay reveals her to be, Marie-Louise Sjoestedt has placed herself at just the spot where Ireland most copiously bleeds its healthy, young, and strong.

She is deeply moved by the sight of them, the lines of emigrants—some thirty thousand a year during this period—waiting to board the little tenders that will ferry them to the steamers anchored in the great harbor. "They appear suddenly from the night outside in interminable procession. The clothes they've bought in the little town, commonplace and ugly, make them look as if they are in costume." The scene stuns her.

> It is as if I recognized them, having met so many of their brothers and sisters before. . . . I spotted here a peasant's short neck, there shoulders stooped from leaning so long over the peat bog. I saw deeply marked faces, expressions clear like water, then sometimes, too, that peculiar Spanish intensity you see in Kerrymen, which to me is so dear.

As they step forward, she sees past them to the world they've left behind, to "the hills swept by the wind, the slender canoe in the froth of the sea, the humble cottages full of wild children, and the savage, epic destitution of this Atlantic coast—all that I will see tomorrow and that they will never see again."

It is September 1929, and Marie-Louise is in Queenstown. Around the same time, a few months either way, so is Mary Kearney, George Thomson's island sweetheart, boarding a steamer for the New World.

Back in 1926, before their trip to Inishvickillaun, Maurice dropped by the house where George was staying to find him seated on a stool, chin in hands, staring into the fire. "You are in love, my boy," Maurice declared with a clap of his palm to George's shoulder. And indeed he was.

Whatever it was to her, George's relationship with Mary Kearney was to him no brief summer's fancy; she occupied a place in his hopes and affections for seven years. In the end, he didn't win her; one might worry for them both if he had. But it was not for want of trying. Convinced Mary felt herself inadequately educated, he at one point offered to pay her way through school, or so it's said in Mary's family today. At another juncture, as we've seen, he talked to Father Paddy Browne in Dún Chaoin about converting to Catholicism. What must have been a third fraught moment occurred across the breadth of Ireland from the Blaskets, outside Dublin, but again within the orbit of Father Browne, and perhaps indirectly through his doing.

In flat countryside about fifteen miles west of Dublin lies the town of Maynooth—from the Irish "Má Nuad," meaning "Plain of Nuadha"— built up around a cozy eighteenth-century streetscape of little houses clustered along a modest tree-lined main street. But if from the center of town you proceeded two or three blocks west, beyond a little stream and the ruins of an ancient castle, you'd pass through a gate and into a world of cloisters, grandly scaled quadrangles, and light-filled chapels. Maynooth's Saint Patrick's College, fed by smaller diocesan schools and seminaries, was Ireland's richest vein of Roman Catholic clergy, the town's two whispered syllables enough to conjure up visions of the Irish priesthood at its most aristocratic.

For five years beginning in 1917, the college's resident medical officer was a Dr. Patrick J. Grogan. In 1922, Grogan resigned his position there, but remained in town, presiding over its Maynooth Dispensary until at least the summer of 1927, when he became medical officer in a nearby county. During these years, he, his wife, Margaret, and perhaps her sister Lily as well, lived in a house on the north side of Main Street, near Courthouse Square, virtually at the center of town. Their maid was a girl from the Great Blasket, Miss Mary Kearney.

Dr. Grogan had come out of west Clare, a farmer's son, the only one of seven boys to get an education, earning a medical degree from the National University of Ireland in 1908. In college, he was active in the Gaelic Athletic Association. He embraced republican ideals; during the Rising, he reputedly harbored a future president of Ireland, Seán T. O'Kelly. "He was very much into the 1916 crowd," reports his nephew, also named Patrick Grogan, inclined to mix more with political friends than with fellow physicians. He was an Irish-language enthusiast, too, a member of the Gaelic League, and for a time in the 1920s went professionally as Pádraig Séamus Ó Gruagain. He was "very keen on the Irish language," his nephew recalls, yet never actually spoke it much himself. "Tea, please" or "Sugar, please" was about the beginning and end of his Irish.

When Mary Kearney's elder sister Cáit returned to the Blaskets after a period in Dublin as a domestic, their father looked at her hands rubbed red and raw by work and burst into tears; he'd never let her go back to that, he vowed. Mary, though, probably had it better; her brother Seán said Dr. Grogan and his wife were good to her. The doctor's nephew, from when he lived with them in the 1930s, remembers another maid from the Blaskets: up early, tending the house; Sundays to early Mass, back in time to tidy up before the Grogans were back from church; meals in the kitchen; little time off, a half-day or two a week; unobtrusive, a background presence, forever scrubbing, serving, fussing. Something like this must have been Mary Kearney's lot, too.

A studio portrait from around this time shows her, in a dark, ornately belted dress, papers on her lap, competent-looking and attractive; the photo is credited to a studio on Upper O'Connell Street, Dublin, not many minutes on the train from Maynooth. But just how had she gotten to Maynooth in the first place, two hundred miles across Ireland from the Blaskets? How *could* she have wound up there, this girl whose command of English was at first probably limited to whatever little she had learned in the island school or from George? She leaves her island home and, at sixteen or seventeen, suddenly winds up outside Dublin?

From the summer of 1924 and for most of the next five years, Mary largely vanishes from island memory, only Dr. Grogan a link to her whereabouts, information about her otherwise blurred and uncertain. This seeming disappearance, the persistence of George's feelings, and the notorious secrecy surrounding sexual matters in Catholic Ireland make it hard to dismiss entirely the possibility that she'd become pregnant. George later wrote an Irish-language short story, "The Illegitimate Child," that described a young woman cradling her baby beside a church door, her father offering her passage money to America if she'd give the child over to an orphanage. He wrote another, "Getting On in the World," about a girl with an illegitimate child who can't get a job and leaves town, only to find work later as a servant girl with a Dublin doctor. Plainly, not all Irish women and their men friends were pure and chaste. One report from before the turn of the century tells of pregnant young women routinely "sent away" from their homes in the country, arriving on Dublin's doorstep to have their babies. Now, during the 1920s, between 2 and 3 percent of recorded births in Ireland—close to two thousand per year—were illegitimate. The figure had climbed almost 30 percent in recent years, stoking much alarm in the new Ireland.

Of course, as far as Mary goes, none of this constitutes evidence. It was common for country girls with no prospects in the economically bereft west to seek jobs that could help them send money to their parents back home, or earn passage money to America—which, with few expenses, they often managed to do. The ten to fifteen pounds a Dublin servant earned annually in cash, together with room and board, tips, and Christmas presents like fabric or books, compared favorably with what she could make elsewhere in Ireland. As servants to merchants, well-off farmers, or, as in Mary's case, professional men in town, such girls were said to be *in aimsir,* "in service"; they numbered a hundred thousand in Ireland during this period. Their circumstances were mostly above reproach, their motivations straightforward, their stories unexceptional. Marie-Louise Sjoestedt would later write, of another West Kerry woman, that her life first stirred one's interest not, as with a young man, in tales of adventure, but on that "day when a little girl was sent into service far from her parents and the home of her childhood."

However Mary got to Maynooth, it is tempting to see at work the able, well-connected hand of Father Paddy Browne, professor at Maynooth and a summer and holiday resident of Dún Chaoin. He may have been trying on his own to defuse an entirely chaste, if awkward, situation between Mary and George. Or, knowing Dr. Grogan—and his uncle knew all the priests at Maynooth, says the doctor's nephew—he may simply have spread word of the opening around Dún Chaoin; or else, the other way around, spread word around Maynooth of Mary's readiness for a move. Then again, as one perhaps muddled account has it, Dr. Grogan may have been vacationing on the island himself and actually brought Mary back to Maynooth when he and his wife returned.

In any case, Máire Pheats Tom Ó Cearnaigh worked for Dr. Grogan as his maid, and sometime during this period, perhaps around 1925 or 1926, was visited by George, who stayed on in Maynooth for a couple of days. We know this because in 1965 George wrote to his wife and told her so. While he was in Greece, a chance meeting with an Irish priest from Maynooth had stirred memories of once spending a night there as Paddy Browne's guest, and how, earlier, "I visited the Blasket girl, Mary Kearney."

George likely took a train from Dublin that left him a few minutes on foot from the center of town. Did he call at the Grogan house, or meet Mary somewhere else? Did they talk of things they'd done and people they knew on the island? Did they resurrect the religious issue? Or was this actually the first time he'd poured out his heart to her?

In 1928, the Irish journal *An Phoblacht,* the republic, published a poem by George. Conceivably, it was the product of an active imagination only, not drawn from his own life. More likely, it enacts a pained moment with

Mary on the island or in Maynooth. The poem tells of the narrator's love for a girl. Lost to her charms, unmanned by lovesick distress, he long remains mute. But then, one cool, crisp night, the sky alive with stars, it all comes tumbling out: His silence has been unbearable. Now, more unbearable yet, is her rebuff. It is "crueler still," he writes, "that she didn't care."

The following year, probably in October, Mary arrived in Queenstown, bound for America.

Typically, a West Kerry emigrant made arrangements for departure through a Dingle travel agency, Galvin's. She or a relative would make a four-pound deposit toward the total fare of about twenty-one pounds; one pound then bought about what seventy-five American dollars does today. An additional seven shillings, for what a clerk recorded as "certs," went to register the emigrant's birth certificate. Transactions were recorded, usually in black ink, in a large, leather-spined ledger two inches thick. A page might record half a dozen transactions, each representing an Irish man or woman lost to his native land. And there, on page 285 of one of these ledgers, on August 6, 1929, was listed "Miss Mary Kearney, Blasket Island, by cheque for fare to U.S., 21.10.4." All together, the evidence suggests that *this* Mary was *our* Mary, and that she left on October 22, 1929, on the Cunard liner *Scythia* from Liverpool, stopping at Queenstown, and bound for Boston and New York.

Queenstown—which since Ireland's split from Britain had been renamed Cobh, pronounced "cove"—was located on the south shore of a large island a few miles east of Ireland's second city, Cork, linked to it since 1862 by a busy rail spur. Convicts bound for penal colonies in Australia had shipped out from Queenstown. The *Titanic* had docked here in 1912, picking up 123 passengers, mostly emigrants from the south and west of Ireland, most of them to go down with the ship. The town occupied a spot commanding fine views of the bay that opened before it. An imposing Roman Catholic church sat perched on the hill above it. The harbor front was crowded with small awninged shops where emigrants could buy food and supplies for the voyage, hotels and cheap rooming houses in which to spend their last nights in Ireland. Queenstown was one great stage on which was enacted the national tragedy of emigration, a place of high hopes and bitter tears.

Mary's first time in Queenstown came sometime before departure, for the much-feared medical examination. "A lot of boys and girls didn't pass," she'd recount years later. You needed to show you could speak and read English, and pass a physical exam. She was "scared stiff"; the medical examiners were said to be ruthless. "We were washed and scrubbed and cleaned, and our hair was washed and cleaned, and we went through doctors and nurses, and we had to be in perfect condition."

After two days in Queenstown, now back on the island, she met her sister Siobhan at the slip, and mischievously told her she hadn't passed. Told you so, said Siobhan, who didn't think Mary even wanted to go to America. Actually, she didn't, Mary would say later. But "I wanted so much to help my father and mother," who by now were in their late forties, with five children at home; money from America would help them "get along better and have better things," maybe help get her brothers and sisters to school in Dingle. It was only once she and Siobhan reached their house at the top of the village that she told her the truth.

Weeks later, with the arrival of her passport, it was really time to go. Her parents took her to Dingle. When her mother came down sick, Mary insisted that she stay in bed and arranged for a friend to get them to the station the next morning in time for the six-thirty train. In Queenstown, it dawned on her that she knew no one boarding the ship with her. "I was all by myself," save for some cousins from Dingle, two boys whom she'd never met before, the barest tendrils of connection. "It was really very sad, you know? At that time, you never thought of going back."

The voyage aboard the six-hundred-foot-long steamer, probably about a week, was not unpleasant. "We used to go up on deck, the whole crowd from Kerry," she'd say. They'd buy cookies and drinks. "The boys who were with us, five or six of them, they were so good to us." She heard shipboard stories of boys who might be up to no good, of course, "that we were too innocent, that we didn't know anything about anything." But there was no trouble that way. The Kerry boys saw the girls to their bunks at night, patrolled the passageways, then would be "waiting for us," their manly protectors, in the morning. On the way over, "all the Kerrys stayed together. But it was lonesome, very lonesome."

Mary was part of what Marie-Louise Sjoestedt had termed the "interminable procession" of emigrants from Queenstown. What did she think aboard the tender? Or as the big liner steamed out of the harbor and into the Atlantic? Did she think of her time in Maynooth? Or of the island? Did she think of her parents, brothers, and sisters? Did she think of George?

Did he think of her?

Maybe not. Late 1929 had been eventful for him. He'd left behind his Cambridge University lectureship and moved back to Dublin; though he retained his King's fellowship, he was no longer tied down by Cambridge's academic shackles. He was hard at work writing now—both scholarly projects, such as a translation of Aeschylus' *Prometheus Bound,* and stories and criticism for Irish-language publications. He was very busy. Late that year, his father died. He may not have known that Mary had left at all.

Chapter 9

Working at Irish

[1932]

A few years later, George was at a festive theater opening in Cambridge when "the wife of a distinguished historian, a professor, got up, looked through her lorgnette, and remarked, in a very superior voice, 'I think everybody who is anybody is here.' " George cringed. Here, the way his wife told the story, was Cambridge at its worst, smug and elitist. All in all, "he'd rather be in Ireland talking to a fisherman than gossiping in Common Room," his daughter Margaret reports him often saying. In 1928, he'd been lecturing at Cambridge. He was a fellow of King's College. His thesis would soon be published as a book. He was proceeding along a well-marked academic career path, Oxbridge-style. And he wanted to get off.

In May 1929, George advised his colleagues at King's he was resigning his lectureship. By July, he had cleaned out his Cambridge digs, left England, and moved to Dublin. There, for the next two years, he lived in Raheny, a suburban enclave stretching back from Dublin Bay north of the city. When he returned for a visit to Dublin almost two decades later, he wrote, "I felt drawn irresistibly to my old haunts at Raheny, where I spent some of the most impressionable years of my life."

In Raheny lived Moya Llewelyn Davies, whose grand old house,

Furry Park, had so impressed Maurice O'Sullivan on his memorable visit to Dublin two years before. Moya herself left an indelible impression on everyone. She was slim and lovely, and sported the kind of intriguing personal history that can stoke personal and sexual allure. Her father, James O'Connor, was an ardent republican who was imprisoned (the year Moya was born) for his political activities, and later served on the council of the Irish Republican Brotherhood. When Moya was nine, her mother and four sisters died, in the span of a few hours, from eating poisoned shellfish; she was spared, she always said, because she'd been sent to her room without supper for misbehavior. When she was twenty-eight, she married Crompton Llewelyn Davies, an official in Britain's Liberal government, thirteen years her senior.

Two years later, at a dance—she was wearing her wedding ring, but introduced herself as Moya O'Connor—a nineteen-year-old man, drinking lemonade, looked over to see a pair of "dazzling blue eyes fringed by a mane of golden hair and a face of extraordinary vitality." This, according to Vincent MacDowell, one of his many biographers, was the young Michael Collins, who was to become one of the chief architects of Irish independence and command the pro-treaty side during the civil war, only to be gunned down in County Cork in 1922. Moya would insist they'd had an affair. In somewhat less doubt is that, during the tumultuous years of the independence struggle, Collins visited her at Furry Park. Moya, it was said, stored guns and ammunition in hat boxes scattered around the house, then delivered them across the city. Delivered them, her granddaughter Melissa Llewelyn-Davies would write, "in an open-topped car, her long hair flying in the wind. Her hair, my father told me, was brushed by a maid a hundred times a night." In March 1921, Moya was arrested and imprisoned at Mountjoy, a Dublin prison, and was released only after the truce that July.

Intoxicating and larger than life, she bathed herself in drama. She never installed electricity at Furry Park, said her granddaughter, "believing she looked more desirable by candlelight." In her mid-forties at the time George first met her, she cut a striking figure to which he was in no way oblivious; why, he'd loved her almost from the time he met her, he told his wife a few years later. In 1932, he dedicated to her his translation of Aeschylus' *Prometheus Bound*. She, Maurice, George, and George's novelist friend E. M. Forster, as we'll see, would make for an unlikely four-leaf clover of a literary team.

George lived about a mile across the sprawling Saint Annes Park from

Moya's home, in a picturesque cottage called Watermill, which looked across to a low, flat island and beyond that to Dublin Bay. He'd remember the "pools left by the low tide, with stretches of shining wet sand, Howth Head and Irelands Eye in the distance, the Dublin mountains across the Bay, and the air full of the music of curlews and oystercatchers and plovers of all sorts." The cottage, which took its name from a mill situated on a nearby creek, was no mere "cottage," really, but a substantial thatched-roof affair, all chimneys, gables, and greenery, that went back at least a century, approached through a gate George had himself painted bright green; his mother, who visited him there, would write of "the velvety peace of Watermill." Later, when he moved to Galway, Forster wrote to him: "I expect I should like Galway . . . but we mustn't expect to find anything like Watermill there."

While at Watermill in 1930, George wrote a piece for a Dublin publication called *The Star*, about the place of Irish among Ireland's intelligentsia. "Every day, when I am not working at Greek, I am working at Irish," he wrote.

> I know a number of other Irish speakers in the neighbourhood—
> some of them native speakers, some of them University men, and
> all of them engaged in working in one way or another for the lan-
> guage. In the evening we meet—they come to my house or I go
> to theirs—and we sit and talk till midnight or the small hours of
> the morning. We acknowledge no restriction in our topics of con-
> versation. We talk about Irish literature, past and future; about
> English and French literature and about the classics; we discuss
> whether Tolstoy is greater than Dostoevsky; we discuss religion,
> philosophy and economics; we talk about Lenin, Mussolini and
> Gandhi; in short, "we tire the sun with talking and send him
> down the sky." And of course we talk nothing but Irish.

He wrote much in Irish during these years, too. He wrote about Irish-language education and a visit to Greece, came out against what he deemed a silly Dublin land-development scheme. He translated Shakespearean sonnets. He wrote a number of short stories, including the two cited earlier about young women with illegitimate children.

Another story, "Barra na Trá" top of the beach, is set on the Great Blasket, above the White Strand. An old man sits alone facing the sea. His reverie is broken by "the bright, long laughter of the young girls, as is usual when they are out walking together at night and know there are boys nearby." The boys corral them. Revelry ensues. "They're lively enough tonight," says a bystander. "They'd want to be," says another, a big man with a deep voice, lying back in the heather. "They have youth, but not for long." Working himself up, he complains that the young people of the day lack courage, generosity, dignity. He turns to the old man at the top of the beach: would they ever again see the likes of the old island worthies? "The old man doesn't move," George's story winds down. The wind is strengthening from the north; it will rain. " 'I don't see them,' " he says flatly, and " 'I never will.' "

In Dublin, George had escaped the maw of Cambridge, was happily immersed in the Irish language, and enjoyed a fecund intellectual and creative life. His words and ideas were appearing in print. He was never far from the irrepressible Moya. He had his cottage; on the wall hung two maps—one of Greece, the other of Ireland. Here was a young man coming into his own.

Two years earlier, after meeting George in Dublin and undergoing months of training with the Guard, Maurice O'Sullivan had been ordered to Inverin, in wild, Irish-speaking Connemara in County Galway. There he was, as he'd write on the train bound west, "I in the Guard's uniform, going out to Connemara to enforce the law." He arrived one fine evening at the barracks, a modest two-story building set back from the coast road. "I looked out of the window. The moon was high in the sky and the night as bright as day. Galway Bay stretched out before me and the coast of Clare over in the south-east. . . . Children were playing up and down the road, calling to each other in sweet, fluent Irish."

Were it not for George's influence, Maurice would doubtless have wound up in America; sooner that, Daniel Binchy once suggested, than suffer "the unknown world of English-speaking Ireland." So he was fortunate to be assigned to the Gaeltacht. A photograph from those days shows him in uniform, looking square into the camera, a little jaunty, hands in pockets, big metal buckle at his waist, jacket closely fitting his trim body. He is twenty-three years old and off to a good start.

But two years later, he was an unhappy man. What was there for him to do? Resolve domestic rows? Settle neighborly disputes over seaweed? He carried no weapon except for a brown billy club of turned and polished wood. Sometimes, in pursuit of evidence, he'd be called upon to barge into people's homes and overturn their mattresses. Or disrupt some lovingly maintained still. "Poteen," the Irish word for its illegal product, helped keep people warm over the winter; what was the harm in that? Altogether, the Guard was an easy life, but boring and dispiriting. In October 1928, Maurice was transferred to Carraroe, a bit farther west into Connemara, but that changed nothing. "His whole nature," George Thomson would write, "rebelled against the idea of using the law against these destitute peasants."

It was probably in 1929 that Maurice wrote him to complain, as George remembered it, that "he didn't have enough to do in the winter." Well, replied his friend, why not write about his youth? Tomás Ó Criomhthain's *An tOileánach,* recently published, was a sensation among Irish-speakers; maybe Maurice could do something like it. He had imagination, it was plain to George, a sharp eye, a broad generosity of spirit. "Nothing would go unnoticed by him, and he was very fond of people." Like his grandfather Daideo, to whose stories George had listened raptly on the island, he was a great storyteller, able "to make a good story out of trivial, everyday things. However long you spent in his company, you'd never feel the time passing." Surely he could bring these qualities to his writing.

Well, he couldn't—not at first, anyway. Telling a story was one thing, writing it another. After reaching Dublin in 1927, Maurice had regaled George, and probably Moya, too, with his riotous tale of getting lost on the train from Tralee. Now George urged him to set it down, "with a view to publication in some form." But it came out flat, a good story that wasn't: "He made the attempt, and failed, and we discarded it." He suspected Maurice was worrying about some great faceless Public out there. Pay no heed to the big world, George counseled. Write for your friends on the island.

Maurice, he all but ordered him, was to "keep writing as the spirit moved him, and to observe everything."

By the time Maurice got much further with the project, George had left Dublin and was living in Galway, beneficiary of a peculiar, once-in-a-lifetime turn of Irish history.

Since the end of the civil war in 1923, Ireland had been in flux, its social and political institutions emerging in new forms, drawing on the pent-up energy of new nationhood. Its universities were no exception, and during the 1920s the question arose of just what was to become of one of the smallest of them, variously known as University College Galway or, since 1908, the National University of Ireland, Galway. Its counterparts in Dublin and Cork were bigger and better established; Galway could seem too small and insignificant to sustain itself. Located on the largely rural west coast a few peninsulas up from Dingle, far from any metropolitan centers, it sat right in the middle of the country's largest Irish-speaking region; Galway City was 40 percent Irish-speaking, areas around it as much as 80 percent.

This last, of course, determined the college's fate; it was to fulfill "the functions of an Irish-speaking University College," it was decided, "through the conducting of University teaching of general subjects through the medium of Irish." *Not* teaching Irish, mind you; that was not the point. But, rather, teaching mathematics, and science, and the classics *through* Irish, to students who spoke it as their native tongue.

In 2007, Irish writer and scholar Muiris Mac Conghail, looking into George Thomson's years in Ireland, told a university seminar in Dublin how he'd long supposed University College Galway's teach-through-Irish talk was, to use an Irish phrase he found apt, just so much *gui i gcéill*, or making a pretense. But his research led him to conclude that, quite to the contrary, it was the product of serious study, firm conviction. A 1926 report devoted to Galway's institutional fate noted that Irish had been "declared to be the National language of the Irish Free State." An across-the-board "Irishising" of all the nation's universities was impractical. "But a beginning should be made and can be made now. The University College at Galway is a small though fairly complete institution and it can be made Irish through and through in a comparatively short time and at comparatively little expense."

All this idealism couldn't last, of course. But it was enough by 1931 to get George Thomson—or Seoirse Mac Tomáis, in Irish—a position at Galway reflecting the university's new mission.

In February of the previous year, two University College emissaries had gone to Dublin to meet with Ernest Blythe. Blythe was successor to Michael Collins as the Free State's minister of finance and, it would be said, an ardent champion of "an Irish culture based on high aesthetic principles"; when Marie-Louise Sjoestedt interviewed him in Dublin in 1929, she pictured him as the language's staunchest—"I would say almost the most fanatic"—patron in government. One of the college men was Liam Ó Briain, professor of romance languages and founder of a local Irish-language theater. Mac Tomáis was "with me here last night on his way to Connemara and we had a long talk with him," Ó Briain had written Blythe. "He is very keen on getting to do language work here, would like to come here, believes in the great possibilities of the scheme, and is full of ideas." He had just finished translating the *Odyssey* into Irish and had gone to Connemara to read it to a member of the Guard there—Maurice O'Sullivan, of course. He could teach Homer, Dante, and Shakespeare, all in Irish, and serve as inspiration to the people of the Gaeltacht.

From the start, George had impressed the people at Galway whom he needed to impress. "He has already done three books of Plato into Irish," Ó Briain wrote to Blythe, "so he would be no fake appointment. Dillon and I are both convinced he is a man worth going a long way to secure." And Blythe knew George already; Moya Llewelyn Davies had introduced them back in 1926, during George's earlier Dublin stay. So it seemed like a lock.

But George had one more bar to clear. In a television interview in 1998, Muiris Mac Conghail told this version of how he did it: The president of the college, though otherwise satisfied with Thomson's credentials, preferred someone else for the job. A *Cambridge* man for Gaelic Galway? So, he said to George when they met, "you must be able to give some small contribution in Irish to the lectures in Greek. Could you give us an example of your capacity in this regard?" Whereupon Thomson, in Mac Conghail's telling, "went to the blackboard, took out his notes, and delivered a long lecture on Plato in Blasket Irish." The nice thing about the story is that, as Mac Conghail himself verified later, it was substantially true: when Thomson presented himself in Irish before the eleven members of the Board of Examinations, he made "a tremendous impression" on them. They "all want to have him here now."

Ever since going up to Cambridge in 1922, George could be seen as split between his Irish and Greek sides. But now the stars had aligned to make it possible for him to say yes to both passions, no to neither. He seized the opportunity: He would teach the classics. He'd do it in Irish. He'd do it at Galway. His tutor at King's, J. T. Sheppard, did his best to dissuade him, but George was determined.

On August 1, 1931, long after the job had become all but his, Thomson applied for it, and early that fall moved to Galway. His mother was proud: "Will you humour me by letting me have a press cutting of your appointment when it is published?" she wrote him. But as a career move, it was not brilliant; he was giving up Cambridge for an academic backwater, presumably to bring the light of scholarship to benighted Irish-speakers barely out of places like the Blaskets themselves. Or, as one colleague summed it up, he was leaving Cambridge "to bury his talents in Galway as a lecturer at a small and remote university college."

Galway did have its yearbooks, catalogues, student clubs, and other trappings of college life. Inevitably, it had its rules: "Students shall not walk on the grass or cycle in the Quadrangle." It had professors of chemistry and physics, German and philology. Its library of sixty thousand volumes included a few rare manuscripts. Its minaret-topped, Gothic-style quadrangle, which dated to its opening as Queens College in 1849, was said to have been inspired by one of the oldest Oxford colleges. Yet small and remote Galway surely was—inhabiting the second, or maybe the third, tier of European universities—far down from the glittering heights of King's. With about seven hundred students enrolled when Thomson arrived, it awarded a hundred or so B.A.'s each year and a handful of advanced degrees. Its unique character lay squarely in its Irishness—in scholarships reserved for Irish-speakers from around the country; courses in mathematics, geography, history, economics, and the like taught in Irish; in Irish-conversation courses made available to everyone.

It was still early in the great experiment, however, and George sometimes had but two or three students in his class. Typically, he taught in a little second-floor gallery adjacent to the college's most stately space, the Aula Maxima. Remembered as a devoted Socrates-like figure with ready command of Irish and a love for obscure phrases heard in the Blaskets, he spoke only Irish on campus. In class, it was Aeschylus, Sophocles, Herodotus, Homer; he'd supply a Greek passage, his students would render it in Irish. (Once, probably in 1933, Marie-Louise Sjoestedt visited his class, spoke briefly with him in Irish, then took up the day's text with everyone else.) A former student remembered him from early in his time there as soft-spoken, fairly caressing words into sweetness; the class met in George's own flat by the river, the few students sitting on the floor.

George lived in a Galway neighborhood known as Wood Quay, in a three-story house with thick stone walls, some hundreds of years old by family reckoning, that sat across the street from a boat club. Corrib Lodge, it was called. It was a ten-minute walk from the university, less by bicycle. He'd ride past the old jail and across bridges spanning five distinct bodies of water; the brawny river Corrib split off through town and made for a multitude of dikes, canals, and other waterways. From his second-floor bedroom window, George could look out over placid waters literally across the street; or else, to the west, the churning rapids of Salmon Weir;

or beyond them both to the railroad-truss bridge on its great stone pillars, and the copper-clad minarets of the university on the far shore.

His lodgings were presided over by a Mrs. Naughten, a tall, fiftyish woman who'd taken to letting out a room of the house after her husband died. George was served meals opposite the kitchen. Then he could retreat to a little nook for coffee or port or to read the paper. It was a place of Irish-linen tablecloths, windows with shutters and blinds—and of spirited talk. Mrs. Naughten was a formidable figure; well read, she knew her history and Shakespeare. Out behind the house stood a big lilac tree. In front, a few steps across the narrow street, right beside the waters of the Corrib, was a bench where on fine days George and his friends could sit out and talk.

It was here that George spent most of the next three years. And it was here, often of a Saturday, that he'd meet with Maurice to talk about his writing. "Dear Maurice, my friend," he'd write in a postcard, "you'll be very welcome if you come to Galway tomorrow morning. Bring the manuscript with you."

In the National Library of Ireland in Dublin reside five large account books, the red lines running down their pages originally to record pounds, shillings, and pence. Inscribed on right-hand pages is Maurice O'Sullivan's original manuscript for the book that became known as *Fiche Blian ag Fás,* or *Twenty Years A-Growing.* The title came from a local proverb:

> Twenty years a-growing,
> Twenty years a-blossoming,
> Twenty years a-fading,
> Twenty years a-withering.

The book celebrates childhood, adolescence, and young adulthood. It is full of rambunctiousness, spirit, mayhem, and fun. Maurice was just twenty-five when he started it.

"There is no doubt but youth is a fine thing though my own is not over yet and wisdom comes with age." That's how it begins. The second paragraph reads:

I am a boy who was born and bred in the Great Blasket, a small truly Gaelic island which lies north-west of the coast of Kerry, where the storms of the sky and the wild sea beat without ceasing from end to end of the year and from generation to generation against the wrinkled rocks which stand above the waves that wash in and out of the coves where the seals make their homes.

In the third paragraph, he tells how his mother died when he was six months old, that he was removed from the island and left in the care of "a stranger woman" in Dingle. When he returns, at age seven, he knows no Irish. At dinner his first day back, his father, grandfather, and two sisters speak Irish, which he can't follow. That night, his sister sweeps the floor and shakes sand over it, a young man comes in with a melodeon, and soon there's dancing. The crowd encourages one of the girls to sing.

It was delightful to listen to her in the stillness of the night, everyone silent, with their chins on their hands, not a word out of them save now and then at the end of the verse, when my grandfather would cry, "My love forever, Eileen," and that was the first bit of Irish I picked up that night.

And from there it's one adventure, one fine day's quest, or hunt, or playful excess, to the next. "My grandfather and I were lying on the Castle Summit," he'd write. "It was a fine sunny day in July. The sun was splitting the stones with its heat and the grass burnt to the roots. I could see, far away to the south, Iveragh painted in many colours by the sun." As many a critic has commented, the sun always shone on Maurice's boyhood. There is little of the time-worn resilience and resignation of Tomás's book.

Even the Great War, when Maurice was an adolescent, gets light treatment. A ship is sunk. Its cargo washes up on the island.

Next day the quay and the strands were a grand sight, big timbers lying here and there and not a curragh with less than a hundred planks.

"By God," one man would say, "war is good."

"Arra, man," said another, "if it continues this Island will be the Land of the Young."

The war changed people greatly. Idle loiterers who used to sleep it out till milking-time were now abroad with the chirp of the sparrow gathering and ever gathering. There was good living

in the Island now. . . . Nothing was bought. There was no need.
It was to be had on the top of the water—flour, meat, lard, petrol,
wax, margarine, wine in plenty, even shoes, stockings and clothes.

Eighty book pages later, George arrives on the island. We learn of
their friendship, Maurice's journey by train to Dublin, his enlistment in
the Guard. The book ends two years after that—about the time Maurice
started writing, in 1929. He returns to the island on holiday: "I took a car
to Dunquin and how my heart opened when I reached Slea Head and saw
the Blasket, Inish-na-Bró and Inish-vick-illaun stretched out before me in
the sea to the west! I was as gay as a starling."

The National Library volumes are written mostly in blue ink, thirty-
four lines to the page, few changes or corrections, the script periodically
washing out as Maurice's pen runs dry, intensifying with each resort to the
ink pot. This, then, is *the original manuscript.* Or that, anyway, is what
George called it in notes he deposited with the library. But three years
passed between the time of Maurice's first, failed attempts and the time
the manuscript went to its publisher in late 1932. "I hadn't known Muiris
long when I realised he had the makings of a writer in him," George would
write. But "makings" or not, Maurice was a novice, facing the inevitable
false starts, awkward detours, dead ends.

"The only help I gave the author," George claimed, "was to guide
him towards adapting for publication the craft he had learnt from his
grandfather as a child by the fire." But even this modest claim suggests
he played a substantial role in the book's making, just as Brian Kelly and
An Seabhac had in Tomás's. With George in Galway and Maurice just
twenty-five miles down the coast road, in Carraroe, the two of them had
"the opportunity to edit it and advise each other," as George put it in an
Irish-language publication later. Sometimes he'd go out to Connemara,
but more often they met on Saturdays, the manuscript in front of them,
at Corrib Lodge.

As one critic, Eibhlín Nic Gráinne, noted when the book came out,
"evidence of mentorship" appears throughout,

in the selection of incidents, the use of proverbs or snatches of
Gaelic poetry which come into his narrative without much rel-
evance but for effect, like the too frequent description of scenery.
These topographical pieces are the "purple patches" that are more
characteristic of English prose style than of Gaelic writing.

George wrote that he did no more than "select and condense," before submitting each new draft to Maurice. *Select?* Choice of word, incident, and order are fundamental to all writing. George may even have helped position paragraph breaks, which so markedly shape the reading experience: the original Irish-language manuscript is written out line by line, page after page, with virtually no such breaks. *Condense?* The published version, in English and Irish alike, is shorter than the original, whole chapters and parts of chapters omitted. Shorter even with the new material Thomson urged Maurice to add; in the words of his friend Tim Enright, George sometimes "reminded the author of incidents he had forgotten." And he prevailed on Maurice to add two new chapters, the final one and one called "American Wake." George himself was proud of his efforts on Maurice's behalf. "I didn't add to it," he wrote, "but I did remove from it a word or two here and a line or half a page there, just as someone would card wool or clean the oats from the chaff."

Whatever help he gave, George was not preoccupied with ruthless fealty to fact. *Twenty Years A-Growing* is classed as memoir, or autobiography, but most critics agree it bears a flavor of fiction and gains much from Maurice's imagination. Some passages, Irish critic Declan Kiberd has asserted categorically, "are not credible if you read them as autobiography."

One instance concerns the author's first meeting with George, which I briefly described earlier, in the prologue. Maurice is "looking after a sheep on the hill-side, the sun yellowing in the west and a lark singing above." He hears lambs clattering on the slopes beneath him, while down at the sea's edge a shoal of mackerel rustle the water. Then he spies a man he doesn't know. "Where had he come from and he approaching me now from the top of the hill in the darkening of the day?" They say hello. They sit down for a smoke. They try to talk. . . .

Only trouble is, George didn't remember it this way. He would tell quite a different story, of his coming up the path from the slip that first day, Maurice descending with a donkey, a wholly different conversation, nothing like Maurice's version at all.

If any did, this discrepancy invited editorial tinkering; after all, he'd *been* there. But he let it pass; it is Maurice's telling that survives in print. George—no scientist, no literal-minded historian, his scholarly life brimming over with Greek gods and heroes and their improbable feats—was later asked about such seeming contradictions. No worries, he as much as said; poetic truth was not the same as narrative truth. Tomás Ó

Criomhthain clung closer to the raw facts, he allowed, whereas Maurice freely took artistic license:

> What he gives us is not primarily a factual account at all but an artist's impression of certain selected episodes. This does not mean that he misrepresents the facts; on the contrary, he is a keen and accurate observer, even of the smallest details; but he has recast his material in retrospect so as to present the essentials of each situation in a concrete and concentrated form. This method may convey more than a factual record, just as an artist's portrait may reveal more than a photograph.

George, in Muiris Mac Conghail's happy phrasing, offered here "an original approach to Muiris's originality."

Thus, a genial coterie of like-minded souls—Maurice, the Irish dreamer and storyteller; George, at home in poetry and myth; and finally, as we'll see, George's cotranslator, Moya Llewelyn Davies, romantic to the core—all sign off on an account rejecting servitude to literal truth.

And whatever its departures from fact, George was surely right that *Fiche Blian ag Fás* did ably represent Blasket life. Declan Kiberd, for example, has cited the book's fidelity to the island's social life. "It's full of people doing things together. . . . In some ways, it's a better rendition of the communal nature of that community than was produced either by Synge or O'Crohan, both of whom admired that element but don't seem to have captured it as fully as O'Sullivan did."

In November 1932, George, serving as Maurice's agent, signed a contract with the book's Irish-language publisher, Talbot Press, putting up a hundred pounds of his own money, several months' salary, to subsidize its publication. His editor at Talbot? Three years after working on *An tOileánach,* An Seabhac was back in the picture. George corresponded with him regularly in the months before publication. Predictably, they had their editorial squabbles, George fighting for Maurice's homegrown Blasket Irish against An Seabhac's preference for language more elevated and refined.

George helped see Maurice's book into print in English as well, through Chatto & Windus in Britain. E. M. Forster wrote the introductory note for it: Readers of the Irish edition, he said, "cannot possibly be as much surprised as we," readers of the translation, "for here is the egg of a sea-bird—lovely, perfect, and laid this very morning." At one point, he, Maurice, and George met at Corrib Lodge, sat out on the bench by the waters of the Corrib, took snapshots memorializing their work together.

Missing from the little party was Moya, with whom George had collaborated on the English translation. Chapter by chapter, he'd do a rough draft, then send it on to her. She'd rework it and return it to him for comments. Maurice got the last word. The translation, wrote George, "was done in some haste in order that it might be available as the Book Club choice for May, and also in order to bring pressure to bear on the Talbot Press, who were making difficulties over the Irish version." It was a hectic, unsettled time.

The bench where Maurice O'Sullivan, at right, and novelist E. M. Forster sit in this 1932 photo stood just across a narrow street from George Thomson's digs, Corrib Lodge, in Galway city.

The book came out in April 1933 in Irish, and by August had sold sixteen hundred copies. In May, it appeared in English. Both editions were widely reviewed, critical response splitting sharply. Ireland's *Catholic Bulletin* complained that *Fiche Blian* stirred "intervals of nausea." The reviewer faulted its Irish, and was horrified to see it "punctuated with offensive expectoration and repeated invocations of the Prince of Darkness." In the United States, where it was a Book-of-the-Month selection, a reviewer for *The Nation,* Ernest Boyd, observed that the author had not seen fit to mention that he inhabited "a part of the world where rain, dampness, and depression are more than ordinarily the portion of the native." O'Sullivan's Blasket, wrote Boyd, was pure Hollywood. Ireland was once more being saddled with a myth—"the charm of life without sanitation, adequate food, and decent housing."

More often, though, reviewers gave themselves over to Maurice's exuberance. One thought of it not so much as a book as a kind of talisman: "The scream of a gull, the wash of a wave, the slow laugh of a peasant, a voice from the pre-historic past, all these sounded in Mr. O'Sullivan's pages, and spirited me away." Another termed it poetry: "For those to whom the rare poetic prose of Synge was a joy and a delight, Maurice O'Sullivan's simple, lilting pages will hold a similar pleasure."

Irish short-story writer Seán Ó Faoláin described Maurice's Blasket as lying three miles from the mainland—and five hundred years away, deep in the Middle Ages. "The life is hard and dangerous but perpetually gay," he said, buying into Maurice's sensibility; "in that respect it is almost a Land of the Ever Young." Never before had he been able to praise a book without reservation, but now he had to: "Whatever this book may be for English readers, it is for Irishmen the most exciting thing that has happened within a hundred years. It is the first piece of literature in Irish since the scattering of the poets in the eighteenth century."

It seemed to George that Maurice's book masterfully integrated its opposing themes, "the gaiety of youth and the magic of the old Gaelic world, the one blooming, the other in decay"; each gathered momentum across the span of the book. "The story moves like a piece of music, revealing a sustained sense of artistic unity." To him, Maurice was a genuine artist who, it could seem, had only to give up the first person to write a full-blown novel.

And yet he never did. "The novel," George observed much later, "is a story of a new type," caught up in the intimately personal, with scant room for what he called "the oral and collective." Private preoccupations like that "lay beyond Muiris's experience," submerged as it was in the communal.

Of all George's experience of the island, its communitarian ways may have left the deepest mark. The sound of Irish on the lips of his friends? Yes, certainly, a distinct pleasure. But it was not just as individuals that he thought of them. He was alive to the uniqueness of the men and women he met, like the quirky islanders Tomás had sketched in *Island Cross-Talk*. But he'd found on the Great Blasket something more, something originally quite new to him—a sense of its collective spirit.

George took numerous photos on his visits, most of them of islanders in groups. One was of Seán Ó Criomhthain, Eibhlín Ní Shuilleabháin, Mícheál O'Guiheen, and Maurice O'Sullivan, lined up together, sitting along a low stone wall. Another was of villagers climbing up the path from the slip. Another of children cavorting on the White Strand. Another of islanders gathered at the well. Did this people-together pattern reveal some deep unmet need in George? Maybe so, but just as likely it was simply what he saw most. The islanders did almost everything together. Visitors invariably reported them collecting above the slip to greet a *naomhóg*, or sweeping down onto the White Strand to gather wreckage, or crowding into the "parliament" house near the well at the top of the village. Synge described using a bit of broken mirror to shave: "As I stood with my back to the people I could catch a score of eyes in the glass, watching me intently." Carl Marstrander depicted islanders as scarcely able to endure solitude at all. It required no special soft spot, then, for George to see what he saw in the village; he was immersed in a living community.

And he loved it. For all its privations, the communal life of the island gave him something he found missing from London and Cambridge. Odysseus, we may recall George writing, called Ithaca " 'a rough place, but a fine nurse of men.' One might say the same of the Blasket Island." Not a nurse only of individuals, however, but of men, women, and children, living humanely and well, together.

The islanders, he observed, "were bound to one another by close ties of blood and marriage, all residing within a stone's throw of each other, all engaged in the same occupations and faced with the same dangers at sea." On the island, over the course of many summers, he'd seen that up close.

But now in Galway, as before in Dublin, he had time and leisure to make sense of it, to trace the new gullies in his brain the Blaskets had worn. Full and alive in him now was a communitarian streak that would lead him to see the world and its workings through new eyes.

Now everything looked different. As a schoolboy, he'd been puzzled by some of his earliest exposure to the Homeric poems, including one particular line from the *Odyssey*, which tells of Achilles lying "full length in the dust, his horsemanship forgotten." George appreciated the cadence of it in the original Greek. "It struck me as magnificent, inspired." And yet he would later encounter the same phrase, exactly, in the *Iliad*. How could this be? "If it was really inspired," he'd write, "how did it bear repetition?"

Then, he'd write, "I went to Ireland. The conversation of those ragged peasants, as I learnt to follow it, astonished me. It was as though Homer had come alive. Its vitality was inexhaustible, yet it was rhythmical, alliterative, formal, artificial." He told of a Blasket woman who'd just given birth, the story reaching him in language both poetic and vigorous. Yet, within the day, he'd heard it the same way from three or four other islanders. "It was common property," as were other verbal niceties he'd gathered, some of them generations old. Here, it struck him, was his Homeric quandary resolved: Homer's was "the language of the people, raised to a higher power"—eloquence not rising up from the rare, fevered brain of genius, but billowing up from the collective intelligence and spirit of the people. "It's in the Blasket," he would unequivocally declare, "that I found the key to the Homeric Question."

Certainly, the times he lived in influenced George Thomson as well. Europe and America had sunk into an economic depression so desperate, cruel, and lingering that some of the most basic tenets of industrial capitalism, with its insistent individualism, were being challenged. The injury and hurt experienced by so many made people look anew at socialism in its many flavors. The cultural and aesthetic fashions of the day—in books by John Steinbeck, in the Socialist Realism of communist Russia, in the art of Diego Rivera, in triumphant visions of men and women joined together, building dams and harvesting wheat—all reflected new interest in the common man and woman. There was a nobility, it seemed, in ordinary people working together.

Some years later, in 1944, Thomson wrote an article for a Celtic-studies journal on the "The Irish Language Revival." Among the impoverished peasants of the Blaskets, he reported, "the language embodied a culture and way of life which in my own country had been lost." He was not deceived, he said, by the simplistic yet seductive ideas of the "Celtic Twi-light." He had no wish to return to the Middle Ages. He had seen enough of the Blaskets "to shed any romantic illusions they may have inspired in me at the start." But, he declared, their rich culture was simply "a fact."

One had only to turn to Maurice O'Sullivan. Readers of *Twenty Years A-Growing,* he suspected, would "agree with me that the author possessed a remarkable imaginative gift," one that, of course, was his own. "On the other hand," he continued, "the eloquence of his language, which is far more striking in the original than it is in the translation, is not his own. It is traditional. I do not think there is a phrase in the whole book which is not current on the lips of the people."

It was *the people* about whom George more and more came to think and care. And while in Galway, he set out on a high-minded project on their behalf, or on what he deemed their behalf. It was all well and good to imagine restoring Irish to Ireland, but more important, he decided, to preserve it among the peasants who already used it:

> I conceived the idea of using the language as a means of giving [the people of the Gaeltacht] a modern education so that they could adapt their culture to modern conditions. I thought that, given an up-to-date education in their native language, they could be introduced to modern life without losing their culture in the process.

Indeed, behind the move to Galway in the first place had been a scheme (apparently hatched with Ernest Blythe) to launch a series of public Irish-language lectures in that spirit.

On Friday or Saturday nights in October and November 1931, soon after arriving in Galway, George began giving lectures on "The Begin-nings of European Civilisation," with a cast including the Egyptians and the ancient gods. He delivered them in Irish, to a packed auditorium in the university quadrangle. But they were aimed not at university students, or not just at them, but at local Irish-speakers generally. "Extension" classes, we call them today. But in Galway, in 1931, delivered by an Irish-speaking exemplar of Oxbridge scholarship, they were quite the thing. No one present for Friday's lecture, said the local paper, would want to miss the next one.

George's ambitions were nothing if not grand. In an article outlining his ideas, he described how lectures in Dún Chaoin, say, might include one on Pierce Ferriter, the local poet and patriot known by name and legendary exploits but little else. Discuss his poetry, his life and times, and you had an entrée into literature and history. Or what about mackerel? Dún Chaoin men fished for it every day. So why not a lecture on how mackerel spawn, their life as marine creatures, the intricacies of their biology? Ultimately, you'd be wandering into economics, meteorology, and chemistry. All in Irish. "If we began in this way, dealing with matters that concern the lives of the people closely, there is no doubt that we would be able to arouse interest in the origins of things." Such lectures were sure to succeed, "if only a start were made."

Or that, anyway, was the idea. As Séamus Mac Mathúna, today the university's director of academic affairs, looks back on the noble experiment, Thomson started with "high hopes and ambitions" but in the end had to reckon his efforts a failure. Ireland, as Thomson would take pains to point out later, was not Greece; you couldn't hold lectures in the open air. You needed a hall, which in most Irish villages meant a school, which normally required the say-so of a parish priest. "I had not proceeded far with my arrangements," he would write, "when it was made plain to me that there was not a priest throughout the length and breadth of Connemara who would dream of permitting his school to be used for anything so subversive" as his lectures. Nor did he get much support from the university, or from the Ministry of Education; Ernest Blythe, his vigorous champion, had been voted out of office.

Three years in Galway left George embittered. As he wrote later, at a time when his political views had hardened:

> The authorities did not *want* the peasants to be educated. It might put ideas into their heads. It might inspire them to demand an improvement in their lot. The authorities saw this more clearly even than I did. . . . No doubt, if the peasants had heard my extension lectures, they would have been stirred to demand an improvement in their conditions, but that precisely is why they were not permitted to hear them.

During these years, he'd write, "I was working to save the culture of the Irish-speaking peasantry"—which betrays some slight taint, at least, of bravado or grandiloquence. George was capable and resourceful, but maybe a little overearnest, too; independent, but also stubborn. When he arrived in Galway, he was only twenty-eight, an age at which he may not yet have learned the interpersonal and political skills needed to pull off such an ambitious project.

Despite these disappointments, George remained busy and productive. He brought out Irish translations of works of Euripides and Aeschylus. He helped translate a play by the Russian dramatist Gogol, which was performed at Taibhdhearc na Gaillimhe, the local Irish-language theater. He translated the Book of Common Prayer.

Altogether, he probably worked too hard. A long-standing ulcer acted up. Even by early 1933, he was apparently weighing a return to Dublin, though for the moment he hung on. "I am sorry that you are not leaving Galway," Forster wrote him on January 31, after learning that Maurice's book had found a publisher. It was a dead end for him there. In Dublin, on the other hand, "you would be in contact with other people's minds, and perhaps with their affections, and in Galway I can't see that you are."

In April 1934, Forster wrote George that he'd recently talked to Jack Sheppard and had news: Sheppard "would and could still take you back to Kings." If he was interested, Forster made it sound, he'd better move fast.

Finally, overwhelmed and exhausted, "my mind in turmoil," as he later wrote, George gave up, and later that year left Galway to take up once more his King's fellowship in Cambridge.

Perhaps while still at Watermill, or else later in Galway, George learned that Mary Kearney had immigrated to America. "I was determined to follow her," he'd write—determined, that is, until he learned that his girl from the Blaskets with the hearty, infectious laugh had become a nun.

It was probably around the beginning of November 1929, after about a week's voyage, that Mary arrived in Boston. Walking down the gangplank, she heard someone call her name. Her sister Cáit, who was working as a domestic for a family with connections in the Springfield police force, couldn't come herself, but arranged for an officer to meet her at the dock. Yes, said Mary, that's me. She was in America, and soon on a train bound for Springfield, ninety miles west.

Like other immigrants, she held visions of America as a land of gold and limitless opportunity. But as the train chugged west across eastern

Massachusetts, she looked out on a trackside landscape of rubbish and old cars. And *that,* she'd remember with a laugh years later, left her oddly comfortable: America was not so daunting, after all, not so rich, not so foreign: "I felt at home."

Cáit, two years older and four years in the New World, was thrilled to have her sister join her in Springfield. When she had time off on Thursday afternoons, she and some friends would round up Mary and set about showing her America. One time, they went to get their portraits taken—the four of them, young women in their twenties, lined up in front of a studio backdrop of a garden trellis, wearing fresh frocks and the little head-hugging cloches fashionable at the time. In another photo, of just the two sisters, Cáit had put on a few pounds; Mary sat prettily and petitely beside her, in a pleated skirt, a string of pearls, faux or not, and a

Mary Kearney, at right, a month or two after landing in America. Her sister Cáit sits second from the left.

scarf tied like a scout bandanna around her neck. A month or two off the ship and Mary looked like a million other American girls.

She'd landed in America at the end of the Roaring Twenties, around the time of the stock-market crash. But the Depression seeped through the country only gradually, and Mary soon got a job in an adjacent town, working for a mixed Catholic-Protestant family with five boys. At one point, she heard the parents talking about possibly placing the last of the boys, still an infant, in an orphanage. "Over my dead body he's going to an orphanage," Mary remembered herself saying, as she marched into the room and plucked the baby from its mother's arms; he'd be safe in *her* care.

But was there something wrong with this picture? During her first weeks and months in America, she would join her sister and friends for a dance or the movies, and "this thing would be in my head all the time, you know, that I shouldn't be there, that there was a place for me"—a place not in the world, but in the church. Anything she did, it was the same, "going around like a record" in her head.

She'd never met a nun on the Blasket, yet the idea had taken hold in her that she wanted to become one. Had she conceived it only in the wake of her relationship with George, in response to some inner storm of confused feeling? Or did it start earlier? Maybe even before she'd met him, quashing chances for any real romance from the outset? "I knew he was sweet on me, but I knew I had a vocation." That, at least, is what she'd say years later, after a lifetime in the church.

She didn't want to take the fateful step right away, but, rather, to get a job, make money, send some of it home to her parents. But it *was* right away. One night, a couple of months after arriving in America, she burst into tears. When Cáit asked why, she told her she wanted to join the convent. "Who's keeping you?" she remembered Cáit saying. "You shouldn't be crying over that. You should be very happy."

It was arranged that she meet Springfield Bishop Thomas O'Leary. She wanted to become a nun, said Miss Mary Kearney, twenty-one years old, late of the Blasket Islands, and virtually just off the boat. She wanted to be a missionary. In China, maybe, or Africa.

Well, she could be a missionary in Springfield, she recalled Bishop O'Leary telling her.

Oh, but how could that be, with her friends and family right there in Springfield? What kind of a missionary was that?

"But you'd still be a missionary—from Ireland. The Sisters of Providence have a lot of work for you to do."

Sisters of Providence went back to 1873 in America, operating a network of hospitals in the Springfield-Holyoke area. They were a relatively well-off order and heavily Irish; of foreign-born nuns joining the order over the years, one came from Poland, one from Italy, ten from England, and 172 from Ireland. Among those with whom Mary entered the novitiate in January 1930, five were Irish girls, but she alone could actually speak Irish.

Six months later, the engraved invitations went out:

The Sisters of Providence
cordially invite you to attend the ceremony of
Reception of the Holy Habit
at Holy Family Institute,
Brightside, Holyoke
Saturday, July 19th, 1930
at nine in the morning.

In a ceremony a year and a half later, on January 6, 1932, Mary took her temporary vows and became Sister Mary Clemens.

In the late 1960s, with the liberalization accompanying the Second Vatican Council, Mary gave up her nun's habit. Before that, all anyone could see of her was a pinched remnant of face that included the eyes and mouth. All the rest of her face and figure were lost in a voluminous sea of cloth, a spotless oval of white around her head. So remembers her niece Kathleen Arduini, daughter of Mary's sister Cáit. On the rare occasions when Mary was allowed to visit her family, she was delivered by limousine, escorted by another nun, who would come into the house with her, sit quietly, and wait.

Her aunt was not overly demonstrative when she came to visit, Arduini remembers, never one for hugging and kissing. She had a "great, great smile," but sometimes seemed too holy to touch.

In the spring of 1934, just before George left Galway, a twenty-eight-year-old musician named Katharine Stewart was visiting Greece with her mother. Six years before, while in her final year at Girton, one of Cambridge University's three women's colleges, she'd been urged to sit in on a lecture by George Thomson devoted to Greek lyric meter. She found the subject, with all its links to music, fascinating, the lecturer no less so. That, however, was that. But now, while she was visiting Greece, a Scottish couple with whom she and her mother were traveling recommended to her a recently published book, written by a peasant fisherman from the far west of Ireland, and translated into English by this same George Thomson.

Later that summer, Katharine had just returned to Cambridge when she learned that Thomson was back, too; by her own account, she sought the chance to see him again. "The opportunity came in July," she remembered. She was playing a Beethoven piano concerto at King's, and during the intermission George approached her. They talked. Soon after, on July 23—the invitation came less than three weeks after Maurice O'Sullivan was married in Connemara—he sent her a note: "Could you come to tea on Friday (4:15), so that we may continue the conversation which was interrupted—very sweetly, I admit—by Handel?"

"That," she wrote later, "was the beginning of our short courtship."

In the months that followed, George told her of his efforts to nurture the Irish language and teach classics in Galway. "George spoke eloquently and passionately," Katharine recalled. Both of them were interested in the classics, both in music. She'd play for him on her new harpsichord, captivating him with her reading of "Callino Casturame," a lilting little Elizabethan air. Sometimes they'd meet in his rooms. Or he'd come to tea at her parents' house, Girton Gate.

Katharine Stewart—"Katten" to her friends, and soon to George—came from a large family prominent in the academic and musical life of the old university town. Her father, Hugh Stewart, dean of Trinity College and a lecturer in French, was an ardent Francophile; the family often spoke French at the dinner table. Her mother, Jessie Stewart, was a first-generation woman classics scholar at Newnham College; she and George liked to talk about Walter Headlam, the King's classicist who'd inspired George's earliest work on Greek lyric meter. Katharine, who would herself contribute to Mozart scholarship and maintain a lifetime's devotion to the keyboard, had three sisters and a brother. All cared for music. All were caught up in the surging political currents of the day; Katharine's sister Frida would drive an ambulance in Spain during the civil war there. They enjoyed their privileges, yet, as Katharine recounted in notes intended to form the basis for a biography of her husband, they all found ways to escape what they experienced as Cambridge's elitist grip. As for Katten and George, it is hard to see them as anything but superbly matched. "We did feel this instant sympathy," she'd say.

By mid-August, three weeks after Katharine's piano recital at King's, they were engaged. "What thrilling, wonderful, lovely news!" Frida, closest to Katharine among her siblings, wrote her. George, it seemed to her, "hits you in the eye as a person of beauty and sincerity and sensitiveness, and I thought him charming but," she went on, "didn't know he was so wise!"

George took Katharine to Dulwich to meet his mother, who welcomed her warmly. She met his brothers and sisters, too, all but one of whom still lived at home on Lovelace Road. Lorlie, the musician of the family, played the cello; she and Katharine tried some sonatas together. The elder sister, Maisie, who'd lost her fiancé in the war, had taken over the family accountancy business when their father died; it had been George's for the asking, had he wanted it. Brother Hugh had served in the merchant marine but was just then unemployed, and discouraged. George's much younger brother, Oscar, just sixteen, was at school.

On October 4, 1934, George and Katharine were married in Girton Church; they might have preferred a civil wedding, Katharine would later explain, but dispensed with it in deference to her father and his mother, who had grown increasingly religious. They honeymooned in Ringstead Mill, north of Cambridge, in Norfolk, where they stayed in the house of a family friend. They walked by the sea, read Shakespeare in the evenings.

Their marriage lasted more than half a century, until George's death in 1987, and was marked by tenderness, honesty, and a profound communion of values. They shared much, felt for each other great respect and love. "I am thinking of you constantly, but after 8 p.m. even more so," he wrote to her from Cambridge one day about a year after their marriage, when she had to leave town for the day. "Outwardly I shall be listening to the high-table chatter, but inwardly I shall be trying to catch strains of your music, and I am saving up for you a kiss for every note. Good night, my sweet love, take care of yourself, and goodbye, my darling, till tomorrow."

Four years later, as addendum to an otherwise chatty note, George wrote her that he'd learned there were thirty-nine ways of saying "darling" in Irish: "So far, I'm ashamed to say, I have only been able to think of about 12, but here they are, all for you: My heart, my bright heart, [illegible], [illegible], my love, my bright love, my thousand loves, love of my heart, my darling, child of my heart, vein of my heart, my heart's secret."

After their honeymoon, the young couple returned to Cambridge and moved into the house her parents had given them as a wedding present. It was called Lavender Cottage.

The following summer, George took his bride to Ireland.

They went first to Dublin, where they stayed in Raheny as guests of Moya and Crompton Llewelyn Davies. "George had told me much about Moya and her romantic history," Katharine would recall, including "her involvement in the 1916 rebellion and her attachment to Michael Collins. . . . She was very fond of George, though she probably disapproved of his marrying an Englishwoman with so little knowledge of Ireland."

Then it was on to Galway. They stayed at George's old digs at Corrib Lodge, overlooking the river, "whence we could watch the leaping salmon."

"I appreciated the warmth and humor of the Irish, who seemed so different from Cambridge academics," she'd write. "But it was only when we reached Kerry and spent two days on the Blasket Island" that she began to appreciate something of what Ireland really meant to her husband.

They were rowed to the island in a *naomhóg* on Sunday, August 4; she was too seasick to enjoy the scenery. A few days later, back on the mainland, in Ballyferriter, she wrote to her mother about what she had seen of the Blasket, and of her new husband in its glow:

> As soon as the villagers spied a boat coming in, they all ran out of their cottages and down the hill to see who it was. And when they recognized George we had the warmest welcome I've ever seen given, and we were overwhelmed with cries of joy and embraces, and all the way through the village people came running out to greet us. They are the most beautiful people and [most] delightful I've ever met. The old women with shawls over their heads, leaning on their sticks, the men in jerseys and caps (which they never take off) and girls in bright colours, and the most enchanting, elf-like children with pointed chins. You could never get tired of looking at them. . . .
>
> And the room full of people and animals ranging from the ubiquitous cat in front of the fire, through chickens, ducklings, and all kinds of wild fowl, to a donkey or cow in the poorer houses. The language is lovely to listen to, but I wish I understood. There were endless stories and jokes, George talking just like a native and completely at home.

The summer before, in the wake of the publication of *Twenty Years A-Growing*, George had made a triumphant return to the Blaskets with Maurice. Now, with his new wife, he was back. Twelve years before, on his first visit, a foreigner's arrival still counted as an event. Now it verged on commonplace. All through the 1930s, there were times when the island seemed to swarm with visitors.

Chapter 10

Visitors, Strangers, Tourists, Friends

[1937]

At the time of his first visit to the Blasket, George Chambers lived in a house on a fine greenery-softened crescent set back from Temple Fortune Lane in London, not far from a Jewish cemetery. He was a man of commerce and industry— he owned, or managed, a good-sized toy factory— but he had a literary streak, too; he later wrote a book of poetry showing evidence of real feeling and considerable craft. He was born in 1873, and married, with three children; one went on to become an artist, another to immigrate to Australia, marry, and become a farmer. In old age, at least, Chambers was remembered as a quiet and gentle man. He had thin, straight hair, a high forehead, and in later years a beard.

Sometime before the summer of 1931, Chambers decided he wanted to see the lighthouse on the Tiaracht, one of the Lesser Blaskets, three miles west of the big island. He was advised that it was difficult to get to the craggy little outcropping, that he ought to make the Great Blasket his base and, as he wrote later, "get the fisherfolk to take me out to the lighthouse."

Having never heard of the Blaskets, he pulled out a map, found the school that served the village, and wrote to its schoolmaster. A reply soon came from Nóra Ní Shéaghdha, its schoolmistress since 1927. "Nora O'Shea," as he'd call her in his own acount, arranged island lodgings for him in the home of Peats Tom Kearney. In late June 1931, he made the usual trip—by rail to Tralee, the narrow-gauge over the mountain to Dingle, and a car ride via Slea Head to Dún Chaoin—which he would describe as "a bleak, impoverished and scattered village lying under a bare mountain side." The sea was too rough for them to reach the island just then, so he stayed overnight at the post office, whose proprietress—"red-headed and unmarried," Chambers described her—put him up and fed him. The next morning, a Saturday, he was rowed to the island in a *naomhóg*.

Late that first afternoon, hiking up the hill behind the village, he met two girls coming down the other way with a pannier-laden donkey bearing turf. They "wore neither shoes nor stockings and were clothed in little more than rags, but two more beautiful girls I have seldom seen and they were as merry and unaffected with me as though I had been an elder brother." One of them was named Lís. Based on the totality of later events, it seems hard to credit any conclusion but that, however unlikely or outlandish it might seem, George Chambers, at the age of fifty-eight, fell in love with her on the spot or in the days that followed. "Was it chance or divinely planned," he'd write in a poem to her published years later, "that my bleak heart should flower once more?"

The object of his fascination, Lís, pronounced "Leesh," was Eibhlís Ní Shúilleabháin, second cousin of Eibhlín Ní Shúilleabháin, recently emigrated to America, and her brother Maurice, just then writing *Twenty Years A-Growing*. She was twenty years old, dark-featured, with a ravishing smile and thick black hair. In one photo Chambers took of her, he aims the camera from up close and below, her eyes and head turned hard to the side, her dark locks flung round her head in careless abandon. It is intimate and intense. It is no routine tourist snapshot.

On the cold, wet, and windy day after his arrival on the big island, Chambers went out to the Tiaracht with Lís and Nóra Ní Shéaghdha, who were friends. They were rowed the six or seven miles along the back face of the Great Blasket, then across open water to the Tiaracht, by Seán Tom Kearney, whom Lís later recalled to Chambers's mind as "the one with the jutting jaw." They had tea there, perhaps at the lightkeeper's station, then went on to Inishvickillaun, where Nóra, Lís, and other islanders—they all wore shoes now—lined up on the stony porch outside the old Daly house for a picture.

Back on the Great Blasket, Chambers stayed on the second floor of the Kearney place, which he remembered as crowded, dirty, and "verminous, with no comfort of any kind." But he really didn't seem to mind.

Lís Ní Shúilleabháin with her husband Seán and daughter Niamh in about 1938, some seven years after she'd met Londoner George Chambers on the island and begun a correspondence with him that would endure for more than a quarter century.

The island was like nothing he'd ever experienced, a place where most of the children had never seen a tree, or a wheeled vehicle, or an electric light. Now and in a subsequent visit, Chambers took pictures wherever he went. Of an island man, the mainland rising behind him across the sound, caught at an idle moment beside the bare latticework of an unfinished *naomhóg.* Of Nóra and her wide-smiling pupils lined up by age in front of the village school. Of sheep-shearing on the Gravel Strand. Of a dozen island men, garbed identically in caps and jerseys, maneuvering an enormous cow into a *naomhóg.*

Sometime after his return to England, he and the young woman he would call "Eilísh of the Island" began to correspond. "I love to read your letters," she wrote to him in November. "I have everyone [sic] of them yet and a couple of days ago I read them all through again. Have you got mine? . . . I never had such a passion for writing to anyone as I feel in writing to you."

Her letters were written at great cost, in a sometimes awkward English that was, after all, her second language; excerpts here appear just as she wrote them, with no cosmetic alteration. She sometimes labored over them for hours. Occasionally, she apologized for their deficiencies. She needn't have: her letters were spirited and heartfelt, never smothered or tight, and, especially in those first months after he left, maybe more than that. On January 12, 1932, two weeks after receiving a Saint Theresa medal she'd asked him to send her, she wrote:

> Today again is a rather bad day. The sea is rough and risen up, also a good breeze is there. No postman, no cable, no wireless, nothing atall from the mainland, but as you wrote yourself: "The scent of sea-wrack and keen salt spray," and from that my heart goes o'er to G.C. on your London shore. On my neck wearing every day, all the time is my dearest thing on earth. Death won't part me from it. Your letters and things has given me a new life, hope and happiness

"I suppose it was a pity," she added, "that I was not twenty when you were thirty."

Each post day, she went down to the slip in expectation and hope. One day the following month, when she feared not hearing from him, she stayed up at the house instead, only to see her sister coming up the path, blue envelope in hand. "My heart came to my mouth with joy, oh dear what would I do if you would not write again. . . . I love your letters and yourself and your family and everything you send me makes me as happy as the day is long."

He did write again, and so did she, often with a fresh, appealing frankness:

> I would love to answer all your questions but it is a task but its for you and indeed no matter how hard I'll try to do everything for you . . . but I am afraid and it is troubling me that I have not as much knowledge in life as to know what to tell you rightly. An Island girl without much education what would she know up to you oh dear me.

In the same letter, she resorts to doggerel: "My ink is bad and my pen is old but my love for you will never grow cold."

She added, "We are together now. . . . . . . .I mean that the two of us are together. We are nearly by our letters." "S.W.A.L.K." on a letter, she explained to him, meant "sealed with a loving kiss," then added:

"I must say Good night now dearest because it is getting late with best love and regards to George from Eilish," followed by a dozen or more kisses—though "I suppose that they'll be cold before they reach you."

From time to time, without shame or artifice, she asked him for something, like the Saint Theresa medal, or "cards" for combing wool, or his wife's cast-off clothes. And he would oblige, or send something on his own—boxing gloves for Lís's brother Seán, or a dictionary. Thank you for the books, she wrote to him early in their correspondence. "It is yourself that knows the best of books. An English song book wouldn't it be nice, I could sing you know."

On June 7, 1932, she reported that Robin Flower—whom Chambers may have known even before his visit—had brought to the island with him a young Cambridge scholar. "I met Kenneth Jackson and had a little talk with him," she wrote to Chambers, but assured him, "I don't ever go down to the strand with him nor either write his name in the sand, oh no indeed. If George was here we would go down to the strand these lovely evening and write in the sand." She realized it was almost a year since they'd spent that day on the Tiaracht. "The very best day in my life I ever enjoyed. Will a day like it never come again?"

In early 1933, Lís's letters took a new turn. Shrove, just before Lent, was the usual time to conclude marriages, but this year, she wrote, there'd been none. That was March 3. But on April 27 she wrote Chambers in these words:

> My best friend, I have every thought of getting married. I hope
> you will love to hear it and your dear Eilish of the Island, stay-
> ing always in her dear Island home. I hope we will be the best of
> friends as always. Would married life be so cruel to change such
> friends. I am very sure in the next letter I will be able to tell you
> everything about it but at present I can't tell you anymore.

Nine days later, on May 6, in a little ceremony in Ballyferriter sparsely attended because of bad weather, she married Seán Ó Criomhthain, son of Tomás, the Islandman. It was the day before her twenty-second birthday. "I love my husband and my home," she wrote Chambers a few days later, "all the world has changed to me, everything for the better. Let us all praise God in Heaven."

Accompanying Lís's letter to Chambers came one from her new husband: "Just a Line to Let you know that I was the lucky one to fall in touch with your Island girl. It was not today or yesterday I was in her company But with the Last Seven years and see now what I have gained by it. To have my whole Heart's desire."

I don't know how Chambers felt on reading this, though I can guess. I do know that their correspondence endured, each occasionally ruffling the other's feathers, but mostly with great affection, and never flagging for too long, for at least the next twenty-five years.

"There are many visitors on the Island already but they are all strangers to us," Lís wrote Chambers early that summer of 1933. "They all have my father-in-law's book." Since its publication in 1929, Tomás's books, especially *An tOileánach,* had put the Blasket on the map, made of it an object of curiosity and interest. In 1931, Tomás wrote to his son Thomas in the States: "Manny the strangers that come heare this summer visiting the Island all of them took my picture, I had to write my name on the book for the whole of them, Professor's Priests, Monks, Brothers, Sisters, every sort off people." By 1933, there was talk of an English translation. But then Flower, who was preparing it, was injured in a fall from a horse; it finally appeared in 1934.

By then Maurice, Moya, and George had beaten Tomás to the English-language punch, with the appearance, in May 1933, of their trans-lation of *Fiche Blian ag Fás.* "It was a great Loss for us for O'Sullivan's book *Twenty Years a-Growing* took the market from us," Lís's husband wrote Chambers in October.

It was, of course, the two together, first Tomás's gritty account and then Maurice's in all its wonderment, in Irish and English both, that did it: "Within the space of four years," Daniel Binchy wrote in 1934, "one small island, with a population of less than 150 souls, has contributed to the scanty stock of original literature in modern Irish the only two works which, in my opinion at least, are worth reading for their own sake." And *they,* in turn, forever altered the Blaskets in the popular imagination, making them into a literary destination. "There is a time and it is not so very long ago," Nóra Ní Shéaghdha would look back from 1940 in an Irish-language memoir published that year, "when a person would prefer to scrape a finger on a rock than think of spending a short time holidaying on the Great Blasket." Now all that had changed.

"Of all years this year was the best," Lís wrote Chambers on August 21, 1933; "never before was the Island so full and taken with visitors." A group of male teachers had come and actually set up a tent, she told him. The islanders furnished them with potatoes and fish. The Kearney place was fairly full to bursting with visitors. Now that they'd finally left, "the Blasket people will have a rest."

This moment in the island's transformation was captured in a cover illustration for the June 1933 issue of *Dublin Opinion,* a literary magazine. It shows a craggy, Blasket-like isle to which cartoonish writers cling, pecking away at cartoonish typewriters, manuscript piling up around them. An old island woman is accompanied by a boy lugging her typewriter. A publisher is being rowed away from the island in a boat sinking under the weight of manuscripts bound for Dublin and London. The caption: "The Literary Wave Hits the Islands."

Predictably, one staple of the new attention was the overwrought recounting of exotic island perils. One writer, Donal O'Cahill, lovingly described the risks of being rowed to the island, picturing "ridge after ridge of hissing water that each moment threatened to overwhelm us." What chance had they in their flimsy boat?

> Boat! It was a slip of a thing of light trellised laths and tarred canvas—a "cockle-shell," incredible, everything, anything, but my conception of what at that instant should be a boat. Feverishly I poked the side with my finger and might have poked it through. I felt the water pulsing, surging, crashing against it. . . . Was this all that was between us and how many fathoms of treacherous sea?

You get the idea.

Seán Ó Faoláin, who made his island stay part of a memoir, *An Irish Journey,* bragged of sitting by the hearth with Tomás Ó Criomhthain—"a pompous old man" whose favorite proverbs he proceeded to challenge or dismiss. "I enjoyed tussling with old Tomás," he allowed, "and he enjoyed tussling with me." On the island at the time were "three professional Gaels," along with a young Englishman from London. At first Ó Faoláin made light of how they skipped across the island in "innocent elation." But then, abruptly, he seemed to correct himself, as he recalled his own first exposure to the Gaeltacht years before. He'd felt just

> the same sense of release. It was like taking off one's clothes for a swim naked in some mountain-pool. Nobody who has not had this sensation of suddenly "belonging" somewhere—of finding

The cover of Dublin Opinion, *June 1936.* By this time, the Great Blasket, population *150,* had produced three important works of Irish-language literature.

the lap of the lost mother—can understand what a release the discovery of the Gaelic world meant to modern Ireland.

Robin Flower, whose first visit to the island by now went back more than twenty years, also kept coming, as did new visitors on his recommendation or in his company. In the spring of 1931, he brought with him a British Museum colleague, forty-two-year-old Edward Meyerstein, novelist, poet, and confirmed curmudgeon; somebody once described him as "throbbing with interior distress." Meyerstein wrote of the men gathering seaweed and stuffing it into panniers. Of the islanders' "grave courtesy." Of "an old woman, with a black shawl enveloping her head, blowing up a fire with her lips, while the light from the kindled turf invests her eyes with a sort of prophetic glow." His fortnight on the island, he wrote a friend, "has shown me very clearly what is wrong with me"; Meyerstein makes his Blasket idyll sound like therapy.

It also gave the bilious Englishman a chance to see Flower in his element. A Dublin student and an umbrella-toting German that Meyerstein apparently loathed, both studying Irish, accompanied them. "We feed together," is how Meyerstein put it, "and Flower spreads the wealth of his ripe and varied knowledge on our bread and marmalade. To him this place is a dream of his youth; everybody loves him and runs up to shake his hand, and he teases the girls to his heart's content—all is laughing and merriment."

George Thomson and Maurice O'Sullivan came back together in the summer of 1934 to celebrate the success of *Twenty Years A-Growing*, posing for photographs in their crisp city duds beside the islanders they'd left behind. The following year, as we've seen, George was back with his bride, Katten. And Chambers returned in the summer of 1938 to see Lís and her new family.

But many came, too, not to solidify ties of many years' standing but to see the island for the first time. All through the 1930s and up to the beginning of World War II they came, in greater numbers than ever. They came because they'd read the books. They came for the love of the language—though, as Daniel Binchy would observe, many had more enthusiasm than they had Gaelic. They came because they *needed* to learn Irish; some jobs in the Free State government required it. And they came to gather what by the 1930s had come to be seen as among the island's chief resources, its stories—imbibed not from books, but from the lips of the islanders themselves.

. . .

A father declares he will give his daughter to whichever of her suitors can show he suffers most for her love. One young man says his suffering is like a thorn against his toe. A second, that the love he suffers is like a knife through his heart. A third, that it is like a crumb stuck in his teeth. The third suitor wins the girl.

This, told in the brisk telegraphic style anthropologists sometimes use to efficiently record their content, is a folktale. So is this:

A young priest, owing to complaints about his behavior, is to be defrocked. But he's allowed to say one final Mass. Forbidding the clerk to light the candles, he lights them himself by simply blowing on them. In the face of this miracle, he is reinstated.

And finally this: A poor widow extracts a fish spine from the flipper of a seal. Years later, she arrives at a house whose host recognizes her: now very much human, he had once been a seal, fated to remain so until a widow should pick a fish spine from his flipper. He marries the widow's daughter.

All these—they "tell" better than they read—are folktales. All were recorded on the Great Blasket between the years 1932 and 1937. The word "folklore" went back only to an English coinage of 1846. Before then there was scant reason to think much about the "folk"; their stories and songs were not yet so threatened as they would be when modern life turned industrial, urban, and fast. Irish folklore encompassed local legends, saints, miracles, supernatural beings, fairies, heroes. Some had diffused through the traditions of several countries. By the time folklorists reached the Blaskets, two scholars, Antti Aarne and Stith Thompson, had fashioned a taxonomy of them, breaking them down into numbered categories. Cinderella, for example, was AT 510.

Folktales were not always chaste: A married couple attends a gathering at which the wife's former lover is present. Her husband's suspicions are aroused when he notices that the two yawn in unison. He weighs drowning her on the way home, but she convinces him of her abiding fidelity.

Nor were folk stories always high-minded: A woman farts in public, but a young man saves her from embarrassment by insisting he's the culprit. Grateful, she marries him. Then, one night, the two of them in bed, the man farts. She leaves him.

These stories were all taken down by Kenneth Jackson, the young English scholar Lís Ní Shúilleabháin met when he first came in 1932 (and with whom, as she assured Chambers, she *didn't* go down to the beach to write their names in the sand). A twenty-two-year-old graduate of Saint John's College, Cambridge, where he'd studied archeology, anthropology, and the classics, Jackson had only just set out on the study of Celtic languages that would occupy his life. Robin Flower had told him, "I must get Peig Sayers to be my teacher [. . . ,] that she had the finest repertoire of folk tales in Corca Duibhne," the Irish name for West Kerry. Jackson, who on the island liked to wear shorts, knee socks, and a brass-buckled belt that made him look like a Boy Scout, had never heard much spoken Irish. But he did know the international phonetic alphabet, used for recording speech in any language. He'd see Peig every day, have her tell him one of her folktales, and "as she recited, I wrote them down by ear in phonetics, though I had no idea at first what they meant. Then I read them back to her and she corrected any mistakes, and told me what it all meant in English, which she spoke fluently and correctly." He came away with "an abiding interest in the folktale as a literary and social phenomenon."

The Irish literary revival of the late nineteenth century had grown in large part through a new appreciation of folklore; Douglas Hyde, Lady Gregory, and Yeats were all drawn to the expiring world it represented. "Folk-lore," wrote Yeats in 1893, "is at once the Bible, the Thirty-Nine Articles, and the Book of Common Prayer, and well-nigh all the great poets have lived by its light. Homer, Aeschylus, Sophocles, Shakespeare, and even Dante, Goethe, and Keats, were little more than folk-lorists with musical tongues." Yeats published two compilations of folklore after 1888. Lady Gregory collected stories from stone-breakers, potato-diggers, even the beggars who came to her door. And long before his seminal essay, "The Necessity of De-Anglicising Ireland," Hyde had recorded stories and songs in his native County Roscommon.

In England, Hyde wrote in 1890, the folktale was a victim of "materialism and civilization"; Kenneth Jackson went so far as to argue that "what we mean by folk culture is almost entirely a thing of the past" there. Ireland, though, was another story. Cut off from the social and economic forces that buffeted England, something of its folk culture hung on. Its bards of old, who'd once served an Irish nobility that no longer existed, had diffused into peasant life. The result, wrote Jackson, was that "learning became popularised. . . . If poets had to become labourers, yet labourers often became poets." Hence, the *seánchaidhthe,* folk historians—preservers, as Jackson wrote, "of every kind of tradition and superstition and belief, of charms and prayers, riddles and rhymes; singers of folksongs and above all tellers of folktales." A vestige of them yet remained in the Irish-speaking west.

It risked dying out there, too, now, especially among the young. "Yet while the older generation lasts we have still a living folk tradition," Jackson wrote, "probably the richest in the world." To him, Ireland's village storytellers were "the cinemas and wirelesses" of their day. He remembered "Peig sitting by the fire in the dim lamplight and the room crowded with half-seen faces, grown-ups as well as children, listening to the stories they often had heard before but never tired of hearing."

By 1935, a new Irish Folklore Commission had begun an ambitious project, bent, as Jackson put it, on rescuing "such of this lore as is left to us." The Blaskets and the neighboring mainland were of special interest. But long before the Commission's collectors arrived, Robin Flower appreciated what he had around him. On April 12, 1930, a British Museum committee authorized "special leave up to 10 days, if found necessary . . . to Mr. R. Flower, Deputy Keeper, to enable him to complete a collection of gramophone records of the folk-lore tales of the Great Blasket Island, Co. Kerry."

"My visit is an extraordinary success," Flower wrote Idris Bell, his boss at the Museum, probably toward the end of May. "I am collecting folktales and folksongs and lilting tunes at a great rate," though it was

> a task of some difficulty sometimes to set the people to work. They feel it an unnatural thing, to speak or sing into a pipe, and the noise of the motor distracts them. They said that the feeling is as though the pipe were draining your breath out of you. It would amaze you to see me wheedling an old man or a girl to tell a tale or sing a song, or dragging up one of the lads to lilt or whistle a tune into the pipe.

Flower was using the Ediphone, an early recording device that bore an enamel plate on the back referring to the Thomas Edison patents that protected it. You wound it up the way you might an old-fashioned mechanical alarm clock. Its spring motor turned a heavy wax cylinder about the size and shape of a modern beer can; these were the "gramophone records," which embodied sound much as flat "vinyl" discs did later in the century. As the informant spoke or sang into a hornlike speaker, the ups and downs in air pressure passed through a gooseneck pipe to the stylus, which cut wavelike grooves in the revolving wax cylinder. No electronic amplifier, no electronic anything; it all worked mechanically. With a box of a dozen cylinders, the equipment was bulky and heavy. Mary Kearney's younger brother Seán would remember how he and other boys were recruited to carry it, their payment in cigarettes dispensed by Flower, who smoked nonstop.

Five or six minutes per cylinder, or about as many typed pages—that's all you got from each one. Storytellers learned to hol-l-d their thought while the collector extracted the old cylinder, replaced it with the new, and set it to turn once more. The result wasn't exactly high-fidelity; on playback, you could hear the contrivance's internal whirrings along with something like what had been said or sung; the far-off magic of its sound could never be confused with the original.

Flower was himself transfixed by the results. Hearing one story reminiscent of a French fable, from an island woman who insisted it had happened just like that in her grandfather's day, he wrote Bell at the Museum:

> I like to think of these tales as independent of time, existing in a kind of folk eternity and only accidentally localised and set in a temporal world. I get the sensation sometimes as I listen to the people rattling them off in the traditional style that by a kind of extension of wireless I am listening to innumerable voices long silent repeating, again and again, the old tales with constant local variation but no sense of the original intention.

Soon, Flower wrote, he had "folksongs enough to make a book," and folktales, too, and had to put in for more wax cylinders from Dublin. "I give concerts in the evenings with the records of the day," he wrote Bell,

> and practically the whole village attends. It's most entertaining to hear their comments on the tales and the songs and the miracle of the machine which has made an extraordinary impression on them. When one of the old ones heard it for the first time, "Now," she said, "now I believe that the other world exists."

Flower's most inspired informant, as she was for Jackson and others, was Peig Sayers. When later, in the 1940s, Peig moved to the mainland, folklore collectors converged on her house in Vicarstown. During one three-year span, one of them filled six thousand pages of manuscript, a million words or more, with stories she'd grown up hearing from her father or had accumulated in the decades since.

Peig Sayers was no islander by birth but had married into the island in 1892, when, at eighteen, she became the wife of Pádraig "Flint" Ó Gaoithín; like many island women, she went by her maiden name. By 1911, she had given birth to ten children, of whom seven survived into adulthood. One of the seven later fell to his death from an island cliff. Five immigrated to America. A smile came readily to Peig's face, it was said, but a hearty laugh only rarely.

It was not anything in her personal history, however, that led to her enduring fame—or, as we'll see, her peculiar notoriety. What did was the wealth of stories she'd absorbed and the flair and finesse with which she told them. "Her changes of mood and face were like the changes of running water," it was said of her. "As she talked, her hands would be moving too; a little clap of the palms to cap a phrase, a flash of the thumb over the shoulder to mark a mystery, a hand hushed to mouth for mischief or whispered secrecy."

Another folklore collector, a Dún Chaoin native named Joe Daly, recalled Peig's

enormous power when she was sorrowful. I heard the story of her son's fall down a cliff. She went into all the details—how his body was brought home, bruised and battered. She cried, and then clapped her hands, like that, turned around and continued her story without a hint of sadness after that. It was as if, by clapping her hands, she'd wiped the sorrow from her mind.

Peig's hard life story was, as published in Irish, later made a high-school graduation requirement; in the Free State, she was seen as the personification of enduring womanhood, rural, poor, and pious. But to many an Irish man or woman of a certain age who grew up having to read her in Irish as a teenager, she seemed the personification, too, of all things old and woeful. She'd look out from the covers of her books—the second of them fittingly titled *An Old Woman's Reflections*—and all you'd see was that wizened oval face, lost in bulky fabric, all shawl, sweater, and apron, and those crinkly eyes. Other photos captured her when she was in the hospital, and blind, and looked more deathly yet. These, and her tales of hardship, pain, anguish, and death, left most Irish students feeling that, once out of school, they wanted nothing ever again to do with Old Peig.

Peig Sayers

The dirty little secret, of course, is that Peig was not always old. Nor is the evidence for this heretical assertion simply that, as mother of ten, she was once, after all, a young mother. Look at an old snapshot that captures her high cheekbones just so and you realize she had the facial structure of a fashion model. That, and unforgettable eyes. When Robin Flower first met her, Peig Sayers wasn't blind, old, sick, and confined to bed, but still in her thirties. And what comes down to us from Flower, Jackson, and others is that it wasn't just her fund of folklore that won them over, but some deep power of personality, or even something like sex appeal.

"She was a rather tall woman, with the most beautiful eyes, violet in color and triangular in shape," said Kenneth Jackson, who met her when she was in her late fifties.

> It was easy to see that she had been a beauty when she was young, and in those days was called Peig Bhui, Blond Peig. . . . She was a strong character, very unlike, apparently, the meek, pious woman on the frontispiece photograph in Mary Kennedy's book on her, called Peig. She had a tremendous sense of humor and of fun. She

was shrewd, and could show a sharp tongue when she wanted to. I became devoted to her, almost fell in love with her.

In fact, she seemed to exert a hold on most who met her, especially men. When folklorist Brid Mahon met her some years later, she was in her seventies, "with a face scarcely lined, dark expressive eyes and hands, and a wonderful voice," all the makings of an inspired actress. "It was clear to me from the start that she was a man's woman," Mahon wrote. Among women, it was gossip, visitors, the weather. "But let a man cross the door and her face changed, her eyes lit up. The male visitor was given a beaming smile, urged to stir up the fire, offered a drop of whiskey or a fill of tobacco. Thus fortified, she flirted with each man as he arrived until the room was filled."

It was this Peig, then, not the withered old lady looking out from a book cover at generations of hapless Irish teenagers who was Robin Flower's leading informant. Peig's son Mícheál remembered how one evening he came back from fishing to find his mother together with Flower. "He had a big box at the head of the table and anyone would declare from all the fuss that there was something good inside it." The Ediphone, of course. "Now, Peig," said Flower, "I suppose you never before saw the likes of this talking machine." Would she "mind at all putting one of the fine stories you have onto it?" She would not. "All that's in me is a poor tormented woman," Mícheál records his mother saying, "but I wouldn't mind if I thought the boys and girls of my own country would profit from my labours."

And soon, what had become precedent and pattern played itself out in one more variation yet: Tomás's book was out. Maurice's came out in 1933. The once-formidable gap between STORYTELLER and WRITER had shrunk. Peig Sayers a writer? She couldn't read Irish, much less write it. But then Máire Ní Chinnéide came to the island, and soon, sure it was, Peig was an author, too.

Born in Dublin in 1878, the daughter of shop owners, Mary Kennedy, as she was known in English, had attended a school in Dublin run by the Dominican Sisters, graduated in 1900, won a scholarship to Queen's University, taken an academic post in 1903, grown interested in the Gaelic League. Early in the summer of 1932, Kennedy's twenty-three-year-old daughter, Niamh, visited the island to improve her Irish, came away bewitched by the place, and cast a spell in turn on her mother, who then visited the Blaskets and met Peig. The two became friends. Kennedy came back with her husband several times more, in time suggesting to Peig that she dictate her life story to her son Mícheál, recently back from a brief, abortive immigration to the United States. At first Peig resisted. But Kennedy, Mícheál recalled, "would never be satisfied at all until we started to write a book." And so they did.

Peig Sayers, Robin Flower would write, had

> so clean and finished a style of speech that you can follow all the nicest articulation of the language on her lips without any effort; she is a natural orator, with so keen a sense of the turn of phrase and the lifting rhythm appropriate to Irish that her words could be written down as they leave her lips, and they would have the effect of literature with no savour of the artificiality of composition.

And now, when the words left her lips, Mícheál did indeed write them down. Later, according to Mary Kearney's brother Seán, their younger sister Eibhlín, adept at Irish, went through the spelling. When the manuscript reached Mary Kennedy, she lightly edited it and, the following summer, brought it back to the island to read to Peig. She would disappear into Peig's house, an island girl remembered. "We used to peep in through the window. Máire would be writing and Peig talking away."

Late in 1936, the first of two books, *Peig,* was published. "Still another remarkable book from the Blaskets," an early review led off, "this one flung warm to the world from the heart of an old woman of the West Kerry fíor-Ghaeltacht!" Her story, said another, in *The Dublin Magazine,* "is told in fine idiomatic Irish, in a plain vigorous and direct style; the narrative is easy, flowing." By July, a "What Dublin Is Reading" column in the capital listed Peig's book right alongside those of Aldous Huxley and John Gunther. The following year, *Peig* received a prize for Irish-language literature.

And it *was* literature, or had become literature. "Because this inherited store of literary tradition is transmitted orally," one critic said of Peig and her storytelling kind, "it is not less literature than the written word turned into the more lasting mould of manuscript or of print. It is the nucleus of the literature of modern Irish."

On August 15, 1937, people from around Ireland descended on the island to pay homage to Peig Sayers. "The day was beautiful, the sea like milk," Seán Kearney recalled. "The island was black with people." A stage set up outside the island school, according to one visitor, was made up of school desks and "some driftwood planks dripping with dead barnacles." Speeches ensued. Peig "took her honours with a warm-hearted smile, clapping with the others." Men and women, boys and girls, got up to sing Irish songs. Soon the fiddles and melodeons were hauled out and people were dancing.

During this day full of ebullience and cheer, one moment of sobriety intruded, when Peig's son Mícheál read a poem lamenting the death, earlier that year, of Tomás Ó Criomhthain.

On March 9, Lís wrote George Chambers from Dingle, where she'd been preparing for the birth of her second child. Two days before, she told him, her husband and her brother had brought with them news:

> And oh Mr. Chambers, they just stayed ten minutes with me for they were in a great hurry for I must tell and write it down for you in deepest regret that my dearest father-in-law died peacefully and passed away to his reward at seven o'clock that Sunday morning, oh may he rest in peace, Amen, and how I missed being from my home and from his funeral yesterday God only knows.

For two years, Tomás had mostly been confined to bed, in Lís's care. Toward the end, hand and leg paralyzed, he couldn't write, couldn't so much as sign a document, "couldn't even raise his hand above his head," son Seán recalled. And now, with the island at the height of its attention from the world, he was gone.

"On landing on the island," Nóra Ní Shéaghdha wrote in an Irish-language obituary, "the first question a stranger always asked was, 'Where is the house of the Ó Criomhthain?' " He had become a tourist attraction; was there any other way to say it? Everybody wanted a photo of him. "Even when his health began to fail him he would often be led like a child to his seat in the yard, just to please the visitor who was anxiously waiting to secure the 'Islandman's' picture."

One day, it was Nóra herself who wanted one. At first he demurred. "But, Tomás," she implored, "you must remember that men like you will not inhabit the island anymore." That, of course, was a reference—was it ironic or sly? it's hard to tell from her account—to the line in *An tOileánach* he had immortalized: *"Ní bheidh ár leithéidí arís ann,"* the like of us will never be again. And now, with this nod to Tomás's book, "his countenance changed, his face brightened, a smile came on his lips," and he agreed.

Among those counting themselves champions of Tomás and his work was the writer Myles na Gopaleen. *Some champion,* or so it might seem from his bizarre Irish-language novel, inspired by *An tOileánach,* which recurrently parodied "Our likes will not be seen again." *An Béal Bocht,* published in 1941, is supposedly the autobiography of a hapless Gael from a mythical Gaeltacht area known as Corkadoragha. More even than Tomás or Peig, Bonaparte O'Coonassa, born in awful poverty in a cabin shared with chickens and pigs, suffers deprivations unimaginable. His mother, Myles na Gopaleen's protagonist declares,

> took a bucket full of muck, mud and ashes and hen's droppings from the roadside, and spread it around the hearth gladly in front of me. When everything was arranged, I moved over near the fire and for five hours I became a child in the ashes—a raw youngster rising up according to the old Gaelic tradition. Later at midnight I was taken and put into bed but the foul stench of the fireplace stayed with me for a week; it was a stale, putrid smell and I do not think that the like will ever be there again.

So it goes, all the book through, one calamity after another, as befits a wretched Gael from the west of Ireland. And always Tomás's catchphrase, intoned as the last word: "Their like would not be seen again."

An Béal Bocht might seem to resist translation, yet translated into English it was, in 1973, as *The Poor Mouth.* Edgy, manic illustrations by the American artist Ralph Steadman memorably captured the dark, sardonic tone of the book. Its author, this Myles na Gopaleen, was actually a pub-roving Dublin civil servant and newspaper columnist, Brian O'Nolan, who also wrote under the name Flann O'Brien. For years he was Ireland's most mercilessly, deliciously, unrepentantly satiric voice. He called *An Béal Bocht,* which others acclaimed a comedic masterpiece, one "prolonged sneer"; he'd polished it off in a week, he boasted. And yet, he'd explain, it was his abiding respect for Tomás's "majestic" book that had led him to write it in the first place.

The impact on him of *An tOileánach* had been "explosive." Here was a book "not to be seen or thought about and certainly not to be discussed with strangers"—like an intimate episode in the life of a couple so intense, for love or grief, it could never be mentioned aloud. It was something so fresh and authentic that, na Gopaleen made it seem, he *feared* for it. And the island life it depicted? Tomás's book was a "noble salute from them about to go away."

And of course it *was* going away.

The sun might yet shine on the Blaskets in those days of the 1930s. You might still find a hint of Maurice O'Sullivan's high heart and spirit there. And Peig was queen that fine August day in 1937. But even if its outward celebrity still mostly masked its economic and social decline, the Blasket could now sometimes seem a withered caricature of itself.

It is a day late in the 1930s, three decades after Synge, Marstrander, and Flower first ventured onto the island. Two islanders and two visitors line up in front of a camera, alternating, like men and women at a

Visitors and islanders, lined up for the camera. Can you tell who's who?

dinner party. Conceivably the picture emerged spontaneously, capping a day of hearty geniality. But I don't think so; hearty geniality is nowhere evident. We know the names of the islanders: they are brothers, Mícheál and Seánín Mhicil Ó Súilleabháin, second cousins of the author Maurice, both in their twenties, both fishermen. Mícheál is the older. Seánín is an accomplished fiddler who played at Peig's "crowning."

As for the visitors, we know nothing of them, except that they are beautiful. Beautiful, that is, in the outward way a prince is beautiful—regardless of his looks, simply owing to the finery in which he's adorned, the ease and self-confidence with which he carries himself. Here are two princes from the mainland, both wearing sport coats, their wide-lapel shirts pulled out over their coat collars—it must be the fashion of the day—standing erect and assured. One holds a cigarette, has a wide, geeky grin. The other, hand in pants pocket, the stripes of his sweater peeking out from his open jacket, is turned three-quarters toward the camera, seems more practiced at this sort of thing, cool and comfortable in his own skin.

And the Ó Súilleabháin brothers? They look like twins in their close-fitting fisherman's sweaters and caps. They are both dark, with black brows, stand slouched, a smile on neither of them, their faces set, resolute. They look a little menacing, actually, or would if the scene were less ceremonial. They don't look gay, or at their ease; it's not hard to imagine them dragooned before the camera, just for the shot: *Here we are on the Great Blasket, with real peasant fishermen.* That may be seeing more in the image than is there. But certainly the comfort that Flower, Thomson, and Marie-Louise Sjoestedt found in the island world, as friends of Tomás, Maurice, and the others, born of days and nights in and out of one another's houses, is absent, any bond between visitor and islander reduced to the duration of a twenty-fifth-of-a-second snapshot.

February 27, 1939. Lís Ní Shúilleabháin writes to George Chambers:

> Tonight is very fine and the moon is shining bright and I feel a promising of summer in the air and sky. I feel very light hearted about that but such a night in the Island ten years ago when I was just young is very different from this night. There is no stir or sound in this Island tonight, no children laughing or shouting in the moonlight nor later on by this hour when children would be off in their dreams you could hear miles away with the echoes

of the strand rows of fair young colleens in four and five in rows after each other singing lovely Irish songs of love and joy and the older folk with their heads out in the open doors gladly listening to them. The Island is just dead I may say but just for old times sake I sang a few verses myself of the old school songs we used to have. Pity you were not listening.

Chapter 11

A Green Irish Thread

[1940]

By the time of Lís's letter to Chambers in 1939, George Thomson was married, with one child and another on the way, but no longer living in Cambridge; he was a professor now, at the University of Birmingham, far removed alike from the great academic centers of England and from the Blasket. By now, though, the Blasket was irreparably part of him.

All his life, the island would billow up through his intellectual and scholarly work, projecting into the thoughts he thought, the books he wrote, the values he held most dear. In what he called "the village I know best," he had met spirited men and women, living amid the seas and cliffs, distant from the dubious comforts and contrivances of the cities. What he had learned from them influenced his social and political views as well as colored his ideas about the ancient Greeks, whose civilization lay at the center of his intellectual life. "From his earliest book, on *Greek Lyric Metre*, through his *Aeschylus and Athens*, to his *Studies in Ancient Greek Society*," Stanford University classicist Richard Martin has asserted, "runs a green Irish thread."

· · ·

When the Thomsons were married in 1934, Katharine's parents had presented them with a house in Cambridge, Lavender Cottage, where they would live for most of the next three years. In the small studio upstairs, George, still a fellow at King's, worked on his new edition of Aeschylus' *Oresteia*. Downstairs, Katharine gave piano lessons. "He must have become immune to the noise of the piano, which he endured stoically for the rest of his life," Katharine would write. Radio chatter drifting upstairs sometimes brought him down to "politely request me to reduce the volume." But live music never did.

An artfully composed photo of George survives from around this time. It shows him in profile, sitting back, puffing on his pipe, absorbed in a newspaper, the folds of its pages mimicking the soft curves of his jacket. He is a young man at the height of his powers, at home in the cocoon he and Katharine happily share.

Outside, though, the world was changing, awash in historical tides that risked drowning out the voices of Aeschylus and Beethoven and embroiling the Thomsons in irresistibly more urgent concerns. Just now, Europe was still at peace, if on the crumbling foundations of the 1919 Versailles Treaty. But all across the Continent, ideas wrangled, reaching for the extremes. Fervency was all.

George Thomson at his ease, mid-1930s

In the year just before she'd become reacquainted with George, while studying piano in Frankfurt during the summer of 1933, Katharine had seen the emergent Nazi Germany up close. Kristallnacht was then still five years away, and Hitler's threats to the Jews and his European neighbors were still mostly talk. But Katharine had seen Nazi rallies, once heard Hitler, who'd become chancellor that January, inflame his audience with anti-Jewish ravings. Many of her teachers at the conservatory had been Jewish; all would lose their jobs. Yet some of her friends in Cambridge, she'd write, "saw some good in the new regime, feeling that the wrongs suffered by Germany through the Versailles treaty were being righted." To some, and not just in Germany, Hitler was a bulwark against Bolshevism, a return to sturdy national roots after the cataclysm of the Western Front.

For most in their circle, however, Soviet communism tugged at them more sympathetically. Stalinist totalitarianism and terror were not then so commonly understood for what they were. Many saw the new Soviet state, and the high-flown Marxist ideas on which it claimed to be based, as answer to the economic hardships besetting Europe. To some, the Soviet Union recently birthed from the ashes of czarist Russia was symbol of a new and better world to come. George was among them.

One of his friends during this period was Austrian-born philosopher Ludwig Wittgenstein, whom he'd met in 1929. "He was nearly always tense," George would remember, "even in his light-hearted moods." They'd dine at high table at Trinity or at a tea shop, later settle in Wittgenstein's rooms to talk. And what they talked about was often Marxism, which, as George put it later, had become "an intellectual force" in Cambridge. Wittgenstein, fourteen years his senior, hadn't much immersed himself in the Marxist classics. But several of Wittgenstein's friends were Marxists; he was "alive to the evils of unemployment and fascism"; he was drawn to Soviet ways and visited Russia in the fall of 1935. Of just such intellectual and political peregrinations Cambridge saw many specimens during these years.

Another of the Thomsons' left-leaning friends, about George's own age, was Roy Pascal, a lecturer in German at one of the Cambridge colleges, and a member of the Communist Party. Pascal gave George Russian lessons. George and Katharine read Trotsky, became intrigued by all things Russian. England suffered from horrendous joblessness, whereas in the Soviet Union, George heard it said, unemployment had been abolished. "We were moving more and more to the left," said Katharine later. Soon, like Wittgenstein, the Thomsons decided to visit the Soviet Union, and after their memorable trip to Ireland in the summer of 1935, they did so.

Joining a tour organized by a theatrical exchange group, they left from Greenwich with Katharine's sister Frida. They toured art galleries in Leningrad, saw a Jewish Theater production of *King Lear* in Moscow, visited factories and day-care centers. They were charmed by friendly Russian soldiers who took to the chessboard at any leisured moment. At one point, George would recount, their car was "held up by throngs of children in festive costume, who greeted us with songs and pelted the car with flowers. When we got to Red Square we found ourselves in a vast sea of colour," children by the thousands dancing and singing.

From what George saw in Russia—and from what he had been told, and what he wanted to believe—the new Soviet state encouraged its minority national cultures, didn't trample them as Britain had Ireland's. National theaters thrived from the Polish border to the Bering Straits, Shakespeare was more vibrant in the Soviet republics than in England: "Not only will these cultures survive," George wrote in a 1944 essay reflecting his early infatuation with the Soviet experiment, "but the modern industrial civilisation into which they have been transplanted will itself be enriched." At least as seen through rose-colored-enough glasses, the Soviet system seemed to work. "This is what might have been, and may yet be, in Connemara," he concluded, referring to his early-1930s efforts in Galway. "Where I had failed with 300,000, they have succeeded with a 100 million."

The Thomsons were won over. English socialist economists Sidney and Beatrice Webb had written a popular book about the Soviet Union with the subtitle *A New Civilization?* To Katharine, "there seemed no need for the question-mark." Back home, they became active in the burgeoning anti-fascist movement and in a Russian-English friendship club. That year, 1935, George Thomson joined the Communist Party. He was thirty-two.

His loyalties would shift over the years to a degree, but he would remain a Marxist all his life. He would write scholarly and interpretive studies, in areas of his scholarly expertise, from a Marxist perspective. In 1947, he would become a member of the Communist Party's Executive Committee. A photograph from this period shows George at a meeting of party comrades in jacket and tie, his formidable swathe of dark hair swept across his forehead, mouth set, gaze straight ahead—more so even than the others, looking very serious indeed.

It is not true that *everybody was doing it,* joining the party, but among politically minded young British intellectuals, certainly, enough were; party membership swelled to fifty-six thousand by 1942. In 1937, George visited Moya in Dublin and wrote Katharine about it: "I had a rather unsatisfactory discussion with Moya about the state of the world. She does not altogether approve of my present opinions, while I feel that her individualism is untenable." To George, of course, communism bore the lingering sweetness of social and communitarian ideals he had tasted in the Blaskets.

In December 1936, George was appointed to a chair in Greek studies at the University of Birmingham, and by January of the following year, he was settled there. His tutor at King's, J. T. Sheppard, was appalled at the news he was going off to "teach the barbarians in Birmingham." Here was a self-consciously working-class city, "city of a thousand trades," where they made chocolate, airplanes, and electrical equipment, not transcendent ideas. Its residents, "Brummies," jabbered in a distinctive accent not pleasing to every English ear. Still, as Katharine wrote, "We were both glad to get away" from Cambridge elitism. Wittgenstein and he had been drawn together, George would say, not by philosophy or politics but by their "common distaste for the intellectual life of Cambridge."

Several times before, his impatience with it had driven him away—to the Blaskets, to Dublin, to Galway. This time, though, it was for keeps. He and Katharine would remain there for the rest of their lives. They'd raise their children there. George would run classes for workers at a local automobile factory. He'd befriend a group of surrealist painters, help launch Katharine's folksinging group, the Clarion Singers.

At first, George went ahead to Birmingham while Katharine stayed back in Cambridge, where she had just given birth to their first child, Elizabeth. George wrote her on January 11, 1937: "Here I am in my room. It is quite a nice one, rather like a business-man in his office, but I don't object to that. I have just seen the lecturers and conferred with them about the time-table." He was teaching Homer on Mondays and Thursdays that first term, Aeschylus' *Agamemnon* on Wednesdays and Fridays. He had lunches to go to, meetings of the Graduates Club, Classical Association teas on Friday afternoons—the familiar round of classes and academic functions that were the lot of any young scholar in his first real professorial job.

But inwardly, George was settling into territory familiar to him for years now, of memories, impressions, ideas, and preoccupations dating back to his days on the Blasket. The Blasket of Maurice and Tomás simmered in his mind together with the Greece of Homer and Aeschylus to create an intellectual stew satisfying to countless readers and thinkers in the years ahead.

When he left Galway in 1934, George left behind him at Corrib Lodge a bound notebook with faux-marble endpapers that over the years would absorb the random scribbles, word games, and impromptu artworks of the children in his landlady's family. Its cover was inscribed:

The Oresteia of Aeschylus
translated into English verse
by
George Thomson

Aeschylus was George's deepest love, in particular the fifth-century B.C.E. trilogy known as the *Oresteia,* which, after Homer, critic D. W. Lucas would say was "the most valuable of the legacies of antiquity."

The *Oresteia,* the story of Orestes, is a story of murder, revenge, justice, and compassion. It begins with *Agamemnon,* first of the trilogy, when a watchman at last spies in the distance lit beacons heralding the fall of Troy, and with it King Agamemnon's return.

> I've prayed the Gods' deliverance from this labour
> A full year's length of watching, couched dog-wise
> On the roof of the Atreidae where I scan
> The congregations of the stars of night.

That's George's translation of it, dating from about 1934.

In 1938, Cambridge University Press issued his two-volume edition of the *Oresteia,* dedicated to Maurice O'Sullivan, complete with an English verse translation that one reviewer lauded as "direct, fluent, and dignified." Now the Watchman's monologue reads:

> I've prayed God to release me from sentry duty
> All through this long year's vigil, like a dog
> Couched on the roof of Atreus, where I study
> Night after night the pageantry of this vast
> Concourse of stars. . . .

George had been *working* at it. He was a professor, and a Marxist—and yet a laborer of sorts, too. Aeschylus, the poetry of the *Oresteia,* Agamemnon's murder, Orestes' revenge, the goddess Athena's inspired intervention—all this was the object of his most devoted attentions, as it had been since he'd first witnessed Sheppard's 1921 production of it in school. But now, almost two decades later, colored over by life experience in the Blaskets and elsewhere, and by his developing ideologies, it held new meaning to him.

In September 1940, in a rudely bound edition rushed into print after the outbreak of the war with Germany, George came out with *Aeschylus and Athens: A Study in the Social Origins of Drama,* which would be translated into at least seven languages. In it, he used evidence from ethnographic and anthropological sources to suggest, as British historian Joseph Needham summed up his argument a few years later, that Greek tragedy owed something to "the primitive collectivism of the Greek people." Before the glory of fifth-century Athens, in other words, came millennia of clans and tribes like the one George had lived among on the Blasket.

You sense something of George's wonder in these pre-modern worlds in notebooks he began to keep in the years before publication of *Aeschylus and Athens.* There are about twenty of them today in the University of Birmingham Special Collections, with cloth or faux-leather covers, stuffed with handwritten citations in English, German, French, and Greek.

"Every native can sing, and most natives have from time to time composed their own songs," George copied out from John Layard's *Stone Men of Malekula.*

From Robert Briffault's *The Mothers:* "The moon is more important to the savage than the sun because it, and not the sun, is the marker and therefore the cause, of time and change, and in particular, of the changes in women's reproductive life."

Or from H. H. Bancroft's *Native Races of the Pacific States:* "Work is equally divided between the sexes." Women prepared food, made baskets and matting. "They are nearly as skillful as the men with the canoe and are consulted on all important matters."

It is page after page like this—insights and accounts bearing on primitive, peasant, and tribal cultures, drawn from rural life in Syria and Lebanon, from Eskimo culture, that of Costa Rican Indians, those of African tribes. *Notes on the Nature of Man,* it could have been called, were it bound and published. Through this anthropological compendium, George seems determined to capture just what men and women were like before cities and states, when they still lived together in tribes. It is hard not to see a specifically Blasket influence in it: beginning with his first visit, the island had shocked him with its example of a complex pre-industrial world that granted pleasure, interest, and rich human relationships for which nothing in his earlier life had prepared him.

At a few points in *Aeschylus and Athens*—which is, of course, a volume rooted in the origins of Greek civilization, not Irish, and cut off from the Blaskets by the full breadth of continental Europe—George's Ireland years surface directly. Delving into how earlier civilizations defined particular social relationships, he offers a dozen Irish words for "grandfather," "cousin," and the like; his list, he notes, was based on "my own knowledge of the West Kerry dialect, of which I am a fluent speaker." At another point he wonders how Athenian audiences might have responded to performances of their tragedies. Londoners, he writes, were apt to tamp down their responses, whereas those in the west of Ireland were more expressive; at critical plot moments, "almost every face wears a terrified look and continuous sobbing may be heard." An Athenian, he concludes, would feel more at home there than in London's West End.

Richard Seaford at the University of Exeter would point out how George Thomson understood key elements of the Aeschylean world, such as the revenge-minded Furies, through insights into pre-modern culture he'd gleaned "from the *inside*," meaning the Blaskets. Indeed, in his preface to *Aeschylus and Athens*, George alluded to the "special debt" he owed to his peasant-fishermen friends on the island,

> who taught me, among many other things that could not have been learnt from books, what it is like to live in a pre-capitalist society. It is true that nominally they fall within the orbit of the capitalist system, because they are liable for rent, but most of them refuse to pay it; and in general their traditions, especially their poetry, date from a time when social relations were profoundly different from those in which I have been brought up.

The house on Lovelace Road. The towering Anglican church across the street. The train that took him along ribbons of track into London. The great libraries of Cambridge: George Thomson never wholly rejected all that, the world in which he had been brought up. But on the Blasket, and the Greek islands of three millennia before in which he saw such parallels to it, he found much of value lost from the modern world, ill-appreciated, forgotten, ignored.

The Blaskets, we've seen, had helped George formulate his solution to the Homeric problem: The compositional mastery of the Homeric epics, he noted, was so great that most could see in them evidence only of individual genius. He saw them, though, as bubbling up from the collective energy of the people—just as "artistically perfect" sagas and folktales, for example, were "progressively shaped and polished by a sort of natural erosion, which has worked away excrescences and fashioned by slow degrees a final unity." Not single authorship, in other words, but work of the highest order that profited from the shaping influences of many. George was wise enough to realize, and candid enough to admit, that aesthetic judgments invariably turn on personal experience. His own judgment of Homer, he asserted in a 1949 book, went back to the Blaskets and the genius of the "ragged peasants" he'd met there. For him, there, on the island, "it was as though Homer had come alive."

Of course, his earliest major work of classical scholarship, *Greek Lyric Metre,* owed much to the Blaskets, too—to its dance, its song, its stories. His daughter Margaret, herself a distinguished classicist, would write that her father had in that book transformed a field belonging to "the driest philologists of the German school . . . into a quest for the lyre strings and dance beats that lie behind Greek lyric poetry." It had emerged "indirectly but profoundly" from his time in the Blaskets, where he found life and art intimately entwined. "I shall never forget," George would write, "the first time I heard some of the Irish poems I had long known in print sung by an accomplished peasant singer in the traditional style." Neither as poetry nor music had he ever heard anything like them.

In a 1976 talk for the Irish-language radio network, Raidió na Gaeltachta, George addressed similarities he discerned between Homer and the Blasket autobiographies, especially those of Tomás Ó Criomhthain and Muiris Ó Súilleabháin. What they'd done, he said,

> was something new in Irish literature. And yet there had been no break with the past. What these writers did was to weave their autobiographical tales, told many times at the fireside, into a continuous narrative in book form. In this way, they succeeded, especially Tomás and Muiris, in carrying over into print the art of the spoken word. It was as if the old Gaelic world had become articu-

late just as it was about to expire. These books are the literature of a preliterate community.

"As one listens to the voice of the passionate scholar speaking his perfect Kerry Irish," Richard Martin observed warmly of the performance, it was not hard to imagine this Englishman, George Thomson, as "the true bard of the Blaskets."

Chapter 12

No Herb or Remedy

[1946]

It took up almost the whole façade, a banner two stories high, plastered above the marquee of the News Theatre, on Birmingham's High Street, not far from where George Thomson taught at the university. "All this week," it announced in capital letters two feet high, they were showing

CHAMBERLAIN

THE

PEACEMAKER

a fifteen-minute newsreel commemorating the historic events in Munich. "SCREEN STORY OF B'HAM'S GREATEST LIVING CITIZEN WHO BY HIS COURAGE & STEADFASTNESS AVERTED A WORLD CATASTROPHE!"

Three years had passed since the Thomsons' trips to the Blaskets and to Russia. All across Europe, war threatened. In Spain, the elected Republican government was fighting a losing civil war against Franco, who was backed by Mussolini and Hitler. Katharine's family helped settle Jewish refugees from Germany. In March 1938, George's old tutor J. T. Sheppard announced to a Cambridge crowd gathered for a theatrical performance that Hitler's goose-stepping legions had just marched into Austria. Then, in September, came the Munich Agreement. Today the signature of British Prime Minister Neville Chamberlain (a son of Birmingham) on an agreement with Hitler to dismember Czechoslovakia is cavalierly dismissed as "appeasement." But, with the carnage of the Western Front still fresh in mind, and Europe on the brink of another descent into war, Chamberlain's assurances of "peace in our time" made him, just then, a hero.

War did come, of course, with the German invasion of Poland on September 1, 1939. Six dark, frightening years followed, years bleak for the Blaskets as well. Though Ireland was officially neutral—"The Emergency," the war was called there—the island's flow of visitors was staunched, its friends, such as Flower and Thomson, kept away, its living conditions made more difficult yet.

In Birmingham, the authorities issued gas masks by the thousands. George and a friend started digging an air-raid shelter in the garden, though, as Katharine would recall, "I don't think they got very far." In November, they received a letter from Maurice O'Sullivan, "showering blessings on us," as George wrote, "for the duration of the war." Thirty-six at the time, the father of two small children, George had been advised that, "unless I provide convincing arguments to the contrary," the university would tell the Ministry of Labour, who oversaw the British draft, "that my services are indispensable to the university." He spent the war years mostly in Birmingham.

The Thomsons accepted an invitation to stay with family on Katharine's side in Scotland but returned after a few weeks, because the war had so far amounted to little; the "Phony War" is what historians today call those seven uncertain months before May 1940, when Germany invaded Belgium and France. After that, things happened fast. France fell within six weeks. An attack on Britain seemed imminent. The Thomson children, now one and four, were evacuated to a cottage owned by Katharine's sister-in-law, looked after by a trusted nurse, visited once a month. "They seemed well and happy," Katharine remembered, "safe from the bombs which were soon to fall on Birmingham."

"We have had it pretty hot here the last few nights," George wrote his mother-in-law in October 1940. "They come in relays at intervals of a quarter of an hour, from seven-thirty till about eleven, starting fires in the centre of the city, and then hurling bombs into the blaze, which lights up the whole town." This wasn't Achilles on the plains of Troy, but war literally in their backyard. At one point, they and their neighbors were told to scour their gardens for a delayed-action bomb thought to have fallen nearby. After a while, they wrote off the search as fruitless, but suddenly "there was a terrific bang, we all flopped into the grass, and guessed that was it."

They slept downstairs "and cowered in the scullery," Katharine would write. She'd never forget the sight of a seemingly endless procession of German bombers passing overhead bound for nearby Coventry. "We've had some disturbed nights—Tuesday was awful, with a 4-hour raid," she wrote her mother. "A lot of anti-aircraft firing, and good few bombs, all on the other side of the town, but we heard quite enough."

At one point, she came down with diphtheria and wound up in the hospital for several months. The children were moved to Cambridge, where her mother tended them. "George remained at Oakfield Road, where he was very lonely," surviving on a dry egg mixture, sometimes visiting the children in Cambridge, about a two-hour train ride away, or else peppering them with picture postcards from Birmingham.

In the days before Christmas 1939, during the "Phony War," George Chambers took up a collection at the factory for Lís Ní Shúilleabháin and her family. The parcel they sent "was a wonderful one full of everything that was wanting," she wrote back gratefully. "Tell my factory friends that they were very kind and generous."

It wasn't long, though, before the war reached Chambers himself. "I was shocked at hearing of what befel or nearly fell so near your house," Lís wrote to him on October 30, 1940. It was the Blitz, London under siege from the air. "Thank God you were safe and also your dear home which I hope you'll never see in ruins."

Wartime travel was restricted, certainly to the Blaskets, which were all but sealed off from the world. Lís's letters were a succession of grim tidings. That first wartime winter was particularly awful, bleak with snow and frost. "We are not able to do anything but sit around the fire warming ourselves," she wrote on January 19, 1940. There was no work, certainly none decently paid. They were on the dole, at five shillings a week, and it took two shillings just to fill Seán's pipe. "Its not worth while to be living on 5/- a week," she added. A house off the island and an ordinary laboring job for Seán "would be heaven to us."

"You would be surprised to hear the real history and hardship of Islanders these days," she wrote in February, "that every family is quite tired of the wind and rain and would prefer to be in any other place in the world than here. Meat and food and flour are all gone up in prices and they with other hardships of Islands together leave no hope atall for Islanders." The rest of the letter verged on unintelligible, but its overall tone was clear enough—glumness, foreboding, and despair. "This Island will be none atall but rabbits some fine evening."

Chambers and Lís both survived the war. So did their correspondence, which continued into the 1950s. "What would you tell me if I would tell you that I would write my own life story from the beginning until getting married?" Lís had wondered back in 1935, the island's early publishing successes fresh in mind. "If my dreams ever come true," she added, "a friend from London will be mentioned no doubt." That book never materialized. But in 1950, Chambers came out with *The Lovely Line and Other Verses,* which immortalized Lís by name in at least two poems. And years after his death—as well as hers, in 1971—a sample of her letters were published as *Letters from the Great Blasket,* which is still in print. Lís's daughter Niamh visited Chambers in London after the war, but following his visit to the island in 1938 he and Lís probably never saw each other again.

Once, early in the war, they fell into what amounted to a lover's spat. In March 1940, Lís wrote Chambers requesting a pair of shoes each for her and her husband. The shoes arrived, but, as she wrote him, "they did not bring any joy or pleasure to me . . . for I knew from your letter you sent them with anger to me and with no pleasure in your own heart." Apparently, he'd read her request as a threat not to write again unless she got the shoes. No, not true, she said. "If I only thought it would give you so much displeasure as it did I would first rather walk out barefoot than tell you to send them. . . . You have thrown everything you ever sent me into my face."

All was soon made up, though. She was glad, she wrote a few weeks later, "to hear all being well again between us. Yes all cuts have been healed since and thank you and thank you for the nice letter, it was so free and gay like years ago when there was no worry or war time."

But there was much more worry to come.

And no end to the war.

. . .

After her trip to Ireland in 1929, where in Cobh she'd seen so many emigrants bound for America, Marie-Louise Sjoestedt visited Dún Chaoin and the Blaskets twice more, in 1933 and 1936. On the first of these, she gave Seán an Chóta an inscribed copy of Maurice O'Sullivan's newly published book. Her friendship with Seán went back a decade, but her affair with him, if that's what it was, was long over. In July 1932, she had married Michel Jonval, a scholar of Lithuanian and Latvian language and culture, whom she accompanied on a 1935 trip to Riga, Latvia, just before his death; she would subsequently write under the name Sjoestedt-Jonval.

Marie-Louise spent the summers of 1935 and 1936 in Wales. Her important articles on Kerry Irish appeared in the 1930s in *Études celtiques.* Finally, in 1940, the book for which she would be most remembered, *Dieux et héros des Celtes,* was published. "It did her the greatest honor," wrote one of her mentors, Joseph Vendryes. "Her friends will never be able to open it without the deepest emotion, for it will serve as the measure for them of the loss Celtic studies have suffered."

The loss was that of Marie-Louise herself, who died by her own hand on December 26, 1940, in Paris, at age forty. The following year, her colleagues prepared a memorial volume with *hommages* to her and her work, her own last essay on contemporary Irish literature, affectionate tributes to her person and her intellect. But with the Germans then occupying Paris, not all that might have been said about her final days could be said.

At the time of the French defeat in June 1940, Marie-Louise had what should have been a long and distinguished career before her. But she took the occupation hard, her tendency to depression much aggravated by events. "A too-late departure from Paris, a return marked by tragic incidents, a whole lamentable succession of circumstances, led to a series of nervous crises." This, anyway, was how one of her colleagues would put it, cryptically enough, in 1941. "A kind of instability dragged her along by intervals towards death. On five occasions she came to be saved just in time."

But this wartime account judiciously skirts the details of just what happened at the end, which, as Seán Ó Lúing put it years later, had to be "shaded and softened." Toward the end of 1940, she married Louis Renou, another Parisian scholar and author of a tender obituary in the memorial volume to her that appeared the following year. When the Germans arrested him, Marie-Louise abruptly took her life—by one account, throwing herself out a window. According to the sanitized version, "she submitted herself to a cruel death, which at least did not allow her time to suffer."

The memorial book included a photographic portrait that catches us a little off-guard. Here is not our Marie-Louise from the Blaskets, garbed in peasant shawl, but an elegant young woman fashionably coiffed, turned out in Parisian finery—gauzy, with a hint of décolletage—all her spirit alive in the directness and intelligence of her gaze.

Brian Kelly was dead by now, too.

On December 28, 1936, about the time George Thomson was named to his Birmingham post and just two months before the death of Tomás Ó Criomhthain, Kelly died of polio at the age of forty-seven. He was laid to rest in Lovrinac Cemetery, in the city of Split, on the eastern shore of the Adriatic Sea, in what was then Yugoslavia, now Croatia; he had been living on the Continent since about 1926. "I felt at the arrival of that news," An Seabhac wrote soon afterward, "that a lonely tragedy had occurred."

Kelly, it might be argued, had done little with his life, at least as far as his career went. His modest jobs in the Irish school system never came to much. His Irish was never really strong. He wrote little. But, it was said of him, he had the gift of friendship. At the time of his death, Eoin Mac-Neill, cofounder of the Gaelic League, compared Kelly to, of all people, J. M. Synge. The playwright Synge, he wrote, had sipped at the fountain of the Irish language in Aran and the Blaskets, using it "to give distinction and power to his English." Kelly, on the other hand, had given us "the well itself to drink from." He meant, of course, Tomás Ó Criomhthain.

The books Kelly encouraged Tomás to write were published in 1928 and 1929. He may never have seen them.

The paths of Carl Marstrander and the Blaskets crossed, briefly, for five months in 1907. After that, he set out on a busy and distinguished scholarly career, and never came back. He did field research in Brittany, the Isle of Man, and Scotland up to 1936; in that year, he returned to Ireland to receive an honorary degree from Trinity College, Dublin. He survived the war years and lived into his eighties, dying in 1965.

"His pen was sharp," another Norwegian scholar once said of him, "and he did not mince words." (Marstrander's opinion of Monte Carlo, the gambling mecca on the Riviera: "All is first class here apart from the inhabitants and the visitors.") David Greene, a student of his during the 1930s who went on to become professor of Irish at Trinity, wrote later that, even though Marstrander sympathized with Ireland's wish to break free culturally and economically from England, "he never really believed that the Irish people possessed the necessary determination and stamina" to do it. And he was revolted by the provincialism of Irish life. Still, he passed the torch of his enthusiasm for the Blaskets to Robin Flower and, through him, numerous other visitors. And he infected the islanders themselves, notably Tomás Ó Criomhthain, with a sense of their own significance.

"A fervent Norwegian patriot," Irish scholar Daniel Binchy called Marstrander. During World War II, with Norway occupied by the Germans, he played some role, at least, in the resistance. At one point—rumor has it he was stopped near Gestapo headquarters with a radio wrapped in a newspaper—he was arrested and interned in a camp outside Oslo. From there, the story goes, he smuggled out a diary to his son, also in the resistance, written in Old Irish. His son was arrested, the diary confiscated and sent to Berlin for examination by language experts there. When they couldn't make sense of it, they returned it to the Gestapo in Norway, advising them that the only person who might be able to translate it was one Professor Carl Marstrander, of Oslo.

Some months before the outbreak of the war, Robin Flower wrote: "I am myself thinking of retiring at the age of 60 to try and do some work"; he meant his own scholarly and literary work, not his duties at the British Museum. He was just then writing an article for the Museum's quarterly journal and acquiring some John Donne letters. "This kind of thing goes on all the time and fritters away all my energies. I have no conviction that this is my real work in life, though of course being paid for it I must do it." He had but so much energy. "I find it difficult nowadays to work in the evenings, tired after the distractions of the day."

The war, of course, halted all thought of retirement. On August 24, 1940, several Museum departments transferred manuscripts and other materials to an underground tunnel at the National Library of Wales for safekeeping; Flower was placed in charge. For the moment, his family remained back in London. "The ghastly bombing of London goes on," he wrote from 12 South Marine Terrace in Aberystwyth, Wales, in November. "The wife of one of our best friends was killed the other day." One of Flower's daughters taught in a school on the outskirts of London. Another was at Oxford. Son Patrick was about to join the Royal Air Force.

If, among visitors to the Blaskets, Brian Kelly, Thomson, Sjoestedt, and Synge each in their own ways bore some tincture of the exotic or irregular, Robin Flower was more like the rest of us, a kind of Everyman, leading a middle-class life in every way familiar to us today. At the British Museum, where he'd worked since 1906, he rose up through the Manuscripts Department, became assistant keeper in 1922, a position renamed "deputy keeper" in 1929. He held some outside posts, too, would eventually become acting director of the Early English Text Society. But the Museum was the only place he ever actually worked, his professional home, stiff in its bureaucracy, subcommittees, and periodic reorganizations, its rules governing promotions or how long clerks and assistants had for lunch. It "was already old at the beginning of the twentieth century," someone once said of it.

All through these years, Flower lived in London, beset by the daily worries of home and work. He and his family moved every few years from one suburb to another, but always within easy rail commute of his job at the Museum. He kept track of his career, monitored his salary, worried about putting his kids through college. At one point, in May 1939, Patrick, then about eighteen, seemed to be gravitating toward life as an artist. "I know only too well the difficulties of the life artistic being the son of a painter whose life was one long struggle," Flower wrote. He wanted none of that for his son, or for himself.

He wasn't in the slightest shy about looking ahead to his pension: "My prospects are good in the Museum," he wrote, "and my salary will steadily rise, and there is a pension at the end. The pension is a vital matter." He quoted from *Richard II:* "The setting sun and music at the close / As the last taste of sweets is sweetest last." This he observed while still in his thirties.

Flower was by any standard a gifted and accomplished man, a true intellectual. He held a senior position, with plenty of leave to exercise judgment. He could recognize the handwriting of scores of English authors, helped decide whether to acquire this manuscript or that, was something of an expert on forgers and their methods. And of course, as we've seen, he had a poetic and literary side. Still, as one obituary had it, Flower's duties at the Museum "were heavy and confining," and he often felt ground down by them. As another obituary said, "he was more remarkable than anything he did," his literary and scholarly production never quite up to his formidable intellect. His life was too packed, too distracted, too busy—or maybe, like a lot of us today, *he* packed it in, he *made* himself too busy. "He could never resist the attraction of a new interest," his boss at the Museum, Idris Bell, wrote of him. Flower took his vacations on the Blaskets just as millions of overworked city slickers take theirs today—like clockwork, every summer, packing up the family to the same mountain retreat, resort, or island camp, seizing an annual few weeks of sweet relief.

During their visit to the island in 1931, Edward Meyerstein wrote how Flower discarded "the cares of the British Museum, and jests with everyone." He was known to all, much liked, respected. From the beginning, Seán Ó Criomhthain recollected, Flower had fallen in easily with the islanders.

> He accepted their ways and the manner in which they put the day past them. He threw off his gentleman's clothes and put on a jersey and old trousers and hob-nailed boots with the boys of the village and away with him into every place along with them. It's often he was on the back of a donkey fetching turf from the hill or sea-weed from the strand or digging his share.

Anytime he'd come, he'd bring whiskey, tobacco, old clothes and shoes for his friends. "He was big-hearted," remembered Seán, "generous, hospitable, with no miserliness about him," good for a hundred pounds or so every year to the villagers. Indeed, Seán's recollections can make Flower seem something like a feudal lord: "The Islanders were very fond of him and their hearts were set on pleasing him, and if he had called them to arms they wouldn't have failed him."

On the island and off, he was identified with the Blaskets. He was a fixture of the place, a bad word never heard of him. "I would confide things to Bláithín I would not reveal to the priest," one islander said. He'd come to the island when it was virtually unknown and kept coming, all through the 1930s. He was the island's ambassador to the larger world, giving press interviews, lecturing on it in England, Wales, and America. If any of the visitors deserved to be called Mr. Blasket, it was he.

By the outbreak of the war, however, Flower was getting on in years; he was just short of fifty-eight, and medically speaking probably older. Even when he was young, he was dogged by health problems, physical and mental: "I have had rather a worse time than I expected. The attack declared itself, like last year's, in migratory pain over the whole field of my body," leaving behind "a legacy of weakness and headaches which effectively blackens the world for me." This was in 1911, when he was thirty.

"I have been ill of late," he wrote ten years later; "a thing called gastric catarrh knocked me out for a fortnight and I cannot get back any power of work. I hope a holiday will soon set me straight."

And in 1929: "I am feeling ill with overwork and many different anxieties."

Long before the three score and ten years he might have hoped was his due, Flower was getting old and sick. And the Blaskets were getting old and sick with him.

"Great hardship has been on islanders with the last 3 and 4 months," Lís wrote Chambers on October 2, 1941. "No flour comes to Dunquin for them as it used to." And for any that was available, "islanders must pay more and more."

The island's economic future, anyone could see, was bleak. In the 1920s, the United States had placed a tariff on salt mackerel, crippling the local market. The best turf on the island's back spine had been cut and burned, leaving its only ready fuel in short supply; islanders had increasingly to rely on driftwood washing up on shore. The 1930s were bad, the war years no better. In 1937, an Irish government agency, the Gaeltacht Services Division, brought in a few hand-operated sock-knitting machines and supplies of yarn and set up shop in one of the houses; two women from Donegal were brought in to train the villagers. By the early 1940s, however, it had been discontinued.

Meanwhile, the islanders continued to leave. In 1911, the Irish census recorded 160 people on the island. The census of 1926 showed 143.

In 1936, there were 110.

The women, especially, left. "The young women weren't willing to settle down anyplace there," author Críostóir Ó Floinn told an Irish radio audience later. "They were going off to London as nurses, or going off to the civil service in Dublin, or anywhere. They wanted to go to the cities, go to America, if they could. You wouldn't blame them, you know."

Back in 1936, Lís had written Chambers, "I am the only girl that got married since you were here" in 1931. "At present nobody thinks of marrying." Four years later, the war on, she responded in this way to Chambers's news that he'd be alone that winter, his wife presumably withdrawing to

Day is done: an islander returns to the village after cutting turf.

safer ground: it was a pity, of course, but she knew "of men who are more lonely and have to live alone through all their lives, who never had the joy of sharing one day of family life and has never now any chance of tasting that joy." She meant the island's men, of course, left behind by emigrating women.

During the 1930s, the first stirrings of a tourist industry propped up the island economy a bit. But with the war, that was gone, too. A "black cloud" hung over the island, Lís wrote in 1940. "It is terrible this summer season, and it is no happiness atall." Only one *naomhóg* had gone out fishing. There was a lobster blight. "Shillings are far and scarce at present." And hardly a visitor to be seen. "Only the one visitor has come to the Island yet," she wrote Chambers two weeks later, on June 29. "It's a hopeless, fruitless year, everyone thinks so."

In August, she told of another house being shut down, the old woman who'd lived there having left for the mainland. "So picture our Island home sinking from day to day."

The following February, the island schoolteacher was ordered to close the school. She "bid the Islanders adieu after about seven easy years teaching," Lís wrote to Chambers, "and left the three poor scholars to run wild with the rabbits—which," she added, "is their delight indeed."

One stormy night the following winter, she and Seán were sitting by the fire. Outside, the wind blew, lashing rain. She had recently visited the mainland, she declared to her husband. Life was better there, easier and more peaceful, with "no swell or surge of the sea washing over their rock," as Seán reported the conversation later. She wanted out. That was it. That was all of it. "This is the last winter here for me," she told her husband, "even if I have to shoulder my own pack!"

"That was the sermon she gave me," Seán recalled, "and it wasn't in Latin either, with every word of it sinking home."

On February 23, 1942, she wrote Chambers: "We have determined at last to leave this lovely Island. . . . Next time you will come to this Island there will not be no Eibhlís but the ruins of the house." She wanted a new life, the sort of life she knew they were missing where they were. Visitors on holiday, from comfortable homes on the mainland, seemingly without care, "would never believe the misfortune on this Island no school nor comfort, no road to success . . . everything so dear and so far away." The fishing was down to nothing. People couldn't live "on air and sunshine."

In July, they left. By the time she wrote Chambers in November, they were well established in Muirríoch, about ten miles away. Daughter Niamh was doing fine at school. By the following February, in the middle of what she ranked as "the severest winter that came with ages," she had to say, "I don't miss my lovely Island so much."

Eight years later, Chambers sent Lís his book of poems, which included ones he had written for her. Among them was "The Song of the Island Girl (Eilish)," for the girl she once was:

> The prison of trees
> Is all you gave,
> For the open seas
> And crested wave
>
> Oh, scent of sea-wrack,
> And keen salt spray,
> How my heart goes back
> The Island way!

He was right about that, she confided to him in a letter in September 1950: "I was very very lonely the time after the Island."

Just then she was back from two weeks spent with her parents on the island. "Its nice to be home once again with mother making the tea like years ago."

In 1935, Flower went to the United States to give a series of lectures on Irish literature. These later became the basis for another book about the Blaskets, *The Western Island.* In it, he told how on one visit Tomás and some of his other friends gathered in one of the houses to welcome him. Inevitably, they recalled those who had died since his last visit, talk veering to what island proverbs had to say about the inevitability of death. Finally, the conversation flagged and silence fell . . . until an old woman leaned forward and piped up in Irish, "Where is the snow that was so bright last year?"

"I sprang up in excitement," Flower wrote, "and cried out: " '*Où sont les neiges d'antan?*' "

> "Who said that?" asked the King, an expert in this lore.
> "Francois Villon said it," I replied.
> "And who was he?" he returned. "Was he a Connaughtman?"
> "No, he lived hundreds of years ago and he said it in French, and it was a proverb of his people."

Now, Flower wrote in his preface, "The King is dead and Tomás and the greater part of that lamenting company, and all this that follows is the song we made together of the vanished snows of yesteryear."

The Western Island was published in 1944. Later that year, Flower suffered a stroke. Some months later, he wrote, or perhaps dictated, a letter describing his condition: "I am still a very long way from actual recovery. I cannot read yet and still write with the greatest difficulty. Every letter is still a struggle for me. . . . I have temporarily lost all foreign languages and a great deal of English."

Since at least 1937, Flower and his wife had been living in the Southgate area of London, at 100 Ulleswater Road, in one of a long line of brick row houses, two or three stories high, with little gardens out front, sheltered from the street by hedges, which dropped down to a broad expanse of park at the base of the hill. One day early in January 1946 after lunch, he went out for a walk and never returned. Around four in the afternoon, police showed up at the house, saying he had been found collapsed in the park and taken to the hospital. When his wife and daughter Jean got there, he didn't recognize them. He died the following morning, age sixty-four.

"I was so sad to hear of Blaheen's death," Lís wrote George Chambers two weeks later. "I could not do anything atall but to think and think and be thinking. Old vivid pictures of the Island and Blaheen and family came before my eyes, of a crowd of Islanders coming down to the pier visiting himself and his family and children and young and old on the Island so merry and happy."

"It was a cause of grief to the people of the Great Blasket," Seán wrote in a tribute to Flower, "to learn of the death of our excellent noble friend. There is no herb or remedy against death."

Around the time of Flower's death, four years after Lís and Seán had reset-tled on the mainland, forty-five people still lived on the island—thirty-two men and boys, and thirteen females. Folklorist Brid Mahon visited the island during this period. "To this day I can recall the modest comfort of the houses on the island, with their raftered ceilings and open fires and the fragrant smell of turf smoke which I love above French perfume." She'd remember the boundless hospitality she enjoyed there, the settle beds and dressers filled with delft dishware, the chairs of woven straw, the walls hung with religious pictures. She visited every inhabited house on the island. All seven of them.

"It's going downhill almost every day," Seán wrote after Flower's death, comparing the village then, in 1946, to when Flower and Marstrander had visited earlier in the century. "There were thirty houses on it at that time and fifty children on the register of the school. To-day it is without a school, without a child."

The Great Blasket "was no place at all for old people," Seán Ó Gui-thín, one of the last of the island dwellers, said before he died. "It was like a ship which requires a certain number of crew members" and now no longer had them.

Emigration sapped all of rural Ireland, of course. But, as a 1947 gov-ernment report had it, "certain features" of Blasket life made matters worse yet—its remoteness, its loneliness in winter, coupled with "the dread of being without food, the danger of not being able to obtain the services of priest or doctor in time of need, the absence of teacher or nurse." As the population dwindled, the lot of the remaining few grew only worse. "Loneliness is accentuated and there is a greater feeling of helplessness in times of emergency."

On Christmas Eve 1946, the emergency arrived. A young island man, twenty-four-year-old Seán Ó Cearnaigh, fell ill, complaining of fever and headache. Most of the Ó Cearnaighs had by now left for America to become Kearneys and Carneys, Seán being among the few who remained. And now there was nothing to be done for him. For days a storm raged; the mainland was inaccessible. A radio telephone that was supposed to connect the island post office to Dún Chaoin didn't work. On the afternoon of January 10, 1947, "with most of the island community helpless at his bedside," as Mícheál de Mordha wrote years later, Seán died. When his body was later brought to Dingle, it was determined that he'd died of meningitis.

Soon after the tragedy, islanders wrote to Éamon de Valera, the Taoiseach, or Prime Minister: "STORMBOUND DISTRESS. SEND FOOD. NOTHING TO EAT. BLASKETS," read their telegram. De Valera, hero of the earliest days of the Irish Republic, visited in July. On his return, he set up a panel that decided there was nothing to do but abandon the island and resettle its inhabitants on the mainland.

For a while, rumors flew in Dún Chaoin of a motor ferry to better link the island to the mainland, or even a bridge. These, of course, came to nothing.

On May 20, 1953, Lís wrote Chambers: "Two men from the 'Land Commission' Dublin visited the Blasket Island lately about [islanders] transferring to the mainland. They have signed for them that they are satisfied to get cottages on the mainland," soon to be built for them. Her own mother and father would be among the last to leave.

They didn't come over all at once, only when a mainland house was ready. From the top of the cliffs in Dún Chaoin, recalled Críostóir Ó Floinn, he'd see them rowing in. "I'd go down to the slip and I used to help the lads bring in the stuff." Wardrobes, cattle, whatever, they all came in on the same little boats, men leaning to one side or another to balance the heavy loads in the surf.

November 17, 1953, was the day designated for the final migration of the twenty-one people then remaining on the island. Cameramen were on hand to record their passage across the sound and onto the mainland. Breandán Feiritéar, a mainlander born in 1943, remembered from his boyhood those last few islanders. It was a bleak time in Dún Chaoin. "A black gloom hung over the valley and remained there into the early 60s." They couldn't so much as muster a football team. Marriage was rare, the local school almost empty. Meanwhile, across the sound stood that "string of islands majestically rising out of the sea." When islanders came over, they stood out from the grim mainlanders. Among them, he remembered no "cantankerous faces or careworn countenances. I can only recall to memory the smiling faces of Seán O Súilleabháin or Paddy Daly, or Peats Tom Ó Cearna. . . ."

> I remember the Island men coming in their curraghs to Sunday Mass in Dún Chaoin. Each face wore a smile, each body a navy-blue suit, a zipped navyblue fisherman's jersey, studded boots and tweed peaked caps. They always spoke to us children, told us what various parts and workings of their boats were called, even gave us rides in and out of the harbour in their curraghs after Mass.

When he saw them in Dún Chaoin, they always walked in single file, "one after the other, looking over their shoulders to talk to the following Islander," as they did on the island's narrow paths.

Sometimes, returning by taxi from Dingle after selling their lobsters or sheep's wool, they had money for a pint of Guinness or two. "Watching them stumbling, staggering and reeling their way down the steep path to the pier, some singing songs," he could scarcely imagine them not falling on their way down, much less navigating across the sound. Yet soon their boats were smoothly slipping from the cove. Anyone "watching them rowing in unison and riding the waves on their way home could swear that not one drop of an intoxicating drink ever passed their lips."

One Sunday when he was seven, he was taken out to the island by one of its last inhabitants. He duly recorded "the little white-washed houses with their black felt roofs leaning into the hill." But what struck him more forcibly was how the islanders treated him, how everyone spoke to him, asked him who he was, how the "old ladies gave me slices of home-made bread and jam and fistfuls of raisins or currants. I never felt so grown up in my life before. These islanders *talked* to children."

Finally, late in 1953, the last families were coming across the sound. "As they approached the pier we could see the three curraghs laden with house-hold furniture and goods. Two oarsmen rowed the first curragh that had across its transom a maroon-painted dresser. An old lady in a black shawl sat in the bow and as the curragh approached the slipway we could see that she was crying profusely."

Later, he and the other children trudged slowly up the path with her to the top of the cliff. "She cried every step of the way."

Chapter 13

The Bottom of the Garden

[1950]

A U.S. passport issued in 1951 to "Mary Kearney known as Sister Mary Clemens," an American citizen since 1943, gave her occupation as seamstress. Records furnished by Sisters of Providence, the convent in Massachusetts where she spent the last fifty-eight years of her life, list her work for most of that time as "Sewing—Habits."

Sisters of Providence presided over numerous hospitals, residences, and care facilities and was a large, respected institution figuring prominently in its community. Its imposing new Mother House, all brick and churchly arches, the name PROVIDENCE spelled out in gilded letters above the entrance, had opened in adjacent Holyoke in 1932. Ten or a dozen young women entered the order each year.

After she joined it in 1930, Mary first went to work in the kitchen at Saint Luke's Hospital, then in a refectory, then in a nurses' dining room. In 1937, she took her perpetual vows. Two years later, she began her years-long service as seamstress, first at Mercy Hospital, Springfield; then at Saint Luke's Hospital, then Holy Family Institute. She sewed habits beside one or two other nuns, a convent spokesperson takes care to explain, not in a factory.

Much later, in her mid-fifties, Mary became a "cottage mother" at the newly opened Children's Center, an orphanage, where she worked with troubled children. "She was fantastic with the boys," her niece, Kathleen Arduini, recalls. In her seventies, she volunteered at Saint Luke's Home, where what was recalled as her "infectious laugh" left those around her feeling somehow all was well, dispelling their woes, earning her the unlikely nickname "Troubles."

In 1951, Mary, then in her early forties, visited Ireland. "One of Pats Kearney's daughters from America—the nun—was home for a month," Lís wrote George Chambers in May. Mary and her father, still living on the island, were driven around the mainland and dropped by to see old friends, including Lís and Seán. One day she went in to the island. "It made her very lonely, she told us."

Her thick hair in old age forming a crown of almost angelic white around her head, Sister Mary Clemens would be remembered for her faith, and for the joy she seemed to draw from life. Nothing in the record of her service over a span of more than half a century, however, suggests the church ever singled her out for any position demanding talent, leadership skills, or intellect beyond the ordinary. When she died, she was laid to rest on church property set apart for the order's own, each among that formidable field of headstones identical save for a family name set in the center, a religious name inscribed in a gentle arc across the top.

Before Mary's death on January 13, 1987, several students of Blasket Island life succeeded in tracking her down and interviewing her. She received such attention, of course, not in recognition of her service to the convent, or for her religious faith, but as a native of the Great Blasket whose life happened to intersect that of George Thomson, who died three weeks after she did, on February 3.

One of these Blasket enthusiasts was Tom Biuso, an American scholar of Irish extraction (with a Sicilian stepfather) who, one October day in 1983, convened a reunion of immigrant Blasket women, all once playmates together on the island, now living in New England. Sister Mary Clemens, he wrote, was "a small woman who is towered over by her sister Eileen." He remarked on the blue habit that set off her white hair, her eyes as bright as the silver crucifix suspended from her neck. "God's world is so beautiful," he took down her words. "If we'd only realise that He made the mountains and the valleys and the lakes and the streams just for us," the world would be better, with "less sadness and war and hatred." Otherwise, Biuso recorded little of Sister that might rank as memorable—nothing, certainly, of her years-earlier relationship with George.

Breandán Feiritéar, the mainland boy who'd witnessed the island exodus in 1953 and then grew up to become an accomplished filmmaker, managed about as well when he visited with her. He was in America working on a documentary, *Blasket Roots, American Dreams,* hoping for reminiscences of George, or memories, or comments, or thoughts, or *something.* But Mary, half a century in America, didn't want to talk about George, didn't want to talk Irish, didn't want to say much of anything to him. "I found her very difficult to deal with," certainly as far as George was concerned. She was "a tough, hard lady," simply unwilling to talk about George if she didn't want to.

Ray Stagles fared a little better. In 1940, Stagles, a nineteen-year-old university student, heard Robin Flower, then ministering to British Museum treasures in Wales, give a talk about the Blaskets. Beginning in 1966, Stagles visited the island with his wife, Joan, many times, and co-authored a book with her. On a trip to America, for a lecture tour, he met up with Blasketers in Springfield. Introduced to Sister Mary Clemens by Tom Biuso, he got her and her sister Eileen in front of the microphone to talk about leaving Ireland and becoming a nun. The tape was prepared at least in part with George in mind, for Stagles at one point asked her to send him a personal message. She did. The one in which, her voice fresh and light, she said: "I remember the times on the Blaskets Islands very well. We had a great time, George." And that was all.

Some time later, in Birmingham, Thomson had the tape played for him. "He listened very intently," a witness to the moment recalled. At one point, the tape whirring, Thomson's daughter Elizabeth entered the room. "Come listen, Liz," said George, "this is the woman who might have been your mother."

Of course, the woman who *was* her mother, and that of her sister Margaret, was Katharine Stewart Thomson. And it's hard to conceive any alternative history working out more satisfactorily than the real one did. Sean Cahillane, the American-born son of Mary's sister Eileen, tells of banter around the table at the family house in Springfield about how, yes, George would have made quite a catch. But the would-have-beens didn't materialize. Mary's life took one turn, George's another.

After moving to Birmingham, the Thomsons settled into a house on Goodby Road, which they came to dislike soon enough, in part because their neighbors played the radio loud and incessantly. So, in December

1938, George, Katharine (now six months pregnant with Margaret), and Liz moved to a five-bedroom house on Oakfield Road, in nearby Selly Park, fifteen minutes by city bus to George's classes near Chamberlain Square. They would remain there for the next twenty years. To this house on Oakfield Road, Margaret dates her most loving memories of her father.

For years, the family read together, the four of them, Mum and Dad, she and Liz. Before about 1950, they'd gather in her father's bay-windowed study on the second floor, overlooking the garden. Later, it was the music room. "Last time . . . ," George would begin, recalling where they'd left off, then plunge into the book for an hour or so. Maybe Sir Walter Scott, or the Bible, or Thomas Hardy, or *The Pilgrim's Progress,* the choice keyed to the ages of the children. To this day, says Margaret, a Greek scholar herself, anything she writes, any translation she attempts, is inexorably influenced by the sound of her father's voice, the rhythms of his speech.

Her father was not physically demonstrative, any more than was her mother. "But he didn't need to be," she says; the bond among them all was so close. He had no patience for small talk, yet when it came to children, to her and her sister, to people they met outside their immediate circle, he could be downright garrulous. With children, "he had a way of getting into their heads." His parenting style, she says, was no 1940s version of *Well, let's set up your next play date,* but engaged and responsive to anything on their minds.

According to Margaret, he had few practical skills. He didn't fix things around the house. He didn't swim. He didn't drive a car. He wasn't particularly graceful; when he rowed, his movements could be a little jerky—not the smooth, flowing strokes of a seasoned rower.

With his brothers and sisters, he maintained dutiful relationships, but was not especially close.

As for his colleagues at the university, he did not always hold them in high regard. He'd come home sometimes, Margaret says, complaining to anyone who'd listen of someone "pompous, mediocre, or both."

Always he held definite views. Always he expressed them doggedly. Popular culture arising from peasant roots, Margaret remembers him asserting, was good. That arising from the influence of American mass culture was bad. He did have American friends, but had no use for what he characterized as American imperialism. In 1941, he got into an extended and vituperative epistolary debate with his friend F. M. Cornford, a classical scholar and poet, in which he pictured Plato offering views of education in *The Republic* "indistinguishable from the theory and practice of fascism." Just after the war, he fell into a correspondence with Marxist historian Christopher Hill, in which he described Shakespeare, later in life a landowner, as "exploiting wage labour, possibly when he wrote Hamlet, and certainly when he wrote Troilus, Othello," and others among his plays. You might not want to slip into debate with George Thomson. Katharine didn't. "You've got the words," she'd say to him as some argument wound down, "but that's my view on the matter." He was relentless. He'd never back down, though he did grow mellower as he aged, says Margaret, ultimately coming to recognize some of the excesses and cruelties of Stalin and Mao.

In 1955, he visited communist China, writing long letters home to Katharine about his trip. "Yesterday evening I went to give my third talk to the Foreign Languages Institute," he wrote in June. "This time I told them how I became a communist, and we had a very good discussion." A friend of the family—Jane Scott, then a child—would remember how after his return he'd sometimes wear a Chinese suit around the house, how the children liked to visit him in his study. "This was no gloomy sanctum," she reported, "but a room full of little treasures, hung with pictures and pieces of Chinese silk, with leaded windows and an elderly gas fire hissing away in the background."

It may have been on the trip to China that he brought home a print of a village—men, women, and children hauling in a net thick with fish, working together as one. Years later, he sent it, or a copy of it, to a friend: "See how my vision of the Blasket is being realised in China today," he wrote. As classicist, professor, writer, Marxist, parent, and friend, he had absorbed the Blaskets in every pore. In China, when a student sang a song from a Chinese opera, "my mind was carried back thirty years to the moonlight nights in the Blasket island, when they used to sing and dance on the edge of the cliffs." Later, when he was old, almost blind, and near death, he worked on a new edition of his book about the Blaskets, *Island Home*. Margaret helped him, but mostly he typed it out himself on an old manual typewriter. Though it was slow going, she recalls, he was "energized" by doing it. Even the *way* he wrote owed something to the island and its oral culture: George, his friend Tim Enright reported, "would never commit anything to print without first reciting it aloud to hear how it sounded."

In 1976, in a trip arranged by Father Pádraig Ó Fiannachta, an impish little Irish priest from West Kerry with whom he'd collaborated on a new Irish-language edition of Maurice's book, George returned to western Ireland after decades away. Ó Fiannachta ferried him around, arranged for him to be interviewed; people who saw his performance voiced astonishment at the old man's ease and facility before the camera. "It was a wonderful experience," George wrote Ó Fiannachta later,

> which has healed the breach in my life that occurred when I left Ireland. I felt a little apprehensive at first, rather like Rip van Winkle, but thanks to you, it was not like that at all. I felt rather like Oisin might have done if he had received from Padraig a special dispensation to revisit the Land of the Young.

During this trip, Father Ó Fiannachta took George to see Cáit, Maurice O' Sullivan's wife. Maurice himself had been dead for many a long year.

The Irish- and English-language editions of Maurice's *Twenty Years A-Growing* both came out in 1933 and did well from the start. If not quite an overnight celebrity, Maurice surely had a new life opening up for him. To Denis Ireland, writing in 1936, Maurice's book was nothing less than "Troy seen in the morning of the world." Ireland told of Moya Llewelyn Davies, whom he met in Raheny, showing off the original manuscript, "written in cheap exercise books in Gaelic." Still in the Civic Guard in Connemara at that point, Maurice sometimes had to give evidence in court and one time, in Ireland's telling, the judge descended from the bench to shake hands with him. Soon, the two of them were strolling down the village's main street, trading thoughts on literature, Maurice's fellow guards "peeking from the window of the barracks."

Maurice did not long remain in the Guard. How could he? How could any young man with success like that thrust upon him? On July 5, 1934, he resigned. Five days later he married Cáit Ní Chatháin, whom he'd met in Carraroe, about twenty miles west of Inverin, site of his first Connemara assignment. It seems that the parish priest, attempting to direct local youths away from dancing and into more wholesome pursuits, organized baking classes for the young women. Cáit was among them. When a local boy annoyed her, in one instance making off with some rhubarb pie she'd baked, she complained. Enter the Guard, in the person of Muiris Ó Súilleabhháin, who'd been transferred to Carraroe in 1928. "Be going off, boy," he admonished the young troublemaker. Cáit, some years younger than he, continued with her classes. Maurice took to walking her home. A romance flowered. "He was a fine block of a man," said Cáit later.

In May 1934, E. M. Forster wrote George, worried that Maurice might come under what seemed to him the not entirely benign influence of Cáit. And worried also that too much by way of royalties might come Maurice's way. So far, he allowed, the money "has not done harm." But he enjoined George to do what he could to keep Maurice levelheaded. "I do hope he'll pull himself together."

Well, if pulling himself together meant steering clear of Cáit and staying in the Guard, Maurice didn't. "Oh Cáit, I don't like it," she remembered his saying when she worried about his leaving a steady job. "I hate getting up at three in the morning, going into houses, moving beds and quilts and mattresses . . . I don't like it. I won't do it even if I have to beg for a living."

Had he confided in George about his plans? "He didn't like the idea," he told her, "but I don't care."

After Maurice quit the Guard and married Cáit, the couple lived for most of the next year in West Kerry with Maurice's sister Máire. One Sunday morning, they took a boat out from Dingle to visit the Blasket. As they approached, a *naomhóg* came out to ferry them into the island. "That's when the chattering started," she'd remember. "You'd think they were wild geese with everyone talking," the islanders saluting their marriage, piling greetings high upon them. On the island, they "drowned him with tears and dried him with kisses." But his childhood home, clinging to the slope of the hill, now stood empty, a big lock on the door. At one point, Maurice approached it, peered through a window, turned sadly away. Then "he put his head under him and started crying."

During their time in Kerry, Maurice tried writing a biography of a local West Kerry character, one Dónal Cháit Bhillí. "Of course, Dónal spoke as though he were reading out of a book," Cáit noted later. "It came out like that." The book was never published. "He sent it to some publisher and he was told there was too much of it. There was nothing to it in a way."

For Cáit, Kerry felt like exile. "I couldn't understand a word of what the people were saying," she said, so strange to her was the dialect at first.

All that year she was homesick. Finally, they moved back to Carraroe, where they built a small two-story house. A son, Eoghan, was born to them in November 1935.

In September 1937, George visited. He and Maurice met in Galway in a pub, then to tea in a local hotel, all the while rattling on in Irish. Maurice wanted him to come back to Carraroe and stay with him and Cáit for the night. "They would have a great welcome for me and dance till morning," George wrote Katharine next day. But it would be one in the morning before they reached Carraroe on the bus, and only then the dancing! "I would have done it once, but not now." As for Maurice, he looked great, and "it was a delight to be with him again. But I am very worried about his future. I feel sure they will be destitute in the end. An added difficulty is that Cáit's health is not good. And he is so improvident."

Of course, now Maurice was homesick, too. He was "heartbroken at leaving Kerry," Katharine had written to her mother after their 1935 trip to the island. "There is tremendous county feeling here, and it is like being in a foreign country to be in another part of Ireland." Still, Maurice adjusted, more or less. It wasn't Kerry, but it was Irish-speaking, wild, and primitive, dotted with little lakes and broad swathes of bog. During these years, he tended his vegetable garden, kept a cow, cut turf, collected seaweed. On a moonlit night, he'd sometimes go down to the graveyard in the place they called Barraderry, a few miles from the house, sit listening to the sound of the sea. "An islander marooned ashore," his son, Eoghan, once called him.

When Seán Ó Faoláin first reviewed *Fiche Blian* in 1933, he voiced the conviction that Maurice O'Sullivan was not "a man of one book." He was wrong. Around the time World War II broke out, Maurice started work on a sequel to *Twenty Years A-Growing*—titled *Fiche Blian Faoi Bhláth,* or *Twenty Years in Bloom,* largely about Connemara and Carraroe. Alan Titley, professor of Irish at University College Cork, got his hands on the manuscript once. It was, he concluded, "an appalling book . . . very badly written," stuffed with loose chatter of the sort you'd encounter "talking in a pub late at night or around the breakfast table, just gabbling on," littered with the Irish equivalents of "You know what I mean" and "So it goes." To Titley, it lacked "the quirky humour and devil-may-care attitude of the first book" and was beyond saving.

Maurice had invested a lot of time in it, of course, and sent it off to publishers. "But what good was that," said Cáit later, "because the reply he got was that it was not like Twenty Years A-Growing," not as good, and needed to be. Maurice went back, worked it over, but to no avail. George didn't much care for it, either. Whatever good his editing might have done—and once Alan Titley saw the sequel, he was convinced George's editorial contribution to the original was substantial—he didn't see the new manuscript as worth it. It remains unpublished.

In a 1944 essay, George recalled Maurice's first day in uniform in 1927 in Dublin, and how he, George, had "had to take him by the arm and guide him through the traffic to the safety of the pavement." In the years since, Maurice had "widened his experience enormously, he had learnt to enjoy books, the theatre, the cinema, and the other amenities of urban life, without losing any of his native independence." But it never quite took, asserted George. With the success of *Twenty Years A-Growing,* Maurice had left the Guard, "purchased a patch of land in Connemara, built himself a house, married a Connemara girl, and now he is living very happily back where I had found him—among the peasantry." To listen to George, Maurice had returned to his roots and "walked out of modern civilisation."

This does not quite ring true. Yes, Maurice lived "among the peasantry" in Connemara and identified with them. But the author of *Fiche Blian ag Fás* in its many editions and translations was a peasant no longer. Year in, year out, in success and in failure, he carved out a life for himself as a writer. Like Tomás Ó Criomhthain, he inhabited a corner of the literary world. He had left the Guard, yes. And he had left the peasantry as well.

By necessity, Maurice wrote shorter, more salable pieces, about people he met in Connemara, snippets of old folklore. He'd cycle for miles into the stark countryside, talk to the old people, tell of the loneliness and isolation he saw around him. He wrote scripts for radio plays, some of which were broadcast, others performed onstage in Carraroe. He wrote a story about Jonah and a shark—not the Biblical whale, but a shark. One about the transatlantic cable, which came ashore near Ventry, just south of Dún Chaoin. He wrote about "life in the bee world," with bees as his characters. Much of it was religious: a blind man comes to Connemara, looking for a holy well, rubs water on his eyes, and is cured. Sometimes he gave his Connemara characters Munster dialects and Kerry sayings. Occasionally, come Christmas or Easter, he'd reminisce in print about the Blaskets. But whatever his stories' strengths and failings, he kept at it—for *The Irish Press,* for Irish-language publications like *Feasta* or *An Iodh Morainn* or *Ar Aghaidh,* for the more widely read *Messenger of the Sacred Heart.* "Disappointment followed on disappointment," Blasket biographer Leslie Matson characterized Maurice's writing life over the years. Yet not entirely so. One compilation of his work listed 132 published pieces. They were darker and sadder, though, than anything in his book, concluded Nuala Uí Aimhirgín, author of an Irish-language biography of him, the youthful exuberance of *Twenty Years A-Growing* by now largely extinguished.

The book continued to earn royalties—about sixty pounds a year, George estimated in 1945. Maurice and Cáit supplemented that by letting out a room or two during the summer. Mostly, though, he just kept writing. In 1944, they had a daughter, Máire Llewelyn, named after Moya Llewelyn Davies, who'd died the year before. Máire remembers her father from when she was a little girl. As a toddler, she'd cycle everywhere with him, propped up on the handlebars. Or else she'd find him upstairs, at his desk, which faced a lake he could look out at by day. The house had neither running water nor electricity, and in the long northern nights he'd write by lamplight. She remembers the pink glow, the play of shadows on the wall, the scratching pen.

It is September 1945, the war finally over. George returns to Ireland once more, the first leg of his trip this time by plane. "The journey from Liverpool to Dublin was wonderful," he writes Katharine, "5000 feet up on a summer afternoon with the coast of N. Wales spread out like a map, every house and hedgerow as clear as if they were toy models." Dublin is a joy to him. "I have never seen it so bright and gay, the streets and cafes full of crowds of people with nothing to do but stroll and talk." Unlike in England, there is no bomb damage here.

His mind thick with memories of Moya and Watermill and on-till-midnight talk in Irish, George is inevitably drawn to Raheny. He takes the bus there; the tram tracks have been taken up. The coast road is being widened, houses and walls razed to accommodate the project. Watermill Cottage is gone, "disappeared, except for a ragged stretch of one wall," its gate intact, though, still the bright green he'd painted it. The garden is gone, reduced to a lumberyard for the road project, "a wilderness of timber, iron and mortar, and in the midst of them my lovely weeping ash, shorn of her tresses and obviously doomed. I stood for a moment feeling utterly desolate."

The next morning, he catches the train to Galway to spend a few days with Maurice and Cáit in Connemara. He presents a teddy bear to little Máire, joins them all at Mass on Sunday morning, then for a wake on a little island just off the mainland. Coming back, the little boat is crowded with more than twenty people, "hilarious on the way home."

He'd worried that it somehow wouldn't be the same with Maurice, but they never stop talking. "He is just the same as he always was," George writes. And being in the Gaeltacht is as exhilarating as ever. "My Irish has returned to me in a flash." It is like being with Maurice back on the Blasket.

A 1949 photo of Maurice shows him in jacket and tie, hair parted on the left, all turned white. He is still a good-looking man—not old, but no longer young, either. He's in his mid-forties now, looks as if he's stepped from one of the many snapshots that come down to us of Blasket fishermen—hearty and vigorous men, their boyish youths only a memory.

By the spring of 1950, George has lived in Birmingham for more than a decade. He is, this academic year, president of the Classical Circle, its aim being "to encourage the appreciation of Greek and Roman Literature, Art and Civilisation, both for their intrinsic value and for their bearing on modern conditions." He is president of the Socialist Society as well. His appointment book notes a visit to Nottingham set for May 22, a garden party for Thursday, June 22, meetings with Russian émigré linguist Nicholas Bachtin and others among his friends.

On Monday, June 26, a telegram arrives:

Maurice Drowned in Galway Yesterday

The day before, Máire, six years old, is out playing. It is four or five in the afternoon. A man in uniform comes to the gate.

The house is full of chatter and music, crowded with Sunday visitors, people in the sitting room singing. When Máire sees the uniform—just like her father's, that of a Guard—she thinks at first that it *is* her father. The man comes to the door, huddles with her mother. He tells her he has some bad news.

It happened at a public beach just outside Galway, in Salthill, at a place called Lover's Strand. A few months earlier, in February, at last giving up on trying to support his family as a writer, Maurice had re-joined the Guard, sixteen years after leaving it. It could not have seemed like much else but failure. Four days before his death, he'd been transferred from Oughterard, a pretty little village on the shores of Lough Corrib, to a station in Galway itself, twenty miles away; a strike was on, police were needed.

Maurice's biographer, Nuala Ní Aimhirgín, doesn't think he killed himself. Neither does his daughter, Máire. "I think he had a heart attack while he was in the water," she has said. He was a good swimmer, but "there was a strong undertow. It was pulling him out to sea. He managed to swim in to the shore. But he seems to have collapsed. And the tide came in. He drowned in about three or four inches of water."

"Sixty I may be," wrote Máire—grown, a wife, a mother—in a poem, "but my soul remains at six / Just as it was on the Sunday you slipped into silence, into serenity / On to another Island, out of sight."

When George got the telegram he was at home. The house he and Katharine had lived in for ten years, one of four such houses built in a closely spaced row around 1930, was from the street an unprepossessing affair. From the back, though, it was memorable for a great sweep of garden that dropped down to a stream. Bourne Brook it was called, and that's where George, in shock, went now. He was "barely able to speak," Katharine recalled.

Today, the banks of the stream are fettered in concrete. In those days, though, George's young daughter Margaret liked to play there, scampering beside the brook, ducking in and out of neighboring properties. A heavy rain could turn the stream into a torrent, rising up enough over root-entangled banks to flood part of the garden. In summer, it was most likely just a trickle; the Thomsons sometimes kept hens and rabbits there. "The bottom of the garden" Meg called the spot, and it *was* somehow the bottom—more, through its particular play of topography than it was the garden's end, or edge, or boundary. A world apart, a leafy enclave far from the eyes of others, far enough from the house that you had to *go* there, a journey. George made his way down the whole length of the garden, two hundred feet from the house, past the apple tree, the little redbrick outbuilding, the vegetable patch at the bottom.

Margaret watched. From the drawing room, looking out the back window, she saw "Dad, walking up and down, up and down, tears in his eyes. Then he went to the very bottom of the long garden and stood and watched the stream."

What's the matter with Daddy? she asked her mother. "It was the first time I'd seen my father so unhappy. I'd seen him worried, but I'd never seen him express such grief. And I don't think he ever felt any person's death so deeply ever again."

Chapter 14

A Dream of Youth

There will never again be on the Great Blasket a village of fishermen and subsistence farmers who live in rude stone houses, fish the surrounding waters in canvas-clad boats, do without electricity, and speak only Irish. Perhaps, as scholars say, human history traces no simple straight line of progress, but this is probably one prediction as safe as any.

Likely, too, is that, around the world, places like the Blasket will grow fewer. "Maybe it will come that all the little islands, all the little places where men do make a livelihood together out of the gathering of the strand and the hunt of the hill and the fish of the sea will be empty and forgotten." These are the words Dylan Thomas gives Maurice O'Sullivan's grandfather in a screenplay, never finished, based on *Twenty Years A-Growing*. And that surely is the pattern of the past century and more, countless versions of the Blasket abandonment being played out in Italy, India, Mexico, and Korea, one village after another vanishing altogether or stepping into the modern age.

The Blaskets lost. London and Los Angeles, Dublin and New York won. Here and there, as with the Pennsylvania Dutch Amish or other religious communities, a few try, and may partially succeed, in squirming free of modernity's grasp. But mostly, the movement goes the other way, toward ease and security, plumbing and packaged goods, cell phones and flat screens, or whatever else constitute the marvels of a time and place.

The visitors to the Great Blasket we've met here likewise valued modern life; they didn't forsake it, anyway. Carl Marstrander did fieldwork in out-of-the-way places like the Blaskets, but spent most of his professional life in the capitals of Europe. Robin Flower? For all the many years he visited the Blaskets, he and his family lived, for eleven-twelfths or more of each year, in comfortable houses in the inner suburbs of London, always near a train to get him to work. George Thomson turned his back on Oxbridge, but chose an alternative that, for all its nuanced points of difference, left him for most of his life in England's second city, imbibing eagerly of politics and ideas. They and the other visitors could, in principle, have rejected big-city life and embraced the Blasket, moving there, living among their island friends not for the summer but throughout the year and for the rest of their lives. But they didn't, all of them acquiescing to one or another version of the modern metropolitan lives for which they'd been groomed.

Of course, one visitor, it could be said, *did* throw in his lot with the Blaskets. This would be Neal O'Moore—or that, anyway, is the name a scriptwriter gave his character. On May 28, 1937, Lís Ní Shúilleabháin wrote George Chambers that some "film stars" were on the island. And I suppose they were, if the likes of Cecil Ford, the unknown actor who played Neal, qualifies. He and a coterie of other unknowns were there to film a movie about the island inspired by Robert Flaherty's instant classic, *Men of Aran,* a dramatized documentary of Aran life that had appeared to much acclaim in 1934. (Robin Flower visited Flaherty on Aran in 1932 and saw some of the early footage. Flaherty seemed to him "a great man . . . [with] a great anger against civilisation and the machine age.")

So our Neal O'Moore, Dublin medical student, comes to the Blasket and falls in love with an island girl, Eileen, who is pledged to another. They draw closer, but she holds back. "I can never mean anything to you," she says, "I will marry Liam," the sturdy island lad she's known all her life, whom Neal befriends as well. Near the end of his stay, they climb up to a rocky outcropping, the sea beneath them. "If I come back again, I'll stay for good and all," says earnest Neal. "I'll become an island man."

He returns to Dublin, but then, one day, hears Eileen on the radio in his college rooms, singing a song she'd sung on the Blasket, captured with the fledgling electronic technology of the day and broadcast across the country. He's smitten all over again, of course, and returns to the island—this time, he declares, to stay. "I'm not returning to the mainland,"

he tells Eileen and Liam. "I'll become an island man, cultivating, turf cutting, cattle breeding. Yes, and if you will help me, Liam, I'll become a curragh man." That is, he'll become strong enough—man enough, really—to
row an island *naomhóg.*

As you may have decided from these bits of dialogue, the film is not
very good. Its American distributor called it *Men of Ireland,* shamelessly
exploiting its Aran forebear. In Ireland and England it was known as *The
Islandman.* But "that Film is not about my father-in-law—may God rest
his soul," Lís wrote Chambers. Rank melodrama it was, down to a worthy
Catholic priest issuing homilies to his "children," wooden acting, and a
nascent *ménage à trois* of a story that managed to remain not just chaste
but bloodless. The film was redeemed only by some nice dancing and
singing—filmed in a Dublin studio—a *naomhóg* race, glorious island vistas, and the two pounds a day villagers got for hauling cameras up the
cliffs.

But if you can pull away from the story long enough—and, believe
me, it will come as a relief—the film raises a serious question: could Neal,
or anyone like him, forsake the intellectual and professional rewards of
medical school, along with Dublin's comforts, stimulations, and seduc-
tions, to live permanently among the islanders? Could Neal ever truly
become "an island man"?

Back in Aran, J. M. Synge apparently once did flirt with going native.
One day, rowing to Inishmaan with some islanders and caught up in a
"dreamy voluptuous gaiety," he finds his friends "so full of divine simplicity that I would have liked to turn the prow to the west and row with them
for ever." He'd return soon to Paris, he tells them, to sell his books and his
bed, and then he'd be "coming back to grow as strong and simple as they
were among the islands of the west."

He did not do it.

Among visitors to the Blaskets, none seems to have gone even so far as
Synge did. Did Flower, Thomson, or Sjoestedt—of a perfect island night,
the peat fire glowing, the west wind outside not too cold or too wet—
never think of settling on the island for good? If so, I haven't heard or read
of it. Flower came so regularly on holiday and was so generally liked that
he was all but an honorary Blasketer. But he, like the others, knew full well
he was a visitor, not an islander, and always would be. And all of them
were clearheaded enough to see that the island culture so precious to them
was becoming extinct.

In Aran, Declan Kiberd has written, Synge fed "off the death of the old Gaelic culture, as do all coroners and morticians"; and was aware, too, that the beauty of the dialect he used in his plays was "the beauty that inheres in all precarious or dying things." Might some similarly dark thought apply to the Blasket visitors? Did their coming accelerate the island's decline? After all, Brian Kelly brought books to the island; these helped inspire Tomás to write his own books, weakening the oral culture; Tomás's celebrity brought tourists, diluting authentic island life; George Thomson induced Maurice to leave the island for the Guard. . . . Still, weighed against the overwhelming economic and social currents lashing at the Blaskets, these must be reckoned secondary influences at best. The "tangled world of to-day" had been reaching out to the Blaskets and its mainland neighbors all through the early twentieth century—and, really, long before.

That phrase owes to Robin Flower. In his book *The Western Island,* he writes of being rowed out to the island, which from a *naomhóg's* perch seemed to recede "behind the dancing company of the waves. 'Say your farewell to Ireland,' cries one of the rowers, and I turn and bid farewell, not only to Ireland, but to England and Europe, and all the tangled world of to-day." In a 1937 talk he gave in Germany, folklorist Séamus Delargy worried that in Europe there were "only a few remaining corners where the old world can find a free place. The storm and violence of modern life, the hustle and bustle of the big cities, the wail of the factory horn, the whirring of machines"—these could be escaped only "in the far west of our remote island," in Irish-speaking places like the Blaskets. But long before the Blaskets were abandoned, they and Flower's tangled world, distinct and apart for so long, had been drawing irredeemably closer.

We've seen how English encroached on West Kerry Irish; Synge and Marstrander lamented as much in the first decade of the century, and Marie-Louise Sjoestedt supplied evidence and detail for it in her 1928 paper. Literacy itself helped pull the island out of its insular past and into the European future. "Having acquired the doubtful blessing of being able to read the newspapers," Daniel Binchy wrote in 1934 of Ireland generally,

> the new generation has turned its back upon the rich storehouse from which the language of the old people drew its savour and its strength, the folk-tales handed down from generation to generation around the kitchen fire. Nowadays let one of the seniors begin a "story," and in a flash the kitchen is emptied of the entire youthful population.

Blasket storyteller Seán Eoin O'Donlevy told Robin Flower once, "It was only the other day that I had all the old tales in my mind." Now, he'd forgotten them, and it was Tomás Ó Criomhthain to blame, he said, "for he has books and newspapers, and he reads them to me; and the little tales, one after another, day after day, in the books and newspapers, have driven the old stories out of my head." Of the islanders George Thomson would observe, "Within the space of a single generation, their whole outlook on life had been transformed by literacy," which had "opened up a new world of commercialised mass entertainment."

In the early 1900s, books began to appear on the island. So did photography. Synge took a few pictures in 1905. In 1920 and then again in 1924, Carl von Sydow took numerous islander portraits. In 1923, from London, George mailed to Maurice's sister Eibhlín the first photographic image of herself she'd ever seen, one he'd taken just before leaving the island that first time.

In 1931, an article in *The Irish Times* reported, Robin Flower attributed the decay of folk culture in part to gramophones, which offered Blasket youth "more popular entertainment than the telling of tales around the fireside. It is strangely ironical that the instrument which does most to preserve Ireland's folklore should be an agent of its decline." Peig Sayers told countless stories into Flower's Ediphone; you can hear her gravelly whisper of a voice today online, or at the Blasket Centre in Dún Chaoin, where hundreds of photos taken on the island, as well as sound recordings and film images, are now digitally enshrined.

By the 1930s, certainly, islanders were well aware of amusements and conveniences they lacked. Lís threw out a suggestion to Chambers in a November 1938 letter:

> What about giving friends a bit of enjoyment and a bit of the world outside which you have and enjoy each day and night and keeping the spirit up for Christmas by collecting the price of a Radio in your own factory and to buy it yourself for me if you like in Dublin and sending it on for Christmas Eve.

A penny from each of the factory's four hundred workers, she figured, would do it. Chambers did not oblige.

Technology had figured all along, of course, in the island's transformation from an isolated, more or less self-sufficient community to the creaking social and economic ruin it was on the eve of its abandonment.

The big motorized French fishing trawlers handled larger catches at lower cost than the little *naomhóg*s ever could. The narrow-gauge railroad that, beginning in 1891, snaked round and through the hills of West Kerry from Tralee to Dingle delivered Synge and other visitors to West Kerry—but also Mary Kearney and countless other emigrants away. Once they reached Cobh, twenty pounds would get them to Boston or New York in a week or two, courtesy of great ocean steamers in all their relentless cost-per-mile efficiency.

Meanwhile, all across the first third of the century, Tomás Ó Criomhthain was slipping out of a fisherman's life and into that of writer and intellectual; at the time of his death in 1937, he may have had more in common with Robin Flower than with Tadhg and Séamus and the other fishermen he'd immortalized in *Island Cross-Talk* and *The Islandman*. Sometime before 1922, he'd tell the story, he'd helped Seoirse Mac Cluin, a Catholic priest visiting the island, compile an Irish phrase book. "We used to be sitting at it eight hours a day in two sessions—four hours in the morning and four in the afternoon—for all that month. That's the most painful work I ever did, on land or sea." Tomás was talking like "knowledge workers" the world over, lamenting the brain-scrunching burdens of sustained intellectual effort. "It is a book that couldn't be found written in any language," he'd brag in English to his son of *An tOileánach* in 1931; "3000 of them is sold now."

In the 1930s, the Great Blasket could be mistaken for a tourist town, with outsiders, drawn by its literary reputation, no longer so rare a sight. "Lá Breágh"'s, the islanders called them, from the Irish for "a fine day," which was about the only Irish most visitors could manage. Peats Tom Kearney's place, next door to Peig Sayers's, was sometimes called Kearney's Hotel, or Pats' Inn. For now, sheer physical inaccessibility saved the island from a precipitous descent into touristic gimcrackery. Still, it was enough to remind you of a Nice, France, say, in its first flush of tourist development 150 years before.

In the 1960s, a black-and-white documentary called *The Village* showed Dún Chaoin and the Blaskets sprinkled with tourists. One well-dressed Englishwoman with an upper-class accent can be heard—with what an anthropologist reviewing the film termed "Protestant incomprehension"—coming near to dismissing local poverty altogether: "I suppose it's their Faith; they know that material things don't matter very much. . . ." This fine lady exulted in "the complete absence of all the modern machinery" in the village. "I think that's what I like best. Not men with tractors, but a man in a field cutting down the oats by hand. And a donkey cart instead of a car. A sort of fairy tale . . . All the nasty, modern things aren't here."

More and more, of course, they were.

The area would soon even feel a breath of celebrity culture. *Men of Ireland* and its shabby little black-and-white excuse for a story was one thing. David Lean's 1970 Hollywood epic *Ryan's Daughter,* filmed in living color on the mainland within sight of the Blaskets, was quite another. Today the locals can direct you to where star Robert Mitchum liked to down his Guinness, or show you the remains of the schoolhouse built for the film. To Séamus Delargy, folklore was an oral "literature of escape" through which spellbound listeners "could leave the grinding poverty of their surroundings, and in imagination rub shoulders with the great, and sup with kings and queens." Film, Delargy would also say, had become "the modern folktale."

The wandering scholars of old were gone, Robin Flower wrote in *The Western Island,*

> and the fashion of life they knew has gone with them. The people read newspapers, and in the police barracks at Ballyferriter . . . a wireless set strikes wonder into the country people. "Yes," said one of the islanders to me the other day, "I sat in the barracks and I saw a man dancing a hornpipe, and a fiddler in London was playing the music for that dance. It is the greatest marvel I ever saw."

There was no escaping modernity's grip.

In August 1969, Tomás Ó Criomhthain's son Seán, by now seventy and living on the mainland, near Smerwick Harbor, dropped by to see his eighty-six-year-old neighbor. "It is a strange world to him today," he would write of the old gentleman, "with the mad rush there is on everybody," and people having so much of everything. " 'This is the modern way of life,' says I to him, 'and if peace lasts and no war breaks out, 'tis only better it will be getting for us, if God spares us to see it. Did you hear,' I went on, 'that men landed on the moon last night?' "

In the inexorable tension between the simple ways of the Blaskets and the push and shove of modern life, the influences, however, don't go just one way. The little village is gone, but its story has a way of sticking. "Their collective narrative," writes Fintan O'Toole of the autobiographies by Tomás, Maurice, and Peig, "haunted, and to a degree still haunts, the Irish imagination." "Haunts" is just the right word, but it's not only the Irish imagination. *An tOileánach* has been translated into English, French, German, Italian, Swedish, and Danish; *Fiche Blian ag Fás* into at least four languages. The three original Blasket books are all still in print and have been joined by several dozen others—books by Seán Ó Criomhthain, Mícheál O'Guiheen, Máire Guiheen, Lís Ní Shúilleabháin, and others among the islanders, as well as by Thomson and Flower. Each year, close to fifty thousand visitors make their way across the Dingle Peninsula to Dún Chaoin's Blasket interpretive center, a handsome museum, archive, and conference center dedicated to the legacy of the island community, its great picture windows looking out at the island from across the sound. Each year scholars from Ireland, England, America, and elsewhere descend on it for a conference, conducted mostly in Irish, devoted to Tomás Ó Criomhthain, say, or George Thomson, to the island's music or its religious faith. Meanwhile, the Blasket books continue to shoot tendrils out into the worldwide community of scholars, captivating students of literature; and also of history, geography, anthropology, and folklore; and, because they stand astride at least two sets of paired languages—Irish and English, oral and written—of translation itself as subject of study.

But the Blasket story matters not alone for the sake of the island itself, or the people who once lived there, or the literature it produced, but for how it reflects back at us our lives today. Almost from the moment Tomás's book first appeared, it's been like that—life on the Blasket seen in stark contrast to modern lives that, in the right light or the wrong mood, can seem too fevered, insubstantial, or inauthentic. The Blaskets speak to us not only of what *they* once were, but of how *we,* the rest of us, are today. "It was a simple culture," Thomson wrote of the island, "but free from the rapacity and vulgarity that is destroying our own." True or not, the assertion, like others over the years from critics and scholars, makes the Blaskets into a kind of half-silvered mirror that, even as we look back through it to the past, shows us ourselves and something of how we live today.

No one anytime soon is returning to live on the Blaskets; the hundreds of islanders who over the years left it behind for America and Canada might scratch their heads, incredulous, at the thought. But this truth doesn't deny another truth, that the island has something for us yet to learn. George Thomson once lamented that he'd "failed in the work I had set out to do—that is, bring the people of the Gaeltacht into modern civilisation while retaining their own culture." But there is other work to do—to confront modern civilization with the story, the example, the contrast, of places like the Blasket: As counterweight to a "progress" that sometimes seems too headlong, or not progress at all; as repository of those old ways of pre-modern life worth reclaiming today, or at least revisiting; as testimony that life's satisfactions lie amid people, individually or together, undistracted by the ceaseless swell of clatter and activity, goods, gadgets, and pixels that constitutes our lives today.

"We were poor people who knew nothing of the prosperity or the vanity of the world," said Peig Sayers. She and the other islanders lived hard lives, buffeted by the extremes of nature, isolated and narrow. Still, most of the time, it was enough. Whereas today—doesn't it seem?—nothing is ever enough.

Or, seen another way, it's too much, leaving us to yearn for just a little less of everything. Today, right beside Facebook Nation and the rest of the twenty-first-century digital world, coexists a twenty-first-century counterculture in sometimes uneasy tension with it: Slow food, locally grown. An intimate urbanism built around compact, walking-scaled city neighborhoods. Vacations offering respite from the hammer and thrum of modern life—camping, long-distance bicycle touring, folk-dancing camps, trekking in Nepal, hiking along the Appalachian Trail. Each offers at least a hesitant, momentary step into a slower, less technology-tangled life; one of less choice, less convenience, closer to nature, maybe some taste of real community. A little, in short, like the Blasket in its prime. The Blaskets "may be a broken-down culture," wrote Thomas Barrington in 1937. "It may be a culture run to seed. But seeds scattered over a field prepared for them will produce a new crop."

Should it surprise us that our visitors loved the Blasket? They were products of a society by now almost a century past, yet much like ours, with many of the urban, technology-bound pleasures and social pathologies we experience today; we need scant imagination to recognize their worries, problems, and preoccupations as our own, their lives like ours. One man a frustrated, bureaucratized intellectual, forever coming down sick, behind in his work, worried about his bills. Another a great playwright, denizen of Paris and Dublin when he wasn't on the road, a sometimes reluctant player in the literary and theatrical world of his day. A Left Bank intellectual, prone to depression. The troubled Brian Kelly, struggling with obscure psychic wounds, finally retreating to an insular little world on the Continent. And of course Thomson, who worked for much of his life against what he deemed the evils of industrial capitalism. All, in the Blaskets, had found a balm, a peace, a happiness.

Thomson, who would insist that he came to see beyond the romantic haze through which he'd first seen the island, nonetheless did view it through a scrim of longing. So did the other visitors. Yeats said of his friend Synge, "It was only when he found Innismaan and the Blaskets, where there is neither riches nor poverty, neither what he calls 'the nullity of the rich' nor 'the squalor of the poor,' that his writing lost its old morbid brooding, that he found his genius and his peace." There, according to Yeats, Synge found men and women who had "refused or escaped the trivial and the temporary, had dignity and good manners where manners mattered." Marie-Louise Sjoestedt wrote in 1925: "I am greatly taken with this place, lonely and wild as it is. . . . I don't think I shall ever get tired of it."

Are we required to judge as distorted or naïve all that these superbly educated men and women experienced on those windy heights above the sea? Must we dismiss it on the simple if undeniable grounds that their place in the island world was temporary and artificial, their immersion incomplete, their insight skewed?

Today they would all be termed "privileged." Each was spared the island's grimmest truths, was buffered from the village's social pressures, could come and go as he or she pleased. What George and Marie-Louise and Marstrander lived was not what the islanders lived. Australian scholar Irene Lucchitti says Synge's sympathetic picture of the Blaskets "recognises neither the realities of poverty nor the ordinary complications of Island life." Synge and the others may have hauled nets, collected turf on the hills behind the village, rowed until their muscles burned. But, unlike the islanders, they weren't consigned forever to labor and hardship. Their livelihoods didn't depend on it. Their prospects ranged beyond the sea-ruffled edge of the island. They were on vacation, or they were on leave, or they were doing research, or they were working on their Irish. Usually it was summer, and the sun shone; come winter, they were back in the city. With no matter what clarity Synge, Thomson, and the others could see the harshness of island life, they nonetheless enjoyed the mental leisure, the freedom from exigency, to see it warmed by softer light. . . .

Or so, voicing this objection, speaks Maturity, the grown-up part of us that insists on being hardheadedly realistic. But of course that was not the part of them the Blaskets claimed. Because for them the Blaskets were their youths, their Land of the Young.

Synge, twenty-seven when he first visited Aran, was older at the time of his visit to the Blaskets, thirty-four. George was twenty. Marstrander was twenty-three. Sjoestedt was twenty-four. Brian Kelly was twenty-eight, as was Robin Flower. "To him," his bilious friend Edward Meyerstein wrote of Flower on a trip to the island, "this place is a dream of his youth." And it was something like that for most of them.

"Dream" suggests unreality, fantasy, nothing to be taken quite seriously, what the crimped adult in us is quick to smack down as ephemeral or silly. But—like Utopia, with its paradoxical intimations of impossible *and* ideal; or for that matter, the Irish Tír na nOg, Land of the Young, itself—"Dream" also suggests something rare and good, on a higher, if elusive, plane, a vision of a happier time or a better world. And it's this we see again and again among the Blasket visitors—their idyllic days on the island transmuted into a personal vision, into sensibilities that reached across their lives and into old age.

Around the time of George Thomson's eightieth birthday, he was visited by Irish scholar Seán Ó Lúing, a native of West Kerry who'd been intrigued by Thomson ever since reading *Fiche Blian ag Fás*. It was a memorable day for Ó Lúing in Birmingham, he and George talking of prospects for the Irish language in Ireland, of links between Greek and Irish. "As he was speaking," Ó Lúing wrote, Thomson "got up and paced the room, a light came into his eyes, his voice which at first has been weak, grew stronger, the years fell away, and I found myself listening to a man who spoke with the animation and fire of youth."

For Thomson, the Blaskets seem to have defined a personal state of grace, a time when he was tied to his fellows in a way he perhaps never was again.

> By the old wooden stove where our hats was hung,
> Our words were told, our songs were sung,
> Where we longed for nothin' and were quite satisfied
> Talkin' and a-jokin' about the world outside.

These are lyrics from a song, "Bob Dylan's Dream," from one of his early albums. Dylan wrote it when he was just twenty-one. Even then, it seems, he cherished the memory of a yet earlier, magical time, full of easy fellowship:

> I wish, I wish, I wish in vain
> That we could sit simply in that room again.
> Ten thousand dollars at the drop of a hat,
> I'd give it all gladly if our lives could be like that.

For Dylan in his dream, at least from the other side of the confounding gates of memory, younger was simpler, and simpler was happy. When we yearn for simplicity, for lives less saddled with stuff, for time less crowded and closed down, it's usually our youthful selves we want back—for the early years when, just out of school, not making much money, as young officers, assistant professors, or junior engineers, we sat "simply in that room again," in pub, bar, or coffee shop, with friends. For the times when, typically, we had less, yet more. "They haven't much worry about material things, really," said the upper-caste Englishwoman in *The Village*. "They prefer to have the extra time to sit around and talk." Insufferable as she could seem, she was on to something, seizing on what, among her friends back in England, she didn't have, or didn't have enough, and what maybe these Irish villagers did.

Some of the islanders' own memories retain this same sense of youth at its delighted ease. Maurice O'Sullivan's book is one long paean to an exuberant youth from which he'd not wholly emerged, full of adventure, games, drinking, and horseplay, steeped in friendship. Mícheál O'Guiheen calls his book *A Pity Youth Does Not Last.* Lís Ní Shúilleabháin "spent the most wholesome part of my childhood and young womanhood" on the island, she wrote George Chambers, "and not a single night passes without me in my happy dreams on the white sand shore." Honeysuckle-sweet nostalgia? A little. But if we ache for the past, maybe it holds something for us.

"The long years have vanished and all I can see today are the old ruined houses where people used to live," Mícheál O'Guiheen recalled in old age. He and one island girl, he remembered, "would walk and walk until we reached the top of the hill. The height wouldn't bother us. We were like a little brother and sister together. I would pick every bright flower growing on the mountain and tie them in a button-hole in front of her dress to please her. We were young and everything looked good to us."

. . .

So much, on that beautiful island off the farthest shore of Ireland, looked good to young George and the others. Yet, in the end, the Blasket community perished. That is the verdict of history, brutal in its finality. Modernity won out. Today, in the big cities of Europe, Asia, and the Americas, traffic roars and restaurants glitter. Suburbs leap across the countryside. Music pounds from the bars of Boston and the *boîtes* of Paris. Online sites herald conferences and conventions. Technologies advance. New companies start up. Food is shipped across the nation and the world. "Social networking" takes some new fashionable form, it seems, every few months. Our world crackles and hums.

The Blasket visitors we've met in these pages had seen vestiges of their own slower, horse-drawn past recede from view, too. They felt some of the ambivalence many today feel at the disappearance of the front porch, the corner market, and the local pub. "It is sad to think," George wrote Katharine in 1937, on a visit with Moya Llewelyn Davies at her new home in Raheny, "that in a year or two the village of Raheny will be swallowed up in the Dublin suburbs"—as indeed it is today. All in our day who chafe at the insistent demands of lives that move too fast, too divorced alike from nature and human community, are a little like Flower, Thomson, Sjoestedt, and the others who found, among their fisherman friends, something they missed in London, Cambridge, or Paris.

The islanders, too, were racked with ambivalence as they left their homes. "Whatever happens on the Island," Lís Ní Shúilleabháin wrote Chambers on February 23, 1942, reporting their decision to leave the Blasket, "I have one gifted thing to tell you of it, I was always happy there. I was happy among sorrows on this island." Another islander, Seán Ó Guithín, when asked about emigrating, said, "The Island will be in my head as long as I live. . . . The coming of each season brought its own charm for us especially when we were young lads. There was the time for making lobster-pots and time for fishing with the pots," which sounds straight out of Ecclesiastes. In the end, there can be no surprise—nor surely is there any contradiction—that people can embrace the blessings of modern life, even reach hungrily for more of them, yet know they've lost something in the bargain, and grieve for it.

It is not entirely mysterious, really, what this something-lost was. We have only to turn to the visitors themselves to see what captured their imaginations; persistent themes run through their writings. They tell of the peculiar dignity and grace of the island people, of their abiding hospitality. They tell of their bravery and strength and capacity to endure. They tell of how, with reading, writing, and pre-packaged distraction such a small part of their lives, vitality shot through their everyday human interactions. They tell of the islanders as creators of joyful music, exuberant dance, and artful language, not mere consumers of them. They tell of time taken to enjoy moments of extraordinary natural beauty. They tell of men and women measured not by one narrow yardstick of performance, doing one thing capably, but of an adaptability that left room for doing much well, living life well.

Such qualities can't easily be figured in to the social and economic equations comparing one society or culture with another. They are hard to stack up against food prices, miles-per-gallon, music downloads, life expectancy, stock options; they don't compute. What, then, should we do with these "losing" graces? As we think of the Blaskets, how they touched the visitors, and what we might draw from them today, how are we to retrieve them, ensure they don't slip irredeemably from sight? How are we to treat virtues too amorphous, soft, and tentative to count, too sweet and admirable for any place but our dreams?

The Blasket books ensure they won't be forgotten; this much, at least, is certain. "It was often," island poet Mícheál O'Guiheen wrote in one of them, that "I spent a while taking my ease spread out on the brown heather, listening to the murmuring of the wind and the moaning of the waves in the coves." Sometimes he'd feel the urge to compose a piece of poetry, yet wouldn't. "It wasn't from laziness I didn't do it, but because those pictures most pleasant to my heart were too much for me to describe."

It would be silly and misguided to imagine the Blaskets as some straightforward model for a richer, better way of life, or from which to draw too-easy lessons of sociology or culture. The visitors themselves, certainly, were not deceived. They were all seasoned intellects. They visited the island. They were seduced by it. But they were clear-eyed and self-possessed enough not to hold it up as an exemplar to be transported bodily somewhere else. They'd been lucky, and they knew it: they'd landed on the island when they were young and had the wisdom to let it change their lives.

"I have been reading the Irish version of Maurice's book," George wrote in 1937 to Katharine while briefly away in Ireland. "It is as fresh as ever, and as beautiful—much more beautiful in Irish than in English, but it leaves me rather sad thinking over the past. Not that I want it back again. What I want is to be back with you. This is a lovely place, but I could not live here because it is too remote from the ugly world, which is less forbidding when one lives in the thick of it."

During the years when our story plays out, then, just as in the years since, and in the years to come, the eternal oppositions remain: To live challenging lives that don't grind us down with their pace and pressure. To sample the best of the "simple" things while enjoying the benefits of a complex and sophisticated society. To exult in the beauty of wild places yet not destroy them through use. To embrace the wisdom of our parents and grandparents while adapting to new situations and passing on new wisdom to our children.

Their time on the Blasket didn't leave our visitors able to resolve such oppositions. In our consumer society, men grow rich by convincing us that the next new product, or exercise regimen, or exotic locale can fix the contradictions nagging at us. But of course they never do. The timeless tensions and lingering mysteries take new form in every culture and in every generation, are never resolved.

Not resolved permanently, anyway. But back then, on that ocean-swept island, for Robin Flower and Carl Marstrander, George and Marie-Louise, the mysteries were clarified, the tensions relieved, and everything, for the blessed days of their youth, was just right.

Acknowledgments

It was Trish Hogan and Ed Barrett who, when Sarah and I were weighing where to go in Ireland for our honeymoon in 2005, suggested a spot at the far western tip of the Dingle Peninsula, the village of Dún Chaoin, County Kerry. Not long after we returned, Trish introduced me to some of the Blasket-related books in her substantial library of Irish literature. In the years since, she has been unfailingly enthusiastic and a wonderful friend. Ed, an MIT colleague, and his wife, Jenny, also took an early interest in the project and, for one of our times in Dún Chaoin, let Sarah and me stay at their house. I owe both of these Cambridge friends many thanks, not the least for pointing me to their own most cherished place in Ireland.

The day after we'd first found our way from Shannon Airport, over the Connor Pass to Dingle and then, around Slea Head, to Dún Chaoin, Sarah and I stumbled on the Blasket Centre; what happened next is briefly told in the Prologue. What's not told there, and needs to be said here, is how much friendliness and cooperation I enjoyed during my research trips to the Centre, which is archive and museum as well as visitor's center. There, Dáithi de Mórdha responded to untold questions and research requests. He tracked down books, papers, and photographs, never protested, never wavered. He and his father, Mícheál de Mórdha, the Centre's director, gave me the run of the place, or so it seemed, routinely advising me of materials just then reaching the archive, introducing me to people, doing spot translations from the Irish. My warmest thanks to them for their dedication, their professionalism, and their many kindnesses.

Thanks as well to others in the Dún Chaoin community who freely offered help and hospitality to me and my wife. Chief among these are Frances and John Kennedy, our neighbors across the road from Ed's house who were so generous— with flowers from their garden, honey from their hives, books from their library, stories from their experience. Through Frances's memorable portrayal of Maurya in a local performance of Synge's *Riders to the Sea,* I came away with an indelible impression of the fortitude and forbearance demanded of the fishing families of Ireland's west.

Much material about the Blaskets is available in English; some is not and can be found only in Irish-language sources. For her translation work, I wish to thank Ruth Úi Ógáin, whose intelligence, skills, and seriousness of purpose helped make this book a better one. Right from the start, she grasped the tack I'd taken and guided me to particular resources of the Blasket Centre, where she had formerly served as guide, translator, and researcher. She did this, I should say, while juggling the demands of home and family, seemingly without breaking a sweat.

Many people, most cited by name in the Notes, granted me interviews, furnished correspondence and photographs, invited me into their homes, or lavished on me the resources of their libraries and archives. My debt to them is substantial. I wish especially to acknowledge Séamus Mac Mathúna, for going far beyond his duties at NUI Galway to talk to me at length about George Thomson's time at Galway seventy-five years earlier; Leslie Matson, for sharing with me his vast trove of Blasket lore and for the hospitality he and his wife accorded me in Waterford; Muiris Mac Conghail, for his generosity in sharing the fruits of his Galway research and his high-spirited conversation in Dublin; Breandán Feiritéar, for driving me around Connemara, where Maurice O'Sullivan lived much of his life after leaving the island, and sharing with me insights and impressions culled from his deep knowledge of the Blaskets. Thanks, too, to Gilberte Furstenberg, who secured for me a rare French-language publication, and Pádraig Ó Healai, for translating substantial excerpts from his mother's book.

Finally, thanks to Meg Alexiou, for our many hours talking about her father, George Thomson, and for her friendship. I met Meg not long after the death of her mother when she was clearing out the family house in Birmingham. Just then, before her father's books and papers had been distributed among various repositories, Meg let me spend time with these precious family materials and through them gain my first real insight into the mind and heart of her father. We were joined in Birmingham by Máire Kavanagh, daughter of Maurice O'Sullivan. The three of us spent the better part of a weekend together, capped with a memorable candlelit dinner. I am grateful to Meg, and to Máire as well, for their openhearted welcome into the lives of their fathers.

Around the time this book appears in the United States, I'll be retiring from MIT where I have been professor of science writing since 1999. These years have left me with friendships, fond memories, and debts unpaid. I wish to thank Nick Altenbernd, Maya Jhangiani, and Magdalena Rieb for their steady help in the headquarters office of the Program in Writing and Humanistic Studies, as well as Susanne Martin before them and Shannon Larkin; my students in the Graduate Program in Science Writing, several of whom gave me good advice on sections of the book; my colleagues in the Grad Program, including Tom Levenson, Marcia Bartusiak, Phil Hilts, Alan Lightman, and Boyce Rensberger; and Deborah

Fitzgerald, dean of the School of Humanities, Arts, and Social Sciences, for her support and sure common-sense advice.

I was honored to receive a Simon Guggenheim Memorial Foundation fellowship for this project. The Guggenheim, supplemented by grants furnished by MIT's School of Humanities, Arts, and Social Sciences, as well as by the MIT provost's office, allowed me to pursue the research and writing of this book with fewer of the financial constraints that can slow, undermine, or distort a substantial book project. For all these, I am extraordinarily grateful.

I wish to thank Michael Carlisle, my agent, who has placed his affirming and high-minded soul in the service of this book—and to Dava Sobel and Robin Henig for pointing me to him. At Knopf, I've been fortunate to have been able to work, easily and agreeably, with editor Ann Close, as well as with her able and tenacious assistant, Caroline Zancan. A word of thanks, too, to Vicky Bijur, whose probing questions early in the book's genesis helped me to see more clearly what I didn't want the book to be as well as what I did.

And Sarah, my dearest? I am she, and she is me, and we are all together.

Notes

I have supplied notes for most quotations as well as for most assertions of fact that might seem debatable, curious, or obscure, or that otherwise warrant reclamation from the great body of available material bearing on the Blaskets and its visitors. I have not, typically, supplied citations for amply documented historical events like the Irish Civil War, or well-known figures like Éamon de Valera; or for routine background information culled from gazetteers, university yearbooks, Web sites, maps, newspaper obituaries, or standard references such as the *Oxford Dictionary of National Biography*.

INTERVIEWS

In addition to the books and documents cited, these notes make reference to interviews, conversations, or, in the cases indicated, e-mail correspondence with the following persons in Ireland, England, and the United States: Margaret Alexiou, Bo Almqvist, Kathleen Arduini, Anna Bale, Seán Cahillane, Mike Colles, Dáithí de Mórdha, Mícheal de Mórdha, Breandán Feiritéar, Linda Francis and Justin Elcombe, Patrick and Una Grogan, Máire Llewelyn Kavanagh, Frances and John Kennedy, Niall R. Livingstone, Gerry Long, Melissa Llewelyn-Davies (e-mail), Máire Mhac an tSaoi, Muiris Mac Conghail, Séamus Mac Mathúna, Sister Mary Justin, Leslie Matson, Brian McGuinness (e-mail), Kerby Miller, Eileen Naughten, Joe Nugent, Seán Ó Coileáin, Tadhg Ó Dúshláine, Father Pádraig Ó Fiannachta, Pádraig Ó Healai (e-mail), Pádraig Ó Siochfhradha (nephew of An Seabhac), Sue Redican, Ann Saddlemyer (e-mail), Ray Stagles, Alan Titley (e-mail), Nuala Uí Aimhirgín, Niamh Uí Laoithe.

MANUSCRIPT SOURCES

Manuscripts, documents, images, and other materials were consulted at the following archives and libraries, or kindly made available by the individuals named:

Alexiou, Margaret: See Thomson Archives, below.

Almqvist, Bo: Correspondence and documents related to Marie-Louise Sjoestedt.

Arduini, Kathleen: Personal papers and photos related to Mary Kearney.

Blasket Centre/Ionad An Bhlascaoid Mhoir, Dun Chaoin, Co. Kerry: Library, archives, and interpretive center devoted to the Blaskets. Irish-language materials translated by Ruth Uí Ógáin.

British Library: Idris Bell papers, mostly Add ms. 59510, ff. 46–108, corrrespondence with Robin Flower and other Blasket visitors.

British Museum: Records of Standing Committee, 1910–1944; Index to Trustees Minutes, 1906–1946; Robin Flower papers

Cahillane, Seán: Personal papers and photos related to Mary Kearney.

Delargy Centre for Irish Folklore, University College Dublin: Robin Flower papers; Eibhlís Ní Shúilleabháin/George Chambers correspondence, manuscripts vols. 1943–45; Schrier notebooks, vols. 1407–11. Many thanks to Jonny Dillon for his extraordinary cooperation.

Dublin City Library and Archive.

Dublin Writers Museum.

Dulwich College archives.

Feiritéar, Breandán: Photos and other materials related to the Blaskets and neighboring mainland communities.

Galvin's Travel Agency, Dingle, Co. Kerry: Emigration records. Courtesy of Maurice O'Connor.

Kennedy, John and Frances, Dún Chaoin, Co. Kerry, Ireland: Willie Long materials and other aspects of local history.

King's College Archives: materials bearing on George Thomson's time at King's.

Mac Mathúna, Séamus, National University of Ireland, Galway: In the notes that follow I treat as interview material, rather than as documents, informal on-the-spot translations by Mr. Mac Mathúna of articles by M. Ó Flathartaigh and Risteard Ó Glaisne, in *Inniu*, January 16, April 17, April 24, and May 1, 1981, as well as of other Irish-language university documents related to Thomson's time at University College, Galway.

Matson, Leslie: Information supplementing his collection "Blasket Lives," his account of 125 islanders and their families, available at the Blasket Centre; his comprehensive survey and summary of the letters of Eibhlís Ní Shúilleabháin at the Delargy Centre, Dublin.

National Library of Ireland: Seán Ó Lúing papers; materials bearing on Seán an Chóta, Robin Flower, Marie-Louise Sjoestedt, and other Blasket visitors; Tomás Ó Criomhthain letters to Brian Kelly; original manuscript of *Fiche Blian ag Fás* with George Thomson's notes.

Royal College of Physicians, Dublin: Materials bearing on Dr. Pádraig Grogan, courtesy of Robert Mills.

Russel Library, National University of Ireland, Maynooth: Materials bearing on Dr. Pádraig Grogan, courtesy of Penny Woods.

Sisters of Providence, Springfield, Mass.: Sister Mary Clemens (Mary Kearney), courtesy of Sister Mary Justin.

Thomson Archives at the Birmingham Archives and Heritage Service, Birmingham Central Library: Accession 2007/144, "Papers of Katharine and George Thomson," some of this material made available to me through Thomson's daughter Margaret Alexiou in the period before they were actually transferred to the archive. Includes fragmentary, mostly handwritten biography of George Thomson, in the form of letters linked by text, by Katharine Thomson. Thomson's letters to his wife, Katharine, found in this collection are normally addressed to "Katten," but I identify them here by her proper name.

Trinity College, Dublin: J. M. Synge notebooks; Robin Flower correspondence.

University of Birmingham Special Collections: George Thomson.

In the notes that follow, I have used the following shorthand to designate some of the more frequently cited books, archives, and other references. I hope readers find this system easier to navigate than the acronyms more typically seen (and which I, at least, can never keep straight):

Another: Muiris Mac Conghail's video documentary, *Another Island: A Portrait of the Blasket Islands.*

Celtic: Seán Ó Lúing, *Celtic Studies in Europe.*

Cross: Tomás Ó Crohan, *Island Cross-Talk.*

Delargy: Delargy Centre for Irish Folklore, Dublin.

Eighty: Gerry Gregg's *George Thomson: Eighty Years A-Growing,* video documentary.

Hidden: Irene Lucchitti's *The Islandman: The Hidden Life of Tomás Ó'Crohan.*

Islandman: Tomás Ó'Crohan's *The Islandman.*

KathFrag: Katharine Thomson's fragmentary biography of her husband, Thomson Archives, Birmingham. Because its pagination is unclear and appears in handwritten and typewritten sections of unknown priority, the citation goes no further.

KerryIsland: Muiris Mac Conghail's *The Blaskets: A Kerry Island Library.*

Lís: Three page-numbered volumes of Eibhlís Ní Shúilleabháin's letters, vols. 1943–1945, located at the Delargy Centre for Irish Folklore, Dublin, of which her published *Letters from The Great Blasket* includes about a third. A foreword by George Chambers appears in vol. 1943.

LísLetters: Eibhlís Ní Shúilleabháin's *Letters from The Great Blasket.*

Memories: Pádraig Tyers, ed., *Blasket Memories.* The untitled nine-chapter first half, pp.7–88, appears in the notes as "Seán Ó Criomhthain, in *Memories.*" The second half of the same volume, pp. 89–190, includes question-and-answer interviews with several other Blasket-related figures (including, again, Seán Ó Criomhthain). These are referred to in the notes as, for example, "Seán Ó Guihín interview, in *Memories.*"

NatLib: National Library of Ireland.

Reflections: Cathal Póirtéir, *Blasket Island Reflections.* Transcription from the audio if not otherwise indicated. Otherwise, with page number, English translation furnished in the accompanying booklet.

RuthTransl: Irish-language materials wholly or partially translated for the author by Ruth Uí Ógáin.

Thomson Archives: Thomson Archives, Birmingham Public Library.

Twenty: Maurice O'Sullivan's *Twenty Years A-Growing,*

PROLOGUE

4   Neolithic civilization: E. M. Forster, introductory note, *Twenty,* p. v.

5   Looking after a sheep on the hill-side: Ibid., p. 220.

5   Will know that the wildest sayings: Synge, preface, *The Playboy of the Western World.*

6   I have done my best: *Islandman,* p. 244.

6   If we put them all together: Thomson, in *Another.*

7   Hurston: See Valerie Boyd, *Wrapped in Rainbows* (New York: Scribner, 2004). See also Tracy Mishkin, *The Harlem and Irish Renaissances* (Gainesville: University Press of Florida, 1998).

9   To express "darling": Thomson to Katharine, April 18, 1939, Thomson Archives.

9   Books of Irish verse: Several can be seen in the Blasket Centre.

I. THE WEST

10   Take advantage: Mrs. D. P. Thomson, p. 104.

11   Jeremiah Curtin: Curtin journal entries (in English), in Uaitéar Mac Craith, "Turusanna Jeremiah Curtin I gCiarraí," in *Thaitin Sé Le Peig,* ed. Pádraig Ó Fiannachta (Baile an Fhirtéaraigh: Oidhreacht Chorca Dhuibhne, 1989).

11   The most fertile and vigorous: *Benét's Reader's Encyclopedia,* 3rd ed., p. 770.

12   The Necessity for De-Anglicizing Ireland: See Pierce, pp. 2–13.

13   Gaelic League: See McMahon, Garvin.

13   Language as a neutral ground: Cited in Kiberd, *Inventing Ireland,* p. 153.

13   It is very much alive now: Cited in *Celtic,* 192.

14   The authentic Ireland: Whelan, p. 184.

14   Part of the creation myth: Kevin Martin, p. 90.

14   Synge: See Grene, *Synge;* Saddlemyer, ed., *Letters of Synge;* Greene and Stephens; quotation in Kiberd, *Synge and the Irish Language.*

15   It gave me a moment of exquisite satisfaction: Synge, *The Aran Islands,* p. 11.

16   So strange and silent: Cited in Foster, "Certain Set Apart," p. 108.

16   An almost Aeschylean: *Benét's Reader's Encyclopedia,* p. 953.

16   Willie Long: Interview, Frances and John Kennedy and census records; see also Richard Irvine Best letter, 1908, in Ó Lúing, "The Scholar's Path"; Marstrander, p. 5.

17   Of course my place is not an out-and-out Hotel: Long to Synge, July 27, 1905, letter 187, MS 4424, Trinity College, Dublin.

17   Myself & household all speak Paddy's language: Ibid.

17   Narrow-gauge steam railroad: See Rowlands and McGrath.

17   A confused mass of peasants: Synge, *Travels,* p. 72.

17   Ah, poor fellow . . . in Saint Louis: Ibid., p. 73.

17   As the night fell . . . heavy night smells: Ibid., p. 74.

18   In the centre of the most Gaelic part: Saddlemyer, ed., *Letters of Synge,* p. 119.

18   Suddenly on the . . . indescribable grandeur: Synge, *Travels,* p. 85.

18   Even more primitive . . . joy at the prospect: Saddlemyer, ed., *Letters of Synge,* p. 120.

18   I came off yesterday: Synge notebooks, Trinity College, Dublin.

18   As we came nearer: Synge, *Travels,* p. 87.

19   I have been here . . . most interesting place: Saddlemyer, ed., *Letters of Synge,* p. 122.

20   Irish-tinged obscurities: Ibid., p. 124.

20   He wrote to Yeats: Ibid., p. 125.

20   Notes in Ballyferriter: Synge notebooks, Trinity College, Dublin.

20 Perhaps from America: Breándan Ferritéar broached this possibility in an interview with the author.

20 The little hostess: In Synge's notebooks at Trinity and in his letters from the island, Synge refers to a little queen and sometimes to a princess—all "royalty" in the house of the king. In the published version, we meet only the little hostess, the notebook's "queen"; the princess has mostly disappeared or perhaps melded with her sister. In a letter to Nathalie Esposito the following month (Saddlemyer, ed., *Letters of Synge,* p. 128), Synge recalls the king's two daughters, one of whom "was married a few months ago and still lives in her father's house—a curiously charming person."

20 Máire Ní Chatháin: See Matson, "Blasket Lives."

21 She is a small, beautifully-formed woman: Synge, *Travels,* p. 88.

21 Heard a story of Connaught man: Synge, *The Aran Islands,* p. 42.

21 Country public house or Shebeen: Pierce, p. 172.

21 Playboy Riots: See, for instance, Lady Gregory, *Our Irish Theatre.*

22 *Streeleen:* Kiberd, *Synge and the Irish Language,* p. 52.

22 one of the most beautiful and living figures: Percival Presland Howe, *J. M. Synge: A Critical Study* (1912), p. 168.

22 Favors actress Molly Allgood: Ann Saddlemyer, e-mail.

22 Prototype: Greene and Stephens, p. 203.

23 Puts him to bed: Synge, *Travels,* p. 90.

23 Well, aren't you . . . company of women: Ibid., p. 101.

23 He was shy and inclined to silence: Greene and Stephens, p. 52.

24 The direct sexual instincts: Synge, *The Aran Islands,* p. 77.

24 As she put her hands on my shoulders: Synge, *Travels,* p. 95.

24 Hadn't enough material: Synge to Joseph Hone, Jan. 17, 1907, in Saddlemyer, ed., *Letters of Synge,* p. 283.

24 The most intimate experience: Grene, ed., *J. M. Synge, Travelling Ireland,* p. xxi.

25 Wonderful air, which is like wine in one's teeth: Synge, *Travels,* p. 85

25 Walked through a boreen: Ibid., p. 89

25 Slights: *KerryIsland,* pp. 133–134.

25 Emphasis on wildness suggests a primitive simplicity: *Hidden,* p. 45.

25 Shows him . . . little of himself: Ibid., p. 46. In her doctoral dissertation, on which her book is based, Lucchitti writes, " . . . gave nothing of himself."

26 A nicer thing: Synge, "Notes in Ballyferriter," p. 24.

26 I am sitting within the four whitewashed walls: Ibid., p. 26.

26 They have an island and I have an ink-pot: Ibid.

26 Awkward English: Mr. Pat Keane to Synge, Jan. 20, 1906, letter 233, TCD MS 4424, Trinity College, Dublin.

27 Aspiring to simplicity: Agostini, p. 161.

2. THE FINE FLOWER OF THEIR SPEECH

30 All the bridges to the outside: Marstrander, p. 5.

30 Children of nature: Ibid., p. 14.

31 Superstitious and blinded: Ibid., p. 15.

31 That the Almighty might lead your boats into destruction: Ibid.

31 It's from these evening gatherings: Ibid., p. 16.

32 Healthy and high: Ibid., p. 20.

32 I have never met . . . thinking back on them: Ibid., p. 21.

32 Marstrander was the son: See *Celtic,* chap. 7; Olsen; Greene, "A Warm and Generous Friend," and "Carl J. S. Marstrander"; Binchy, "Norse Scholar"; Oftedal obituaries; McGrath, " 'The Vikings' Great Gaelic Studies"; Ó Lúing papers, NatLib.

33 London, not Athens: Bo Almqvist pointed this out at a conference devoted to Marstrander at the Blasket Centre, Oct. 2007.

33 *Hic Rhodus:* Ó Lúing papers, NatLib.

33 Fertile scholarly ground: Olsen, p. 55.

33 Teetotal Hotel: Marstrander, p. 2.

33 The living Irish: Seán Ó Criomhthain interview, in *Memories,* p. 90.

33 I did not . . . difficult Irish language: Marstrander, p. 4.

34 My enemy is just behind my ear: Seán Ó Criomhthain interview, in *Memories,* p. 90.

34 An honest attempt to get my tongue right: See also, Robin Flower to Idris Bell, before July 17, 1910, in which he tells the story he heard from Marstrander himself.

35 To learn the spoken tongue: Details offered in these pages do not reflect reading or speaking knowledge of Irish on my part but are drawn from a number of authoritative sources: Ó Cuív; Ní Chartúir; Ó Siadhail; Kenneth Jackson, "Some Mutations in Blasket Irish"; a variety of dictionaries, standard texts, and online sites devoted to the language. Thanks to Jennifer Hogan for a short course in Irish Gaelic given at Massachusetts Institute of Technology in Jan. 2006; and to Ruth Uí Ógáin for reviewing this brief treatment.

    "I still find the same difficulty in understanding [the locals]: they all speak so terribly fast. . . . I never had such an experience before with language," writes Richard Irvine Best in frustration while staying with Willie Long in Ballyferriter in 1908. "I attribute it altogether to the absurd antiquated spelling. The spoken word and phrase has no identity with the written word. That is why so few native speakers can read Irish. Again, final vowels are elided, terminations vanish, and words are quite obscured by accent or lack of accent." (Ó Lúing, "The Scholar's Path.")

35 When I . . . disgusted and pessimistic: Marie-Louise Sjoestedt, cited in *Celtic,* p. 114.

36 After a fortnight in Balleyferriter: Marstrander, p. 5.

36 The speech is like a big river: Ibid., p. 14.

37 His business was to get the fine flower of the speech: *Islandman,* p. 224.

37 Fine with him: Ibid.

38 We'll manage. I won't refuse you: Seán Ó Criomhthain interview, in *Memories,* p. 91.

38 Improving moderately: Marstrander to Richard Best, in Irish, Sept. 15, 1907, Ó Lúing papers, NatLib.

38 Vocabulary lists: *KerryIsland,* p. 102.

38   Rude sketches: Ibid., p. 88.

38   Marstrander bridged this gap: Oftedal, "Carl J. S. Marstrander."

38   Had little . . . Healthy as a salmon: Seán Ó Criomhthain interview, in *Memories,* p. 90.

38   Aboard their joined hands: Ibid., p. 91.

38   Charms the young ones: Marstrander, p. 15.

38   Accepted like . . . as an Islander: Ibid., p. 14.

38   A fine man: *Islandman,* p. 224.

39   Convinced . . . a special people: Marstrander conference, 2007.

39   I haven't heard . . . many a long day: *Islandman,* p. 225.

40   One of the most . . . elemental phenomena: Ó Lúing, *Kuno Meyer,* p. 240.

40   School of Irish Learning was already taking shape: For the early years of the school, see *Ériu: The Journal of the School of Irish Learning* (Dublin), beginning in 1904; *Celtic;* Ó Lúing, *Kuno Meyer.*

40   Garden party: *Bláithín,* p. 26.

41   Infixed pronouns; the vagaries of the copula: Robin Flower to Idris Bell, before July 17, 1910, British Library.

42   By common consent: Bell, p. 362.

42   Three weeks' leave: Records of Standing Committee, 1910–1944, p. 2718, British Museum.

42   What human beings . . . gift of eternal youth: Robin Flower to Idris Bell, c. July 1910, British Library.

42   A bit of a trickster: Bo Almqvist, at Marstrander conference, Blasket Centre, Oct. 2007.

42   Robin Ernest William Flower: See Bell; Robinson; *Celtic,* chap. 5; Prescott; *Bláithín.*

43   String bag: Patrick Flower, p. 23.

43   His pockets always bulged: Bell, p. 355.

44   British Museum, Manuscripts Department: See P. R. Harris; Wilson.

44   Home from home for the great reader: Patrick Flower, p. 25.

44   His practice of wandering about the Department: Bell, p. 360.

44   Pangur Ban: Robin Flower, *The Irish Tradition,* p. 24.

44   I am safe here in the royal palace: Robin Flower to Idris Bell, Aug. 9, 1910, British Library.

45   Tír na nÓg: Robin Flower's poem is in his *Eire and Other Poems.*

45   Talking with Cáit: Robin Flower to Idris Bell, Aug. 9, 1910, British Library. On Aug. 7, 1911, Cáit wrote the Flowers thanking them for the parcel she'd received from them, "but sorry to say I cannot ware it here, because they don't ware such dresses in Kerry. I thought it rather tight around but I know they are the latest fashion." (Delargy.)

46   Two-week leave: Records of Standing Committee, 1910–1944, p. 2779, British Museum.

46   Glorious time: Flower to Best, Aug. 9, 1911, NatLib.

46   And did some rather nice sketches: See Robin Flower, *The Western Island.* Mrs. Flower was "much more observant in my view than her husband Robin in some respects," suggests Muiris Mac Conghail in an RTÉ program aired Oct. 22, 2002.

46   Pen-and-ink she made . . . of the king's house: Ibid., p. 43. An exhibit at the Blasket Centre represents this image.

46   As good lodgings: *Celtic,* p. 127. But see Marstrander, p. 9, where he recalls being less pleased, recording that he had to ask his host, the king, to make a window for his room, that "the rain made small streams on the floor," that mold grew "thick on my clothes after a couple of days."

46   In another country: Máire Mhac a tSaoi, interviewed on RTÉ, broadcast Oct. 2003.

47   Posed beside the slipway: *KerryIsland,* p. 99.

48   My high-spirited friend: As translated in Mac Conghail's *Another Island.* For a variant, *see KerryIsland,* p. 138.

49   You may imagine . . . ingenious and complicated: Robin Flower, *The Western Island,* p. 37.

49   Foaming crests: Ibid.

49   Dear young gentleman: Tomás Ó Criomhthain to Flower, Aug. 29, 1910, Delargy.

49   A sudden feeling: Robin Flower, *The Western Island,* p. 12.

3. BRIAN'S CHAIR

50   Gaelic League teacher: Nic Gráinne, p. 94,

50   In the Protestant school: "The origins of his literacy in Irish are more likely to derive from the legacy of the Protestant missionary school on the island," which operated from about 1839 to 1863; the Roman Catholic primary school opened the following year (*Oxford Dictionary of National Biography* entry for Tomás Ó Criomhthain).

51   Until I got a taste for the business: *Islandman,* p. 223.

51   Calligraphic art: Ms. 15,785, NatLib.

51   A cramped little house, roofed with rushes: *Islandman,* p. 2.

51   My father . . . great man for work. Ibid., p. 3.

52   The Troubles of Life: *Islandman,* chap. 20.

52   I was told . . . like iron: Interview, in *Another.*

52   Eveleen Nichols: See Ó Dubhshláine, *A Dark Day on the Blaskets;* Matson, *Méiní,* chap. 12.

52   One day: *Islandman,* p. 197.

52   He let out a scream: Ó Dubhshláine, *A Dark Day on the Blaskets,* p. 97.

53   Dónall's Scholar: *Reflections,* p. 6.

53   Only island name: *KerryIsland,* p. 131.

53   A small, lively man: Robin Flower, foreword, *Islandman,* p. ix.

54   Tremendously close friends: In *Another.*

54   Cross the Irish Sea: Tomás Ó Criomhthain to Mrs. Flower, Aug. 30, 1915. Delargy Centre.

55   It is horrid work: Flower to Best, NatLib, in Seán Ó Lúing, *Saoir Theangan* (Coiscéim, 1989).

55   Stood off to the side: Matson writes, in "Blasket Lives," that when a ship went aground on the island in 1916, Tomás was not part of a regular crew, perhaps

"because some of the fishermen did not regard him as being a regular fisherman or looked on him as an unusual person who might not fit in, or who might look on himself as a cut above them."

56   Roger Casement: This account broadly follows Mac Conghail, "Brian Ó Ceallaigh."

56   We understood each other: An Seabhac, "Tomás Ó Criomhthain, Fisherman and Author," p. 30, RuthTransl.

57   Are there limpets: *Cross,* p. 20.

57   Printed word was not quite so alien: See, for example, *Hidden,* p. 110.

58   Pebbles of language: Ibid., p. 195.

58   Qualified to congratulate: Ó Criomhthain to Flower, Sept. 18, 1911, Delargy.

58   Irish Professor: Ó Criomhthain to Mrs. Flower, n.d., Delargy.

58   Everyone knows: Cited in Enright, introduction, *Cross,* p. 4.

58   For people . . . uncomplicated existence: Kelly.

59   Write about what you see at this moment: Ibid.

59   The Voice in the Afternoon: *An Lóchrann,* Dec. 1917.

59   You can't live on scenery: Kelly.

59   I don't think: "Radharc na nIontas," *Fáinne an Lae,* Oct. 12, 1918.

59   The nights are getting longer: Quoted in Lucchitti, p. 117.

60   Exacting in his standards: Bell, p. 367.

60   He had an instinct . . . true literary taste: Eoin MacNeill.

60   Cherished that pen: Account follows Seán Ó Criomhthain interview, in *Memories,* p. 113.

62   He said it would be a pity if I were idle: Cited in Enright, introduction, *Cross,* p. 2.

62   Sit down a bit: *Islandman,* p. 86. Another translation in *KerryIsland,* p. 141.

62   Sheep killed by neighbors: A translation of this poem appears in Ó Scannláin, pp. 73–77.

62   Phonetic script: *Islandman,* p. 87. "I set about scribbling down the words as they came out of his mouth. It wasn't in the usual spelling that I wrote them, for I hadn't enough practice in it in those days."

62   I thought it a pity: Kelly.

62   Séamus and His Cravings: *Cross,* p. 11.

62   Tadhg the Joker: Ibid., p. 12.

63   The mountains were aglow: Ibid., p. 80.

63   I have the seven cares: Ibid., p. 66.

63   I had forgotten: Thomson to Pádraig Ó Fiannachta, Oct. 29, 1975, Thomson Archives.

63   The great pearl: *Reflections,* p. 38.

64   They lived there in each other's shadow: *Reflections,* p. 39.

64   He was a mason: Kelly.

64   Wouldn't it delight: *Cross,* p. 191.

64   One crowned King: Ibid., p. 51.

65   A currach: Ibid., p. 78.

66   I am writing this: *Cross,* p. 208.

4. NICE BOY WITH A CAMERA

67   He occupied rooms: King's College Archives.

67   Classicist, below a budding mathematician: Ibid.

67   Markby, and a French peasant girl: Markby, Thomson's family generally, letters quoted, marriage certificate, and other family records, photographs, etc., from Thomson Archives.

68   Derwentwater: Margaret Alexiou, interview.

68   Lending library: Birmingham.

68   Dulwich College: Dulwich College archives; Piggott; *Dulwich College Register,* 1629–1926, compiled by Thomas Lane Ormiston; issues of Dulwich College *Alleynian.*

69   Six years of unbroken bliss: Piggott, p. 217.

69   Forged a letter: Katharine Thomson, in *Eighty.*

69   Chiton and sandals: *Alleynian,* 1921, Dulwich College archives.

69   A production of the *Oresteia*: Thomson to Sheppard, June 27, 1929, Thomas Archives. See also *Alleynian,* Feb. 21, 1921: "J. T. Sheppard [O.A.], Fellow of King's College, has the production of the 'Oresteia' of Aeschylus in his hands; the play is to be performed at Cambridge this month."

70   Sheppard: Wilkinson, pp. 194–95.

70   At the risk of appearing sentimental or gushing: Thomson to Sheppard, June 27, 1929, Thomson Archives.

70   Classics was second best: Margaret Alexiou, interview. See also Thomson to Pádraig Ó Fiannachta, Oct. 29, 1975, Thomson Archives, in which Thomson speaks of his youthful "intention to give up Greek for Irish. I was put off Old Irish by the specialists who (with the exception of Robin Flower) seemed to treat it as philology and nothing more."

70   During the last years: Statement by Thomson, in KathFrag.

71   *Tess of the D'Urbervilles:* Thomson to Arnold Kettle, Sept. 22, 1953, Thomson Archives: "Ever since I read Tess at sixteen . . ."

71   Rescued: George Thomson, "Thomas Hardy and the Peasantry," p. 633.

71   The burning anger: Thomson, China journal, May 24, 1955, Thomson Archives.

71   Evokes so many forgotten memories: Ibid., May 18, 1955.

71   I spent my holidays in Dorset: Thomson to Arnold Kettle, Sept. 22, 1953, Thomson Archives.

71   Black-and-Tan terror: Thomson, China journal, May 24, 1955, Thomson Archives.

71   An ardent Sinn Feiner: George Thomson, "Irish Language Revival," p. 7.

72   About seventeen: According to Thomson, China journal, May 24, 1955, Thomson Archives, it was "a year or two" after reading *Tess of the D'Urbervilles* for the first time, at age sixteen (see above note to p. 71), that he joined the Gaelic League in London.

72   As soon as . . . cadet uniform: Katharine, in *Eighty.*

72   *The Pursuit of Diarmuid and Gráinne:* In Blasket Centre library, as well as the others mentioned.

72   Of "fear" and "ban" and "rann": The three Irish words meant "man," "white," and "verse," while the final phrase referred to a rule of grammar. ("To con" meant to learn by rote.)

73 Waley suggested: Thomson, in *Another;* Enright, "George Thomson: A Memoir."

73 Arrived in Dingle: See Raidió na Gaeltachta Collection, Blasket Centre, CD 0945 (04), RuthTransl.

73 Just a slip of a school girl: Quoted in Enright, "George Thomson: A Memoir," 119.

73 Pointing to the pot rack: Ibid., p. 121.

73 By listening to them reciting it by heart: Ray Stagles, interview.

74 Their family name: On Irish names, see, especially, Matson, "Blasket Lives."

74 Six Seán Ó Cearnaighs: Matson, "Blasket Lives," p. 2.

76 He was . . . studious and introspective: George Thomson, foreword, O'Guiheen, p. vi.

76 He's a nice boy. He has a camera: Ní Loingsigh, entry for Sept. 7, 1923, RuthTransl.

76 I have not seen the young Englishman: Máiréad Ní Loingsigh, entry for Sept. 2, 1923, RuthTransl.

76 Beginish just behind them: Photograph, Blasket Centre.

77 Because I've never seen my own picture: Máiréad Ní Loingsigh, entry for Sept. 29, 1923, RuthTransl.

77 Maurice: See, for example, *Twenty;* Uí Aimhirgín, *Reflections.*

77 That this girl . . . And they'd believe him: Máire Mhic Ní Shúilleabháin, interview by Mícheál de Mórdha, 1993, Blasket Centre, RuthTransl.

77 Ghost in her coat: Ibid.

77 Meeting George Thomson: *Twenty,* chap. 19.

77 If everyone in Ireland . . . Gaels again: *Twenty,* p. 222.

78 Happy as children: Ibid., p. 223.

78 It is a pity . . . Not in the city of London: Ibid., p. 224.

78 Daideo: Matson, "Blasket Lives."

79 If I had been listening with eyes closed: Thomson, China journal, June 14, 1955, Thomson Archives.

79 Men meet but not the hills or mountains: Mac Conghail, "An English Scholar of Ireland and Greece."

79 I never took much notice: Thomson to Joan V. Robinson, Jan. 1, 1939, King's College Archives, JVR/7/444.

79 George left us today: Ní Loingsigh, Sept. 30, 1923, RuthTransl.

79 Picture slipped out. Ibid.

79 He was in Bodley's Court: King's College Archives; site visit.

79 I went to the Blasket: George Thomson, "Irish Language Revival," p. 7.

80 Ten or eleven years: Ibid. See also Raidió na Gaeltachta Collection, Blasket Centre, CD 0945 (02), RuthTransl.

80 Gifts: Muiris Ó Guithín, in *Eighty.*

80 George had better Irish: Quoted in Enright, p. 146. See also Seán Ó Criomhthain interview, in *Memories,* p. 93.

80 Up to the fire: Seán Ó Guithín interview, in *Eighty.*

80 Fistful of dirt: Seán Pheats Team Ó Cearnaigh, interview by Mícheál de Mórdha, 1993, Blasket Centre, RuthTransl.

80 Seven sons to America: George Thomson, *The Human Essence,* p. 68.

80   Poetic lament: Thomson to Pádraig Ó Fiannachta, Oct. 29, 1975, Thomson Archives.

81   That was the first fiddle of their own: Seán Ó Criomhthain, in *Memories*, p. 82.

81   They had little else to do: Ibid., p. 84

81   Many other activities: Ibid., p. 85

81   The room would be lit: Account follows Síle Flower, interviewed in *Another*.

81   The sharp sounds: Marstrander, p. 17.

82   In their naked feet: Synge, *Travels*, p. 102.

82   Rise up now: Robin Flower, *The Western Island*, p. 47.

82   An island with a population of wreckers, smugglers: Synge, "Idea for play," in reworked version of original notebook, in "Notes in Ballyferriter."

82   While life . . . there was little talk: Seán Ó Criomhthain, in *Memories*, p. 45.

83   Boccaccio: See Almqvist, "The Mysterious Mícheál Ó Gaoithín, Boccaccio and the Blasket Tradition"; James Stewart, *Boccaccio in the Blaskets*.

83   On our way back: Synge, *Travels*, p. 98.

83   The girls are shouting: Marstrander, p. 17.

84   Might hop in over a fence: Seán Ó Criomhthain interview, in *Memories*, p. 135.

84   There were lots of young people: Thomson, in *Eighty*.

84   Dancing steps in Paradise: Quoted in Jean Pace [Katharine Thomson's older sister], "George Thomson, 1903–1987," unpublished typescript, Thomson Archives.

84   As unmusical as he seemed: Margaret Alexiou, interview.

84   Pipes hanging: Breandán Feiritéar, at Blasket Commemoration No. 4, Ruth Transl.

84   He could step it out: *Eighty*.

85   Secret smile: Ibid.

85   There was one girl in particular: Ibid.

85   Mary Kearney: McGrath, "The Nun of the Blaskets: Biuso, "The Poet's Ring"; records furnished by Sister Mary Justin, Sisters of Providence, Holyoke, Mass.; reminiscences, private papers, and photographs furnished by family members Seán Cahillane and Kathleen Arduini; Breandán Feiritéar, interview; photographs, Blasket Centre; Seán Ó Cearnaigh, interview by Mícheál de Mórdha, Blasket Centre; Mary Kearney and her sister, interview by Ray Stagles, Blasket Centre; Leslie Matson, "Blasket Lives," account of Muintir Cheárnaigh; visit to site of family home on the island.

86   Tee-hee: Kathleen Arduini, interview.

86   Lively young thing: Seán Pheats Tom, Irish-language account, in McGrath, "The Nun of the Blaskets," translated by Dáithí de Mórdha and Ruth Uí Ógáin.

86   Fresh, strong, and youthful: Stagles, audiotape interview.

87   I remember: Stagles, audiotape interview.

88   Bronze medal: On display at Blasket Centre.

88   No patience with the frivolous or mediocre: Jean Pace, "George Thomson, 1903–1987," unpublished typescript, Thomson Archives.

88   Deeply serious: Obituary, unknown source, King's College Archives.

88   Old studio portrait: Thomson Archives.

88   I'd say he was in love: *Eighty*.

89 It's not me that will marry you: Seán Pheats Tom Ó Cearnaigh, interview by Mícheál de Mórdha, 1993, Blasket Centre, RuthTransl.

89 1926 is as good a guess: At several junctures in the relationship between George and Mary we know something happened but cannot say just when. Máire Mhac an tSaoi remembers the meeting between George and her uncle at her uncle's house, An Cill, which he occupied only after 1925. In a telephone interview, she estimates her age at the time as between four and ten, which seems to fix the earliest possible date for the meeting as 1926.

89 I remember him coming to our house in An Cill: *Eighty.*

89 Paddy Browne: See Corish; MacGreevy; Máire Cruise O'Brien, *The Same Age as the State;* Meehan; Titley, pp. 313–15.

89 As refuge: M. C. O'Brien, *Same Age as the State,* p. 49. The house stands today, with the same magnificent views but as a sad relic and wreck.

90 Maverick . . . altogether uninhibited: Meehan, p. 456

90 From the knees down: Máire Mhac an tSaoi, telephone interview.

91 My uncle Pádraig: *Eighty.*

91 The merest episode: Hardy, p. 197.

91 Dissolved into an uninteresting outer dumb-show: Ibid., p. 198.

91 It struck me suddenly: Thomson, China journal, May 18, 1955, Thomson Archives.

5. INISHVICKILLAUN

93 White streaks: *Twenty,* p. 231.

94 No plants could survive: Richard M. Barrington.

94 Inishvickillaun had distinctive character: See Ó Dubhshláine, *Inisvickillane.*

94 The whole island . . . sense of loneliness: Robin Flower, *The Western Island,* p. 115.

94 The most pleasant and mysterious: George Thomson, *Island Home,* p. 67.

94 Song of the Fairies: See Mac Amhlaoíbh, both bibliographical entries.

95 Jigs and reels . . . hurrying tunes: Robin Flower, *The Western Island,* p. 116.

95 Before long: *Twenty,* p. 234.

95 The magic waters: Robin Flower, *Eire and Other Poems.*

96 What do you see?: *Twenty,* p. 234.

96 I looked west: Ibid., p. 235.

97 Ever travelled through the empty lands: Letter to the editor, *Irish Statesman,* July 9, 1927, p. 423.

97 A rough place, but a fine nurse of men: George Thomson, *Island Home,* p. 71.

97 A nursery for raising human beings for export: Seán Ó Dúbhda, in Schrier notebooks, vol. 1407, p. 201, Delargy.

98 Nearly all the characteristics . . . near to penury: Synge, *Travels,* p. 145.

98 Arnold Schrier: The Schrier notebooks are located at the Delargy Centre, Dublin, vols. 1407–11, from which much of this account is drawn.

98 Inspired dissatisfaction: See Miller, especially chap. 8, sect. 3.

99 I have a great mind: *Twenty,* p. 216.

100 A mournful look: Ibid. p. 218.

100 Oh, Mirrisheen: Ibid., p. 219.

100 Western peasants: Miller, p. 425.

100 Springfield, Massachusetts: Seán Cahillane and Kathleen Arduini, interviews.

101 Of nothing but America: *Twenty,* p. 216.

101 This place . . . drowned vessel: Ní Loingsigh, entry for Sept. 30, 1923.

101 There's a curse on America: *Cross,* p. 40.

101 A vicious, materialistic: Miller, p. 456.

101 Rosy-faced. Ibid.

101 Having had . . . good-natured ways: Schrier notebooks, vol. 1407, Delargy.

102 Listen here: *Twenty,* p. 236.

102 There was the reluctance of the world: Ibid., p. 235.

102 'Tis the fine, rich Irish: Ibid., p. 238.

103 I give you my blessing: Ibid., p. 241.

103 Journey to Dublin: Following account is adapted from *Twenty,* pp. 240–70.

105 The Prometheus Trilogy: Thomson's thesis, with acknowledgments, may be seen in King's College Archives.

106 As soon as I read it: Ibid., appendix.

106 Craven Studentship: King's College Archives.

107 Only 235: King's College Council, March 9, 1928, in ibid.

107 Leeson Street: *Twenty,* p. 282.

107 I was blinded by the hundred thousand lights: Most of the following is adapted from *Twenty,* pp. 271–77.

109 Capitol Theatre: See Frederick O'Dwyer, *Lost Dublin* (Dublin: Gill and Macmillan, 1981). See also George Kearns and Patrick Maguire, *The A to Z of All Old Dublin Cinemas* (self-published, 2007). The Capitol was also the site for the screening of Ireland's first talking picture, on April 21, 1929. The Fianna Fail meeting is marked by a stone plaque.

6. THE LAST QUIET TIME

111 Boys played football: Seán Ó Criomhthain interview in *Memories,* p. 132.

112 The pressure: Seán Ó Criomhthain, in *Memories,* p. 63.

112 Hardly any of . . . close clustering: Hockings, p. 145.

112 You'd have a drink: Seán Ó Criomhthain interview, in *Memories,* p. 105.

113 I was young and light-hearted: Nóra Ní Shéaghdha interview, in *Memories,* p. 154.

113 Even if a gale of wind: Ibid., p. 150.

113 They'd shake it off like ducks: Ibid.

114 Very keen on English: Ibid., p. 151.

114 We were thinking . . . life beyond the Island: Seán Ó Criomhthain interview, in *Memories,* p. 120.

114 It was our business: *Islandman,* p. 243.

114 The *naomhóg*s: See, for example, *Memories,* chap. 4; Creedon; *naomhóg*s on display at Blasket Centre.

115 Would laugh at this little toy: Marstrander, p. 7.

115 A census counted: "A Socio-Economic Study of Fisheries in Counties Cork, Donegal, Kerry and Galway," Marine Institute, Dublin, Aug. 2000, p. 50.

115 Huddled in a lump: Patrick Flower, in *Bláithín,* p. 34.

115   Rabbit pelts: Seán Ó Criomhthain interview, in *Memories,* p. 101.

115   Demonstrate for the cameras: McCarty and Hockings documentary.

116   Wreckage and wood: Matson, *Méiní,* p. 142.

116   The world . . . every twenty years: Seán Ó Criomhthain, in *Memories,* p. 43.

117   One and a half hours: See Robert Cresswell, *Une Communauté rurale de l'Irlande* (Paris: Institut d'Ethnologie, 1969).

117   A rabbit might jump out: Seán Ó Guithín interview, in *Memories,* p. 173.

117   Were certainly poor: Nóra Ní Shéaghdha interview, in ibid., p. 154.

117   My two eyes: O'Guiheen, p. 76.

117   They had dancing and music: Seán Ó Criomhthain interview, in *Memories,* p. 93.

118   They can't speak English: Almqvist, "C. W. von Sydow agus Éire," p. 14, Ruth-Transl.

118   Talk Irish to Barbara: Tomás to Flower, Aug. 12, 1912, in summary of Tomás-Flower correspondence, Delargy.

118   We have a real boy . . . of disposition angelic: Flower to Best, July 3, 1921, NatLib.

118   The girls: Flower to Best, April 23, 1929, NatLib.

119   We children had the most idyllic time: Patrick Flower, "My Father," in *Bláithín,* p. 35.

119   Sheer rock precipice: Photo in Ní Ghaoithín, p. 28.

119   It was an incredibly primitive life: In *Another.*

119   Lost in reverie: Raidió na Gaeltachta Collection, CD 0895, Blasket Centre.

119   Happiest times: *Celtic,* p. 100.

119   Roasted mackerel: Raidió na Gaeltachta Collection, CD 0895, Blasket Centre, RuthTransl.

119   Too preoccupied: Osborn Bergin, review, *Irish Statesman,* July 9, 1927, p. 423.

119   Has all the freshness: Tadhg Ó Dúshláine, "Robin Flower: The Creative Cataloguer," in *Bláithín,* p. 143.

119   In the Blaskets: *Celtic,* p. 100.

119   Marie-Louise Sjoestedt: See *Celtic,* chap. 6; *Marie-Louise Sjoestedt (1900–1940);* Pierre-Yves Lambert entry, *Dictionary of Irish Biography;* correspondence kindly made available by Bo Almqvist. See also Davis.

121   Her solidity of thought: Vendryes, in *Marie-Louise Sjoestedt,* p. 17.

121   Seán an Chóta: See *Celtic,* chap. 8; Ní Chuilleanáin; Seán O Lúing files on Seán an Chóta, MS. 24,596, NatLib.

122   Sexual jaunts: Ní Chuilleanáin, p. 10.

122   A prize-fighter's face: Ibid., p. 53.

123   *Fanai:* Excerpt from Sean Óg Ó Caomhánaigh, *Fanai,* RuthTransl. See also O'Leary, p. 193; *Celtic,* p. 153.

123   In response to the undefined promptings: *Celtic,* p. 153.

123   He was from the first day . . . my kind, loyal teacher: Quoted in Ó Lúing, *Seán an Chóta,* trans. by Dáithí de Mórdha.

124   Clogher Head: Niall Ó Brosnacháin, sect. 1.9, p. 33, RuthTransl.

124   Only sea-birds: Ibid.

124   Engagement ring he had for her into the Seine: Ó Lúing, *Seán an Chóta;* also Bo Almqvist to Pierre-Yves Lambert, Sept. 24, 2004, courtesy of Bo Almqvist.

124 Did Marie-Louise merely use Seán: Marie-Louise would be remembered by a friend who knew her for more than twenty years, Marie-Jeanne Durry, as fiercely independent, reserved, a woman who kept her distance even with friends. "It's only the work that counts," she'd say. *Marie-Louise Sjoestedt,* p. 33.

124 An artist in life: *Celtic,* p. 152.

124 Record of Kerry Irish: As a way of getting across Seán an Chóta's preoccupation with fine shades of Kerry Irish meaning in his dictionary, Bo Almqvist imagines him parsing the color blue into every conceivable shade and variant of blue, bluish, sort-of-blue, trace-of-blue, etc.

125 Counted vignettes: Niall Ó Brosnacháin, sect. 1.9, p. 33.

125 Was neither very remote: Sjoestedt, *Celtic Gods and Heroes,* p. xiv.

125 I cannot help but feel: *Celtic,* p. 114.

126 Parisian coiffure: Ní Ghaoithín, pp. 62–64.

126 Sound-info: Ibid.

126 English's influence: This and subsequent discussion follows Sjoestedt's paper, "L'Influence de la langue anglaise sur un parler local irlandais."

127 A literature . . . for love of Irish: Sjoestedt, review of Tomás Ó Criomhthain's *An tOileánach* and *Allagar na hInise,* 212.

7. GORKY'S PEASANTS

129 Plain, straightforward: *Islandman,* p. x.

129 St. Thomas's day: Ibid., p. 1.

130 In and out . . . untidy-haired babbler: Ibid., p. 2.

130 A great mug: Ibid., p. 21.

130 Couldn't keep a glass of whisky: Ibid., p. 68.

130 the shining glory: Ibid., p. 45.

130 Gathering her skirts: Ibid., p. 23.

130 A field is only described: McGahern, "An tOileánach," p. 56

131 Has a flavour . . . almost taste: Máire Cruise O'Brien, "An tOileánach," p. 26.

131 Hemingwayesque quality: Kiberd, in *Reflections.*

131 There's an authenticity: Ó Coileáin interview.

131 More ambitious work: An Seabhac, "Tomás Ó Criomhthain, Fisherman and Author," RuthTransl.

131 Ó Siochfhradha: Pádraig Ó Siochfhradha, interview (nephew bearing the same name who supplied news reports, census records, and other materials).

131 I don't believe he ever spoke a word of English: Ibid.

132 Sign his name in English: "An Seabhac Had to Sign Name in English," *Irish Independent,* Dec. 29, 1952.

132 Backs bent: McMahon, p. 120.

132 Fresh story?: Account follows An Seabhac, "Tomás Ó Criomhthain, Fisherman and Author," RuthTransl.

133 Time after time: Loti, p. 28.

133 Endemic plague: Gorky, vol. I, "My Childhood," p. 11.

134 I declare to the devil: Seán Ó Criomhthain interview, in *Memories,* p. 114.

134 Knut Hamsun: Ibid. See also Jeffrey Frank, "In From the Cold: The Return of Knut Hamsun," *New Yorker,* Dec. 26, 2005.

134 Tomás was offered: *Hidden,* p. 124.

134 The cornerstone: Ibid., p. 172.

135 Brian did not have an easy life: An Seabhac, "Tomás Ó Criomhthain, Fisherman and Author," RuthTransl.

136 May have been homosexual: Ó Coileáin interview.

136 I could use them: An Seabhac, "Tomás Ó Criomhthain, Fisherman and Author," RuthTransl.

136 Entirely innocent in their naiveté: Sjoestedt, review of Tomás Ó Criomhthain's *An tOileánach* and *Allagar na hInise,* p. 213.

136 Big lumps of girls: *Reflections,* p. 36.

137 Often simply arbitrary: Sjoestedt, review of Tomás Ó Criomhthain's *An tOileánach* and *Allagar na hInise,* p. 213.

137 Preserves the odd earthy expression: Máire Cruise O'Brien, "An tOileánach," p. 35.

137 Recognise that repetition inhered: *Hidden,* p. 127.

138 Anyone at all: O'Leary, p. 135.

138 Textual tampering: James Stewart, "An tOileánach—More or Less," p. 241.

138 I may as well give some brief account: *Islandman,* p. 26.

138 If King George: Ibid., p. 29.

138 The swell would be rising: Ibid., p. 243.

139 Untrained in the craft: Fitz Gerald, p. 288.

139 The greatest humourous writer: Beaslai.

140 Were made to save face: Stewart, "An tOileánach—More or Less," p. 235.

141 He said he never regretted: Pádraig Ó Siochfhradha (nephew of An Seabhac), interview.

141 Made clear that he was being asked to write: *Hidden,* p. 124.

141 With perfect frankness: Robin Flower, foreword, *Islandman,* p. vii.

141 I would not have left: Cited in *Hidden,* p. 125.

141 Emerged with a little help from his friends: In "The (Original) *Islandman?,*" p. 252, John Eastlake offers an attractively broad-minded view of these and related issues: "The pursuit of the original," he writes, "is much like chasing a mirage. It recedes before us as we track it through the process of [literary] production. It quickly becomes apparent that the original is not located in the published text; so, we look for manuscripts and drafts. At this point, we determine that there are factors at work that challenge the integrity of the working drafts, if integrity means 'uninfluenced' or 'produced in perfect isolation.' Now the original has receded beyond the recoverable text to an inchoate pre-textual stage." The original and authentic, in other words, are apt to prove elusive, even in principle.

141 It was a wonder: Enright, introduction, *Cross,* p. 1.

141 Still lingers . . . silver bell: Binchy, "Two Blasket Autobiographies," p. 547.

141 The effects of oral states: Ong, p. 30.

142 Preamble . . . reciting Ossianic lays: Robin Flower, *The Irish Tradition,* p. 105.

142 Built around admiration: Kiberd, in *Reflections.*

143 Inborn genius for speech: Quoted in Binchy, "Two Blasket Autobiographies," p. 552. See also Thomson to Pádraig Ó Fiannachta, Oct. 29, 1975, Thomson Archives: "There is no reason to doubt that [in *Allagar na hInise*] Tomás is reproducing faithfully what they [the islanders] actually said, and they spoke in the same style. This is true of all of them, though naturally some were more eloquent than others. They differed from Tomás in only one respect, that they were unable to write. Some people seem to think that, interpreted in this way, Tomás's stature as a writer is diminished. It seems to me, on the contrary, that it is enhanced; for it means that Tomás speaks not only for himself but for his people, and not only for his contemporaries but for his ancestors."

143 among the most important life-stories: *Irish Times,* Nov. 26, 1962.

143 Profoundly skeptical: Binchy, "Two Blasket Autobiographies," p. 552.

8. INTERMINABLE PROCESSION

144 Thatched-roof house: The following account is drawn from Sjoestedt, "L'Irlande d'aujourd'hui" (my translation).

145 It is towards . . . rare parishes: Ibid., pt. 1, p. 842.

145 Hills as supportive . . . Corsican maquis: Ibid., p. 844.

145 Magnificent chorus: Ibid., p. 845.

145 I see him . . . alone in his canoe: Ibid., p. 849.

145 Deprived: Ibid., p. 857.

145 To all that is powerful or strange: Ibid., p. 858.

146 They appear suddenly: Ibid., p. 841.

147 You are in love, my boy: *Twenty,* p. 238.

147 Offered to pay her way: Kathleen Arduini interview.

147 Patrick J. Grogan: Account of Grogan built up from Patrick Grogan (Dr. Grogan's nephew) and his wife, Una, interview; records of Royal College of Physicians; local history references.

148 As Pádraig Séamus Ó Gruagain: *Thom's Almanac,* 1928 and 1929, lists Grogan in this way. *Thom's* also tracks his moves during these years.

148 Rubbed red and raw: Kathleen Arduinim, interview.

148 Dr. Grogan and his wife were good to her: Breandán Feiritéar, interview.

148 Studio portrait: Courtesy of Kathleen Arduini.

149 "The Illegitimate Child," "Getting On in the World": Thomson's two stories were enough to inspire Philip O'Leary's opinion in *Gaelic Prose in the Irish Free State, 1922–1939,* p. 213, that Thomson "dealt sympathetically with the issue of illegitimacy."

149 On Dublin's doorstep: Ferriter, 56.

149 Between 2 and 3 percent of recorded births: Ferriter, 56, 126; see also Luddy.

149 Almost 30 percent: Ferriter, 101.

149 Ten to fifteen pounds: My estimate based on Hearn as a whole.

149 Compared favorably: Hearn, 151.

149 A hundred thousand in Ireland: Hearn, 148.

149 Day when a little girl: *Marie-Louise Sjoestedt (1900–1940): In Memoriam,* 71.

149 Hand of Father Paddy Browne: In an interview, Father Pádraig Ó Fiannachta sup-

ports this scenario: "There's no other way she would have been able to get that job" with Dr. Grogan. Likewise, Dr. Grogan's nephew says that the most natural way for his uncle to secure the services of a maid would have been through the priests at Maynooth. In an interview, Muiris Mac Conghail also sees the involvement of Paddy Browne as likely.

149   I visited the Blasket girl: Thomson to his family, Sept. 5, 1961, Thomson Archives. Just when George met Mary in Maynooth is uncertain, not least because George's own correspondence is contradictory. For example, in this letter he writes that he visited the Blasket girl in Maynooth two years before visiting Father Paddy Browne at Saint Patrick's College in 1926, making it about 1924. But in an earlier letter to his wife and children, on Sept. 7, 1945, he writes that he first set foot in Dublin only in 1925.

149   Poem by George: 24 March 1928 issue. RuthTransl.

149   More likely, it enacts: This possibility was suggested by Breandán Feiritéar at Blasket Commemoration no. 4, Account RuthTransl.

150   Arrangements for departure: Based on surviving record books at Galvin's today, courtesy of Maurice O'Connor.

150   October 22, 1929: This and subsequent chronology is not certain but very likely, pointed to from several directions, including Galvin's record books, the known Atlantic schedule and ports of disembarkation of the *Scythia,* the Stagles audiotape interview of Sister Mary Clemens, interview with Kathleen Arduini, and Sisters of Providence records pointing to an approximately three-month period in America before Mary took the veil.

150   Queenstown: See St. Leger; Sjoestedt, "L'Irlande d'aujourd'hui," pt. 1, pp. 839–41; Schrier notebooks, Delargy; site visit, Cobh emigration museum.

150   Mary's first time in Queenstown: Account largely follows Stagles, audiotape interview.

152   His father died: KathFrag. "One of my greatest happinesses," his father wrote him on Aug. 16, 1929 (Thomson Archives), "is that I have been able to give you help in some small way to enable to you do work you liked. You have repaid me a thousandfold."

9. WORKING AT IRISH

153   The wife of a . . . everybody who is anybody: *Eighty.*

153   I felt drawn irresistibly: Thomson to his family, Sept. 7, 1945, Thomson Archives.

153   Moya Llewelyn Davies: Melissa Llewelyn-Davies, both citations in bibliography; e-mail correspondence; Lowth.

154   Dazzling blue eyes: MacDowell, p. 18.

154   In an open-topped car: Melissa Llewelyn-Davies, unpublished personal reminiscence.

154   Believing she looked more desirable by candlelight: Ibid.

154   He'd loved her: KathFrag.

155   Watermill. See Dennis McIntyre, *The Meadow of the Bull: A History of Clontarf* (apparently self-published, 1987): "The 'Water' roads come from the local Naniken 'waterway' with the 'mill' being adapted from an old mill which once operated on

the river close to today's Watermill Bridge." See also photographs, Birmingham. Saint Annes Park was part of a fifty-two-acre site purchased by the Guinness family, of beer fame, in 1835; see also photos, EMF/27/450 and 452, King's College Archives.

155   Shining wet sand: Thomson to his family, Sept. 7, 1945, Thomson Archives.
155   Painted bright green: Ibid.
155   The velvety peace: Thomson's mother to Thomson, Oct. 26, 1931, Thomson Archives.
155   I expect . . . but we mustn't expect: Forster to Thomson, Aug. 1, 1931, Thomson Archives.
155   Every day: George Thomson, "Irish and the Intelligentsia."
155   "Barra na Trá": In Thomson, *Gach Órlach De Mo Chroí,* RuthTransl.
156   I in the Guard's uniform: The following account draws largely from *Twenty,* 247–77.
156   The unknown world: Binchy, "Two Blasket Autobiographies," p. 559.
156   Square into the camera: In *Eighty.*
156   An unhappy man: My account of Maurice's Guard service is built up from Uí Aimhirgín interview.
157   His whole nature: George Thomson, "The Irish Language Revival," p. 8.
157   He didn't have enough to do in the winter: Thomson, in *Eighty.*
157   Nothing would go unnoticed: Thomson, "Fiche Blian ag Fás," RuthTransl.
157   He made the attempt . . . we discarded it: Thomson, in *Another.*
157   Keep writing: Ibid. Maurice wrote George later that he was indeed observing everything, "even the fly flitting past his ear."
158   But a beginning should be made: Preamble, "Conference on Galway University College: Report on the Conference, 1926," University College, Galway.
158   University College emissaries: Account of Thomson in Galway is generally drawn from Mac Conghail, "De Blaghd agus Mac Tomáis"; Mac Conghail, *Aghaidheanna Fidil agus Púicíní,* RuthTransl; Mac Conghail, interview; *Celtic,* chap. 10.
158   I would say almost the most fanatic: Sjoestedt, "L'Irlande d'aujourd'hui," pt. 2, p. 175.
159   Went to the blackboard: Mac Conghail, "An English Scholar." He tells a similar story in *Eighty.*
159   Will you humour me: Mrs. Thomson to George, Oct. 26, 1931, Thomson Archives.
160   To bury his talents: Quoted in Enright, "George Thomson: A Memoir," p. 128.
160   Two or three students: Mac Mathúna interview.
160   Sjoestedt visited: Diskin.
160   Caressing words into sweetness: Mac Mathúna interview.
160   Corrib Lodge: Site visit; Eileen Naughten interview and subsequent correspondence.
161   Bench: See Thomson and Forster, Sept. 1932 photo, EMF/27/541, King's College Archives.
161   There is no doubt but youth is a fine thing: *Twenty,* p. 1.
162   It was delightful to listen: Ibid., p. 27.
162   My grandfather . . . Castle Summit: Ibid., p. 75.

162 Next day the quay: Ibid., p. 142.

163 I took a car to Dunquin: Ibid., p. 297.

163 I hadn't known . . . makings of a writer: Thomson, "Fiche Blian ag Fás," Ruth-Transl.

163 The opportunity to edit it: Ibid.

163 Evidence of mentorship: Nic Gráinne, p. 97.

164 Select and condense: Thomson, notes on O'Sullivan's manuscript, G1309/1, NatLib.

164 Reminded the author: Enright, "George Thomson: A Memoir," p. 129.

164 I didn't add to it: Quoted in Muiris Mac Conghail, "Ollan a Chíoradh . . . ," *Blianiris*, 2003, pp. 198–215, RuthTransl.

164 Are not credible: Kiberd, in *Reflections*, disc 2.

164 Looking after a sheep: *Twenty*, p. 220.

164 Maurice descending with a donkey: See Raidió na Gaeltachta Collection, Blasket Centre, CD 0945 (02), RuthTransl; Máire Llewelyn Kavanagh, in *Eighty*; Pádraig Ó Fiannachta interview.

164 Poetic truth: See Raidió na Gaeltachta Collection, Blasket Centre, CD 0945 (02), RuthTransl. Says Father O'Fiannachta of Thomson, in an interview with the author, "He would admit that Muiris had a wonderful imagination." Here was a potentially tedious account of a routine climb up from the slip, so Maurice refashions it: "He makes the meeting magical."

165 What he gives us: George Thomson, *Island Home*, p. 65.

165 An original approach: Muiris Mac Conghail interview.

165 It's full of people . . . better rendition: Kiberd, in *Reflections*, disc 2.

165 Editorial squabbles: See Mac Conghail, *Aghaidheanna Fidil agus Púicíní*, Ruth-Transl.

165 Cannot possibly be . . . egg of a sea-bird: Forster, introductory note, *Twenty*, p. vi.

166 Was done in some haste: Thomson, notes on O'Sullivan's manuscript, G1309/1, NatLib.

167 Intervals of nausea: "A Sea-Bird's Egg," p. 562.

167 A part of the world where rain, dampness, and depression: Boyd, p. 221.

167 The scream of a gull: Roger Pippett, in *Daily Herald*, May 4, 1933.

167 For those to whom . . . lilting pages: Hutchison.

167 The life is hard . . . Land of the Ever Young: O'Faoláin, "A Wild Bird's Nest."

167 The story moves like a piece of music: George Thomson, *Island Home*, p. 59.

168 Lay beyond Muiris's experience: Ibid., p. 60.

168 George took numerous photos: These and others can be found in George Thomson, *Island Home*.

168 As I stood . . . a score of eyes: Synge, *Travels*, p. 100.

168 Were bound to one another: George Thomson, *Island Home*, p. 84. See also p. 74, where Thomson quotes tellingly from F. E. Hardy's *Life of Thomas Hardy*: "London appears not to *see* itself. Each individual is conscious of *himself* but nobody is conscious of themselves collectively."

169 Full length in the dust, his horsemanship forgotten: George Thomson, *Marxism and Poetry*, p. 35.

169 I went to Ireland: Ibid.

169 The language embodied: George Thomson, "The Irish Language Revival," p. 7.

170 On the other hand: Ibid.

170 I conceived the idea: Ibid., p. 8.

171 If we began: Quoted in Enright, "George Thomson: A Memoir," p. 132.

171 High hopes and ambitions: Mac Mathúna interview.

171 I had not proceeded: George Thomson, "The Irish Language Revival," p. 9.

171 The authorities: Ibid.

171 I was working to save: George Thomson, *Marxism and Poetry*, p. 55.

172 Ulcer acted up: KathFrag.

172 I am sorry: E. M. Forster to Thomson, Jan. 31, 1933, Thomson Archives.

172 Would and could still take you back to King's: E. M. Forster to Thomson, April 30, 1934, Thomson Archives.

172 My mind in turmoil: Quoted in *Celtic,* p. 169.

172 I was determined to follow her: Thomson to his family, Sept. 5, 1961, Thomson Archives.

172 Mary arrived in Boston: This account follows Stagles, audiotape interview; Seán Cahillane and Kathleen Arduini, interviews and photographs and documents furnished by them; Sister Mary Justin, Sisters of Providence, telephone interview; McGrath, "The Nun of the Blaskets."

174 Over my dead body: Stagles audiotape interview.

174 This thing would be . . . a place for me: Ibid.

174 Going around like a record: Ibid.

174 I knew he was sweet on me: Ray Stagles interview.

175 Sisters of Providence went back: See Liptak and Bennett.

175 She alone could actually speak Irish: Stagles, audiotape interview.

175 Great, great smile: Kathleen Arduini, interview.

175 Katharine Stewart: KathFrag, source for details of their brief courtship.

176 Could you come to tea: Letter quoted in KathFrag.

176 "Callino Casturame": Alexiou, "George Thomson: the Greek Dimension," p. 56.

176 Katharine's sister Frida: See Angela Jackson.

176 We did feel this instant sympathy: Katharine, in *Eighty.*

177 Hits you in the eye: Letter quoted, in KathFrag.

177 I am thinking of you: Thomson to Katharine, Oct. 30, 1935, Thomson Archives.

177 Ways of saying "darling": Thomson to Katharine, April 18, 1939, Thomson Archives.

178 George had told me: KathFrag.

178 Whence we could watch the leaping salmon: Ibid.

178 As soon as the villagers: Katharine to her mother, Jessie Stewart, Aug. 7, 1935, quoted in KathFrag.

10. VISITORS, STRANGERS, TOURISTS, FRIENDS

180 George Chambers: Seán Ó Coileáin, who edited, and wrote an introduction to, the published *LísLetters,* says of Chambers in an interview that he "remains a kind of shadowy figure." Information about him here is drawn from his own unpublished introduction to Lís's letters in Delargy; from a kind of "implied biography" I've

pieced together from Lís's many specific and detailed references to him in her letters; from photographs he took while on the island; from his published poetry; and from a few references to him in accounts by Lís's daughter Niamh—for example, Raidió na Gaeltachta, broadcast, Jan. 3, 1995, CD 0999, RuthTransl. On the internal evidence of the letters, Chambers was probably born in March 1873, and died sometime after 1957.

180   Temple Fortune Lane: Seán Ó Coileáin, introduction, *LísLetters*, p. 1.

180   Get the fisherfolk: *LísLetters*, p. 8.

181   A bleak, impoverished and scattered village: Ibid.

181   Wore neither shoes nor stockings: Ibid., p. 10.

181   Was it chance or divinely planned: Chambers, p. 8.

181   Eibhlís Ní Shúilleabhháin: See Matson, "Blasket Lives." "Certainly he took a fancy to her," said Seán Ó Coileáin, editor of the published letters, in an interview with the author.

181   Daly house for a picture: *KerryIsland*, p. 70.

181   Verminous: Chambers foreword, Lís, vol. 1943, [p.] d.

182   I love to read your letters: Lís, Nov. 28, 1931, vol. 1943, p. 33.

182   At great cost: For example, Lís, Oct. 1, 1932, vol. 1943, p. 40: "Ah, you understand how hard it is to me to put english sentences together and trying to write them, imagine if you were to write to me an Irish letter, of course it would be hard on you. So dear Mr. Chambers you shouldn't be hard on me for not having very long letters sometimes. I always must have a couple of hours to spare to write you a long one. I always do my best for you, and I'm glad of it."

183   Today again is a rather bad day: Ibid., Jan. 12, 1932, vol. 1943, p. 35. The week before, she'd written in what seems a similar, if coyer, vein: "Pardon me for saying so. Something was a pity. Would you ever guess what would it be. Now it is time that I should say funny things too to you. If you would visit Blaskets 20 years ago and by at the same time I would be 20 would anything strange happen I don't know? Lost time is never found again so there is no use in getting talking now." (Ibid., Jan. 3, 1932, vol. 1943, p. 34.)

183   My heart came to my mouth: Ibid., Feb. 14, 1932, vol. 1943, p. 36.

183   I would love to answer all your questions: Ibid.

184   I met Kenneth Jackson: *LísLetters*, p. 50.

184   My best friend, I have every thought of getting married: Lís, April 27, 1933, vol. 1943, p. 15.

184   I love my husband: Ibid., May [?], 1933, vol. 1993, p. 16.

184   Just a Line . . . my whole Heart's desire: Ibid., p. 17.

185   There are many visitors: *LísLetters*, p. 50.

185   Manny the strangers: Tomás Ó Criomhthain to his son Thomas, Nov. 15, 1931, Blasket Centre.

185   Fall from a horse: *LísLetters*, p. 26. On June 21, 1932, Flower writes Idris Bell from the Aran Islands, tells of being thrown when the horse, Silver Mane, broke into a gallop on the beach (British Library).

185   It was a great Loss: *LísLetters*, p. 27.

185   Within the space of four years: Binchy, "Two Blasket Autobiographies," p. 548.

185 There is a time . . . scrape a finger: Ní Shéaghdha, p. 67.

185 Of all years: *LísLetters,* p. 53.

186 Ridge after ridge: O'Cahill, p. 145.

186 A pompous old man: O'Faoláin, *An Irish Journey,* p. 143.

186 Innocent elation: Ibid., p. 144.

188 Throbbing with interior distress: *Celtic,* p. 226.

188 Grave courtesy: Meyerstein to R. N. Green-Armytage, "Vigil of Easter Day," 1931, Blasket Centre.

188 An old woman: *Celtic,* p. 227.

188 has shown me . . . what is wrong with me: Ibid., p. 228.

188 We feed together: Ibid., p. 226.

188 More enthusiasm than they had Gaelic: Binchy, "Two Blasket Autobiographies," p. 559.

189 All these . . . are folktales: See Kenneth Jackson "Scéalta ón mBlascaod"; Wagner and Mac Congáil.

189 Irish folklore: See Delargy; Briody; Ó Giolláin; Kenneth Jackson, "The International Folktale in Ireland"; Clodagh Brennan Harvey, "Some Irish Women Storytellers and Reflections on the Role of Women in the Storytelling Tradition," *Western Folklore,* vol. 48 (April 1989), pp. 109–28; Alan Dundes, ed., *International Folkloristics: Classic Contributions by the Founders of Folklore* (New York: Rowman & Littlefield, 1999); Kathleen Vejvoda, " 'Too Much Knowledge of the Other World': Women and Nineteenth-Century Irish Folktales," *Victorian Literature and Culture,* vol. 32 (2004), pp. 41–61.

190 I must get Peig Sayers to be my teacher: Jackson, in *Another.*

190 Is at once the Bible: W. B. Yeats, "The Message of the Folk-lorist," *Speaker,* Aug. 19, 1893, p. 186.

190 What we mean by folk culture: Kenneth Jackson, "The International Folktale in Ireland," p. 264.

190 Learning became popularised: Ibid., p. 265.

191 The cinemas and wirelesses: Jackson, in *Another.*

191 Special leave: Records of Standing Committee, 1910–1944, p. 4651, British Museum.

191 My visit is an extraordinary success: Flower to Idris Bell, annotated as "after 27 May 1930," ff67, British Library.

191 Ediphone: Demonstration and informational film furnished by Anna Bale, Delargy.

192 Payment in cigarettes: Seán Pheats Team Ó Cearnaigh, interview with Mícheál de Mórdha, 1993, Blasket Centre, RuthTransl.

192 Independent of time: Flower to Idris Bell, May 27, 1930, ff66, British Library.

192 Folksongs enough: Flower to Idris Bell, annotated as "after 27 May 1930, ff67, British Library."

192 I give concerts: Ibid.

193 Hearty laugh only rarely: Joe Daly, in *Another.*

193 Her changes of mood: W. R. Rodgers, introduction, Sayers, *An Old Woman's Reflections,* p. xiii.

193 Enormous power: Joe Daly, in *Another.*

193 Graduation requirement: "I don't think it is, or was, a book for teenagers," said Cathal Póirtéir of Peig's books. Póirtéir was being interviewed on RTÉ, May 1, 2008, about his production of *Blasket Island Reflections*. They "didn't want an old woman moaning about how hard her life was when really they were interested in the Beatles, the Rolling Stones, and U2."

194 She was . . . most beautiful eyes: Jackson, in *Another*. See also *Reflections*, p. 18: "Those who knew Peig Sayers paint a picture of a woman noted for her good looks, earthy sense of humour and occasionally racy language." Pádraig Ua Maoileoin refers to "her frankness in sexual discussions." Almqvist says, "Peig was very far from the prude she has often been made out to be" ("The Scholar and the Storyteller," p. 45).

195 With a face scarcely lined: Mahon, p. 141.

195 It was clear . . . a man's woman: Ibid., p. 142.

195 He had a big box: O'Guiheen, p. 79.

195 Mary Kennedy: Biographical details translated and summarized from two Blasket Centre Irish-language articles, RuthTransl; also, "Gentle, Gracious and Gifted—Peig of the Blaskets," *Irish Independent*, Jan. 12, 1952.

196 Would never be satisfied: O'Guiheen, p. 78.

196 So clean and finished a style: Robin Flower, *The Western Island*, p. 49.

196 We used to peep in through the window: Máirín Bean Uí Bheoláin interviewed by Mícheál de Mórdha, 1993, Blasket Centre, RuthTransl.

196 This one flung warm to the world: O'Hanlon.

196 Is told in fine idiomatic Irish: Nic Gh., p. 93.

196 "What Dublin Is Reading": *Irish Times*, July 4, 1936.

196 Because this inherited . . . it is not less literature: Nic Gh., p. 94.

196 The day was beautiful: Seán Pheats Team Ó Cearnaigh, *Fiolar an Eireaball Bhán*, pp. 41–42, RuthTransl.

197 Some driftwood planks: Lockley, *I Know an Island*, p. 134.

197 And oh Mr. Chambers: *LísLetters*, p. 33.

197 Couldn't even raise his hand: Seán Ó Criomhthain interview, in *Memories*, p. 116.

197 On landing: In Lís, vol. 1943, p. 58, Eibhlís describes this as Ní Shéaghdha's own translation of the Irish obituary she wrote for a local paper.

198 Myles na Gopaleen: See his (writing as Flann O'Brien) *The Hair of the Dogma* (London: Grafton Books, 1977); Danielle Jacquin, " 'Cerveaux Lucides Is Good Begob': Flann O'Brien and the World of Peasants," in Genet, ed., *Rural Ireland, Real Ireland?*, pp. 223–33; "An Béal Bocht: Myles na gCopaleen (1911–1966)," in *The Pleasures of Gaelic Literature*, ed. John Jordan (Dublin: Mercier Press, 1977), pp. 85–96; Sarah McKibben, "*The Poor Mouth*: A Parody of (Post) Colonial Irish Manhood," *Research in African Literatures*, vol. 34, no. 4 (Winter 2003), pp. 96–114.

198 Took a bucket full of muck: Flann O'Brien, p. 16.

198 Prolonged sneer: Flann O'Brien, *The Hair of the Dogma*, p. 181. See also Mac Conghail radio interview, Oct. 22, 2002.

199 Two islanders and two visitors: Photo at Blasket Centre. Thanks to Dáithi de Mórdha for identifying the two islanders.

200 Tonight is very fine: *LísLetters*, p. 79.

II. A GREEN IRISH THREAD

202   The village I know best: George Thomson, *Marxism and Poetry,* p. 6.

202   Runs a green Irish thread: Richard Martin, p. 87.

203   He must have become immune to the noise: KathFrag.

203   It shows him in profile: Thomson Archives.

204   Katharine had seen the emergent Nazi Germany: KathFrag.

204   Saw some good: Ibid.

204   He was nearly always tense: Thomson, "Note on Wittgenstein," Thomson Archives.

205   We were . . . more to the left: KathFrag.

205   Took to the chessboard: Ibid.

205   Held up by throngs of children: Thomson, quoted in KathFrag. A slightly different version appears in George Thomson, *Aeschylus and Athens,* p. 297.

205   Not only will these cultures: George Thomson, "The Irish Language Revival," p. 11.

205   There seemed no need for the question-mark: KathFrag.

205   A photograph from this period: W. J. West, in *The Truth About Hollis: An Investigation* (London: Duckworth, 1989).

206   I had a rather . . . her individualism is untenable: Thomson to Katharine, Sept. 11, 1937, Thomson Archives.

206   Teach the barbarians: Quoted in KathFrag.

206   We were both glad to get away: KathFrag.

206   Common distaste: Thomson, "Note on Wittgenstein," Thomson Archives.

206   Surrealist painters: See *Surrealism in Birmingham, 1935–1954,* publication accompanying exhibit at Birmingham Museums and Art Gallery, Dec. 9, 2000–March 11, 2001.

206   Here I am: Thomson to Katharine, Jan. 11, 1937, Thomson Archives.

206   Homer on Mondays: Date books, George Thomson, University of Birmingham Special Collections.

207   Bound notebook: Courtesy of Eileen Naughten.

207   Most valuable of the legacies: Review of Thomson's *The "Oresteia" of Aeschylus,* D. W. Lucas, *The Nineteenth Century,* vol. 125, no. 744, 1939, p. 231.

207   Direct, fluent, and dignified: Review of Thomson's "The Oresteia of Aeschylus," *Times Literary Supplement,* Nov. 12, 1938.

208   The primitive collectivism: Joseph Needham, "Historical Materialism and the Ancient World," journal article, no other information, p. 231.

208   Notebooks he began to keep: University of Birmingham Special Collections.

209   Blasket influence: George Thomson to Hubert Butler, July 21, 1951: "It has always seemed to me that Irish literature is a goldmine for the study of primitive society, but unfortunately very few of those who are qualified to study it know anything about primitive society, and so they don't know what to look for" (10304/75/364/205–209, NatLib).

209   My own knowledge . . . I am a fluent speaker: George Thomson, *Aeschylus and Athens,* p. 390.

209   Almost every face . . . continuous sobbing: Ibid., p. 381.

209   From the *inside:* Seaford, from unpaged online version.

209   Special debt: George Thomson, *Aeschylus and Athens,* p. vii.

210   Progressively shaped and polished: Quoted in Richard Martin, p. 88.
210   Aesthetic judgments turn: George Thomson, *Studies in Ancient Greeek Society*, p. 539.
210   Ragged peasants: Ibid., p. 540.
210   The driest philologists: Alexiou, "George Thomson: The Greek Dimension," p. 55.
210   Indirectly but profoundly: Ibid., p. 57.
210   I shall never forget: George Thomson, *Marxism and Poetry*, p. 5.
210   Was something new in Irish literature: George Thomson, *The Blasket Homer.*
211   The true bard of the Blaskets: Richard Martin, p. 91.

12. NO HERB OR REMEDY

212   Above the marquee: McKenna, n.p.
212   Helped settle Jewish refugees: KathFrag.
213   Peace in our time: He was no hero to Thomson. In a letter to E. M. Forster on Sept. 23, George referred to a time "before Chamberlain's airplane darkened the sky on its flight to Berchtesgaden," going on to express his hope that the Czechs would fight Germany, Thomson Archives.
213   Air-raid shelter: KathFrag.
213   Showering blessings: George to Katharine, Nov. 1, 1939, Thomson Archives.
213   That my services are indispensable: George to Katharine, April 18, 1939, Thomson Archives.
213   They seemed . . . safe from the bombs: KathFrag.
213   We have had it pretty hot here: Thomson to Mrs. Stewart, Oct. 1940, quoted in KathFrag.
214   There was a terrific bang: Thomson to Mrs. Stewart, Oct. 27, 1940. Thomson Archives.
214   And cowered in the scullery: Katharine to her mother, n.d., quoted in KathFrag.
214   George remained . . . very lonely: KathFrag.
214   Tell my factory friends that they were very kind and generous: Lís, Dec. 20[?], 1939, vol. 1944, p. 5.
214   I was shocked . . . befel or nearly fell: Ibid., Oct. 30, 1940, vol. 1944, p. 9.
214   We are not able . . . warming ourselves: *LísLetters*, p. 81.
215   You would be surprised . . . no hope atall: *LísLetters*, pp. 81–82.
215   Continued into the 1950s: The last letter in the Delargy collection seems to be one Lís wrote on March 11, 1957 (Lís, vol. 1945, p. 14G], reporting on daughter Niamh's return from a trip.
215   If my dreams . . . friend from London: Lís, March 4, 1935, vol. 1943, p. 45.
215   They did not bring . . . with no pleasure in your own heart: Lís, April [15?], 1940, vol. 1944, p. 6.
215   To hear all being well: Lís, May 6, 1940, vol. 1944, p. 7.
216   Inscribed copy of Maurice O'Sullivan's newly published book: Pierre-Yves Lambert to Bo Almqvist, n.d. [c. Sept. 2004], Almqvist papers.
216   It did her the greatest honor: Vendryes, p. 432.
216   At the time of the French defeat: "She was a victim of 1940," that iconic year of France's debasement and defeat. *Marie-Louise Sjoestedt, 35*

216   A too-late departure: Quoted in *Celtic,* p. 122.

216   Shaded and softened: Ibid., p. 123.

216   She married Louis Renou: Francoise Bader, "Une anamnése littéraire D'E. Benveniste," in *Incontri Linguistici,* vol. 22 (1999), Pisa, Roma: Istituti Editoriali e Poligrafici Internazionali, p. 23.

216   Out a window: Bo Almqvist, interview.

216   She submitted herself: *Celtic,* p. 122.

217   I felt . . . lonely tragedy: Quoted in Mac Conghail, "Brian Ó Ceallaigh," p. 186.

217   The well itself: Eoin MacNeill.

217   His pen was sharp and he did not mince words: Copy of talk, n.a., "Carl Marstrander's Work with the Manx Language," Seán Ó Lúing papers, NatLib.

217   All is first class: *Celtic,* p. 136.

218   He never really believed: David Greene, "A Warm and Generous Friend," p. 6.

218   A fervent Norwegian patriot: Binchy, "Norse Scholar," p. 6.

218   Stopped near Gestapo headquarters: Oftedal to Ó Lúing, Oct. 11, 1983, Ó Lúing papers, NatLib.

218   I am myself thinking of retiring: Flower to Best, Jan. 28, 1939, NatLib.

218   The ghastly bombing: Flower to Best, Nov. 13, 1940, NatLib.

219   He kept track of his career: For one example, see Flower to Best, March 4, 1913, Nat Lib: "I'm on private time. I am describing a collection of illuminated mss for which work I have to get £1500, a very satisfactory scale of pay. But the work is very heavy and keeps my nose down on the grindstone. Still it frees me of any financial cares and that is a great deal."

219   I know . . . difficulties of the life artistic: Flower to Best, May 21, 1939, NatLib.

219   My prospects are good: Flower to Best, July 3, 1921, NatLib.

219   Were heavy and confining: Robinson, p. 543.

219   He was more remarkable: Bell, p. 374.

220   He could never resist the attraction of a new interest: Ibid., p. 369.

220   The cares . . . jests with everyone: *Celtic,* p. 228.

220   He accepted their ways: Seán Ó Criomhthain, obituary of Flower written in Irish, trans. Flower's daughter Barbara, *Lís,* vol. 1944, pp. 129–32.

220   He was big-hearted: Ibid.

220   I would confide . . . I would not reveal to the priest: Ann Lucey, "How Flower Made an Island Bloom," Blasket Centre.

220   I have had rather a worse time: Robin Flower to Idris Bell, Oct. 10, 1911.

221   I have been ill of late: Flower to Best, July 3, 1921, NatLib.

221   I am feeling ill with overwork: Flower to Best, July 9, 1929, NatLib.

221   Great hardship: *Lís,* Oct. 2, 1941, vol. 1944, p. 77.

221   Sock-knitting machines: Keogh, p. 56. See also Tyers, *West Kerry Camera,* p. 170.

221   The young women weren't willing: Ó Floinn, in *Reflections.*

221   At present nobody thinks of marrying: *LísLetters,* p. 22.

222   Of men who are more lonely: *Lís,* Oct. 30, 1940, vol. 1944, p. 9.

222   Black cloud: *LísLetters,* p. 84.

222   It's a hopeless, fruitless year: Ibid.

222   So picture our Island home sinking from day to day: Ibid., p. 85.

223 And left the three . . . run wild with the rabbits: Ibid., p. 86.
223 This is the last winter here for me: Séan O'Crohan, *A Day in Our Life*, p. 27.
223 We have determined at last to leave this lovely Island: *LísLetters*, p. 87.
223 I don't miss: Ibid., p. 92.
223 "The Song of the Island Girl": Chambers, p. 7.
224 I was very very lonely: Lís, Sept. 22, 1950, vol. 1945, p. 22.
224 Where is the snow?: Robin Flower, *The Western Island*, p. viii. (George Chambers encouraged Flower to write *The Western Island*. See Patrick Flower, p. 42.)
224 I am still a very long way from actual recovery: Flower to Best, Jan. 21, 1945, NatLib.
225 Didn't recognize them: Mrs. Flower to Best [?], March 5, 1946, NatLib.
225 I was so sad: Lís, Feb. 10, 1946, vol. 1944, p. 127.
225 It was a cause of grief . . . no herb or remedy: Appended to Lís, April 7, 1946, vol. 1944, p. 129.
225 To this day I can recall the modest comfort: Mahon, p. 138.
225 It's going downhill: Appended to Lís, April 7, 1946, vol. 1944, p. 132.
225 Was no place at all: Seán Ó Guithín interview, in *Memories*, p. 161.
226 Loneliness is accentuated: Quoted in Keogh, p. 54.
226 With most of the island community helpless at his bedside: Mícheal de Mórdha, "Bereavement and Bravery on the Great Blasket," *An Caomhnóir,* 2007.
226 Resettle its inhabitants: See Keogh.
226 Two men from the 'Land Commission': Lís, May 20, 1953, vol. 1945, p. 30.
226 I'd go down to the slip: Ó Floinn, in *Reflections.*
227 A black gloom: Feiritéar.

13. THE BOTTOM OF THE GARDEN

229 A U.S. Passport: Kindly furnished by Kathleen Arduini.
229 First went to work: Interview with Sister Mary Justin, Sisters of Providence, who furnished Mary Kearney's record of ministries.
230 Infectious laugh: "Excerpts from the Homily of Rev. Robert W. Thrasher at Sister M. Clemens' Mass," Providence Mother House, Jan. 15, 1987, courtesy of Kathleen Arduini.
230 Troubles: Ibid.
230 One of Pats Kearney's daughters: Lís, May 13, 1951, vol. 1945, p. 5.
230 Laid to rest: Thanks to Seán Cahillane for help in finding her grave.
230 Convened a reunion: Account follows Biuso, "The Poet's Ring."
231 A tough, hard lady: Feiritéar, interview. Kathleen Arduini remembers her aunt as "a toughie, really a tomboy."
231 Trip to America: Account follows Ray Stagles, "A 26-Years Journey"; Stagles, audio-tape interview and interviews with the author.
231 He listened very intently: Interview with person who requests anonymity.
231 Loud and incessantly: KathFrag.
232 Her most loving memories: Margaret Alexiou, interviews; also Alexiou, in *Eighty.*
233 Indistinguishable from the theory and practice of fascism: Thomson to F. M. Cornford, series of letters, 1941, Thomson Archives. In 1986, Katharine and George sent photocopies of the correspondence to Cornford's son Christopher, who replied: "I

found myself turning my head left and right like a spectator at a Wimbledon final, admiring the deftness & power of each shot & each recovery: also moved by the mutual respect, affection & good humour shown by both players."

233   Exploiting wage labour: Thomson to Christopher Hill, May 1946, Thomson Archives.

233   You've got the words: Margaret Alexiou, interview.

233   Yesterday evening: Thomson, China journal, June 16, 1955, Thomson Archives.

233   See how my vision of the Blasket: Enright, p. 150.

233   My mind was carried back: Thomson, China journal, n.d., Thomson Archives.

233   Would never commit . . . hear how it sounded: Enright, "George Thomson: A Memoir," p. 126.

234   Which has healed the breach: Thomson to Pádraig Ó Fiannachta, June 21, 1976, Thomson Archives.

234   Troy seen in the morning of the world: Ireland, p. 100.

234   Baking classes: Nuala Uí Aimhirgín, interviews; similar account by Cáit Bean Uí Mhaoilchiaráin [Maurice's wife], in *Memories,* p. 177.

235   Fine block of a man: Cáit Bean Uí Mhaoilchiaráin interview in *Memories,* 178.

235   Has not done harm: Forster to Thomson, May 13, 1934, Thomson Archives.

235   The chattering: *Memories,* 180.

235   Of course, Dónal spoke: *Reflections,* p. 46.

235   Couldn't understand a word: *Memories.*

236   They would have . . . dance till morning: George to Katharine, Sept. 13, 1937, Thomson Archives.

236   Heartbroken at leaving Kerry: Katharine Thomson to her mother, Aug. 11, 1935, Thomson Archives.

236   Cut turf, collected seaweed: Nuala Uí Aimhirgín, interviews.

236   Place they called Barraderry: *Memories,* 188.

236   An islander marooned ashore: Fragment of unidentified newspaper article, Blasket Centre.

236   A man of one book: Ó Faoláin, "Irish Magic." Daniel Binchy held to the same view: "With his remarkable powers of observation he should find materials for many more books in his experiences during the second stage of life—the 'twenty years a-blooming' (*fiche blian fé bhláth*)—on which he has now entered" ("Two Blasket Autobiographies," p. 557).

236   An appalling book: Titley, in *Reflections.*

236   The quirky humour: Titley, e-mail correspondence.

236   But what good was that?: In *Reflections,* p. 46.

237   Contribution to the original: Titley, in *Reflections.*

237   Had to take him by the arm: George Thomson, "The Irish Language Revival," p. 8.

237   He'd cycle for miles: Nuala Uí Aimhirgín, Breandán Feiritéar, interviews.

237   Life in the bee world: Máire Llewelyn Kavanagh, interview.

238   Disappointment followed: Matson, "Blasket Lives."

238   Sixty pounds a year: Thomson to Katharine, Sept. 15, 1945, Thomson Archives. The book did well thereafter, too, being reprinted in an Oxford World's Classics edition in 1953, reprinted again and again all through the sixties and seventies, then

by Oxford University Press beginning in 1983, with whom it has remained in print ever since.

238   Pink glow: Máire Llewelyn Kavanagh, interview.

238   The journey from Liverpool: Account follows Thomson to family, Sept. 7, 1945, and subsequent letters, Thomson Archives.

239   All turned white: Photo in *Eighty.*

239   This academic year: See Thomson date books, University of Birmingham Special Collections.

239   Maurice drowned: Telegram displayed at Blasket Centre. (O'Sullivan died the same day the Korean War broke out.)

239   Máire, six years old: Máire Llewelyn Kavanagh, interview, also in *Eighty.*

240   Four days before his death: Garda Museum/Archives, Dublin record, in Ceiliúradh an Bhlascaoid 5, devoted to Muiris Ó Súilleabháin.

240   A strike was on: Ibid., 187.

240   Killed himself: Nuala Uí Aimhirgín, interview. "It's still an open question," says Margaret Alexiou. Her father, she says, "couldn't get it out of his mind that it might have been suicide."

240   I think he had a heart attack: Maurice's daughter, in *Eighty.*

240   Sixty I may be: Máire Ní Shúilleabháin [Máire Llewelyn Kavanagh], "Do Mhuiris," *An Caomhnóir,* vol. 25 (2004), p. 3.

240   Barely able to speak: Katharine, in *Eighty.*

14. A DREAM OF YOUTH

242   Maybe it will come: Thomas, p. 82. Or, as George Thomson says, in *Another:* "What has happened to the Blasket Islands has happened, or is happening, to hundreds of other small communities" around the world. The Blasket books "raise questions in the reader's mind about the future of his own culture."

243   Film stars: *LísLetters,* p. 56.

243   A great man . . . great anger against civilisation: Flower to Bell, June 1, 1932, British Library.

243   Neal O'Moore, Dublin medical student: Account and quoted dialogue from *Men of Ireland,* directed by Dick Bird.

244   That Film is not about my father-in-law: *LísLetters,* p. 57.

244   Filmed in a Dublin studio: *Scannán: The Islandman,* 1937.

244   Dreamy voluptuous gaiety: Synge, *The Aran Islands,* p. 76.

244   Off the death . . . all coroners and morticians: Kiberd, *Inventing Ireland,* p. 173.

245   The beauty . . . all precarious or dying things: Ibid.

245   Tangled world of to-day: Robin Flower, *The Western Island,* p. 6.

245   Only a few remaining corners: Quoted in Ó Giolláin, p. 137.

245   Having acquired the doubtful blessing: Binchy, "Two Blasket Autobiographies," p. 553.

246   It was only the other day: Robin Flower, *The Western Island,* p. 70.

246   Within the space . . . transformed by literacy: George Thomson, *Island Home,* p. 62.

246   It is strangely ironical: "The Blaskets," *Irish Times,* June 12, 1931.

246   What about giving friends: Lís, Nov. 17, 1938, vol. 1944, p. 42.

247   We used to be sitting: Cited in Enright, introduction, *Cross,* p. *6.*

247   Kearney's Hotel: *LísLetters,* Oct. 14, 1932, p. 51.

247   Remind you of a Nice, France: See Robert Kanigel, *High Season* (New York: Viking, 2002).

247   *The Village:* McCarty and Hockings documentary.

248   Literature of escape: Quoted in Ó Giolláin, p. 138.

248   And the fashion of life: Robin Flower, *The Western Island,* p. 106.

248   It is a strange world: Seán O'Crohan, *A Day in Our Life,* p. 47.

249   Their collective narrative . . . haunted . . . the Irish imagination: O'Toole, p. 9.

249   Fifty thousand visitors: Dáithi de Mórdha, e-mail.

249   It was a simple culture: George Thomson, *Island Home,* p. 85.

250   Failed in the work: Thomson, in *Eighty.*

250   We were poor people: Translation from Peig Sayers, *Peig,* in O'Leary, p. 160. See also English translation by MacMahon, p. 211.

250   May be a broken-down culture: Thomas Barrington, p. 120.

251   It was only when he found Innismaan and the Blaskets: Yeats, "Synge and the Ireland of His Time."

251   I am greatly taken with this place: Quoted in *Celtic,* p. 113.

251   Recognises neither the realities of poverty: *Hidden,* p. *46.*

252   To him . . . dream of his youth: *Celtic,* p. 226.

252   As he was speaking . . . got up and paced the room: Ibid., p. 166. See also interview with Margaret Alexiou in *Eighty:* "I can remember how in his declining years he became a different person when somebody Irish came in the room and had the Gaelic. . . . You would see in his face it became like it was when he was a young man."

253   They haven't much worry about material things: McCarty and Hockings documentary.

253   Spent the most wholesome part: Lís, vol. 1945, p. 53, March 4, 1952.

253   The long years have vanished: O'Guiheen, p. 82.

253   Would walk and walk . . . pick every bright flower: Ibid., p. 87.

254   It is sad to think . . . Raheny will be swallowed up: Thomson to Katharine, Sept. 9, 1937, Thomson Archives.

254   Whatever happens on the Island . . . one gifted thing: *LísLetters,* p. 88.

254   The Island will be in my head: Seán Ó Guithín interview, in *Memories,* p. 174.

255   It wasn't from laziness: O'Guiheen, p. 120.

255   It is as fresh as ever: Thomson to Katharine, Sept. [7?], 1937, Thomson Archives.

Selected Bibliography

SEE BELOW FOR IRISH-LANGUAGE BIBLIOGRAPHY

Aeschylus. *The Oresteia Trilogy.* Edited by Robert W. Corrigan. Translated with a special introduction by George Thomson. New York: Dell, 1965.

Agostini, René. "J. M. Synge's 'Celestial Peasants.'" In Genet, ed., *Rural Ireland, Real Ireland?*, pp. 159–73.

Alexander, S.M.D. "The Birds of the Blasket Islands." *Bird Study*, vol. 1, no. 4 (December 1954), begins p. 148.

Alexiou, Margaret. "Fifty Years Later . . ." In Ní Chéillechair, ed., *Seoirse Mac Tomáis,* pp. 132–135.

———. "George Thomson: The Greek Dimension." In Ní Chéillechair, ed., *Seoirse Mac Tomáis,* pp. 52–74.

Almqvist, Bo. "The Mysterious Mícheál Ó Gaoithín, Boccaccio and the Blasket Tradition." *Béaloideas,* vol. 58 (1990), pp. 75–140.

———. "C. W. von Sydow agus Éire: Scoláire Sualannach agus an Léann Ceilteach." *Béaloideas,* vol. 70 (2002) (English summary, pp. 45–49).

———. "The Scholar and the Storyteller: Heinrich Wagner's Collections from Peig Sayers." *Béaloideas,* vol. 72 (2004), pp. 31–59.

Almqvist, Bo, and Pádraig Ó Héalái. *Peig Sayers: I Will Speak to You All.* Dublin: New Island, 2009. In English and Irish.

"An Seabhac Had to Sign Name in English." *Irish Independent,* December 29, 1952.

Barrington, Richard M. "Report on the Flora of the Blasket Islands, Co. Kerry." *Proceedings of the Royal Irish Academy,* vol. iii (1883).

Barrington, Thomas. "Telescope and Microscope." *Bonaventura,* November 1937, pp. 114–23.

Beaslai, Pieras. "An Seabhac—A Giant of the Gaelic Movement." *Irish Independent,* December 2, 1964.

Bell, H. I. "Robin Ernest William Flower, 1881–1946." *Proceedings of the British Academy,* vol. 32 (1946), pp. 352–79.

Binchy, D. A. "Two Blasket Autobiographies." *Studies: An Irish Quarterly Review,* December 1934, pp. 545–60.

———. "Norse Scholar Whose Irish Dictionary Caused a Furore," *Sunday Independent,* January 16, 1966, p. 6.

Bird, Dick. *Men of Ireland* [also known as *Island Man* and *West of Kerry*]. Irish National Film Corporation, 1938.

Biuso, Thomas. "The Poet's Ring." *An Caomhnóir,* umh 26.

———. "Looking Into Blasket Island Photographs." *Eire-Ireland,* Winter 1987, pp. 16–34.

———. "Tobar an Phuncain: A Story from the Great Blasket Island & Hungry Hill, Springfield, Massachusetts." *Irish America Magazine,* June 1990, pp. 38–42.

———. "Blasket Islanders in Springfield." *An Caomhnóir,* 2004, pp. 4–6.

Blasket Roots, American Dreams. Video documentary, directed by Breandán Feiritéar. Radio-Telefis Éireann, 1997.

Boyd, Ernest. "Twenty Years' Romancing." *The Nation,* vol. 137, no. 3555 (August 23, 1933), p. 221.

Brathnach, Ciara. *The Congested Districts Board of Ireland, 1891–1923.* Dublin: Four Courts Press, 2005.

Briody, Mícheál. *The Irish Folklore Commission 1935–1970.* Helsinki: Finnish Literature Society, 2007.

Browning, Robert. "George Thomson and Modern Greek Studies in England." Typescript of talk given at Colloquium on the Life and Work of George Thomson, January 7, 1989. Thomson Archives, Birmingham.

Burns, Maggie. *George Thomson in Birmingham and the Blaskets.* Birmingham, U.K.: Birmingham Library Services, 2000.

Carney, Mike. "From the Blaskets to Springfield." *Irish Echo,* n.d.

Castro del Rio, Plácido. Journal of visit to the Blaskets, c. 1928. Typescript translation, Blasket Centre.

Chambers, George. *The Lovely Line and Other Verses.* Colchester, U.K.: Oyster Press, 1950.

Coleman, Michael C. " 'Some Kind of Gibberish': Irish-Speaking Children in the National Schools, 1850–1922." *International Review of English Studies,* January 1, 1998.

Coman, B. J. "The Last of His Tribe." *Quadrant,* vol. 49, no. 3 (March 2005).

"Conference on Galway University College: Report on the Conference, 1926." National University of Ireland, Galway.

Corish, Patrick J. *Maynooth College, 1795–1995.* Dublin: Gill & Macmillan, 1995.

Crane, C. P. *Kerry.* London: Methuen, 1914.

Creedon, Ted. "The Currach—Oldest Seagoing Craft in Western Europe." *Cork Holly Bough,* Christmas 1981.

Crohan, Martin J. " 'The Great and the Good . . . The Worthless and Insignificant': A Case Study of Tomás O'Crohan's *The Islandman.*" In Genet, ed., *Rural Ireland, Real Ireland?*

Cultural Committee of the Irish Workers' League. "Culture in Ireland To-day: The Present Position and What We Should Do About It." Typescript, August 1952, Thomson Archives, Birmingham.

Davis, Natalie Zemon. "Women and the World of the *Annales.*" *History Workshop Journal,* vol. 33, no. 1 (1992), pp. 121–37.

Delargy, J. H. "The Gaelic Story-Teller." *Proceedings of the British Academy,* vol. 31 (1945), pp. 177–221.

de Mórdha, Dáithí, ed. *Cuisle Deoil na nOileán.* Proceedings of Ceiliúradh an Bhlascaoid 11. Baile Átha Cliath: Coiscéim, 2008.

de Mórdha, Mícheál. "Bryan MacMahon, Peig Sayers, and the Publication of *Peig* in English." In Gabriel Fitzmaurice, ed., *The World of Bryan MacMahon* (Cork: Mercier Press, 2005).

de Mórdha, Mícheál, ed. *Bláithín: Flower.* An Daingean: An Sagart, 1998.

———, ed. *Na Lochlannaigh.* Proceedings of Ceiliúradh an Bhlascaoid 12. Baile Átha Cliath: Coiscéim, 2008.

Diskin, Patrick M. "Professor George Thomson." Typescript, National University of Ireland, Galway.

Doan, James E. "Revisiting the Blasket Island Memoirs." *Irish Studies Review,* vol. 9, no. 1 (2001), pp. 81–86.

Dunnett, H. McG. *Eminent Alleynians.* Cranbrook, Kent, U.K.: Neville & Harding, 1984.

Eastlake, John. "Orality and Agency: Reading an Irish Autobiography from the Great Blasket Island." *Oral Tradition,* vol. 24, no. 1 (2009), pp. 125–41.

———. "The (Original) *Islandman?*: Examining the Origin in Blasket Autobiography." In Nessa Cronin et al., *Orality and Modern Irish Culture* (Newcastle upon Tyne, U.K.: Cambridge Scholars Publishing, 2009), pp. 241–56.

Enright, Tim. "George Thomson: A Memoir." In George Thomson, *Island Home.*

———. Introduction, Seán O'Crohan, *A Day in Our Life.*

———. Introduction, Tomás O'Crohan, *Island Cross-Talk.*

———. "Padraig Keane—King of the Blasket." *Evening Echo,* February 25, 1984.

Feiritéar, Breandán. "The Last Days of the Blasket Community As Seen from the Mainland." Typescript of talk given at Colloquium on the Life and Work of George Thomson, January 7, 1989.

Ferriter, Diarmaid. *Occasions of Sin: Sex and Society in Modern Ireland.* London: Profile Books, 2009.

Fitz Gerald, Joan. "From Orality to Literacy on the Blasket Islands." In Giuseppe Serpillo and Donatella Abbate Badin, eds., *The Classical World and the Mediterranean* (Cagliari, Italy: Tema, 1996), pp. 284–93.

Fleming, Deborah. *"A Man Who Does Not Exist": The Irish Peasant in the Work of W. B. Yeats and J. M. Synge.* Ann Arbor: University of Michigan Press, 1995.

Flower, Patrick. "My Father." In Mícheál de Mórdha, ed., *Bláithín.*

Flower, Robin. Foreword, Tomás Ó Crohan, *The Islandman,* pp. v–xi.

———. *Eire and Other Poems.* London: Locke Ellis, 1910.

———. "An Irish Island: The Story of the Blaskets." *Transactions of the Honourable Society of Cymmrodorion,* 1931–32, pp. 1–33.

———. *The Western Island.* New York: Oxford University Press, 1978.

———. *The Irish Tradition.* Dublin: Lilliput Press,1994.

———. *Poems and Translations.* Dublin: Lilliput Press, 1994.

Foley, Patrick. *The Ancient and Present State of the Skelligs, Blasket Islands, Donquin and the West of Dingle.* Baile Átha Cliath: An Cló-Cumann Teóranta, 1903.

———. *History of the Natural, Civil, Military and Ecclesiastical State of the County of Kerry.* Dublin: Sealy, Bryers & Walker, 1907.

Foster, John Wilson. "Waking the Dead: *The Islandman* and the Irish Revival." *Irish Renaissance Annual,* Spring 1982, pp. 47–58.

———. "Certain Set Apart: The Romantic Strategy—John Millington Synge." In John Wilson Foster, *Fictions of the Irish Literary Revival: A Changeling Art* (Syracuse, N.Y.: Syracuse University Press, 1987).

———. "The Island Man: The Rise (and Fall) of the Peasant Author—Tomás Ó Crohan." In John Wilson Foster, *Fictions of the Irish Literary Revival: A Changeling Art* (Syracuse, N.Y.: Syracuse University Press, 1987).

Garvin, Tom. "The Politics of Language and Literature in Pre-Independence Ireland." *Irish Political Studies,* vol. 2 (1987), pp. 49–63.

Gathercole, Peter. "Aeschylus, the Blaskets and Marxism: Interconnecting Influences on the Writings of George Thomson." In *The Lure of Greece: Irish Involvement in Greek Culture, Literature, History and Politics,* eds. John Victor Luce, Christine Morris, and Christina Souyoudzoglou-Haywood (Dublin: Hinds, 2007).

Genet, Jacqueline. "Yeats and the Myth of Rural Ireland." In Genet, ed., *Rural Ireland, Real Ireland?,* pp. 139–57.

Genet, Jacqueline, ed. *Rural Ireland, Real Ireland?* Gerrards Cross, Buckinghamshire, U.K.: Colin Smythe, 1996.

"Gentle, Gracious and Gifted—Peig of the Blaskets." *Irish Independent,* January 12, 1952.

"George Thomson." *Feras,* ed. In L. Varcl and R. F. Willetts, pp. 11–17.

Goldring, Maurice. *Irlande: Idéologie d'une révolution nationale.* Paris: Éditions Sociales, 1975.

Gorky, Maxim. *Autobiography of Maxim Gorky.* London: Elek Books, 1953.

Greene, David. "Carl J. S. Marstrander (1883–1965). *Studia Celtica,* vol. 1 (1966), pp. 204–5.

———. *The Irish Language.* Published for the Cultural Relations Committee of Ireland at the Three Candles, Ltd., Dublin, 1966.

———. "A Warm and Generous Friend." *Sunday Independent,* January 16, 1966, p. 6.

Greene, David H. "J. M. Synge—A Centenary Appraisal." In *J. M. Synge: Centenary Papers,* ed. Maurice Harmon (Dublin: Dolmen Press, 1971).

Greene, David H., and Edward M. Stephens. *J. M. Synge, 1871–1909.* New York: New York University Press, 1989.

Gregg, Gerry. *George Thomson: Eighty Years A-Growing.* Video documentary. Dublin: Vermillion Films for RTÉ, 1998.

Gregory, Lady. *Our Irish Theatre.* New York: Capricorn Books, 1965.

Grene, Nicholas. *Synge: A Critical Study of the Plays.* London: Macmillan, 1975.

Grene, Nicholas, ed. *J. M. Synge, Travelling Ireland: Essays 1898–1908.* Dublin: Lilliput Press, 2009.

Hamsun, Knut. *Growth of the Soil.* Translated by W. W. Worster. Sioux Falls, S.D.: NuVision Publications, 2008.

Hardy, Thomas. *Tess of the D'Urbervilles.* New York: Modern Library, 1951.

Harris, John. "Orality and Literacy in Tomás Ó Criomhthain's Narrative Style." *Canadian Journal of Irish Studies,* vol. 19 (1993), pp. 20–30.

Harris, P. R. *A History of the British Museum Library, 1753–1973.* London: British Library, 1998.

Harrison, Alan. "Review Article: Blasket Literature." *Irish University Review,* vol. 31, no. 2 (2001), pp. 488–94.

Hart, Peter. *Mick: The Real Michael Collins.* New York: Viking Penguin, 2006.

Headlam, W. "Greek Lyric Metre." *Journal of Hellenic Studies,* vol. 22 (1902), pp. 209–27.

Hearn, Mona. "Life for Domestic Servants in Dublin, 1880–1920." In Maria Luddy and Cliona Murphy, *Women Surviving* (Dublin: Poolbeg, 1989).

Hirsch, Edward. "The Imaginary Irish Peasant." *PMLA,* vol. 106, no. 5 (October 1991), pp. 1116–33.

Hockings, Paul. "Gone with the Gael: Filming an Irish Village." In *Anthropological Filmmaking,* ed. Jack R. Rollwagen (Amsterdam, Netherlands: Harwood Academic Publishers, 1988), pp. 143–59.

Hughes, A. J. "Advancing the Irish Language." *New Hibernia Review,* vol. 5, no 1 (Spring 2001), pp. 101–26.

Hutchison, Percy. "Youth and the Irish Islanders." *New York Times,* August 6, 1933.

Ireland, Denis. *From the Irish Shore: Notes on My Life and Times.* London: Rich & Cowan, 1936.

Jackson, Angela. *British Women and the Spanish Civil War.* London: Routledge, 2002.

Jackson, Kenneth. "The International Folktale in Ireland." *Folklore,* vol. 47, no. 3 (September 1936), pp. 263–93.

———. "Scéalta ón mBlascaod," *Béaloideas,* vol. 8 (1938), pp. 3–96.

———. "Some Mutations in Blasket Irish." *Éigse,* vol. 3, pt. 4 (1943), pp. 272–77.

Jackson, Kenneth Hurlstone. *A Celtic Miscellany.* London: Penguin Books, 1971.

Jacquin, Danielle. "Les Autobiographies gaéliques: Voix personnelle, voix collective, voix mythique." *Études irlandaises,* vol 23, no. 1 (1998), pp. 13–25.

———. "L'exil dans les autobiographies gaéliques des Îles Blasket." *Cycnos,* vol. 15, no. 2 (1998), pp. 99–110.

Kelly, Brian. "How He Came to Write." No other information, Blasket Centre.

Keogh, Dermot. "Leaving the Blaskets 1953: Willing or Enforced Departures?" In *The Lost Decade: Ireland in the 1950s,* eds. Dermot Keogh, Finbarre O'Shea, and Carmel Quinlan (Cork: Mercier Press, 2004), pp. 48–71.

Kiberd, Declan. "Decolonizing the Mind: Douglas Hyde and Irish Ireland." In Genet, ed., *Rural Ireland, Real Ireland?,* pp. 121–37.

———. *Inventing Ireland: The Literature of the Modern Nation.* Cambridge, Mass.: Harvard University Press, 1995.

———. *Synge and the Irish Language.* 2nd ed. Dublin: Gill & Macmillan, 1993.

———. *Irish Classics.* London: Granta Books, 2000.

Liptak, Dolores, and Grace Bennett, eds. *Seeds of Hope: The History of the Sisters of Providence, Holyoke, Massachusetts.* Holyoke: Sisters of Providence, 1999.

Llewelyn-Davies, Melissa. Unpublished personal reminiscence of her grandmother, Moya Llewelyn Davies.

———. "My Grandmother, the Revolutionary." *Daily Mail,* June 2, 2007.

Lockley, R. M. *I Know an Island.* London: George G. Harrap, 1938.

———. "In Search of an Island." *Irish Digest,* August 1938, pp. 65–70.

Loti, Pierre. *An Iceland Fisherman.* Translated by M. Jules Cambon. Charleston, S.C.: BiblioBazaar, 2007.

Lowth, Cormac F. "James O'Connor, Fenian, and the Tragedy of 1890" (paper read to the Old Dublin Society on October 24, 2001). *Dublin Historical Record,* vol. 55, no. 2 (Autumn 2002), pp. 132–53.

Lucchitti, Irene. "Bláithín and the Islandman: The Blaskets Translated." *New Literature Review,* vol. 37 (2000), pp. 43–58.

———. *The Islandman: The Hidden Life of Tomás O'Crohan.* Oxford, U.K.: Peter Lang, 2009.

Luce, J. V. "Homeric Qualities in the Life and Literature of the Great Blasket Island." *Greece and Rome,* ser. 2, vol. 16, no. 2 (October 1969), pp. 151–68.

Luddy, Maria. "Sex and the Single Girl in 1920s and 1930s Ireland." *Irish Review,* vol. 35 (Summer 2007), pp. 79–92.

Lysaght, Patricia. "Food-Provision Strategies on the Great Blasket Island: Strand and Shore." In *Northern Lights, Following Folklore in North-Western Europe: Essays in Honour of Bo Almqvist,* ed. Séamas Ó Catháin et al. (Dublin: University College Dublin Press), 2001.

———. "Some Thoughts on the Decline and Fall of the Great Blasket Island, Co. Kerry, Ireland." In *The Decline and Fall of St. Kilda,* ed. John Randall (Isle of Lewis, Scotland: Islands Book Trust, 2006).

Mac Amhlaoíbh, Feargal. "Port na bPúcai and Its Concerns," English translation of " 'Port na bPúcai' agus a Mbaineann Leis." In Proceedings of Ceiliúradh an Bhlascaoid 11. Baila Átha Cliath: Coiscéim, 2007.

———. "Port na bPúcaí—the Fairy Music of the Blaskets." *Kerry Archaeological and Historical Society Journal,* ser. 2, vol. 7 (2007).

Mac Cárthaigh, Críostóir, and Barry O'Reilly. "Ó Bhun Go Barr An Bhaile: Recent Settlement on the Great Blasket Island." In *Northern Lights, Following Folklore in North-Western Europe: Essays in Honour of Bo Almqvist,* ed. Séamas Ó Catháin et al. (Dublin: University College Dublin Press, 2001).

Mac Conghail, Muiris. "A Note on the Author." In Robin Flower, *Poems and Translations.*

———. *Another Island: A Portrait of the Blasket Islands.* Video documentary. Dublin: RTÉ, 1984.

———. *The Blaskets: A Kerry Island Library.* Dublin: Country House, 1987.

———. "An English Scholar of Ireland and Greece." *Irish Times,* February 11, 1987.

———. "Tomás Ó Criomhthain: Islandman." *Études irlandaises,* no. 12. December 1987, pp. 155–64.

———. "Aspects of Blasket Literature." Unpublished typescript of talk given at Colloquium on the Life and Work of George Thomson, January 7, 1989.

———. "Brian Ó Ceallaigh, Tomás Ó Criomhthain and Sir Roger Casement." *Journal of the Kerry Archaeological and Historical Society,* vol. 23 (1990), pp. 175–87.

———. Radio interview. RTÉ, October 22, 2002.

———. Radio interview. RTÉ, February 19, 2004.

———. "De Blaghd agus Mac Tomáis." Unpublished personal notes and references for a talk given at Maynooth, November 22, 2007.

MacDowell, Vincent. *Michael Collins and the Irish Republican Brotherhood.* Dublin: Ashfield Press, 1997.

MacGreevy, Thomas. "Monsignor Padraig de Brun." *Italy Speaks,* July 1960, pp. 8–9.

MacIntosh, Fiona. "Amid Our Troubles. *Arion,* ser. 3, vol. 11, no. 2 (Fall 2003), pp. 137–48.

MacKillop, James. "An Authentic Voice." *Irish Literary Supplement,* vol 6, no. 2 (1987), p. 50.

Mac Mathúna, Séamus. "UCG and the NUI." Unpublished typescript, courtesy of the author.

MacNeill, Eoin. "Unique Service to Ireland: The Late Mr. B. Kelly." *Irish Independent,* January 1, 1937.

MacNeill, Máire. Review of *Seanchas ón Oileaán Tiar. Journal of American Folklore,* vol. 71, no. 280 (April-June 1958), pp. 169–70.

Mahon, Bríd. *While Green Grass Grows: Memoirs of a Folklorist.* Cork: Mercier Press, 1998.

Marie-Louise Sjoestedt (1900–1940) : In Memoriam. Paris: Librairie Droz, 1941.

Marstrander, Carl. "Impressions from Ireland." Translated by K. H. Moe. Norwegian Geographical Society, Radio Telefís. Courtesy of Blasket Centre.

Martin, Kevin. "How the West Was Wonderful: Some Historical Perspectives on Representations of the West of Ireland in Popular Culture." *ITB Journal,* December 2001, pp. 89–94.

Martin, Richard. "Homer Among the Irish: Yeats, Synge, Thomson." In *Homer in the Twentieth Century,* eds. Barbara Graziosi and Emily Greenwood (New York: Oxford University Press, 2007).

Mason, Thomas H. *The Islands of Ireland: Their Scenery, People, Life and Antiquities.* London: B. T. Batsford, 1936.

Matson, Leslie. "Blasket Lives: Biographical Accounts of One Hundred and Twenty-Five Blasket People." Unpublished manuscripts. Blasket Centre.

———. *Méiní, the Blasket Nurse.* Cork: Mercier Press, 1996.

McCabe, Carol. "To the Great Blasket." *Islands,* December 5, 2006.

McCarty, Mark, and Paul Hockings. *The Village.* Black-and-white documentary. University of California Extension Media Center, Berkeley, Calif, 1968.

McGahern, John. "An tOileánach." *Irish Review,* 1989, pp. 55–62.

———. "Island Days." *Irish Times,* November 22, 1991.

McGrath, Walter. "Seoirse Mac Tomáis—Colossus of Greek and Gaelic Worlds." *Evening Echo,* December 20, 1983.

———. "Just 75 Years Ago—Double Tragedy Struck Blasket's White Strand." *Evening Echo,* August 7, 1984.

———. " 'The Viking's' Great Gaelic Studies." *Echo,* December 10, 1984.

———. "From Paris to a Blasket Cottage." *Examiner,* March 10, 1990.

———. "The Nun of the Blaskets." *Cork Holly Bough,* 1993.

McKenna, Joseph. *Birmingham Between the Wars.* Birmingham, U.K.: Birmingham Library Services, 1991.

McMahon, Timothy G. *Grand Opportunity: The Gaelic Revival and Irish Society, 1893–1910.* Syracuse, N.Y.: Syracuse University Press, 2008.

McNab, Gregory. "The Hard Life: Gaelic Autobiography and the Image of the Irish Language." *Eire-Ireland,* vol. 14, no. 3 (1979), pp. 133–40.

Meehan, Denis Molaise. *Maynooth Again Remembered.* Tralee, Ireland: The Kerryman, 1982.

Messenger, John C. Review of *The Village,* by Mark McCarty and Paul Hockings. *American Anthropologist,* new ser., vol. 74, no. 6 (December 1972), pp. 1577–81.

Mhac an tSaoi, Máire. Interview. RTÉ, October 2003.

Miller, Kerby A. *Emigrants and Exiles: Ireland and the Irish Exodus to North America.* New York: Oxford University Press, 1985.

Moreton, Cole. *Hungry for Home: Leaving the Blaskets—A Journey from the Edge of Ireland.* New York: Viking, 2000.

Nash, Catherine. " 'Embodying the Nation'—The West of Ireland Landscape and Irish Identity." In *Tourism in Ireland: A Critical Analysis,* eds. Barbara O'Connor and Michael Cronin (Cork: Cork University Press, 1993).

Ní Aimhirgín, Nuala. "British Scholars and the Discovery of Blasket Culture." Typescript of talk given at Colloquium on the Life and Work of George Thomson, January 7, 1989.

Nic Craith, Mairéad. "Primary Education on the Great Blasket Island 1864–1940." *Journal of the Kerry Archaeological and Historical Society,* vol. 28 (1995), pp. 77–137.

Nic Eoin, Máirín. Review of *I Will Speak to You All: Peig Sayers,* ed. Bo Almqvist and Pádraig Ó Héalaí. *Irish Times,* January 23, 2010.

Nic Gh., E. Review of *Peig,* by Peig Sayers. *Dublin Magazine,* January-March 1937, pp. 93–94.

Nic Gráinne, Eibhlín. Review of Irish- and English-language editions of *Twenty Years A-Growing,* by Maurice O'Sullivan. *Dublin Magazine,* April-June 1936, pp. 94–97.

Ní Chartúir, Darerca. *The Irish Language: An Overview and Guide.* New York: Avena Press, 2002.

Ní Chéilleachair, Máire, ed. *Seoirse Mac Tomáis, 1903–1987.* Baile Átha Cliath: Coiscéim, 2000.

Ní Chuilleanáin, Eiléan. *As I Was Among the Captives: Joseph Campbell's Prison Diary, 1922–1923.* Cork: Cork University Press, 2001.

Ní Mhóráin, Bríd. "Women's Lives in the Time of Seán Ó Conaill." *Journal of the Kerry Archaeological and Historical Society,* vol. 29 (1996).

Ní N., M. Review of *The Western Island,* by Robin Flower. *Béaloideas,* vol. 14 (1944 [1945]), pp. 294–97.

Ní Shúilleabháin, Eibhlís. *Letters from the Great Blasket.* Dublin: Mercier Press, 2008.

Ní Shúilleabháin, Máire. "Do Mhuiris," *An Caomhnóir,* uimh. 25 (2004).

O'Brien, Flann. *The Poor Mouth.* London: Flamingo, 1993. [Translation by Patrick C. Power of *An Béal Bocht,* "edited" by Myles na Gopaleen.]

O'Brien, Máire Cruise. "An tOileánach: Tomás Ó Criomhthain (1856–1937)." In *The Pleasures of Gaelic Literature,* ed. John Jordan (Dublin and Cork: Radio-Telefís Éireann in collaboration with The Mercier Press, 1977).

———. *The Same Age as the State.* Dublin: O'Brien Press, 2003.

O'Cahill, Donal. "We Went to the Blaskets." *Capuchin Annual,* 1938, pp. 145–49.

O'Carroll, Audrey. "Tradition, Culture and Difference in the Music of Blasket Islanders." Translation of talk given in Irish at Ceiliúradh an Bhlascaoid, Dún Chaoin, Co. Chiarraí, 2006.

O'Crohan, Seán. Untitled nine-chapter first half of Pádraig Tyers, ed., *Blasket Memo-*

ries, pp.7–88, referred to in endnotes as "Sean O'Crohan, in *Memories.*" The second half of the same volume includes separate question-and-answer interview with Seán O'Crohan, referred to in the endnotes as "Séan O'Crohan interview, in *Memories.*"

———. *A Day in Our Life: The Last of the Blasket Islanders.* New York: Oxford University Press, 2004.

O'Crohan, Tomás. *Island Cross-Talk: Pages from a Blasket Island Diary.* New York: Oxford University Press, 1986.

———. *The Islandman.* Oxford at the Clarendon Press, 1951.

Ó Cuív. Brian. *A View of the Irish Language.* Dublin: Stationery Office, 1969.

Ó Dubhshláine, Mícheál. *A Dark Day on the Blaskets.* Dingle, Co. Kerry: Brandon, 2003.

———. *Inisvickillane.* Dingle, Co. Kerry: Brandon, 2009.

O'Faoláin, Sean. "A Wild Bird's Nest," *The Listener,* 3–33.

———. "Irish Magic." *Commonweal,* August 11, 1933, pp. 371–72.

———. *An Irish Journey.* London: Longmans, Green, 1940.

Ó Fiannachta, Pádraig. "An tOileánach/The Islandman," in *Proinsias O'Conluain,* ed., *Islands and Authors* (Cork: Mercier Press, 1983), pp. 44–58.

———. "Scholarship, Culture and Education in Ireland Today." Apparently unpublished typescript, c. 1985.

Oftedal, Magne. "Professor Carl Marstrander (1883–1965)." *Studia Celtica,* vol. 1 (1966), pp. 202–4.

———. "Carl J. S. Marstrander." *Lochlann,* vol. 4 (October 1969).

Ó Giolláin, Diarmuid. *Locating Irish Folklore: Tradition, Modernity, Identity.* Cork: Cork University Press, 2000.

O'Guiheen, Mícheál. *A Pity Youth Does Not Last.* New York: Oxford University Press, 1982.

O'H., T. "An Old Man of the Blaskets." *Sunday Independent,* November 14, 1934.

Ó Háinle, Cathal G. "Deformation of History in Blasket Autobiographies." In *Biography and Autobiography: Essays on Irish and Canadian History and Literature,* ed. James Noonan (Montreal: Carleton University Press, 1993), pp. 133–47.

O'Hanlon, Terence. "Another Great Book from the Blaskets." *Irish Independent,* July 19, 1936.

Ó Héalaí, Pádraig. "Pregnancy and Childbirth in Blasket Island Tradition." *Women's Studies Review,* vol. 5 (1998).

O'Leary, Philip. *Gaelic Prose in the Irish Free State, 1922–1939.* University Park, Pa.: Pennsylvania State University Press, 2004.

Olsen, Angun Sønnesyn. "Carl Marstrander: His Life and Work." In Mícheál de Mórdha, ed., *Na Lochlannaigh.*

Ó Lúing, Seán. "Robin Flower, Oileánach agus Máistir Léinn. *Journal of the Kerry Archaeological and Historical Society,* vol. 10 (1977).

———. "The Scholar's Path to Kerry's West." *Cork Holly Bough,* Christmas 1982.

———. *Kuno Meyer, 1858–1919: A Biography.* Dublin: Geography Publications, 1991.

———. *Celtic Studies in Europe.* Dublin: Geography Publications, 2000.

Ong, Walter. *Orality and Literacy.* London: Methuen, 1982.

Ó Scannláin, Séamas, transl. and ed. *Poets and Poetry of the Great Blasket.* Dublin: Mercier Press, 2003.

Ó Shea, Nora. "The Passing of the Islandman." *An Caomhnóir,* December 1997. [Translated from the original Irish of March 12, 1937.]

Ó Siadhail, Mícheál. *Learning Irish.* 3rd ed. New Haven: Yale University Press, 1995.

Ó Súilleabháin, Seán. "Peig Sayers." *Eire-Ireland,* vol. 5, no. 1 (1970).

O'Sullivan, Carol. "Retranslating Ireland." In *Translating Others,* vol. 2. ed. Theo Hermans (Manchester, U.K.: St. Jerome Publishing, 2006), pp. 380–91.

O'Sullivan, Maurice. *Twenty Years A-Growing,* translated by Moya Llewelyn Davies and George Thomson. New York: Oxford University Press, 1983.

O'Toole, Fintan. "The Clod and the Continent: Irish Identity in the European Union." Essay published by EurUnion, Spring 2002.

O'Tuama, Sean. "The Other Tradition: Some Highlights of Modern Fiction in Irish." In *The Irish Novel in Our Time,* eds. Patrick Rafroidi and Maurice Harmon (Villeneuve-d'Ascq: Publications de l'Université de Lille, vol. 3, 1975).

Pierce, David, ed. *Irish Writing in the Twentieth Century: A Reader.* Cork: Cork University Press, 2000.

Piggott, J. R. *Dulwich College: A History, 1616–2008.* London: Dulwich College, 2008.

Póirtéir, Cathal, producer, *Blasket Island Reflections.* Audio documentary, RTÉ, with accompanying booklet, 2003.

———. Radio intervew. RTÉ, May 1, 2008.

Prescott, Andrew. "Robin Flower and Laurence Nowell." *Old English Scholarship and Bibliography: Essays in Honor of Carl T. Berkhout,* ed. Jonathan Wilcox (Kalamazoo, Mich.: Medieval Institute, Western Michigan University, 2004), pp. 41–61.

Quigley, Mark. "Modernity's Edge: Speaking Silence on the Blasket Islands." *Interventions,* vol. 5, no. 3 (2003), pp. 382–406.

Robinson, F. N. "Robin Ernest William Flower." *Memoirs of Fellows and Corresponding Fellows of the Mediaeval Academy of America,* vol. 23, no. 3 (July 1948), pp. 543–44.

Ross, Ciaran. "Blasket Island Autobiographies: The Myth and Mystique of the Untranslated and the Untranslatable." *Translation and Literature,* vol. 12 (2003), pp. 114–42.

Rowlands, David, and Walter McGrath. "The Dingle Train in the Life of Corkaguiny." *Kerry Archaeological and Historical Society Journal,* vol. 11 (1978).

Saddlemyer, Ann, ed. *Letters to Molly: John Millington Synge to Maire O'Neill, 1906–1909* (Cambridge, Mass.: Belknap Press, 1971).

———. *The Collected Letters of John Millington Synge,* vol. 1, 1871–1907. Oxford, U.K.: Clarendon Press, 1983.

St. Leger, Alica. *Gateway to the New World.* Cobh, Co. Cork: Cobh Heritage Trust, n.d.

Sayers, Peig. *An Old Woman's Reflections: The Life of a Blasket Island Storyteller,* translated by Séamus Ennis, introduction by W. R. Rodgers. New York Oxford University Press, 1962.

———. *Peig: The Autobiography of Peig Sayers of the Great Blasket Island,* translated by Bryan MacMahon. Dublin: Talbot Press, 1974.

Scannán: The Islandman, 1937, Booklet. Ceilúradh An Bhlascaoid: Dun Chaoin, n.d.

Scott, Jane. "A Tribute to George Thomson, 21st November 1987." Typescript. Thomson Archives.

"A Sea-Bird's Egg.": *The Catholic Bulletin,* vol. 23, no. 2 (1933), pp. 562–73.

Seaford, Richard. "George Thomson and Ancient Greece." *Classics Ireland*, vol. 4 (1997), pp. 121–33.

Sjoestedt, Marie-Louise. "L'Influence de la langue anglaise sur un parler local irlandais." In *Étrennes de linguistique offertes par quelques amis á Émile Benveniste* (Paris: Librairie Orientaliste Paul Geuthner, 1928).

———. "L'Irlande d'aujourd'hui." *Revue des deux mondes*. In two parts: "Gens de la terre et de la côte," June 15, 1930, pp. 839–64; and "Dublin," July 1, 1930, pp. 158–91.

———. Review of Tomás Ó Criomhthain's *An tOileánach* and *Allagar na hInise*. In *Revue celtique*, vol. 47 (1930).

———. Review of *Peig*, by Peig Sayers. *Études celtiques*, vol. 3 (1938), pp. 156–58.

———. *Celtic Gods and Heroes*. Mineola, N.Y.: Dover Publications, 2000.

Stagles, Joan. "Nineteenth-Century Settlements on the Lesser Blasket Islands." *Journal of the Kerry Archaeological and Historical Society*, vol. 8, (1975), pp. 73–88.

Stagles, Joan and Ray. *The Blasket Islands: Next Parish America*. Revised ed. Dublin: O'Brien Press, 2006.

Stagles, Ray. Unpublished audiotape interview of Mary Pheats Taim and Eileeen Pheats Taim Kearney. Blasket Centre.

———. "Blaheen's Ashes—The Last Rites." *An Caomhnóir*, August 1977.

———. "A 26-Years Journey to the Great Blasket Island." *Cork Holly Bough*, Christmas 1978.

———. "Who Was the First? In Search of Blasket Islanders in Springfield, Mass." *Evening Echo*, November 24, 1982.

———. *Blasket Island Guide*. First published in 1982 as *Day Visitor's Guide to the Great Blasket Island*. Revised and enlarged. Dublin: O'Brien Press, 1990.

Stanley, Nick. "The New Indigènes: Culture, Politics and Representation in Contemporary Europe." *Journal of Art & Design Education*, vol. 16, no. 3 (October 1997), pp. 341–46.

Stewart, James. "An tOileánach—More or Less." *Zeitschrift für Celtische Philologie*, vol. 35, no. 1 (1976), pp. 234–63.

———. *Boccaccio in the Blaskets*. Galway: Officina Typographica, 1988.

Stewart, Jesse. "Memories of the Cambridge Background." In *Feras*, ed. L. Varcl, L. and R. F. Willetts, pp. 19–22.

Symes, David G. "Farm Household and Farm Performance: A Study of Twentieth Century Changes in Ballyferriter, Southwest Ireland." *Ethnology*, vol. 11, no. 1 (January 1972), pp. 25–38.

Synge, J. M. "Notes in Ballyferriter and the Great Blasket Island, August 1905." Unpublished notebooks. Trinity College Dublin.

———. *The Playboy of the Western World*. In *Irish Writing*, ed. Pierce.

———. *Travels in Wicklow, West Kerry and Connemara*. London: Serif, 2005.

———. *The Aran Islands*. Sligo: HardPress, 2006.

Thomas, Dylan. *A Film Script of Twenty Years A-Growing*. London: J. M. Dent, 1964.

Thompson, D. P., Mrs. *A Brief Account of the Rise and Progress of the Change in Religious Opinion Now Taking Place in Dingle, and the West of the County of Kerry, Ireland*. London: Seely, Burnside, and Seely, 1846.

Thomson, George. "Irish and the Intelligentsia." *The Star,* June 14, 1930.

———. "A Report from Mr. Thompson [sic]" to the Academic Council of UCG. Type-script, c. 1932. National University of Ireland, Galway.

———. "The Irish Language Revival." *Yorkshire Celtic Studies,* vol. 3 (1944).

———. *Studies in Ancient Greek Society: The Prehistoric Aegean.* London: Lawrence & Wishart, 1949.

———. "Thomas Hardy and the Peasantry." *Communist Review,* August 1949.

———. "Vision Turns to Reality." *New Central European Observer,* August 4, 1951.

———. *Greek Lyric Metre.* New York: Barnes & Noble, 1961.

———. *Aeschylus and Athens.* New York: Haskell House, 1972.

———. *Marxism and Poetry.* London: Lawrence & Wishart, 1975.

———. *The Human Essence: The Sources of Science and Art.* London: China Policy Study Group, 1977.

———. "Note on Wittgenstein." Typescript, February 1979. Thomson Archives.

———. *Island Home: The Blasket Heritage.* Dingle, Co. Kerry: Brandon, 1998.

———. *The Blasket Homer/Hoiméar sa Bhlascaod.* Radio recording of lectures given by Thomson in Irish and English in 1976. Indreabhán, Co. na Gaillimhe: Cló Iar-Chonnachta, 1999.

Thomson, Katharine. "Message from Katharine Thomson . . ." In *Seoirse Mac Tomáis,* ed. Ní Chéilleachair, pp. 143–45.

Thrasher, Robert W. Homily offered at Sister M. Clemens' Mass (excerpts). Typescript, January 15, 1987. Sisters of Providence Mother House.

Titley, Alan. "Turning Inside and Out: Translating and Irish, 1950–2000." *Yearbook of English Studies,* vol 35, pp. 312–22.

Tracy, Honor. *Mind You, I've Said Nothing: Forays in the Irish Republic.* London: Methuen, 1953.

"Tragedy of Great Blasket." *Irish Independent,* June 13, 1931.

Tyers, Pádraig. *West Kerry Camera.* Cork: Collins Press, 2006.

Tyers, Pádraig, ed. *Blasket Memories: The Life of an Irish Island Community.* Dublin: Mercier Press, 1998.

Tzovias, Dimitris. "George Thomson and the Dialectics of Hellenism." *Byzantine and Modern Greek Studies,* vol. 13, no. 1 (1989), pp. 296–305.

Ua Maoileoin, Pádraig. *Na Blascaodaí/The Blaskets.* Dublin: Stationery Office, Government of Ireland, 1996.

Uí Ógáin, Ríonach. Notes accompanying *Beauty an Oileáin: Music and Song of the Blasket Islands,* audio. Dublin: Claddadh Records, 1992.

Varcl, L., and R. F. Willetts, eds. *Feras: Studies Presented to George Thomson on the Occasion of His 6oth Birthday.* Prague: Charles University, 1963.

Vendryes, J. "Marie-Louise Sjoestedt." *Études celtiques,* vol. 4.

Vincy, Michael. "The Wild Island." *Irish Times,* September 13, 1966.

Wagner, H., and N. Mac Congáil. "Oral Literature from Dunquin, County Kerry." Belfast: Institute of Irish Studies, Queen's University of Belfast, 1983.

Whelan. "The Revisionist Debate in Ireland." *Boundary,* vol. 2 (Spring 2004), pp. 179–205.

Whiston, Steven. "George Thomson and China." Manuscript of talk given at Colloquium on the Life and Work of George Thomson, January 7, 1989.

Whitaker, Ian. "Core Values Among the Blasket Islanders." *Folk Life,* vol. 24 (1986), pp. 52–69.

Wilkinson, L. P. *Kingsmen of a Century: 1873–1972.* Cambridge, U.K.: King's College, 1981.

Wilson, David M. *The British Museum: A History.* London: British Museum Press, 2002.

Yeats, W. B. "Synge and the Ireland of His Time." In *Essays and Introductions* (London: Macmillan Press, 1911).

04-11-13 04:55PM

A MeLCat request has been placed on the following item by the
patron listed below. Please pull this item, check it out to this
library on MeLCat, and send it to the library location given below.

Three Rivers Public Lib   Three Rivers Public Library
920 W Michigan Ave   CALL NO: 941.96 KANIGEL
Three Rivers MI 49093   AUTHOR: Kanigel, Robert.
zv327   TITLE: On an Irish island
                                           BARCODE: 313695
                                            REC NO: i2521357l4
                                          SHELVING:Adult - Nonfiction

JOSEPH PATRICK MCGARVEY   517-349-3599
Okemos
Capital Area Dist Library
LOCATION: Okemos
MeL Public Library Adult

04-11-13 04:55PM

The item below is now available for pickup at designated location.

Capital Area Dist Library
zv194 CADL Okemos

Three Rivers Public Library
CALL NO: 941.96 KANIGEL
AUTHOR: Kanigel, Robert.
TITLE: On an Irish island
BARCODE: 3113695
REC NO: i252135714
PICKUP AT: Okemos

JOSEPH PATRICK MCGARVEY
Okemos

517-349-3599

7:40

Selected Bibliography in Irish

EXCERPTS TRANSLATED BY PERSON INDICATED

Mac Conghail, Muiris. *Aghaidheanna Fidil agus Púicíní: Seoirse Mac Tomáis in Éirinn, 1923–1934*. Baile Átha Cliath: Sáirséal/Ó Marcaigh. 2009. [Ruth Uí Ógáin]

Ní Ghaoithín, Máire. *An tOileaán a Bhí*. Baile Átha Cliath: An Clóchomhar Tta. 1978. [Dáithi de Mórdha]

Ní Loingsigh, Máiréad, ed. *Cin Lae Eibhlin Ní Shúilleabháin* [Ruth Uí Ógáin]

Ní Shéaghdha, Nóra. *Thar Bealach IsteachI*. Baile Atha Cliath: Oifig an Solathair, 1940. [Pádraig Ó Healai]

Ó Brosnacháin, Niall. *Éist Leis an gCóta*. Maigh Nuad: An Sagart, 2001. [Ruth Uí Ógáin]

Ó Caomhánaiggh, Sean Óg. *Fánái*. Baile Atha Cliath: An Gúm, 1928. [Ruth Uí Ógáin]

Ó Ceallaigh, Brian. "Ag Tagairt don Leabhar," introduction to *Allagar na hInise*. [Ruth Uí Ógáin]

Ó Cearnaigh, Seán Pheats Tom. *Fiolar an Eireabaill Bháin*. Coscéim, 1992. [Ruth Uí Ógáin]

Ó Coileáin, Seán. "Tomás Ó Criomhthain, Brian Ó Ceallaigh agus an Seabhac." *Scriobh*, vol. 4 (1979). Republished in *Tomás an Bhlascaoid*, ed. Breandán Ó Conaire. [Joe Nugent, Boston College, and Áine de Paor, in Irene Lucchitti, *The Islandman: The Hidden Life of Tomás O'Crohan*]

Ó Conaire, Breandán, ed. *Tomás an Bhlascaoid*. Indreabhan, Conamara: Cló Iar-Chonnachta, 1992. [Áine de Paor, in Irene Lucchitti's *The Islandman: The Hidden Life of Tomás O'Crohan*]

Ó Criomhthain, Tomás. "An Guth ar Nóin" and "Radharc na nIontas." In *Bloghanna ón mBlascaod*. [Ruth Uí Ógáin]

Ó Lúing, Seán. *Seán an Chóta*. Coiscéim, 1985. [Dáithi de Mórdha]

Seabhac, An. "Ón Eagarthóir." Editor's comment, *Allagar na hInise*. [Ruth Uí Ógáin]

———. Translated as "Tomas O Criomhthain, Fisherman and Author." *Bonaventura*, vol. 1, no. 1 (1937). [Ruth Uí Ógáin]

Thomson, George. "Fiche Blian Ag Fás." article about O'Sullivan book, *Comhar*, November 1958. [Ruth Uí Ógáin]

———. *Gach Órlach De Mo Chroí*. Baile Atha Cliath: Coiscéim, 1988. [Ruth Uí Ógáin]

Uí Aimhirgín, Nuala, ed. *Ó Oileám go Cuilleán*. Baile Atha Cliath: Coscéim, 2000. [Ruth Uí Ógáin]

Index

Page numbers in *italics* refer to illustrations.

PERMISSIONS ACKNOWLEDGMENTS

Grateful acknowledgment is made to the following for permission to reprint previously published material:

Áine de Paor: English translation by Áine de Paor of an untitled poem by Tomás Ó Criomhthain originally published in *Scriobh,* vol. 4 (1979). Subsequently published in *Tomás an Bhlascaoid,* ed. Breandán Ó Conaire. [Joe Nugent, Boston College, and Áine de Paor, in Irene Lucchitti, *The Islandman: The Hidden Life of Tomás O'Crohan*]. Reprinted by permission of Áine de Paor.

The Estate of Maurice O'Sullivan: Excerpt from *Twenty Years A-Growing* by Maurice O'Sullivan, translated by Moya Llewelyn Davies and George Thomson. Oxford University Press, 1983. Reprinted by permission of The Estate of Maurice O'Sullivan.

Mercier Press: Excerpts from *Blasket Memories: The Life of an Irish Island Community* by Pádraig Tyers, copyright © 1998 by Pádraig Tyers; excerpts from *Letters from the Great Blasket* by Eibhlís Ní Shúilleabháin and Niamh Leahy, copyright © 1978 by Niamh Bean Ui Laoithe. Reprinted by permission of Mercier Press Ltd., Cork.

Oxford University Press: Excerpts from *Island Cross-Talk* by Thomas O'Crohan, translated by Tim Enright, copyright © 1986; excerpts from *Western Island* by Ida M. Flower and Robin Flower, copyright © 1978. Reprinted by permission of Oxford University Press.

Special Rider Music: "Bob Dylan's Dream" by Bob Dylan, copyright © 1963, 1964 by Warner Bros. Inc.; renewed 1991, 1992 by Special Rider Music. All rights reserved. International copyright secured. Reprinted by permission of Special Rider Music.

page

15: Dublin City Gallery the Hugh Lane

19: The National Library of Ireland

31: Courtesy of the University of Oslo

41: Courtesy of the Blasket Centre

43: Courtesy of the Flower family and the Blasket Centre

48: Courtesy of Ionad an Bhlascaoid Mhóir and the Blasket Centre

54: Photo by Carl Wilhelm von Sydow © the National Folklore Collection, University College Dublin

61: Courtesy of the Blasket Centre

78: Courtesy Professor Margaret Alexiou and Birmingham Archives and Heritage

85: Photo taken by George Thomson, Courtesy of the Blasket Centre

87: Courtesy of the Blakset Centre

90: Courtesy Máire Cruise O'Brien, from her autobiography *The Same Age as the State,* the O'Brien Press Ltd, Dublin

96: Courtesy Professor Margaret Alexiou and Birmingham Archives and Heritage

108: Courtesy Professor Margaret Alexiou and Birmingham Archives and Heritage

113: © Daniel MacMonagle / macmonagle.com

122: © The Artist's Estate

140: Courtesy Pádraig Ó Siochfhradha

166: Courtesy Máire Ní Shuilleabháin and Kenny's Bookshop

173: Courtesy of the Blasket Centre

182: Courtesy of the Blasket Centre

187: Courtesy of the Blasket Centre

194: Portrait by Harry Kernoff, reprinted Courtesy of the Blasket Centre

199: Courtesy of the Blasket Centre

203: Courtesy Professor Margaret Alexiou and Birmingham Archives and Heritage

222: Photo taken by George Chambers, Courtesy of the Blasket Centre

Robert Kanigel is the author of six previous books. He has been the recipient of numerous awards, including a Guggenheim Fellowship and the Grady-Stack Award for science writing. His book *The Man Who Knew Infinity* was a finalist for the National Book Critics Circle Award and the Los Angeles Times Book Prize. His work has appeared in numerous publications, including the *New York Times Magazine,* the *New York Times Book Review, Harvard Magazine,* and *Psychology Today.* He now lives in Baltimore.

A NOTE ON THE TYPE

This book was set in Adobe Garamond. Designed for the Adobe Corporation by Robert Slimbach, the fonts are based on types first cut by
Claude Garamond (c. 1480–1561). Garamond was a pupil of Geoffroy
Tory and is believed to have followed the Venetian models, although
he introduced a number of important differences, and it is to him that
we owe the letter we now know as "old style." He gave to his letters
a certain elegance and feeling of movement that won their creator an
immediate reputation and the patronage of Francis I of France.

Composed by North Market Street Graphics,
Lancaster, Pennsylvania

Printed and bound by Berryville Graphics,
Berryville, Virginia

Designed by Soonyoung Kwon